Representations of Political Power

Representations of Political Power

Case Histories from Times of Change and Dissolving Order in the Ancient Near East

Edited by

Marlies Heinz and Marian H. Feldman

Winona Lake, Indiana
Eisenbrauns
2007

www.eisenbrauns.com

Library of Congress Cataloging-in-Publication Data

Representations of political power : case histories from times of change and dissolving order in the ancient Near East / edited by Marlies Heinz and Marian H. Feldman.
p. cm.
Includes bibliographical references and index.
ISBN 978-1-57506-135-1 (hardback : alk. paper)
1. Middle East–History–To 622. 2. Middle East–Politics and government. 3. Middle East–Social conditions. I. Heinz, Marlies. II. Feldman, Marian H.
DS62.23.R47 2007
939′.4–dc22

2007015133

The paper used in this publication meets the minimum requirements of the American National Standard for Information Sciences–Permanence of Paper for Printed Library Materials, ANSI Z39.48-1984.♾™

Contents

Preface vii

Abbreviations ix

List of Contributors xi

Introduction: Representation–Tradition–Religion 1
MARLIES HEINZ AND MARIAN H. FELDMAN

Part 1
Reestablishment of Order after Major Disruption

Emar and the Transition from Hurrian to Hittite Power 21
REGINE PRUZSINSZKY

Frescoes, Exotica, and the Reinvention of the Northern Levantine Kingdoms during the Second Millennium B.C.E. 39
MARIAN H. FELDMAN

Sargon of Akkad: Rebel and Usurper in Kish 67
MARLIES HEINZ

Part 2
Changing Order from Within

The Royal Cemetery of Ur: Ritual, Tradition, and the Creation of Subjects 89
SUSAN POLLOCK

The Divine Image of the King: Religious Representation of Political Power in the Hittite Empire 111
DOMINIK BONATZ

Nabonidus the Mad King: A Reconsideration of His Steles from Harran and Babylon 137
PAUL-ALAIN BEAULIEU

Part 3
Perceptions of a New Order

Cyrus the Great of Persia: Images and Realities 169
AMÉLIE KUHRT

The Migration and Sedentarization of the Amorites from the Point of View of the Settled Babylonian Population 193
BRIT JAHN

Index of Authors 211

Preface

Change is the only constant in history. Proceeding from this thought and inspired by the many political changes that are occurring today, especially in Europe and Asia, the present volume emerged. Former great powers have collapsed, so-called "Third World" countries are ascending to become economic superpowers, familiar world orders are displaced by new locations and shifts in centers and peripheries. In numerous discussions, the effects of globalization are being debated. Many feel that change and the substitution of the traditional known world order with a new world organization are affecting their lives. Change is being experienced either as a threat to a familiar way of living or as a chance to reject traditions and develop new concepts of life. Many of the discussions concerning the effects of globalization and change focus on the sphere of influence and the meaning of traditions and the customs that express these traditions, on who benefits from maintaining traditions, who is disenfranchised, and who controls the processes of change. The coherence of communities and the stabilization of communal identities are preserved not only by traditions but also by religion. Religion especially has been and still is used frequently by politicians and religious spokesmen to forge community and communal identity, particularly in the context of globalization and the world-wide merging of political and economic interests. Continuity and change, tradition and innovation have far-reaching consequences for communal life and for the consolidation of the ruling order. Controlling these resources is thus one of the most important facets for any politician and must be tackled on a local, regional, and global level.

If then, as stated initially, change is the only constant in history, archaeologists interested in the historical, social, economic, religious, and political development of the Near East (and not only there) are obliged to study the makeup and implications of the metamorphoses that characterized the history and development of ancient Near Eastern societies. Who initiated change in which areas and how? Are certain aspects of society more exposed to change, or does the archaeological record simply preserve some aspects better than others? Which domains of social cooperation clung more tenaciously to the established traditions, and in which did innovation succeed more rapidly? Who was affected by change and how? And how did the politicians and the religious leaders of 5,000 years ago confront and control change and continuity? Further questions that arise query the significance attached to different traditions by a range of people and who profited or lost in each case. What were the social, political, economic, and cultural conditions under which change or continuity took place? In addition, the role that religion played in these processes is of central importance for investigations of this sort.

Continuity and change are thus the main focus of our interests in the present study—they influence our way of living as they did 5,000 years ago.

In keeping with the theme of change, modern innovation in the area of transportation and communication made this book possible. The editors, from Freiburg and Berkeley, met at an international conference in Berlin and established the initial communication from which the plan for a coedited volume developed. The rapid communication of e-mail brought together an international group of scholars to participate in writing the book together. But, in the end, the traditional forms of communication—one-to-one conversation, the personal acquaintance of our colleagues, and the knowledge of their scholarly work—have produced a book in the traditional manner.

The editors would like to thank heartily all the authors for their constructive cooperation, for the time they invested to make the project succeed, for their patience in fulfilling all the editors' requests, and for the intellectual stimulation they have provided in their contributions.

The editors sincerely thank Beverly McCoy, who has worked tirelessly on the manuscript and has accompanied us up to the moment of the book's appearance.

And our concluding sincere thanks go in particular to Jim Eisenbraun, who, with his ready acceptance to publish the study, provided an ideal venue in which our common work could come to fruition.

Marlies Heinz and Marian Feldman
Freiburg and Berkeley
March 2007

Abbreviations

General

A.	Louvre Museum siglum
AO	tablets in the collection of the Musée du Louvre
BM	tablets in the collections of the British Museum
CBS	tablets in the collections of the University Museum of the University of Pennsylvania, Philadelphia
DB	Behistun inscription of Darius
DSk	inscription of Darius I on a brick from Susa
E	siglum for texts from Emar
M.	registration number of texts from Mari
Msk.	registration number of tablets from Meskene/Emar
NBC	tablets in the Babylonian Collection, Yale University Library
PFS	registration number of an inscribed Persepolis Fortification Cylinder Seal
RE	texts in the collection of Jonathan Rosen
RS	field numbers of tablets excavated at Ras Shamra
Sm.	tablets in the collections of the British Museum

Reference Works

ARM	Archives royales de Mari
AuOr	*Aula Orientalis*
CM	Cuneiform Monographs
ETCSL	The Electronic Text Corpus of Sumerian Literarture
FM	Florilegium Marianum
KBo	Keilschrifttexte aus Boghazköi
KUB	Keilschrifturkunden aus Boghazköi
MSL	Materialien zum sumerischen Lexikon
MVN	Materiali per il vocabolario neo-sumerico
RlA	*Reallexikon der Assyriologie*
TCL	Textes Cunéiformes du Louvre
UET	Ur Excavations, Texts
VS	Vorderasiatische Schriftdenkmäler der Königlichen (staatlichen) Museen zu Berlin (Leipzig)
ZA	*Zeitschrift für Assyriologie*

List of Contributors

Paul-Alain Beaulieu is Professor at the University of Toronto. He is the author of several works on the Neo-Babylonian period, including *The Reign of Nabonidus, King of Babylon, 556–539 b.c.* (Yale, 1989) and *Legal and Administrative Texts from the Reign of Nabonidus* (Yale, 2000).

Dominik Bonatz is Professor of Ancient Near Eastern Archaeology at the Free University in Berlin. He has carried out field research since 1990 in Syria, Lebanon, and Indonesia. He has a special interest in the social and cultural context of ancient Near Eastern visual arts and in comparative studies ranging from the Mediterranean to the Southeast Asian world. Publications in the field of visual arts include *Das syro-hethische Grabdenkmal: Untersuchungen zur Entstehung einer neuen Bildgattung im nord-syrisch-südostanatolischen Raum der Eisenzeit* (Mainz, 2000) and *Bild–Macht–Geschichte: Visuelle Kommunikation im Alten Orient* (Berlin, 2002; edited with Marlies Heinz).

Marian Feldman is Associate Professor of Ancient Near Eastern Art at the University of California, Berkeley. Her research focuses on the mediating role of art in the intercultural relations of the Near East, Egypt, and the Aegean. She has excavated in Syria and Turkey and is the author of *Diplomacy by Design: Luxury Arts and an 'International Style' in the Ancient Near East, 1400–1200 b.c.e.* (University of Chicago, 2006).

Marlies Heinz is Professor of Near Eastern Archaeology at the Albert Ludwigs University in Freiburg. Her field research encompasses excavations in Syria, Bahrain, and Lebanon, where she is currently working in Kamid el-Loz. Her research interests concern the field of political power and its expression in art and architecture, processes of urbanization and deurbanization, and globalization and its impact on cultural development. Publications concerning these fields include *Bild–Macht–Geschichte: Visuelle Kommunikation im Alten Orient* (Berlin, 2002; edited with Dominik Bonatz) and *Zwischen Erklären und Verstehen? Beiträge zu den erkenntnistheoretischen Grundlagen archäologischer Interpretation* (Tübingen, 2002; edited with Manfred K. H. Eggert and Ulrich Veit).

Brit Jahn studied classical archaeology and ancient Near Eastern studies in Leipzig from 1997 to 2003. In 2003, she concluded this study with a Master of Arts on a philological theme about the archives and dossiers of the so-called Manana'a Dynasty. Since 2004, she has been part of the Collaborative Research Centre 586, "Difference and Integration: Interaction between Nomadic and Settled Forms of Life in the Civilisations of the Old World" with a project supervised by Prof. Michael Streck entitled, "Between Pasture, Town and Palace: Nomads and Settled Population in the Mari Kingdom (19th/18th Century b.c.)."

Amélie Kuhrt, Professor of Ancient Near Eastern History, University College London, and Fellow of the British Academy. She is the coordinator and editor of the Achaemenid History Workshops series (Achaemenid History 1–8 [Leiden, 1987–1994]) and the editor/author (with S. M. Sherwin-White) of *Hellenism in the East* (London, Berkeley, 1987) and *From Samarkhand to Sardis* (London, Berkeley, 1993). In 1995, she published *The Ancient Near East, c. 3000–330 B.C.* (2 vols., London), which was awarded the Breasted Prize by the American Historical Association in 1998. Work in progress includes a collection of sources for Achaemenid history.

Susan Pollock is Professor of Anthropology at Binghamton University. She specializes in the archaeology of the Middle East and has conducted fieldwork in Iran, Iraq, and Turkey. Her research addresses issues such as political economy, ideology, the constitution of subjectivities, and archaeology in the media. Her publications include *Ancient Mesopotamia: The Eden That Never Was* (Cambridge, 1999) and a volume coedited with Reinhard Bernbeck, *Archaeologies of the Middle East: Critical Perspectives* (Blackwell, 2005).

Regine Pruzsinszky studied Altsemitische Philologie und Orientalische Archäologie in Vienna, Berlin, Würzburg, and Helsinki. Her doctoral thesis was on the personal names in the archives of Emar (Vienna, 2000). From 2000 to 2004, she was a research assistant in the Viennese special research program "The Synchronization of Civilizations in the Eastern Mediterranean in the Second Millennium B.C." with the research project "Chronological Data in Mesopotamia." Since October 2004, she has held a scholarship from the Austrian Academy of Sciences (Austrian Programme for Advanced Research and Technology) with the research project "The Singers in the Ancient Near East."

Introduction: Representation–Tradition–Religion

Marlies Heinz and Marian H. Feldman

Representation of political power seems to have been necessary at all times in all complex urban societies. Representation, so we assume, serves to legitimate political power, to strengthen, and to intensify it. Indeed, it can be seen as instrumental in the construction of power. Representation, whether as texts, rituals, visual images, or architecture, gives form to the ideas of order that the ruling elite seek to normalize or make *common sense*. To secure order—to construct a certain social, ideological, religious, economic, and cultural stability—seems to be one of the main intentions of representation. When order breaks down or is threatened, political power comes under threat, as well as the cohesion of the community. In times of impending change, crisis, or disorder, special effort is required to reassure the community of the rulers' ability to maintain stability.

Two parameters seem to be especially effective in convincing the public that the situation is under control: tradition and religion. The maintenance, and even crafting, of tradition is one of the most powerful means to constitute "community," to establish a "we," and to support the development of group identity. Tradition promises continuity, stability, order; it therefore works along "normative" lines. Yet, tradition cannot be said simply to "exist"; it is not a "thing" but a process. Tradition comes into being and is shaped only through the actions of members of a society; in other words, tradition needs a carrier. Tradition becomes all the more powerful if the carrier is particularly effective in supporting its given potentials, and one such carrier is religion. Religion, as an essential structural element of the ancient Near East, was connected inextricably to the organization of every aspect of life; it was a fundamental frame anchoring the order of social life. Religion legitimated and strengthened the social, political, economic, and cultural structures of society by making certain aspects of the actions of human beings appear as if unchangeable and unassailable. Tradition and religion—controlled and used according to the aims of the rulers—helped rulers to represent themselves as the "true" keepers of order and as the guarantors of prosperity for the whole community, especially in times of change and dissolving order. What those in power did to convince the affected communities of their qualities as rulers, that is, their representational strategies—especially in times of change—is the subject of this book.

The volume is divided into three thematic parts: "Reestablishment of Order after Major Disruption," "Changing Order from Within," and "Perceptions of New Order." Each section is presented in the following part of the introduction, along with a brief consideration of how the individual articles contribute to the different themes. There are, of course, many connections among the contributions across sections, and the multiple ways that they intersect to generate a larger dialogue on representations of political power are advanced in the last part of the introduction, in which more detailed discussions of each essay are provided.

Part 1
Reestablishment of Order after Major Disruption

Major political disruption can come both from without and from within a social system. In either situation, the resulting newly installed power can exercise many options in its quest to continue political domination: from retaining preexisting systems that are controlled according to the needs of the new rulers to introducing foreign or exotic elements for the creation of new traditions to radically changing the entire structure of the community. The most obvious external threat for a prevailing political and social order is military aggression. The violent interference itself is a first offense against the order of the attacked society, affecting the political, social, economic, and cultural spheres. Rebellion and usurpation exemplify crises internal to a community that can result in significant reorganization of hierarchies. Complete societal collapse and regeneration are further means by which major ruptures in the order of society can occur. The effect of any of these scenarios may result in a range of degrees of continuity, from the destruction of the entire structure of order to only a change in leadership within the elite circles. This first part of this book examines how new order is imposed after a major disruption in rule and how the new ruling body engages with or rejects tradition. The three contributions in this part concentrate on representational strategies of newly established rulers and their use of traditions, social order, religion, and identities after they have taken over power.

Pruzsinszky's study on Late Bronze Age Emar explores how a foreign power, the Hittites, acted in Emar to establish a new order in the dominated culture. In theory, various political strategies were possible to establish and to secure the new power, from imposing pure military force to controlling and manipulating cultural activities. An intrusive power might have considered it necessary to be highly visible in order to strengthen its power locally. Or more subtle assaults on the local social and political order might avoid any sign of alteration under the pretense that although a new political power had been installed nothing had changed and life went on as usual. At Emar, the Hittites embarked on a strategy of this sort; they inserted themselves within preexisting traditions and religious rituals, subtly lessening the power of these traditions without their wholesale replacement. Wherever possible they deployed the existing system and structure of political and religious order, while at the same time the insertion of new dignitaries and princes with ties to Hatti allowed them to achieve their political aims. The shift at Emar, however, shows that, while a new concept of authority accompanied the change to Hittite control, it was limited by traditional elements of the indigenous Syrian politics, resulting—at first glance—in an equal co-existence between the local and Hittite power. Possible two-way impacts that could potentially have developed out of the encounter between Emar and the Hittites cannot be reconstructed.

Feldman's essay touches on questions of intentionality in using traditions–in this case, specifically foreign and exotic traditions–to reshape power after a major collapse (whose cause still eludes us). A major component in the regeneration involved a return to an urbancentric focus for power, and within this process a new group of elites sought to present (and represent) their authority by references to the acquisition and use of exotica, namely, frescoed walls and floors executed in an Aegean fashion that were prominently displayed in the main administrative structures of the cities. To negotiate a potentially problematic situation of establishing (or reestablishing) order, the new elite needed symbols that could signal their belonging while excluding others. Because the preexisting symbol system had been profoundly shattered by collapse, the new elite constructed a representational system by using an exotic style of decoration for their palaces as a means of establishing a common "we" that simultaneously reassured themselves about their status. The construction of this exclusive representational system appears to have manifested itself fairly late in the process of establishing new order (at the end of the Middle Bronze Age or even possibly the beginning of the Late Bronze Age), well after the reemergence of dynastic power. The construction, and perhaps more important the maintenance, of these elite identities resulted from ongoing competition among the new dynasties, creating a tradition to fill the vacuum left by societal collapse.

Sargon of Akkad, a rebel who asserted his power over southern and northern Mesopotamia as well as to the west, chose a different strategy to demonstrate the new order that he had created. He blatantly displayed his politics through the physical forms and spaces of almost all aspects of society, reoganizing the layout of important villages either by rebuilding and restructuring or by destroying them, changing the political systems, severing traditional economic connections, and reorienting them toward more Akkad-friendly alliances. In short, Sargon pursued a radical strategy of breaking and reformulating traditions to bend them to Akkadian concerns. Heinz's contribution presents these activities that left noticeable and obvious traces through the Akkadian realm and that indelibly realigned the structures of order in Mesopotamia.

Part 2
Changing Order from Within

Violation of, or threats to, order may also occur without abrupt political disruptions; they may also arise from changes and developments internal to a community, such as the emergence of a new class of individuals (kings in the case of Pollock's article; an intelligentsia for Beaulieu). And representational strategies are necessary to maintain order or avert disorder, as is the case during the Hittite Empire period examined in Bonatz's paper. The essays in the second part of this book explore how changes of order were effected within a more-or-less continuous trajectory of rule–that is, without major disruptions within the ruling base.

The role of religion in both the maintenance and alteration of tradition and order is preeminent and forms a central theme in the three essays that constitute this section. The death of a leading figure, as explored in Pollock's article on the Royal Cemetery at Ur, may cause severe disturbances within the social fabric of a community. Leaders who controlled traditions and behavior within the community had to find solutions for keeping the threatened order together. Religion and, more important, its rituals as a link that constituted identity and strengthened social order especially in times of upheaval proved to be a powerful means for overcoming threats of this sort. Rites associated with celebratory feasting helped to prepare a group of people to be willing to go to their deaths and a newly emerging ruling group to mark the transition from "elected" to inherited rule during the Early Dynastic period in southern Mesopotamia.

Bonatz and Beaulieu both discuss the uses of religious ideology in the maintenance (either successful or not) of power, Bonatz mainly through images and Beaulieu principally through texts. Bonatz demonstrates the close relationship between political and religious iconography that solidified the Hittite rulers' control over their empire through an ambiguously defined unity between king and gods. The ways in which anomalies in rules (*doxa*) lead to changes and new norms allow Bonatz to argue for a "life" of images separate from the life of texts–images that permitted an ill-defined analogy between the Hittite king and the gods. Images of the Hittite king tending to the gods appeared late in the Empire period (thirteenth century) and could thus serve as references to earlier royal ancestors in their capacity as divinized rulers, effectively blurring the line between living and deceased, human and divine.

That the activities of a ruler "at home" undermined the order and survival of the community was the accusation made against Nabonidus. As argued by Beaulieu, the Neo-Babylonian ruler was ineffective in drawing upon earlier Mesopotamian traditions of religious practice as he confronted the growing power of the scholarly community. Nabonidus had tried to develop a religious system according to the political interests of those who had supported his rebellion at Babylon, namely, the religious "lobby" of Sin of Harran. Creating a religious system centered on Sin of Harran was perceived, by Nabonidus's contemporaries as well as by the men who later controlled the cultural memory, as a disregard of Marduk, the principal god of Babylon, and as such presented a threat to the order and survival of that community; that it was also a disempowerment of the priesthood and sages of Marduk goes without saying. That Nabonidus did not share this view and indeed represented himself precisely as the one who prevented society from suffering chaos and disorder in introducing the Sin cult is hardly surprising. Yet it appears that Nabonidus and his supporters overestimated their power to sway the population of Babylon. In particular, the traditional elite in Babylon, who suffered greatest by the demotion of Marduk's cult, sought to counter Nabonidus's reforms. But, while they were successful in helping to shape an image of Nabonidus as a negligent ruler, thus undermining his authority, ultimately they too lost out to an altogether different and new power, Cyrus the Great of Persia.

Part 3
Perceptions of a New Order

Because major shifts in power were almost always accompanied by new representational strategies that supplanted the old ones, it can be difficult to disentangle the superimposed "realities" that the different representations created. Thus, we are often beholden to highly biased or uneven sources in our reconstruction of these past power shifts. Two such shifts in the Near East occurred with the sudden appearance of the Amorite dynasties in the early second millennium and the creation of the Achaemenid Empire under Cyrus. The two essays in this final part, by Kuhrt and Jahn, explore the disparate textual evidence that has contributed to both ancient and modern perceptions of these new powers, addressing issues regarding the representation and perception of newcomers to power.

Among the men who attained renown as usurpers and charismatic rulers at home and over a wide empire and who actively intervened in local, regional, and international traditions and religions—and thus of interest for the topic of this book—is Cyrus the Great. However, it is not his deeds and modes of self-representation themselves that Kuhrt makes the focus of her article. Rather, it is the disentanglement of the later constructions of his heroic image that she investigates. Asserting the need for a critical reading of the sources, Kuhrt carefully analyzes the disparate strands of evidence that have contributed to a portrait of Cyrus as a "wise and tolerant statesman." Effectively deconstructing the evidence, she paints a rather different portrait of Cyrus as a Near Eastern ruler on a quest for imperial domination. How much of the later profile (as tolerant leader) can be directly attributed to Cyrus's own propagandistic activities remains difficult to disentangle, but certainly his actions (even actions of potentially constructing this self-representation) speak to the calculated nature of his motivations. And he worked most effectively by using the cultural elements and iconography of the local populations that he incorporated into his vast realm both at home in Persia and abroad. Somewhat paradoxically, Cyrus used the very upheaval of order to create an image of himself as a culturally tolerant ruler, one who not only respected the cultural achievements of those subdued by the Persian military but who even took care of and cultivated them. Kuhrt's close reading of the sources indicates that Cyrus's representational strategies created a strong, positive image of himself as the keeper of order, tradition, and culture, while in fact it was he who permanently destroyed the prevailing order of the ancient Near East.

Though appearing in less dramatic fashion than military coups or invasions, steady processes involving the acculturation of one group into the realm of another also significantly affect traditions. Migration and sedentarization, by their very nature, involve rather significant breaks in tradition, both for the traditions of those who migrate and settle as well as for the societies that face the integration of the "others" into their social and cultural system. Traditions, values, norms, cultural habits, religious thinking, and last but not least the political order are potentially exposed to change, if not threatened in their existence by these processes. The complexity of this dynamic is compounded in the case of the Amorites' transition to sedentarization because of the absence of written records for the nonsendentarized populations and the diversity of documentation for the settled groups, as illustrated in Jahn's essay. Thus, attempts to track a fundamental change in order that occurred through the process of the Amorite migration and integration into the urban society of the Near East must rely on an extremely uneven and highly biased set of written evidence. The sedentarization of nomadic Amorite populations resulted less from a massive influx than from a gradual infiltration, a slow process of acculturation and assimilation, a process that occurred for the most part without open violence but as a fusion of different communities, cultures, and ways of living that caused a multitude of changes within the organization of all involved parties. Nonetheless, the encounter of urban versus nomadic ways of living was, according to the written testimony of the urban society, seen as a basic threat. The assimilation of the migrant Amorites that resulted from their acquisition of the cultural habits, organizational traditions, and structures of urban communities on the one hand stabilized the order of the communities that emerged from this process. But on the other hand their increasing presence was a major threat to the existing authorities, creating tension in how the Amorites were both received and perceived by the already established Near Eastern groups.

Organization and Summary of Contributions

As manifold and multifaceted as the processes and forms of each particular disruption of order are, so too are their causes and backgrounds, as well as the strategies and efforts to establish new social order out of the chaos. Each particular case has to be investigated through its own cultural specificity regarding the causes of the breakdown and the subsequent realignments of social order; yet at the same time, it remains a worthwhile goal to try to find, in the abundance of cases, something like a thread running through the causes, backgrounds, and developments that propelled both subtle and radical shifts in social and political organization. This is the underlying motivation of this book.

We begin our volume with Regine Pruzsinszky's essay, "Emar and the Transition from Hurrian to Hittite Power," in order to highlight the subtlety and complexity by which representational strategies of new power may be deployed. Rather than the expected, coerced imposition of Hittite power upon the formerly Hurrian/Mittanian ruled city of Emar, the new Hittite overlords mastered the area through subtle shifts in control, bespeaking a highly sophisticated strategy. As a foreign power, the Hittites avoided obvious visibility, whether in restructuring public spaces or in any sizable presence of Hittite functionaries or military personal in the city. Emar was not destroyed, and the texts describe much continuity in social traditions.

The Hittite interference in tradition and order took a subtler course. The Hittites controlled Emar through the cultural and religious life of the city, an effective means that operated within already established normative expectations. Cultural force substituted for military violence and led to the effective control of the instances that were of elementary importance for intellectual life in Emar—and thereby for the legitimation of order. The securing of Hittite power in Emar was carried out through new configurations of the contents of social, cultural, and political order—an effective means for controlling the cultural and spiritual life—and in this way gained economic and political control over the city. The Hittites did not do away with the existing political structures that supported the local order; rather, their control resulted from inserting aspects of Hittite cultural practices into the traditional Syrian practices, which led to an altogether new political significance. This modification—keeping the form of the traditional order while changing the personnel and meaning—ultimately created a far more effective transition than outright cancellation and replacement would have.

After the Hittites had created a new and loyal political elite in Emar, they began similar modifications to the religious concerns of Emar. They did not change the composition of the pantheon or the rituals; rather, they shifted the control of responsibilities and the personnel of the existing offices to fall in line with Hittite interests. Only to outward appearances did Emar seem to function "as it always had." The seeming continuity of the familiar offered those affected the possibility of coming to terms with the new circumstances and maybe even of identifying with the new order. The "new" pretended not to supersede the "old," a clever strategy of the Hittites, who, through their control of the political and religious organizations, monitored exactly the areas that had been significant in guarding the exertion of political power and rulership.

The second essay, by Marian Feldman, "Frescoes, Exotica, and the Reinvention of the Northern Levantine Kingdoms during the Second Millennium," presents an alternative means of asserting authority—through the appropriation and control of foreign technologies and traditions. At the beginning of the second millennium, a widespread change in the political order of the northern Levant followed the collapse of large-scale urban societies at the end of the third millennium. While both the collapse and the subsequent revitalization appear less homogeneous than once thought, new political order is attested in the area, best exemplified by the emergence of Amorite dynasties in control of many of the major city-states. The northern Levantine dynasties that now ruled over city-states such as Alalakh and Qatna signaled their ability to access, acquire, and manipulate knowledge through the physical presence of Aegean-type frescoes on the walls of the very buildings of their administration. Not only were the motifs strikingly non-Levantine in their appearance, but the technique of true fresco—applying pigments directly onto a damp lime plaster ground without binding agents—would have been clearly obvious to the naked eye in contrast to the primary Near Eastern wall-painting technique of tempera, which uses binding agents such as egg to adhere to an already dry wall surface, seen for example at Mari.

The architecture of the administrative buildings at Alalakh, Qatna, and Tel Kabri, where the Aegean-style frescoes appear, offers clues to the social behaviors and norms that would have taken place within them, and thus to larger cultural expectations of order. These buildings can, in turn, be situated in a broader cultural horizon of the northern Levant comparing them with administrative buildings at Ebla and Tell Sakka, the latter having unusual wall paintings of its own. This exercise reveals general similarities that tie all the buildings together, arguing for a common social organization at the level of the ruling elites in the northern Levant and thus reflective of the new order created by them. Yet at the same time, differences in architectural planning, particularly in the structures at Alalakh, Ebla, and Tel Kabri and the structures at Qatna and Tell Sakka, indicate a degree of separation or competition among these same elites. The northern Levant, as it emerges from collapse, can be seen as both culturally unified and politically fractured. Any representational strategies of a new elite would have operated within this dualistic framework. Indeed, the appeal of exotica from the distant area of the Aegean may have gained in usefulness because of this tension between competition and cohesion.

However, significantly, the patterns evident in architectural decoration and planning cannot be correlated with any single "ethnic" ruling group, such as the Amorites. Although all of the cities in which Aegean-style frescoes appear had either new Amorite dynasties or Amorite elements in the population, other cities, most notably Mari, that were also under new Amorite rule did not exhibit this blatant Aegean connection. In fact, at Mari, the decoration of the palace, though exhibiting some possible Aegean motival inspiration, is executed in the tempera technique, which visually creates a strikingly different effect from true fresco. It seems then that the geographic region and its longstanding cultural traditions (even when regenerated after collapsed) carried a greater weight than any "ethnic" affiliations in terms of the representational strategies of leaders who assumed power.

Following the first two contributions, which explore relatively subtle strategies for establishing and maintaining new forms of authority, the third essay, by Marlies Heinz, "Sargon of Akkad: Rebel and Usurper in Kish," investigates the effects of radical and blatant breaks in tradition that Sargon instituted in his pursuit of a comprehensive new order. The rebellion in Kish led first to the modification of the traditional political order in that city. Its priests were disempowered, new groups were elevated as landowners, and the military became the most powerful confidant of the new king. Sargon knew well where and how to keep, change, or break political, economic, and religious traditions to secure the new order established by his rebellion. As a central strategy, he shifted power from the religious to the more worldly spheres of the palace and military and replaced officials to create loyal supporters.

These changes, especially in the sphere of officials, might not have been so obvious to the larger populace and could have left the impression of continuity, similar to what Pruzsinszky argues for at Emar. However, Sargon's intentions were quite the opposite; his policy was to make the change of order highly visible and unarguable. The building code of Kish was altered and a new population settled there—a change that affected the entire population of Kish. This severance of traditions in the sphere of daily life made the irrevocable change of order unambiguously obvious. The alterations in Kish were then surpassed by the most extreme of breaks: the founding of a new capital, Akkad, and the massive and complete disempowerment of the traditional seat of power, Kish. Clearly the new king, the rebel Sargon, was in an extraordinarily powerful position that he dared to modify and even break with traditions on such a large scale—or should the abandonment of the traditional center of power be seen as sign of political failing? In either case, the rebellion of Sargon in Kish escalated into an expansion of his newly established power that led to the destruction and refashioning of the political, economic, and cultural order throughout southern Mesopotamia. The destruction of local order was followed by the destruction of the political system. The independent city-state organization vanished and was substituted by the centralized Akkadian power system.

With the destruction of both the social order and physical structure of the traditional capital and the establishment of a new capital, Akkad, the former identity of the inhabitants of Kish was likewise ruptured and a new identity created that connected the king as well as the new order geographically and ideologically with the new structure Akkad, and Akkad with power, success, and prosperity. In other words, Akkad became the synonym and identifier for Sargon's imperial rule.

Besides controlling political power and subsistence and resource management, the Akkadian rulers also controlled the cultural and religious spheres by seemingly integrating themselves into the ruling traditions but actually misusing this integration in order to destroy the local orders. Destroying the order, creating new rules according to the rebel's needs, and then representing this violation as the salvation of order became the sophisticated strategy that Sargon used wherever he interfered in local affairs. Outwardly, Sargon perpetuated the religious traditions, whereas in fact the disempowerment of the priests was a stinging intervention. Local elites were blamed as the ones who had acted against their own gods' will and therefore had forfeited their authority to the newcomer. The destruction of the local political order went hand in hand with the severance of community solidarity with the accused kings. With Sargon's claims of attaining the sympathy and support of the local gods, he alone could guarantee the "good life" for the community and its future. Because, in this representation, the gods supported the new order, the "new" became "naturalized"—and the "natural," normative—and change paradoxically became the only way of ensuring continuity. Formally, Sargon was integrated into the religious system and a "servant of the local gods," but in fact he abused the system for his own advantage. The brilliance of the Akkadian ideology and propaganda lay in its success in presenting the very person who had overthrown the cultural rules as the one who was in perfect harmony with the given order (that he had just destroyed).

The change of order following the rebellion of Sargon and his policy of expansion thus encompassed all levels and all fields of social existence. In order to gain control of all essential resources—politics, economy, security, religion—Sargon played with rules, norms, values, and traditions as it pleased him and as it served his interests. All destruction and the imposition of a new order were made openly; no attempt to hide the Akkadian actions seems to have been necessary or desirable. Sargon, according to his representations, turned out to be a master in planning and leading military actions and in establishing control by openly breaking with the preexisting rules and traditions. His strategies brilliantly molded the local cultural and religious value systems to fit the Akkadian ideology and dealt deftly with the various traditions he encountered—carrying them forward, modifying or breaking them—in order to suit the needs of the new Akkadian politics.

The next essay, Susan Pollock's "Royal Cemetery of Ur: Ritual, Tradition, and the Creation of Subjects," explores a case of equally high impact and visibility: the practice of "ritual sacrifice." The death of a member of the political and/or religious elite often meant a profound disturbance of continuity on the family and clan level as well as in the political sphere. The community had to reestablish order to avoid further erosion of social life. In third-millennium Ur, the celebrated Royal Cemetery appears to have been an extremely ostentatious form of securing order after the death of an important person. The sumptuous burial rituals at the site, for people of presumably the highest status in the community, included not only the building of elaborate tombs and their endowment with costly burial objects but also the accompaniment of the dead with a great number of personnel. The question of how these individuals were convinced to go to their death "voluntarily" (no signs of violence were found on their bodies) has rarely been considered in any depth. That is, what ideological framework existed that was persuasive enough to do this, and why was this framework so critical for Early Dynastic society at Ur?

The initial impression is that the threat to social order caused by a "natural" incidence such as the death of an elite figure could only be contained through the politically sanctioned breaking of another order–namely, the social order of the individuals who accompanied the deceased. While the first social rupture (the elite's death) threatened to destabilize society, the second (the "sacrifice" of personnel) may have been initiated to repair the rupture in the name of safeguarding the society. However, a closer inspection of the cultural structures and conditions of Early Dynastic society presents a rather different picture in which ritual and ideology played key roles in the process of obtaining the consent of the "sacrificed" personnel.

Several indicators suggest that the attendants who accompanied the deceased were highly placed members of the deceased's household. These personnel naturalized their social identity as an indisolvable unit within the household through feasts, routines of daily ceremonial life, and tradition. Participation in feasts, public rituals, and tradition served to establish conformity and to strengthen the prevailing order. In a society that correlates the death of the head of a household with the "death" of the household as such, following the deceased into a "new life," the netherworld, became natural and persuasive. The metaphorical death of a household at the time of the death of the head of the household was part of an ideological denial of the very heritability of resources and wealth–that is, an abnegation of dynastic relevance (which Pollock argues marks the transition during the Early Dynastic period from appointed individual authority to inherited). Feasting and making food and drink offerings to the gods and the dead acted as mundane, everyday practices that naturalized this ideology during life and made persuasive the ultimate feast of poison and the offering of one's life. Rehearsals of cooperation in feasts and rituals during the active members' lifetimes and conformity in habitual daily routines may have lessened the weightiness of the "next step": taking part in the "final ritual" and celebrating the cooperation in death. Such intimacy in life with the ritual practices also linked to death may have served to lessen the fear of the unknown.

When the natural death of the elite individual and the "unnatural" death of the personnel had been accepted by all concerned as "natural," the cultural and religious practices and traditions that went hand in hand with the ideology strengthened the prevailing order, an order that neglected the interests of the people who were not in control. These practices made one's actions seem natural, even if in the end the actions went against one's self-interest (the question of whether staying alive was even imaginable remains unanswered).

Religion and practices are also the focus of the subsequent essay, by Dominik Bonatz, "The Divine Image of the King: Religious Representation of Political Power in the Hittite Empire." As with Pollock, religion and politics, defined by Bonatz in terms of praxis (the "doing") rather than institutional characters, appear at least on the surface to have functioned smoothly within the cultural continuum of the Hittite Empire. Yet it is through the very notion of praxis–in particular visual praxis, in which the acts of making and seeing construct "reality" for different social groups–that order and tradition can be shaped, changed, and even manipulated.

One aspect of the imperial politics of the Hittites was the dissolution of order in occupied territories. The Hittites must have been aware of the danger that every attack on the order of "others" could and would be answered with the same weapon: an attack on the Hittite order. In addition, the Hittites must have reckoned that events within the Hittite community also posed a threat to "law and order" at home. One threat of this kind for the ruling order was the death of the Hittite king, when, for a short period, the affected community lost their supreme servant of the gods, their intermediary between the terrestrial and numinous sphere. The potential successors warded off this threat primarily by keeping and establishing religious rituals–albeit with slight modifications in the performance of these rituals, such as royal burial–if they were beneficial for the representation of their own power. The maintenance of tradition as a form of crisis management, therefore, could acquire individual traits. However, the continuity of tradition and ritual in the commemoration of the deceased connected the present with the glorious past. In representing themselves as successful rulers who could rely on the support of the deceased, they positioned themselves as guarantors of the preservation of the community and thus connected the present with the future (for example, the death of Tudhaliya IV and the actions of his successor, Shuppiluliuma II, connected the burial ritual for the deceased father with the portrait of the son's own power).

Religious images strongly shaped the introduction of a political iconography into the Hittite royal propaganda ("rhetoric") late in the Empire period (thirteenth century). An analysis of the visual practice reveals that politics and religion were inseparable components in the legitimation of rulership. The forms of this visual representation were, however, contigent on their dynamic contextualization in various places and with various audiences. This in turn provided the potential for assaults on the Hittite order, both from within Hittite society and without. The annexation (or appropriation) of the specific visual tradition by "others" and the ability of images to promote and protect self-interests highlight their double-edged power that contributed to a crisis of Hittite power.

The ambivalence inherent in images of the Hittite king documents both the attractiveness of the ruling order and its failings, which permitted vassals and tributaries of the Hittites to deploy the images in representing their own world views and ruling orders. Where it became possible for the vassals to use the iconography and terminology of the Hittites to declare themselves in public as "great kings" (as in the relief of Kurunta), they presented their low estimation of the validity of the prevailing order and thereby made the crisis of the Hittite power highly visible. When appropriated and manipulated in this manner, the traditions of the Hittite superpower experienced a dramatic devaluation as stabilizers of Hittite culture and rulership. How, other than as a direct attack on the validity of the prevailing political order, can one understand the visual self-representation of the viceroy of Carchemish? In it he expressed his respect not to the Hittite great king but to the storm-god and thereby declared the god and not the king as the representative of the prevailing order.

Succession to the throne constituted another potentially critical moment for the stability of social and political order. In case the succession was contested (as happened when Murshili III claimed power), those responsible had to find legitimacy for obtaining power beyond the traditional means. The visual representation of the ruler experienced strong modifications, if indeed it did not break with tradition completely. The direct ancestor was no longer presented as legitimating the new order, but instead, a new ruler represented himself with numinous iconography during his lifetime. Crisis management and the legitimation of the prevailing order was no longer represented only with reference to ancestry. Not until the new king represented himself as a member of the numinous sphere was his rulership supported and challenges to it prevented (in theory and according to the cultural rules of interacting with the gods). However, religion and tradition were used by all parties, not just the Hittite king. While the kings modified their own Hittite traditions, the vassals broke with them entirely when they presented themselves as great kings, thus constructing their identity through a reference to the traditions of the Hittites and yet at the same time reducing the validity of the prevailing Hittite order *ad absurdum.*

Paul-Alain Beaulieu's essay, "Nabonidus the Mad King: A Reconsideration of His Steles from Harran and Babylon," differs from the preceding contributions in that it explores a negative instance of using religion to shape new political order. For Nabonidus, attempts to draw upon the traditional modes in the construction of his own self-representation were ineffective against the rising power of the scholarly and priestly groups who opposed his rule. Ultimately, it came down to a struggle over who had the authority to interpret and validate religious ideology: Nabonidus or the religious scholars. With the growing strength of the scholars, who self-servingly acted as royal advisers, Nabonidus's authority weakened. And it is the representation of Nabonidus as constructed by his opponents that has survived in large part in the later traditions that labeled him as mad. Nabonidus, king of Babylon, came to power as a usurper. His own "self-portrait," of course, did not represent himself as mad but as the keeper of tradition who had to exclude his precursor from office because, according to the proclamation of the gods, he had ruled against the gods' will. Being in the gods' favor is a familiar justification for taking power violently and a classic means of legitimation for the new order. Although Nabonidus did not descend from the traditional political circles and families of Babylon, as a member of the Babylonian court, he was nevertheless familiar with local norms and traditions and through these sought to create a connection with the legitimate kings of Babylon: Nebuchadnezzar and Neriglissar.

Nabonidus seems to have come to power through the influence of his mother, herself a high priest in the service of Sin of Harran. As a result, Nabonidus was heavily dependent on the supporters surrounding his mother, who did not belong to the traditional power circles of Babylon but to the priesthood of Sin of Harran. This, however, did not serve Nabonidus well in his search for supporters in Babylon for his new political and religious program. His dependency on the Harran elite created virtually inescapable opposition from the local Babylonian circles, not only in the political realm, but, even more problematically, among the religious and scholarly groups. While a change "only" within the political sphere and at the highest level of power (that is, the king) might have found support among some local Babylonian elites, Nabonidus framed his usurpation with a radical change to the religious system–a logical result of the intentions of his supporters from Harran but one that was perceived as a sacrilege to the Babylonian elites. Changing the religious order was one of the most delicate political acts a ruler could undertake in Mesopotamia, because it not only attacked the basis of communal and spiritual life but also potentially angered all interest groups. To attempt this feat, one would have to have been extremely powerful, or "mad" (the fate assigned to Nabonidus's reputation in later traditions). Only with support from outside Babylon was this attempt thinkable–that is, from interests groups (like the Sin Harran clique) that could only win, not lose ground in this process: the power of the Sin elite in Harran need not necessarily have been affected by a failure in Babylon.

Nabonidus presented the systemic change as the reestablishment of a demolished order, demolished by forces in Babylonia who, according to his point of view (and political propaganda) had disobeyed the Babylonian gods, had not fulfilled religious duties, had violated rituals and religious traditions, and because of this had caused chaos in Babylonia. Ironically, the very same allegations were made by Nabonidus's opponents, who added to these charges the accusation that he monopolized religious, ritual, and cultural knowledge spheres and broke with the tradition of keeping a sage as his adviser. Thus, both the "reformers/rebels" who pushed for change and the representatives of Marduk in Babylon who wanted to prevent religious reform described the intentions of each other as leading to chaos, sacrilege, and disorder–in general, threatening culture and community. Control over the religious sphere, proper use of traditions, and accusations by the opposition of flouting the traditional religious rules and customs turned out (once more) to be of central importance for keeping (or gaining) political power in Babylonia.

Clearly, the camps involved in the struggle for power in Babylon understood the inextricable integration of politics and religion. However, Nabonidus and his backers may have underestimated the power of the Babylonian circles and overestimated the power of the Sin clique in Harran. Changing the religious system made it extremely difficult to create loyalty to the new power, even for those who might otherwise have been willing to support Nabonidus. What would form the basis of identity in a situation in which (by changing the "god") the whole legitimation of life and existence that had depended on Marduk was lost? What did Nabonidus offer the populace to gain their support when reducing or even taking away the power of Marduk? He seems to have overestimated the power of his own propaganda in establishing a new order while underestimating the power of the local religious traditions to create the identity of the Babylonians.

Ultimately Nabonidus did not succeed in his changes, either in politics or in religious reform. However, the Marduk supporters did not succeed either. Attempting to keep Nabonidus and his reforms out, they supported the Persians. The discrediting of Nabonidus worked, but at the same time it led to the disempowerment of Babylon as a whole. The city and its elites lost what they had intended to keep: Babylon's position as the center of the political and religious world and their authority as its representatives.

Although located in a different section of the book (according to the theme of later perceptions of new order), Kuhrt's article on Cyrus immediately follows Beaulieu's investigation into Nabonidus, permitting, when read sequentially, a relationship between them that focuses on the same period of time: the end of Neo-Babylonian rule and the formation of the Achaemenid Empire, with paths crossing in the episode of Cyrus's capture of Babylon. Nonetheless, we chose to place Kuhrt's essay not in the same section as Beaulieu's but near Brit Jahn's on the Amorites (see more below) in order to highlight the difficulties that we, as modern scholars, encounter in trying to reconstruct the ancient "realities" of royal or elite manipulations of order. These difficulties arise precisely because the ancient representational strategies (as well as other–both complementary and competing–strategies) for instituting changes in order often obscure and confuse the very presentation of the transition. And it is this aspect of how later or competing representations of charismatic rulers have distorted our modern perceptions of them that Amélie Kuhrt takes as her central theme in the essay, "Cyrus the Great of Persia: Images and Realities."

Cyrus, considered the first Persian king, was renowned in later traditions as a dazzling character, but getting at any kernel of historical accuracy is challenging, not least because his "images," which have conditioned the reception of him as a ruler, derive from numerous disparate sources that do not primarily reflect Cyrus's own (controlled) self-representation. From his death onward, the portraits of Cyrus reflect instead the vision of the diverse historians who recorded his deeds and qualities from their own perspective and, one cannot exclude this, serving their own interests rather than being bound to any historical "truth."

The lineage of Cyrus, according to one of the most propagated stories, is unknown. One particularly trenchant narrative treats Cyrus as a usurper without a past and as the liberator of the Persians from Median rule. According to this narrative, Cyrus, with his violent accession to power, became the "self-made-king" of the Persians. As always, when one order was replaced through the installation of a new person at the top of the elite hierarchy (that is, the ruler), the new beginning needed to be legitimated. And if the legitimation could not derive from the existing tradition, as is usually the case for a usurper, it had to be constructed. According to the sources composed after his death, Cyrus did not ground his legitimacy in the physical power that propelled him to kingship; rather, he integrated himself into a glorious past. According to his titles, he saw himself not as the founder of a dynasty but as the successor of royal ancestors and, as such, as the historically legitimated ruler.

Cyrus's use of tradition to legitimate the new order was a classic strategy deployed by illegitimate rulers of the ancient Near East beginning in at least the third millennium. With the aid of massive military support and tactical brilliance, Cyrus created a world empire of hitherto unknown dimensions. In creating a new world order, he dismantled the regimes, traditions, value systems, and cultural rules of all the incorporated communities; yet, he was glorified as a ruler who was tolerant, even supportive, of the cultural traditions and religions of those he conquered. Thus was the positive image of Cyrus handed down; the ideology of power and the power of propaganda fully exploited its virtue. As a foreign ruler, at least according to the later traditions, Cyrus knew how to shape his actions in order to conform to the traditions of the conquered communities in a way that was always beneficial for his authority yet at the same time created the appearance that he was acting in the best interests of the subject societies. Cyrus integrated himself into the rituals and cultural traditions of these communities and in this way concealed the actual disruption of political order by maintaining the religious traditions.

Cyrus legitimated his take-over of Babylon by vilifying the wrongdoings of his predecessor–another classic pattern of legitimation used by usurpers and foreign rulers in the ancient Near East–in order to declare the coup an act of reestablishing "law and order." In contrast to Sargon's strategies that highlighted his powerful break with tradition, Cyrus sought to emphasize continuity by taking care of the local temples and maintaining the spatial structure of the cities, although of course he had changed the political order significantly. The limitation (and perhaps even falseness) of his tolerance is evident in the case of Babylon, where Cyrus performed the important local religious ceremonies but did so in traditional Persian costume. Subtleties of this sort in his dealings with the religious and cultural traditions of his conquered subjects clearly reflect his all-embracing awareness of political imperatives.

Yet another strategically effective move was Cyrus's political integration of the elements of the conquered that contributed most forcefully to the creation of group identity in order to establish a new feeling of "us" not only in the individual, subject regions but also and above all in the center of political power in Persia. When building his prestigious capital of Pasargadae, Cyrus drew upon the cultural symbols and religious images of the subdued communities to adorn the buildings. In mixing these elements in a hybrid way, he positioned himself as the guardian of the cultural heritage of all the conquered lands, while at the same time creating something that was uniquely Persian and would become the shared heritage of the entire Persian Empire. In using the cultural elements of "others" at home, Cyrus could "prove" that he was a caretaker of all cultures and societies, and not, as he was in reality, an intruder who occupied the land of "others" and appropriated them for Persian interests. He had nothing that he could declare as originally "Persian," so he had to use the cultural elements of others to construct his architecture. But he turned this "failing" into a positive attribute, effectively claiming that the Persians took care of the other traditions and cultural heritages; the foreign delegations that came to Persia saw only a stewardship of their tradition and culture. At the same time it seems that the use of cultural elements of the "other" for visibly creating Pasargadae was another strategic move on the part of Cyrus. The propaganda was clear: not exclusion but integration of the subdued into the sphere of power as a way of creating a "global" identity. Cultural diversity and acceptance of the "other" became a symbol of political grandeur for the Persians. The integration of the cultural symbols of conquered societies into the building program of Persian political power not only acknowledged the "real" political position of the "others" but helped to convince them that they ranked on the same level with the Persians.

The propaganda of a militarily mighty power, one that had caused changes, disruptions, and dissolutions of political and social order throughout the Empire, sought, through the hybrid design of Pasargade, to convince the conquered of the exact opposite. The ideology of power, the power of the images, and the propaganda of those in power served to establish the image of a tolerant Cyrus who created a new global order and a new global community that came to be remembered as the natural order among his contemporaries as well as in the memory of the ensuing ages.

We end the volume with Brit Jahn's contribution, "The Migration and Sedentarization of the Amorites from the Point of View of the Settled Babylonian Population," which tackles one of the more enigmatic transitions in Near Eastern history: the emergence of Amorite dynasties after a long, slow process of infiltration into the established urban centers of the Near East. When urban society and the nomadic way of life meet, the question arises: which pattern of life had what to offer the other? Describing the "other" (here the Amorites) as barbarians who knew nothing about urban traditions, knowledge and culture, proper living, religion, or the proper handling of the dead was surely intended to reinforce the superiority of urban life compared with nomadic life. It also suggests, however, that the urban culture of the Near East was not stable enough to handle the immigration of "others" into their society as a "normal" routine of daily life. While urban life was seen has having much to offer "others," the nomadic lifestyle, according to the "folk literature" of the settled people, had nothing to offer "civilized" (that is, urban) society. Migration and sedentarization were thus constituted in the traditions of the urban societies as a severe affront to the urban traditions. The written transmission of this perception illustrates still another aspect that is central to power: it was only the urban culture as a literate culture, in contrast to the nomadic communities, that was able to perpetuate their perspective on "us and them" for the future (and in particular for the "future" that includes Assyriological scholarship). Those who controlled writing thus controlled the future.

Yet, practically speaking, it was not the urban society but the people who had to change their way of living radically through migration and sedentarization who faced a far greater change and even loss of their cultural traditions. It was they who lost their traditional way of living and, with it, presumably many aspects of their culture, values, and norms. Nevertheless, the Amorites managed to acculturate themselves and assimilate into the urban societies, although today it is hard to determine how the majority of Amorites confronted their new situation. In contrast, one can clearly follow the actions taken both by the settled Amorite leaders and the urban elites in establishing their positions in the emerging arrangements. The new order revealed potential opportunities for powerful newcomers from nomadic backgrounds as well as from elite precincts in the periphery to achieve rulership in the newly developing societies. At the same time, the configuration of new social communities showed the potential for threatening the urban establishment with the loss of their traditional authority within the urban communities.

Rebellion in the periphery against the urban centers of political power was one way to achieve power by those who were legally not (yet) in positions of authority. Rebels and usurpers exploited the migration process of the Amorites into southern Mesopotamia as a way of legitimating their own seizure of power by force. Claiming to need ultimate power in order to prevent the destruction of order threatened by the Amorites' settlement activities, they concealed their own violation of the ruling order and propagated a representation of themselves as the guardians of tradition. Ibbisin and his rebellion against Ur is a good example of this kind of political action. For the traditionally established political elite, their own political operation became an ambivalent issue. While the local kings took care to control the immigration process and provide the basic parameters for a successful acculturation and assimilation, they not only permitted but forced the immigrants to assimilate into the structures of power and political organization. This strategy, however, allowed the Amorite elite eventually to become a threat to their "hosts," whose positions of power they usurped in several cases. The chosen politics of the urban political elite resulted thus on the one hand in the stabilization of their community and on the other hand in the destabilizing of their own power. Paradoxically, then, perpetuating the traditional social order could result in the destruction of the political order and in the loss of rulership. With the successful integration of the "others" into their community, the urban elite had created their own rivals.

Assimilation and acculturation of the Amorites thus allowed some members of the Amorite ruling classes to assume power in their new environment. The newcomers represented themselves as keepers of the local traditions by adopting the traditional royal titles. Thus, in public they demonstrated continuity, where in fact disruption had occurred–a familiar pattern in the ancient Near East as elsewhere. In some cases, they invented new royal titles without relation to either a local or an Amorite tradition, but the new Amorite elite still acknowledged their lineage; even as kings in a new urban environment, they retained their Amorite personal names. In this way, they bridged the two populations: Amorite and traditional urban. They appeased the local population by suggesting continuity and the Amorite tribesmen by displaying their Amorite heritage. The Amorite past was not forgotten, but at the same time this background did not hinder the new kings. Connecting the past and the traditions of the urban as well as the traditions of the nomadic societies with the present thus helped the new Amorite elite secure their future.

The process of migration and sedentarization affected the ruling orders of all societies involved. The changes and disruptions of order seem to have produced winners and losers on both sides–among the nomads as well as among the urban societies–and likewise on different levels of society. Every group affected responded individually to the inevitable change. In learning the traditions of the respective "others," the nomad population lost its traditional way of living and was forced to integrate into the urban structures, and ultimately it was the urban society, though it nursed "grievances" about being threatened, that survived.

Part 1

Reestablishment of Order after Major Disruption

Chapter 1
Emar and the Transition from Hurrian to Hittite Power

Regine Pruzsinszky

Introduction

The history of Emar presents some valuable insights on Hurrian/Mittanian rule and the succeeding Hittite hegemony over northern Syria in the second half of the second millennium B.C. and, as a result, on changes of power and their effects on controlled cities. Emar which was situated along the Middle Euphrates, always played a strategically important role as a center of commerce on the border between political units. The two distinct scribal traditions reflected in the private legal documents found at Emar combined with prosopographical observations reveal a chronological separation of the tablets that roughly date to the second half of the second millennium B.C. With the recognition of this chronological division, institutional changes become apparent that can be linked directly to the transition from Mittanian to Hittite power. The textual evidence elucidates the way the local rulers and administrative and religious institutions were affected by the change of political power and how the overlords maintained control and power over the Middle Euphrates region. Thus one needs to distinguish between the local Syrian tradition and the Hurrian and Hittite influences and innovations found in the texts, because there is hardly any documentation on political affairs. While comparably little can be said about Mittanian rule and its impact on the local Syrian traditional administrative units of the city elders and the city god, we can say that the Hittites exercised control via their viceroy at Carchemiš and seem to have changed the local administration to some extent. Although the local institutions continued to exist, the newly installed rulers and the diviner of Emar evidently collaborated extensively with the Hittite overlords. This enabled the Hittites to control not only the political but also the cultural and religious life of Emar. This essay presents an overview of the most significant features of life in Emar, which seems to have undergone some modification caused by the change of foreign powers during the time that these texts were written.

Author's note: This study has been conducted with the financial support of APART (Austrian Programme for Advanced Research and Technology), funded by the Austrian Academy of Sciences. The complete list of publications of the Emar texts can be found in Pruzsinszky 2003: xxv–xxvii. CM 13 designates the publication number of Emar texts in Westenholz et al. (2000); CM page numbers refer to accompanying commentary. I would like to thank Marian Feldman for her help with the English text.

Two Different Scribal Traditions and Their Impact on the Dating of the Legal Documents of Emar

The numerous texts found at Emar, situated on the Euphrates approximately 100 km southeast of Ḫalab, display two different scribal traditions: the so-called "Syrian" and the "Syro-Hittite" scribal tradition or style. Not only do the tablets differ in shape, format, grammatical features, orthography, and the application of seal impressions, but also the formulations employed by these mostly legal documents show differences.[1] Arnaud, the field epigrapher and editor of the excavated Emar texts, believed that the two scribal traditions coexisted during the period beginning with the foundation of the "new" Emar[2] by the Hittites (ca. 1325 B.C.) until its end in 1187 B.C., based on the preliminary excavation reports of Margueron. However, a number of scholars consider the two scribal traditions to reflect to some extent two chronologically distinct phases in the history of Emar: a period when Emar belonged to the Mittanian Kingdom (beginning ca. 1400 or later) and the period when it was integrated into the Hittite Empire (ca. 1325 or later).[3] This view is now confirmed by the recent excavation report by Finkbeiner, who proved that Emar was not newly founded by the Hittite overlord but had earlier occupation levels as well.[4] The object of this study is to shed more light on the two distinct phases, which are concurrent with the change of sovereignty around 1325, when Šuppiluliuma I took control of northern Syria. Emar eventually became a vassal kingdom of the Hittite Empire under the jurisdiction of Carchemiš, the seat of the viceroy of the Hittite emperor. Unfortunately, the exact date of Emar's annexation and the time of transition to the new power remain unknown.[5]

1. Note, for instance, Seminara 1998a. The absence of some types of contracts, such as security texts, cannot be clearly attributed to the coincidence of finds or social or historical reasons, as Skaist (2001: 236) pointed out.

2. The "old" city, known from the Ebla and Mari texts of the third and second millenniums B.C., was believed to be located somewhere else (see, e.g., Yamada 1995: 297 n. 1).

3. Most notably Skaist (1998a), who separated the chronology into two distinct phases that are represented by two local royal dynasties. An important site situated close to Emar is Ekalte (Tell Munbāqa), which is roughly contemporary with the phase before the Hittite domination of Emar (see Werner [2004: 23–24], who carefully suggested dates of ca. 1400–1325 B.C.). Another revised chronology of the Emar tablets, based on letter E 536, has been proposed by Durand (Durand and Marti 2003: 156–60), who dates them all to the thirteenth century. According to him, the dynasty of Iaḫṣi-Dagān began around 1235 B.C. and is synchronized with Kaštiliašu IV and Tukulti-Ninurta I. The preceding Emarite "dynasty" is dated to the time of the Assyrian king Šalmaneser I and the end of Adad-nīrārī I's reign. In contrast, Skaist (1998a) proposed following chronological periods for each of the scribal traditions: ca. 1400–1220 B.C. (Syrian) and 1275–1210 B.C. (Syro-Hittite). In 2005, he suggested the period between ca. 1325 and 1180 B.C. for the local dynasty of Emar, beginning with Baʿal-kabar I. Di Filippo's valuable conclusions (2004) suggest that the early Syrian tablets of Emar are not from as early as 1400 but sometime later, before Šuppiluliuma's Syrian campaigns. On p. 198, he argues that Liʾmi-šarra, who is "clearly titled king" in FK 6, was a contemporary of Baʿal-kabar. Thus the change of dynasties due to the coming of the Hittites must have taken place at the time of Liʾmi-šarra.

4. For a summary, see Faist and Finkbeiner 2002: 190–95.

5. Di Filippo (2004: 198 n. 100), who just presented a new, careful study on the chronology of the legal texts of Emar, considers Muršili II to have been responsible for the change of dynasties in Emar—shifting the dates for the Emar archives downward (see below).

How can we trace this change within the textual evidence of Emar, and which differences can be observed in regard to the control of the region around Emar in the land of Aštata (which is also referred to as "the land of Emar" in texts from Ugarit)[6] before and after ca. 1325 B.C.? Because the documentation mainly concerns private and legal matters, we lack what we would consider the "most helpful" evidence, such as historiographical texts like treaties, royal declarations, and the like.[7] The historical and social background can only be reconstructed by external textual evidence or by hints within the Emar texts, such as date formulas referring to events (Zaccagnini 1995; Vita 2002) or kings, officials, and institutions mentioned throughout the tablets.[8] Only a few texts allude to historically interesting facts. Nevertheless, the abundance of private legal texts allows us to reconstruct the transition of power at Emar from Mittani to Ḫatti from an internal view. Changes and innovations within the legal clauses represented in the Syrian and Syro-Hittite texts of Emar,[9] which provide us with an idea of the economic, legal, and administrative situation in second-millennium Syria can be linked to a certain extent with the political changes in this area.

The importance of Emar throughout its history beginning in the third millennium B.C. is due to its strategically important location at the crossroads of commercial routes along the Euphrates connecting the Levant and Syria with Mesopotamia. During the first half of the second millennium (Old Babylonian period), Emar was the most remote outpost of the kingdom of Ḫalab, bordering the kingdom of Mari. As Fleming (2004: 213) remarks: "Imar's distance from the shadow of the major kingdoms allowed its local political traditions to thrive with relatively little interference from outside powers, and these local traditions were markedly collective." During the Hittite period, Emar and Tell Faqʿūs, situated ca. 12 km farther southeast of Emar, were again the easternmost military outposts of the Hittite Empire, bordering Assyria, whose growing expansive power was threatening Ḫatti. According to his annals, Muršili II went to the "city (of) Aštata" and built a fortress that he garrisoned (KBo IV 4 ii 59–68). This city is generally identified with Tell Faqʿūs,[10] which is considered

6. Yamada 1994b: 264–68. Yamada thus believes Emar to be the main city of the land of Aštata.

7. Note the essay by Cancik (1993) with special emphasis on the meaning of "sovereignty" in these texts (especially contracts). In his summary on p. 130, Cancik stresses the issues that seem to be essential with regard to cognition of "others" and self-perception. "Die vorgeführten Texte zeigen eine genaue Fremdwahrnehmung . . . ; dem entspricht eine besondere Eigenwahrnehmung und entsprechend 'Selbstbewußtheit.'" On the structure and the relevant issues in vassal treaties, see p. 125 (protection of and respect for defined borders, the vassal's agreement not to become involved in foreign affairs, loyalty toward other vassals, performance of military backup, etc.).

8. The texts from Emar are considered additional evidence to the state archives of Ḫattuša for the study of Hittite society (see, e.g., Yamada 1995: 298; Bellotto 2002).

9. Faist 2002; Westbrook 2003 (with a useful summary of legal issues referring to previous studies; see pp. 683–84 with characteristics of Syrian and Syro-Hittite sale documents). Note that the shape of the Syro-Hittite styled tablets resembles the format of the tablets from Carchemiš, which had a separate scribal tradition from the tablets of Ḫattuša, the Hittite capital (Faist 2002: 132).

10. Note already Bunnens (1989: 24–25), who stressed that Emar should not be identified with the capital of Aštata. He viewed Aštata as a confederation or province of which the kingdom of Emar was part. One of its representatives could have been the UGULA KALAM.MA ('Chief of the Country'), who is mentioned several times in the texts. Adamthwaite (2001: 224), who follows Margueron's and

to have served as a defensive site for Emar, forming part of a system of fortresses along the Euphrates (Margueron 1981–82). Due to similar (specifically architectural) remains at Emar (Tell Meskene), Margueron believed that it was also a new foundation by the Hittites, with no earlier traces of occupation. This widely accepted view of the past 20 to 30 years has been challenged recently by the Syrian-German excavations at Emar, as stated above.

Mittanian Rule of Emar

Little is known about the period preceding Hittite hegemony over Emar and the political situation before 1325.[11] This is mainly due to a general lack of textual evidence during this time within the region (for the main texts, see table 1, pp. 26–27). Most studies have emphasized instead Emar under Hittite domination and influence, since this period is much better documented. We are left with very few hints concerning the governing of Emar in its earlier phase as documented in the textual evidence. The texts do not even identify the name of the Mittanian ruler of this time.

Generally, only a few (royal) Mittanian sources have been found in northern Syria that provide hints to political actions from the period of Mittani's political strength: the newly discovered texts from Tell Bazi recording donations of land by Sauštatar and Artatama (I?) to the "sons of the city of Baziri," the city elders;[12] the tablet from Umm el-Marra granting manumission (*ḫanigalbatūtu*) to several individuals in the presence of Šuttarna II; and two legal documents from Tell Brak, which were written in the presence of Artašumara and Tušratta.[13] After the reign of Šuttarna II, Mittani's situation became unstable and relations with Egypt deteriorated. Šuppiluliuma I finally put an end to the power of Mittani and its ruler Tušratta[14] and annexed northern Syria and parts of upper Mesopotamia to the Hittite Kingdom.

Various (local) Old Syrian features of the "Syrian" tablets of Emar can be identified that are not to be found in "Syro-Hittite" texts and that may also be used as an indication for an earlier dating of those texts.[15] In general, Old Syrian features can be detected in paleography, language, the dating of documents, the formulations and legal clauses/phraseology, sealing practices, rituals and their calendar, and archaeological remains. Parallels to legal practices that are considered local and "Old Syrian," such as the satisfaction clause and penalty clause containing a payment, are found in texts

---

Arnaud's proposal for the chronology of Emar, identifies Aštata with another town: modern El-Qitar. In contrast, Yamada (1994b: 267) believes that the city of Aštata should be identified with Emar.

11. For a reconstruction of the history of Mittani, see, e.g., Kühne 1999.

12. Otto and Einwag 2005: 27. Donations by the king of Mittani to the people of Aštata are recorded in the treaty between Muwatalli II and Talmi-Šarrumma of Aleppo (CTH 75).

13. Sallaberger et al. 2006; Cooper et al. 2005; eidem in Oates et al. 1997. Further evidence, as yet unpublished, from the early Mittanian era comes from Terqa mentioning Parrattarna II and probably Šuttarna (I) and Sauštatar (Rouault 2004: 56–57).

14. Note the Šattiwaza treaty (CTH 51), which also lists the places that were given to Piyaššili of Carchemiš (see Yamada 1994b; and note T. Richter 2005 on behalf of Qaṭna texts).

15. Seminara 1998; Fleming 2000; Sallaberger 2003 in his review of Adamthwaite.

from Ekalte and Nuzi and even earlier in the third millennium (for example, ceremonial actions of breaking bread and anointing a table at the end of transactions). Table 1 lists texts belonging to the phase before Hittite domination of Emar and thus are not contemporary with the "Syro-Hittite" scribal tradition that appears after the transition of power. They contain the most characteristic features of the "Syrian" documents, including "eponym-like" dating, a satisfaction clause, a *ḫazannu* ('mayor')[16] in the witness list, a penalty clause in case of a vindication, with payments to the deity ^{d}NIN.URTA (= ^{d}N)[17] and the city. Most of these tablets derive from the antiquities market (those from regular excavations were found in the M_1 building[18]).

The sale document E 153,[19] which also contains the *arana*-clause, can be attributed to one of the family members according to its witness list. E 12, written by Eḫli-Kuša, belongs to the earlier texts as well; but unlike the others, it was recovered in the "palace" of Emar.

The eponym-like dating "month x, year PN 1st/2nd time" only occurs in these early nonroyal Syrian type tablets. Fleming (2000: 224) has pointed out its origin in the "collective governance identified as the 'city', associated in part with elders or free citizens. Parallel eponym and city administrative systems . . . must have arisen out of the older social pattern."[20] CM 13:4, which is described by its editor as "classical Old Babylonian," also contains this dating formula and uses clauses that are characteristic for these early documents. These include most notably the ceremonial clause concluding the legal transaction, an extra payment (*ku-ub-bu-ru*)[21] to the "brothers" or the fraternal clan ($^{LÚ.MEŠ}$AḪ.ḪI.A, *aḫ-ḫu*) and the penalty clause (compare with E 171 and RE 34 in table 1).[22] All these observations point to a strong urban authority as is also suggested by the historically interesting text FK 6, which was ratified by the seal of ^{d}NIN.URTA but not by a royal authority. The dynastic seal, with the exception of AuOrS 1 14 and E 148, is never attested on these early tablets, while NIN.URTA's seal can always be found on tablets from the beginning of the Emar archives onward. In FK 6, Ir'ib-Dagān is rewarded for his expenditures for the "city and his lord" by "the king and the city of Emar."[23] In comparison with the evidence from Ekalte and Azû,

16. See Mayer (2001: 23–24) for the mayors attested in the documents from Ekalte and in the eponym-like datings.

17. For discussion of the reading of ^{d}NIN.URTA, see Westenholz 1999.

18. An exception may be E 12, which was found in the "palace."

19. Note the restoration made by Skaist (1998a: 62 n. 45) based on the witness list of E 150.

20. Unfortunately, the texts do not inform us about the administrative function of the persons who serve as eponyms. The eponym-like dating is also attested at Ekalte, which names the mayor.

21. On this term, see Zaccagnini 1989: 37–40.

22. Only rarely is a palace referred to in these early documents: for example, in AuOrS 1 14 ^{d}NIN.URTA, the city and the palace (!) are named as recipients of the penalty. In other known cases where the palace is named in the penalty clause, members of the royal family are usually quoted within the document.

23. The city of Emar and its lord are also referred to in RE 34 listed above. Here Ikūn-Dagān, the owner of a house, has his house taken away because of an 'offense' (*ḫīṭu*) committed against his city and his lord (URU^{KI}-*šu ù be-lí-šu*). As a consequence, ^{d}NIN.URTA and the 'great ones of Emar' ($^{LÚ.MEŠ}$GAL-GAL ^{URU}*E-mar*^{KI}) sold the house (the penalty-clause names the city and ^{d}NIN.URTA as recipients). On additional *ḫīṭu*-clauses at Emar that do not refer to the king (LUGAL), see Adamthwaite 2001: 89–97. Ekalte text no. 3, 36 states that the buyer of a house is to hand over the acquired house

Table 1. Texts Explicitly Dating to the Earlier Local "Dynasty" of Irʾib-^{d}IŠKUR

Text	*Parties*	*Penalty Clause*	*Witness*	*Other*	*Additional Comments*
AuOrS 1 14 Sale (plot of land)	^{d}N+elders (sellers) Izraʿ-Dagān, son of Ḫimaš (buyer)	^{d}N+city+ **palace**	Irʾib-^{d}IŠKUR-EN and brothers	[ ]-mālik, scribe	***arana***, the witnesses are also mentioned in ZA 89 4 and AuOr 5 3
AuOr 5 17 Testament	Ištabu son of Zū-Aba (testator)		Igmil-Dagān	Dagān *-ba-aḫ-li* scribe	
AuOrS 1 15 Sale (hills and fields)	lost (^{d}N+elders sellers?)	^{d}N+city	Igmil-Dagān	Rašap-ilī scribe	The city of Emar demanded 2,000 šeqels of gold, they sold hills and fields for silver and gold, which they gave to the ***a-ra-na***[a]
E 150 Sale (plot of land)	^{d}N+elders (sellers) Ḫimaši-Dagān, son of Abī-Dagān (buyer)	^{d}N+city	Igmil-Dagān and Liʾmi-šarra	Dagān-EN scribe, ^{d}IŠKUR-EN *ḫazannu*	
HCCT-E 4 Sale (plot of land)	^{d}N+elders (sellers) ^{I}DUMU.MEŠ Aḫī-ḫamiṣ (buyers)	^{d}N+city	Igmil-Dagān and Liʾmi-šarra	Rašap-ilī scribe	***arana*** (payment in garments)
HCCT-E 11 Loan of silver	var. private persons	–	^{d}IŠKUR-GAL son of Liʾmi-šarra	Rašap-ilī scribe	
RE 91 Sale (plot of land)	^{d}N+elders (sellers) ? (name lost, buyer)	^{d}N+city	Igmil-Dagān and Liʾmi-šarra	Dagān-EN scribe, ^{d}IŠKUR-EN *ḫazannu*	
FK 6 Appointment of a SANGA-priest of the Nergal temple by the king and the city of Emar			Liʾmi-šarra together with the city of Emar	Eḫli-Kuša scribe Abī-Rašap *ḫazannu*	*i-na* U$_{4}$*-ma-ti* ^{I}*Li*-LUGAL DUMU *Ir-ib*-^{d}IŠKUR; reference to the **Hurrian king**!
AuOrS 1 16 Sale doc. (field)	^{d}N+elders (sellers) Milki-Dagān, son of Iḫi-Rami (buyers)	^{d}N+city	Liʾmi-šarra	Eḫli-Kuša scribe Abī-Rašap *ḫazannu*	
AuOrS 1 17 Sale (field)	^{d}N+elders (sellers) Šamaš-gāmil, Igmulu, Dagān-mālik, Ikūn-Dagān (buyers)	^{d}N+city	Liʾmi-šarra	Eḫli-Kuša scribe Abī-Rašap *ḫazannu*	
AuOrS 1 18 Sale (field)	^{d}N+elders (sellers) ^{I}LÚ.MEŠ Abī-Rašap son of Ḫinna-^{d}IŠKUR (buyers)	^{d}N+city	Liʾmi-šarra	Eḫli-Kuša scribe	

Table 1. Texts Explicitly Dating to the Earlier Local "Dynasty" of Irʾib-^{d}IŠKUR (cont.)

Text	*Parties*	*Penalty Clause*	*Witness*	*Other*	*Additional Comments*
AuOrS 1 87 Foundation document (Nergal temple)		+ (recipients not named)	Liʾmi-šarra	Elders of Emar Pilsu-Dagān LÚ.SANGA Eḫli-Kuša scribe Abī-Rašap *ḫazannu*	*i-na* U_4-*ma-ti* ^{I}*L*[*i-mi*-LUGAL] DUMU *Ir-ib*-^{d}[IŠKUR], **curse**[b]
RE 22 Gift (plot of land)	^{d}N+elders to Išbi-EN, the physician (recipient)	^{d}N+city	Liʾmi-šarra	Eḫli-Kuša scribe	
E 148 Sale (plot of land)	^{d}N+elders (sellers)[c] Ilī-Gašru s. of Zū-Baʿla	^{d}N+city	Išbi-Dagān, son of Liʾmi-šarra	Eḫli-Kuša scribe Abī-Rašap *ḫazannu*	
E 149 Sale (field)	^{d}N+elders (sellers) Baia (buyer)	^{d}N+city	lost (Išbi-Dagān son of Liʾmi-šarra)	Eḫli-Kuša scribe Abī-Rašap *ḫazannu*	
E 171 Sale (plot of land)	Zū-Baʿla son of ^{d}IŠKUR-x[ ] (seller) Zū-Aštarti son of Itū[r- (buyer)	lost	–	[ ]-^{d}IŠKUR scribe	^{d}IŠKUR-GAL son of Liʾmi-šarra is named as one of the neighbors, **ceremonial clause *kuburu*-payment**
RE 34 Sale (house)	^{d}N+elders (sellers) Itūr-Dagān son of Iaḫṣi-Dagān (buyer)	^{d}N+city	Ilī-abī son of Liʾmi-šarra	Alal-abu scribe Dagān-kabar *ḫazannu*	*ḫīṭu* against the city and his lord **ceremonial clause**
AuOrS 1 19 Sale (field)	^{d}N+elders (sellers) Ṣilla-Baʿla (buyer)	^{d}N+city	Zū-Baʿla son of Išbi-Dagān	Alal-abu scribe Pilsu-Dagān *ḫazannu*	

General note: The texts listed here name members of this family in their witness list (exception: E 171). The family tree by Skaist (1998a: 60) can be extended (see the catalog in Pruzsinszky 2003).

a. Skaist 1998b. Compare also with AuOrS 1 14, where this Hurrian term for 'tribute' (*a-ra-*[*na* LUGAL] is attested as well. It is unknown whose "palace" in this penalty clause is referred to (theoretically it could refer to the LUGAL mentioned in connection with the *arana*). Since E 153 also dates to the same early phase of Emar (compare with the testimonies in E 150), all attestations seem to refer to a tribute payment to the Hurrian (Mittanian) king before 1325 B.C.

b. A clause stating that, if anyone alters the words, Nergal will destroy his house and his seed. Only early texts involve Nergal, as noted by Fleming 2000: 24 n. 33.

c. Beyer (2001: 432) notes that a dynastic seal is impressed on this tablet ("E 2a?"). However, according to pl. 17, cylinder seal E 2b seems to be found on this tablet.

these features hint at a fairly strong position of the urban authority including the city elders, the Temple of ^{d}NIN.URTA, and the body that is referred to as "brothers." As pointed out by Yamada (1994a: 59), both institutions of Emar, the elders and

to the Temple of Dagān in the case of an "offense" commited by the buyer (*ḫi-ṭá-am ša* PN). According to Westbrook (2003: 688), this term signifies treason or a range of crimes against the state. The (local) king (of Emar) can only be identified in text FK 6. Otherwise, no evidence exists for a local king in the texts from Emar. More evidence on local kings comes from Ekalte, which may have belonged to the administrative district of Emar (see Mayer 2001: 14).

^dNIN.URTA, can be divided into two different bodies, a civil and religious, both of which constituted a corporate body of urban authority at Emar.[24] This close relationship between the city god and the "elders" or "brothers" is also attested at Ekalte and Azû. Clearly, Ekalte, Azû, and Emar share a common sociocultural heritage, which exemplifies the local Syrian traditions. The local king–best represented in FK 6–plays only a minor role in the earlier texts from Emar and the documents of Ekalte.

One of the most important terms identified by Skaist (1999) is the Hurrian word for 'gift, tribute', *arana*, which is attested in these early documents. The city, represented by the elders together with dNIN.URTA, is reported to have sold land in order to pay its *arana*.[25] FK 6 also refers to a payment consisting of gold, silver, and jewelry to a Hurrian king. Apparently the city of Emar was liable for a certain amount of silver and gold to be paid as tribute to the Hurrian king.[26]

Hittite Rule of Emar

Emar did not suffer destruction during the course of the Hittite take-over, and the texts demonstrate that the local inhabitants retained their legal rights despite political and administrative changes.[27] Under Hittite hegemony over Aštata, Emar's "own" institutions (local dynasty and the representatives of the city-community), also referred to as "its own political identity" (Vita 2002: 114), continued alongside princes of Carchemiš and Hittite dignitaries, who were involved in the administration of Emar.[28] Fundamental to the structure of the Hittite state according to Klengel (2003: 288) was:

> Die Erkenntnis, dass jenseits des Taurus eine Kontrolle fremder Territorien schwer dauerhaft auszuüben war, hat nicht zuletzt auch zur Entscheidung Šuppiluliumas I. beigetragen, in Syrien ein hethitisches Vizekönigtum mit Sitz in der Euphratfestung Karkamiš einzurichten . . . indem man in Karkamiš–zeitweilig in Ḫalab–hethitische Prinzen als Herrscher etablierte . . . Dementsprechend galt fortan im Bereich von

24. Yamada concludes that dNIN.URTA "was a figure central to the elders" (1994a: 59 n. 7; and see Yamada 1993: 454 n. 7). On the city elders and their function in Late Bronze Age towns in Syria and the Levant, most notably Ugarit, see Heltzer 2004. For interesting differences between the elders and the body termed "brothers," see Bunnens 1989: 30–31. On further observations on "elders," "fathers," and "brothers" as part of city government, see Mayer 2001: 25–26. Furthermore, there are 'great ones' (LÚ.MEŠGAL-GAL or *rabbū*) referred to in the Emar texts.

25. See also Durand and Marti 2003: 157. Interestingly, *arana* is attested at neither Ekalte nor Azû, which also indicates their less important role among cities along the Euphrates bend.

26. Skaist 1998a: 171. Freu (2003: 83) suggests that this Hurrian king is Artatama I, who ruled at the beginning of the fourteenth century and is known to have had strong relations with Egypt. The ultimate identification depends on the overall chronological setting of the Emar archives, which is still under discussion (see lately Di Filippo 2004). Too little is known about the political situation in the Middle Euphrates region and Mittanian status during this period to identify with certainty a specific Mittanian ruler. However, it seems very likely that the *arana*-payment was due to a Hurrian king before Emar was annexed to the Hittite Empire.

27. Salvini and Trémouille (2003) published the Hittite texts found at Emar (two letters and four divinatory protocols). Among the texts is Msk. 73.1097, which parallels CM 13: 32, a letter by the Hittite king concerning the confiscation of Zū-Baʿla's property by a Hittite official at Emar.

28. On the institution of the Hittite administration, see the overview by Westbrook 2003: 660–61.

> Karkamiš die hethitische Rechtsordnung in weit stärkerem Maße als in anderen syrischen Fürstentümern. Die Hethiter haben somit versucht, ihr bereits nach der Staatsgründung in Ḫattuša eingeführtes Herrschaftssystem der *An*gliederung, nicht der *Ein*gliederung auch auf nicht-anatolisches Gebiet zu übertragen, d.h. ohne es zugleich auch wirtschaftlich oder kulturell zu integrieren. . . . Gleicherweise sind offenbar auch keine spezifischen hethitischen Gottheiten im syrischen Reichsteil verehrt worden.

Anatolian rituals recorded in Akkadian, such as E 470–491 and CM 13: 31, prove that rites for the gods of Ḫatti were performed at Emar. These rites are understood as a result of the foreign religious practice of Hittite officials stationed in Syria. According to Fleming (2000: 228), "these texts demonstrate the results of the most immediate borrowing conceivable." Other than that, little Hittite impact on religious life at Emar is detectable; only a few Hittite words and practices are observed in the Emar ritual texts. Hittite dignitaries and members of the Hittite royal family did not actively participate, nor were they honored in the local festivals (Fleming 2000: 226–27). However, the local king, possibly put in place by the Hittites, took part in the festivities (for example, the *zukru*) by funding them, an event that does not appear in the earlier tradition of the texts.[29] Older versions of the ritual known as "the installation of the NIN.DINGIR" show that the elders (not the king) were present at the enthronement of the NIN.DINGIR priestess and thus represented the local authority. Also the king (LUGAL) of Emar and Šatappu, another town near Emar, are mentioned in the banquets for dignitaries celebrating the NIN.DINGIR installation (E 369), a topic extensively dealt with by Fleming (1992b: 99–102). According to Sallaberger's observations (1996: 144–47), the text naming these local kings belongs to the latest phase of a longer tradition of this ritual, which shows parallels to the ones at Ebla. Apparently, the local kings were now included in the ritual installing the NIN.DINGIR-priestess, continuing a tradition that had previously involved the city elders. However, one notices a general absence of the local king in these ritual activities, particularly in contrast to the evidence from Ugarit, Ḫatti, and Assyria, where they play a prominent role.

Furthermore, the pronounced Hittite interest in the family of the diviner (LÚ.ḪAL) Zū-Baʿla might indicate that Emar was a center of divination for Hittite monarchs, as stated in Singer's commentary (in Westenholz et al. 2000) on the Hittite letter CM 13:32.[30] The family of Zū-Baʿla was the "semi-autonomous local religious establishment" responsible for the administration of the city's cult and divination and shared close relations with the administration of Carchemiš. Thus Fleming (2000: 44–45) and others have suggested that the position of this family strongly depended on the Hittite leadership, who had some interest in preserving the city's religious life by controlling the ritual tradition. In contrast to this, the earlier texts FK 6 and AuOrS 1 87 indicate that religious life, including the appointment of priests, was under the authority of the city alone. Moreover, the texts of the diviner's archive of M_1 belonging

29. See, for example, Fleming 2000: 56 in connection with the *zukru* festival.

30. Note also Sallaberger (1996: 142), who concludes that by analogy with the texts from Ḫattuša the, LÚ.ḪAL (diviner) played a major role in divination at Emar.

to the scribal center and school of Emar suggest strong (traditional) ties continued with Mesopotamia as shown by lexical and literary texts, while Fleming (2000) has demonstrated that ritual tablets and the calendars or religious activities are native to Syria and contain many earlier elements that remained throughout Hittite hegemony.

As stated above, the Hittites installed Hittite sovereigns in Carchemiš and partly in Ḫalab in contrast to the Assyrians in the first millennium B.C., who substituted administrative officers for the local institutions. It seems that at Emar they kept the local traditions in order to guarantee stability in an area that was far from the Hittite heartland and always threatened by raids. After Tušratta's son Šattiwaza fled to Šuppliluliuma, the Hittite king installed his own son Piyaššili as viceroy of Carchemiš and launched another campaign against Mittani, which was now governed by the usurper Artatama II and his son Šuttarna. This campaign sought to establish Šattiwaza as ruler of what was left of imperial Mittani (Ḫanigalbat) in order to integrate its lands into the Hittite Empire, creating a buffer state between Ḫatti and Assyria (east of Carchemiš, including Taide; Kühne 1999: 220–21). Despite the treaties between Mittani and Ḫatti (KBo I 1 and 3), "Hurrian troops" continued to attack the city of Emar, as the Emar texts report during the time of Pilsu-Dagān.[31] As documented in year names, Emar was attacked on numerous occasions during the thirteenth century ("year of distress and war,"[32] "year when ṬÁR-PI troops besieged the city of Emar") This was a result most likely of its geographical situation at the edge of the Hittite Empire which bordered Assyria, between the two rival political powers that were fighting over the remains of the Mittanian state. Despite having its own troops (Vita 2002: 123–27), Emar was dependent on the presence and protection of the Hittites, who engaged in (external) political issues on their behalf.[33] Some Emarites had to perform the GIŠ.TUKUL-obligation and the *ilku*-service (see CM 13: 2 for its existence) in turn, which obviously derived from and belonged to the Hittite social world.[34] More references to military service can be found in E 17 and 18. The *ilku*-service might be connected with the Hittite terms *šaḫḫan* and *luzzi* that are attested in the Hittite letters Msk. 73.1097 and CM 13: 32, in which the diviner is freed from these obligations. However, these clearly went beyond military tasks and could have referred to "work squads," as originally proposed by Beckman (1996) for RE 78. In Hittite laws, *ilku* involved land tenure that was assigned by the palace, as noted in CM 13, p. 6, and that included the *šaḫḫan* obligation.

31. Adamthwaite 2001: 261–80; Vita 2002 (especially pp. 117–21: here, Vita argues that Pilsu-Dagān is a contemporary of Tukultī-Ninurta I instead of Adad-nīrārī as proposed by Skaist 1998a: 64–67). The synchronism between Pilsu-Dagān and Adad-nīrārī I is based on an unpublished text from Tell Fray, that reports a Ḫanigalbatean attack on Emar.

32. As pointed out by Vita (2002: 116), the phrase "in the year of distress and/or war" is attested in both Syrian and Syrian-Hittite style tablets.

33. Archaeological remains seem to prove an elaborated defense system erected by the Hittites and supplemented by the fortress of Tell Faqʿūs according to the French excavators. However, the city wall already existed during the Middle Bronze Age, as the excavations by Finkbeiner have shown. Thus, the influence of the Hittites on the urban topography of Emar should be questioned anew. See Faist and Finkbeiner 2002: 192–93.

34. Westbrook 2003: 663 (a feudal duty is expressed by the term 'bearing a weapon' [GIŠ.TUKUL *našû*]); see also Bellotto 2002; Yamada 1995 (on *arawannu* people, who are said to perform the GIŠ.TUKUL-obligation/service).

The installation of (local) dynasties in Syria by the Hittites possibly had an effect on Emar as well, if we accept the chronology proposed at the beginning of this essay; the local dynasty of Iaḫṣi-Dagān coincided with the period of Hittite domination at Emar and therefore has been described as a "relatively new feature of Emar society."[35] However, these kings ruled under Hittite jurisdiction, and their power was limited. This might be demonstrated by the fact that a resident from Emar (the diviner Zū-Baʿla) could hold feudal land (*šaḫḫan* and *luzzi*) directly from the Hittite king and not the local king.[36] Furthermore, the local city government and the Temple of ^{d}NIN.URTA continued to play an important role until the city's end, around 1180 B.C.[37] Thus, both the local city administration (of the past) and the newly established local dynasty coexisted side by side, and the existing legal system concerning internal affairs (in contrast to external political affairs, which the texts from Emar do not touch upon) was not completely altered after the take-over by the Hittites. However, it might be argued that the power of the city's administration must have been diminished considerably by the local royal family that gained importance thanks to the Hittite overlords and that took over some of the tasks of the city elders, as shown above. Nonetheless, the role of the local king (LUGAL) cannot be compared with the Mesopotamian king but should be seen more as an official such as the *rabiānum* ('mayor, headman'), who was ultimately dependent on the ruler of Carchemiš.[38] Of course this picture could be altered by a discovery of palace archives comparable to the archives at Ugarit. No such archives have been found yet, nor can a palace be clearly detected. Interestingly, the royal family of Iaḫṣi-Dagān is attested in various transactions of property, which may demonstrate a transition from the communal property system to royal power.[39] But, unfortunately, attestations for members of the royal family as buyers are few.

Summary

One can tentatively conclude that the Hittites employed two "institutions" to serve as mediators between the traditional Syrian system and the new Hittite overlord represented mainly by the administration of Carchemiš. While we observe more or less direct Hittite influence in the "Syro-Hittite" documents, including the texts of the diviner's family, communication with the collective city-community and consequently

35. Fleming 1992a: 70–71: it was "not yet able to overshadow other traditional authorities," and "the institutions of an earlier age . . . remain visible below the covering kingship."

36. See Cooper et al. 2005: 50 on CM 13: 32. Salvini and Trémouille (2003: 228) identify the king in Msk. 73.1097 with Muršili II and propose the years 1312–1311 for the Hittite letters Msk. 73.1097 and CM 13: 32. Here, the important and privileged role of the diviner is revealed once again.

37. Furthermore, Heltzer (2001: 236) concludes that there was limited royal power in Emar but points to features that survived from the earlier tribal society. He refers to a "more archaic society" at Emar compared with the society at Ugarit. Unfortunately, Heltzer did not differentiate between the two chronological phases adopted in this study. Note also CM 13: 2, in which a legal decision is made before the overseer of the land (LÚ.UGULA KALAM.MA) and the (city) elders (LÚ.MEŠ.ŠU.GI).

38. Sallaberger (personal communication) kindly pointed out that the LUGAL-LUGAL at Ebla designated some kind of an official rather than a king (perhaps a governor?). For a broader meaning of LUGAL at Emar, see Seminara 1996.

39. CM 13, p. xv. In contrast, the Irʾib-^{d}IŠKUR-family is never directly involved in these transactions but appears only in the list of witnesses.

control over Emar was probably exercised through the installation of a local royal family, the lowest level of authority from the Hittite point of view. Both city elders and a local Emarite king are attested in tablets of the "Syrian" scribal tradition, thus demonstrating the Syrian affiliation. However, before the Hittite take-over, the figure of the king is only rarely documented (FK 6 and two attestations in the Ekalte texts). The postulated kings, Irʾib-ᵈIŠKUR and his sons, are never referred to as "kings," and the *arana*-payments to the Hurrian king were "managed" by the city elders and ᵈNIN.URTA. Also, rituals of the old Syrian tradition add to the reconstruction of a strong urban authority. The "eponym-like" dating system—most likely according to people connected with the city government—was abolished as soon as the local royal family of Iaḫṣi-Dagān, which had loyal relations with the Hittite king and the rulers of Carchemiš, came to power.[40] This drastic change can be seen as evidence of the changes in local politics due to the Hittites, who clearly restrained the role of the city elders.

Although it is clear that the local inhabitants of Emar kept their rights, as evidenced in the legal documents in the archive of the M_1 building, some changes in their rights might be observed, for example, in "innovative" clauses in contracts that can be assigned to external influence (such as the so-called TÉŠ.BI-clause, the redemption clause only attested in Syro-Hittite tablets). Other clauses, such as the satisfaction- and penalty-clauses, are missing in Syro-Hittite texts. Yet some of the legal clauses, and therefore presumably some issues of legal practice, that can be traced to the beginning of the second millennium were maintained and adapted in the Syro-Hittite tablets. The local dynasty clearly continued to employ its own scribes, who worked within the Syrian tradition. In contrast, the contemporary legal texts from Ugarit, a Syrian kingdom in the west, when referring to internal issues, reveal less Hittite influence than the texts from Emar (Faist 2002: 130–34 and 140). Only the texts dealing with rights between two different states, that is, external political issues, show Ugarit's political dependency on Ḫatti or Carchemiš.

Hittite dignitaries appear to have respected the indigenous, traditional institutions of Emar and to have acknowledged those local authorities equally, as was shown by Yamada (1993: 453–60) with regard to E 194 and other evidence.[41] Even if "Hittite politics in Syria enabled Emar to have its own political identity" (Vita 2002: 14), Emar never occupied a politically relevant position, seeming always to have been dependent on external powers. It appears that Ḫatti installed at Emar a (local) kingdom, as it did to a greater extent at Ḫalab and Carchemiš. However, in contrast to Carchemiš, at Emar there was only a "limited kingship" (comparable to the contempoary one of Šatappu); the internal administrative power remained in the hands of the traditional institutions, namely, the elders of the city and the Temple of ᵈNIN.URTA (the ᵈNIN.URTA-seal continues to be used to the end of the Emar archives, as shown by Yamada 1994a: 60–61; and Beyer 2001: 206–7 and 432–35). It appears that the viceroys

40. An exception may be RE 16, in which Iaḫṣi-Dagān and his son ᵈIŠKUR-kabar I act as witnesses; however, the strong urban authority of the elders and ᵈNIN.URTA is expressed here by the *ḫīṭu*-clause (see n. 23, above).

41. In this respect, the 'oath of Emar' (*māmītu ša* ᵁᴿᵁ*Emar*), according to which certain decisions were regulated, is to be noted as one of the traditions respected by the rulers of Carchemiš.

and officials of Carchemiš did not interfere to any large extent but, rather, shared power with the local institutions and fully acknowledged them as local authorities. Interestingly, they also seldom appear together in the texts. In connection with E 194[42] and HCCT-E 8, Yamada (1993: 456–59) pointed out that there were tablets sealed with both the "dynastic seal" (usually used in royal documents) and ᵈNIN.URTA's seal (used from the earliest phase on and specifically of tablets dealing with issues of the city administration), which were presented to the king of Carchemiš. Furthermore in the testament E 181, the official of Carchemiš (DUMU LUGAL) Tuwatta-ziti, Puḫi-šenni, 'overseer of the land' (UGULA KALAM.MA), and the city elders (LÚ.MEŠ *ši-bu-ti* URU.KI) are mentioned together at the end of the document among the witnesses and sealers. Because the local king, most likely installed by the Hittites, and the city elders are attested together more frequently, the administration of Carchemiš clearly exercised control and had contacts by means of the local kings of Emar. Despite being dominated by larger empires, Emar was always able to preserve its individual cultural traditions and identity, which helped to stabilize and strengthen its commercial and political position. This was certainly the case during the hegemony of the Hittites, who managed to link the local institutions with their own institutions, thus avoiding a radical break. A complete reorganization of local institutions might have been too costly and risky and not necessarily effective for the Hittite interests. However, one needs to consider that, due to the new authorities installed by the Hittites and the influence upon the religious and scholarly center of Emar represented by Zū-Baʿla, the position of the local institutions certainly was weakened to a great extent. Gallagher (2003: 180) is right in describing the diviner of Emar as a powerful priest and "international chaplain," diplomat, schoolmaster, and author, "molder of young minds," controller of the intellectuals, who was totally aware of his importance and wide range of power.

For the time before Hittite domination, our evidence for the nature of governance at Emar is very weak; it seems that tribute payments to the Hurrian king were part of the system, which sometimes forced the city government to sell communal land. The exceptional text FK 6 may reveal an active Mittanian rule in its report on four (Emarite) princesses who were taken as hostages by the king of the Hurrian land. Aside from that text, no activity by the Hurrian king or any other Mittanian political agents is attested in the city of Emar. Further evidence on the local LUGAL is missing as well. Therefore the local city government, represented by a civil and religious body, seems to have been fairly autonomous and continued with its administrative tasks to the end of Emar.

42. The "Carchemiš document" was restored by Yamada (1993: 456–59), according to whom the mentioned "king," who sealed one of the three documents (with his dynastic seal), should be identified with the king of Emar, whose son is involved in this settlement over fields in the presence of the king of Carchemiš.

Appendixes

Appendix 1. General Time Table

	Mesopotamia	*Emar (Syria)*	
1800	Old Baylonian Period	Old Syrian Period (Mari, Ḫalab)	
1700			
1600			
1500		Mittanian Period	
1400	Middle Babylonian Period	↓ Syrian tradition: ca.1400 or later, but before 1325–ca. 1189 B.C.	↓ Syro-Hittite tradition: ca. 1325–ca.1189 B.C.
1300			
1200			
1100			

Appendix 2. The Royal Dynasties of Emar according to Skaist (1998a)

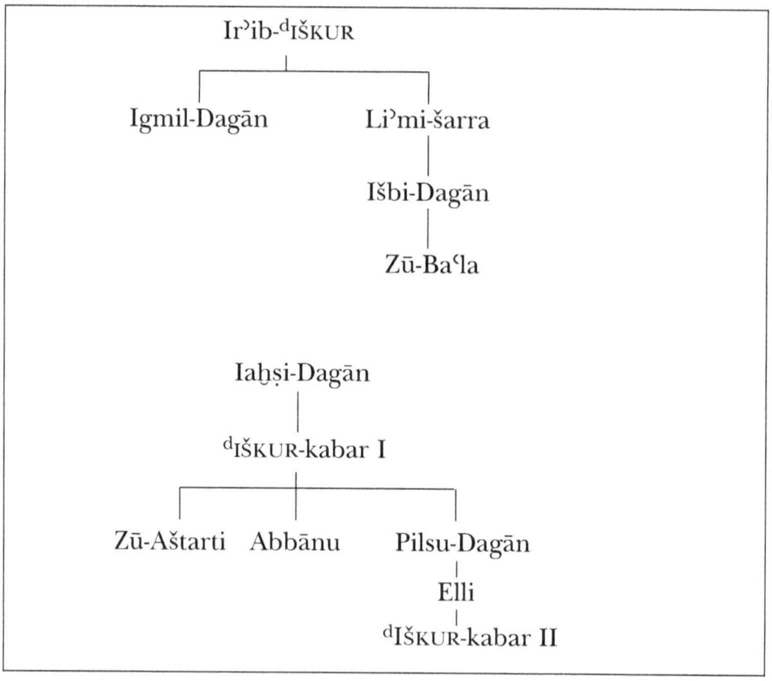

Changes as to the succession of rulers of the 2nd Emarite dynasty have been recently proposed by Skaist (2005, with table on p. 572). According to Di Filippo (2004: 198), these two “dynasties” are overlapping.

References

Adamthwaite, M. R.
2001 *Late Hittite Emar: The Chronology, Synchronisms, and Socio-Political Aspects of a Late Bronze Age Fortress Town.* Ancient Near Eastern Studies Supplement 8. Louvain: Peeters.

AuOrS 1 = *Arnaud, Daniel*
1991 *Textes syriens de l'âge du Bronze Récent.* Aula Orientalis Supplement 1. Barcelona: AUSA.

Beckman, Gary
1996 *Texts from the Vicinity of Emar in the Collection of Jonathan Rosen.* History of the Ancient Near East Monograph 2. Padua: Sargon.

Bellotto, N.
2002 Alcune osservazioni sull'istituzione GIŠ.TUKUL a Emar. *Altorientalische Forschungen* 29: 128–45.

Beyer, D.
2001 *Emar IV: Les sceaux.* Orbis Biblicus et Orientalis Series Archaelogica 20. Göttingen.

Bunnens, G.
1989 Emar on the Euphrates in the 13th Century B.C.: Some Thoughts about Newly Published Cuneiform Texts. *Abr-Nahrain* 27: 23–26.

Cancik, H.
1993 'Herrschaft' in historiographischen und juridischen Texten der Hethiter. Pp. 115–34 in *Anfänge des politischen Denkens in der Antike,* ed. K. Raaflaub. Schriften des Historischen Kollegs, Kolloquien 24. Munich: Oldenbourg.

CM 13: *see* Westenholz et al. 2000

Cooper, J., et al.
2005 A Mittani-Era Tablet from Umm el-Marra. Pp. 41–56 in *General Studies and Excavations at Nuzi 11/1.* Studies on the Civilization and Culture of Nuzi and the Hurrians 15. Bethesda, MD: CDL.

CTH = Laroche, E.
1971 *Catalogue des textes hittites.* 2nd ed. Paris: Klincksieck.

Di Filippo, F.
2004 Notes on the Chronology of Emar Legal Tablets. *Studi Micenei ed Egeo-Anatolici* 46: 175–214.

Durand, J.-M., and Marti, L.
2003 Chroniques du Moyen-Euphrate, 2: Relecture de documents d'Ekalte, Émar et Tuttul. *Revue d'Assyriologie* 97: 141–80.

E = Arnaud, D.
1985–87 *Récherches au pays d'Aštata: Emar VI. Les textes sumériens et accadiens.* 4 vols. Paris: Éditions Recherche sur les Civilisations.

Faist, B.
2002 Die Rechtsordnung in Syrien nach der hethitischen Eroberung: Wandel und Kontinuität. Pp. 129–46 in *Brückenland Anatolien? Ursachen, Extensität und Modi des Kulturaustausches zwischen Anatolien und seinen Nachbarn,* ed. H. Blum et al. Tübingen.

Faist, B., and Finkbeiner, U.
2002 Emar: Eine syrische Stadt unter hethitischer Herrschaft. Pp. 190–95 in *Die Hethiter und ihr Reich: Das Volk der 1000 Götter, Ausstellungskatalog,* ed. Kunst- und Ausstellungshalle der Bundesrepublik Deutschland. Bonn.

FK = Sigrist, M.
1993 Seven Emar Tablets. Pp. 164–84 in *kinattūtu ša dārâti: Raphael Kutscher Memorial Volume,* ed. A. F. Rainey. Tel Aviv: Institute of Archaeology.

Fleming, D. E.
1992a A Limited Kingship: Late Bronze Emar in Ancient Syria. *Ugarit-Forschungen* 24: 59–71.
1992b *The Installation of Baal's High Priestess at Emar.* Harvard Semitic Studies 42. Atlanta: Scholars Press.
2000 *Time at Emar: The Cultic Calendar and the Rituals from the Diviner's Archive.* Mesopotamian Civilizations 11. Winona Lake, IN: Eisenbrauns.
2004 *Democracy's Ancient Ancestors: Mari and Early Collective Governance.* Cambridge: Cambridge University Press.
Freu, J.
2003 *Histoire du Mittani.* Paris.
Gallagher, J.
2003 An Extraordinary Everyday for Emar's Diviner. Pp. 171–81 in *Life and Culture in the Ancient Near East,* ed. R. E. Averbeck et al. Bethesda, MD: CDL Press.
HCCT-E = Tsukimoto, Akito
1990–92 Akkadian Tablets in the Hirayama Collection (I–III). *Acta Sumerologica Japan* 12: 177–259; 13: 335–45; 14: 289–310.
Heltzer, M.
2001 The Political Institutions of Ancient Emar as Compared with Contemporary Ugarit (13.–Beginning of the 12. Century B.C.E.). *Ugarit-Forschungen* 33: 218–36.
2004 The "Elders" (*šībūtē*) and the "Great Ones" (GAL.MEŠ) in the Levant in the XIII Cent. B.C.E. *Zeitschrift für Altorientalische und Biblische Rechtsgeschichte* 10: 213–18.
Klengel, H.
2003 Einige Bemerkungen zur Struktur des hethitischen Staates. *Altorientalische Forschungen* 30: 281–89.
Kühne, C.
1999 Imperial Mittani: An Attempt at Historical Reconstruction. Pp. 203–21 in *Nuzi at Seventy-Five.* Studies on the Civilization and Culture of Nuzi and the Hurrians 10. Bethesda, MD: CDL.
Margueron, J.-C.
1981–82 Tall Faqʿūs. *Archiv für Orientforschung* 28: 217–18.
Mayer, W.
2001 *Tall Munbāqa–Ekalte II: Die Texte. Ausgrabungen in Tall Munbāqa–Ekalte.* Wissenschaftliche Veröffentlichungen der deutschen Orient-Gesellschaft 102. Saarbrücken: SDV.
Oates, D., et al.
1997 *Excavations at Tell Brak, Vol. 1: The Mittani and Old Babylonian Periods.* London: British School of Archaeology in Iraq.
Otto, A., and Einwag, B.
2005 Ein Tempel für den Ältestenrat. *Alter Orient aktuell* 6: 27–29.
Pruzsinszky, R.
2003 *Die Personennamen der Texte aus Emar.* Studies on the Civilization and Culture of Nuzi and the Hurrians 13. Bethesda, MD: CDL.
RE: *see* Beckman 1996
Richter, T.
2005 Qaṭna in the Late Bronze Age: Preliminary Remarks. Pp. 109–26 in *General Studies and Excavations at Nuzi 11/1.* Studies on the Civilization and Culture of Nuzi and the Hurrians 15. Bethesda, MD: CDL.
Rouault, O.
2004 Chronological Problems concerning the Middle Euphrates during the Bronze Age. Pp. 51–60 in *Mesopotamian Dark Age Revisited,* ed. H. Hunger and R. Pruzsinszky. Contributions to the Chronology of the Eastern Mediterranean 6. Vienna.

Sallaberger, W.
1996 Review of D. E. Fleming, *The Installation of Baal's High Priestess at Emar* (Harvard Semitic Series 42). *Zeitschrift für Assyriologie* 86: 140–47.
2003 Review of M. R. Adamthwaithe, *Late Hittite Emar. Zeitschrift für Assyriologie* 93: 271–78.
Sallaberger, W., et al.
2006 Schenkungen von Mittani-Königen an die Einwohner von Basīru: Die zwei Urkunden aus Tell Bazi am Mittleren Euphrat. *Zeitschrift für Assyriologie* 96: 69–104.
Salvini, M., and Trémouille, M.-C.
2003 Les textes hittites de Meskéné/Emar. *Studi Micenei ed Egeo-Anatolici* 45: 225–71.
Seminara, S.
1996 Il "lugalato" da Ebla a Emar: Sopravivenze emarite della terminologia e della prassi eblaite della gestione del potere. *Aula Orientalis* 14: 79–92.
1998 *L'accadico di Emar.* Materiali per il Vocabolario Sumerico 6. Rome.
Skaist, A.
1998a The Chronology of the Legal Texts from Emar. *Zeitschrift für Assyriologie* 88: 45–71.
1998b A Hurrian Term at Emar. Pp. 167–71 in *General Studies and Excavations at Nuzi 10/2.* Studies on the Civilization and Culture of Nuzi and the Hurrians 9. Bethesda, MD: CDL.
2001 Emar. Pp. 237–50 in *Security for Debt in Ancient Near Eastern Law,* ed. R. Westbrook and R. Jasmow. Culture and History of the Ancient Near East 9. Leiden: Brill.
2005 The Order of the Rulers of Emar. Pp. 568–74 in *"An Experienced Scribe Who Neglects Nothing": Ancient Near Eastern Studies in Honour of Jacob Klein,* ed. Y. Sefati et al. Bethesda, MD: CDL.
Vita, J.-P.
2002 Warfare and the Army at Emar. *Altorientalische Forschungen* 29: 113–17.
Werner, P.
2004 *Tall Munbāqa-Ekalte–III: Die Glyptik.* Wissenschaftliche Veröffentlichungen der deutschen Orient-Gesellschaft 108. Saarbrücken: SDV.
Westbrook, R.
2003 Anatolia and the Levant: Emar and Vicinity. Pp. 657–91 in *A History of Ancient Near Eastern Law,* ed. R. Westbrook. Handbuch der Orientalistik 72/1. Leiden: Brill.
Westenholz, J. Goodnick
1999 Emar: The City and Its God. Pp. 145–67 in *Languages and Cultures in Contact: At the Crossroads of Civilizations in the Syro-Mesopotamian Realm—Proceedings of the 42nd RAI,* ed. K. van Lerberghe and G. Voet. Orientalia Lovaniensia Analecta 96. Leuven.
Westenholz, J. Goodnick, et al.
2000 *Cuneiform Inscriptions in the Collection of the Bible Lands Museum Jerusalem: The Emar Tablets.* Cuneiform Monograph 13. Groningen: Styx.
Yamada, M.
1993 Division of a Field and Ninurta's Seal: An Aspect of the Hittite Addministration in Emar. *Ugarit-Forschungen* 25: 453–60.
1994a The Dynastic Seal and Ninurta's Seal: Preliminary Remarks on Sealing by the Local Authorities of Emar. *Iraq* 56: 59–62.
1994b The Northern Border of the Land of Aštata. *Acta Sumerologica Japonica* 16: 261–68.
1995 The Hittite Social Concept of "Free" in the Light of the Emar Texts. *Altorientalische Forschungen* 22: 297–316.
Zaccagnini, C.
1989 Ceremonial Transfers of Real Estate at Emar and Elsewhere. *Vicino Oriente* 8/2: 33–48.
1995 War and Famine at Emar. *Orientalia* n.s. 64: 92–109.

Chapter 2

Frescoes, Exotica, and the Reinvention of the Northern Levantine Kingdoms during the Second Millennium B.C.E.

Marian H. Feldman

The Middle Bronze Age (ca. 2000–1600 B.C.E.) in the northern Levant represents a period of fundamental changes and transitions both politically and culturally. After the collapse of a major period of urbanization in the mid- and late-third millennium, newly emerging regional powers embarked on an intense and ongoing process of redefinition and reinvention that was to lay the foundation for the rest of the Bronze Age. As Akkermans and Schwartz (2003: 288) have recently remarked, "In the succeeding Middle Bronze period, we encounter one of the most compelling issues of Bronze Age archaeology: how did Syrian complex societies reinvent themselves after 'collapse'?" It is also during the Middle Bronze Age that frescoes of distinctly Aegean style and technique appear in palatial buildings of new regional powers. This essay explores the conjunction and possible codependency of Aegean-type frescoes and a reinvention of power and authority in the northern Levant during the Middle Bronze Age. Given the exotic nature of the frescoes within their Levantine context of use and reception, I examine the implications for their conscious and active placement in palatial structures and argue for their centrality in constructing and presenting a new ruling elite.

Wall and floor paintings in the Near East, including the Levant, have a long history stretching back to at least the Neolithic period, so the mere presence of painted architectural surfaces would hardly qualify as novel or exotic (Nunn 1988). However, during the second millennium several Levantine sites provide evidence of a radically different technique and style of architectural surface decoration (both wall and floor) that contrast strikingly with previous and contemporary paintings from the region and elsewhere in the Near East. Thus far, three main sites have yielded Aegean-type frescoes in the Levant. From north to south they are: Alalakh (Tell Atchana) in the Amuq plain in present-day Turkey, Qatna (Tell Mishrife) along the middle Orontes River in Syria, and Tel Kabri along the coast of the northern Akko valley in Israel.[1]

1. In addition to these three Levantine sites, wall paintings have been excavated at Tell Sakka near Damascus, which the excavator claims were executed in a technique similar to the Qatna paintings (Taraqji 1999), and, most recently, at Tell el Burak near Sidon in Lebanon (Sader 2006). The imagery at Sakka, however, is strongly Egyptianizing, as is that at Burak. Until further publication of these two

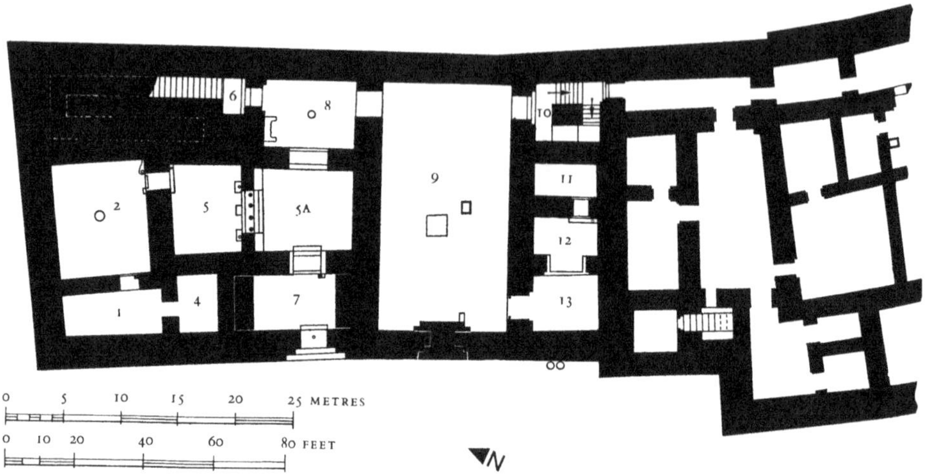

Figure 1. Plan of "Yarim-Lim" palace at Alalakh, Level VII (after Frankfort 1996: fig. 283; reprinted, courtesy of Yale University Press).

The Levantine examples join the well-known paintings from Tell ed-Daba (ancient Avaris) in the eastern Delta of Egypt[2] and less publicized examples from Miletus along the southwestern coast of Turkey (Niemeier 1998: 34) and Trianda on Rhodes (Immerwahr 1990: 190; Mee 1982: 4–7; Monaco 1941: 68–72, 88–89, 117, 128) that form a geographic bridge with the profusion of frescoes found throughout Crete and the Cyclades, including Akrotiri on Thera, Phylakopi on Melos, and Ayia Irini on Kea (Immerwahr 1990).

At Alalakh, Woolley (1955: 228–34) excavated fragments from two rooms of the Level VII palace (so-called Palace of Yarim-Lim; see fig. 1).[3] Though Alalakh chronology is notoriously contentious, Level VII can be assigned generally to the late eighteenth and/or seventeenth century B.C.E. (MB II in the north Levantine/Syrian chronology; Heinz 1992). Imitation marbling covered stone dados in Room 5, and fragments of a griffin's wing, a bull's horn, and swaying grasses appear to have fallen from an upper room, landing in the ground floor storerooms 11–13 (figs. 2–5). At Tel Kabri, another late Middle Bronze Age palatial structure has produced an *in situ* painted floor in a large room (no. 611) measuring 10 × 10 meters (Niemeier and Niemeier 2002; see figs. 6–9 here). Fragments attributed to a miniature frieze were found

sites, it is not clear exactly how these paintings relate to the other Levantine material. Architecturally, Sakka presents an illuminating counterpoint to the three main sites discussed in this essay (see below). The excavator of Burak has compared its palace to the Middle Bronze Age palace at Tell Bi'a, though comparisons with Alalakh and Tel Kabri might also be relevant.

2. The bibliography on the Tell ed-Daba paintings is large and appears in diverse publications; final reports have not yet appeared. For some overviews and recent discussions, see Bietak 1996; Bietak and Marinatos 1995; Bietak, Marinatos, and Palyvou 2000; and Morgan 1995, 2004.

3. Woolley (1955: 231) also found paintings in the Late Bronze Age Level IV.

Figure 2. Reconstruction of fresco fragments of griffin from the Alalakh palace, Level VII, by B. Niemeier (Niemeier and Niemeier 2000: fig. 22; reprinted, courtesy of W.-D. Niemeier).

in a secondary context under a later resurfacing of one of the doorways off of this room, which have been reconstructed to decorate the upper parts of Room 611's walls (figs. 10, 11).[4] The Qatna frescoes also derive from a palace that was probably begun in the Middle Bronze (Novák 2004; see fig. 12 here).[5] The first few fragments—all nonfigural designs—were discovered in the 1920s and dated to the Mitannian period (Du Mesnil du Buisson 1935: 143). In renewed excavations, the German component of a Syrian-Italian-German team has uncovered further examples from a mixed, late MB and early LB context (Novák and Pfälzner 2002: 226–31; Novák and Pfälzner 2003: 138; see figs. 13–16 here). The scholar in charge of the restoration and study of the frescoes has recently proposed that they date most likely to an LB I phase of the palace, though she considers them part of a longer tradition in Syria in which Aegean-

4. Recently, Lyvia Morgan (2006) has suggested that the miniature frieze might have decorated the walls of the adjoining room, 740.

5. Debate continues over the dating of the Qatna royal palace, which continued in use into the Late Bronze Age (Morandi Bonacossi 2006).

Figure 3. Fresco fragment of bull's horn from the Alalakh palace, Level VII, Ashmolean Museum, Oxford, 1957.36–37 (reprinted, courtesy of the Ashmolean Museum).

style paintings of this sort occur in the context of Syrian material culture.[6] More than 3,000 small pieces were found in collapsed fill from Room N and Room U in a cistern in the basement room of Room U. Isolated fragments from two other locations in the palace (Rooms P and AG) suggest even more extensive use of wall paintings in this building. While the date of the wall paintings remains uncertain, the probable earliest building phase of the palace during the later Middle Bronze Age, along with the comparisons from palaces at Alalakh and Kabri suggest a very late Middle Bronze or very early Late Bronze Age horizon.[7]

These paintings can be classified together as a coherent group according to their shared technique of execution, motival repertoire, and style of depicting this repertoire. Foremost in setting this group apart from other architectural painting in the region is the technique. All were executed to some degree in the true fresco method, which entails applying pigments without the aid of binding media onto damp lime plaster (Brysbaert 2002; Immerwahr 1990: 14–15; Nunn 1988: 5–17). The use of a damp lime-based surface is essential for the pigments to adhere to the wall or floor (through the physical penetration of the pigment into the plaster). Secondary tech-

6. Von Rüden 2006: personal communication. Von Rüden also stresses that by the early LB I period this use of Aegean-style wall paintings appears to be more integrated into the indigenous material culture of Syria.

7. An early Late Bronze Age date for the Qatna frescoes would align them with the newly proposed lower dates for the Tell ed-Daba frescoes that Bietak assigns to the early Eighteenth Dynasty. In the context of a possible later date for the Qatna frescoes, it might be noted that the purported break between the Middle and Late Bronze Ages is not very distinct, particularly in terms of material culture, despite what appear to have been rather significant historical shifts that led to the general demise of many Amorite dynasties in Syria and Mesopotamia—a point with relevance for my argument presented below (Akkermans and Schwartz 2003: 326).

Figure 4. Reconstruction of fresco fragment of bull's horn from the Alalakh palace, Level VII, by B. Niemeier (Niemeier and Niemeier 2000: fig. 15; reprinted, courtesy of W.-D. Niemeier).

niques that are associated with the true fresco method of application and apparent in the dried plaster today include the use of string guidelines that were snapped against the damp plaster, polishing or rubbing of the plaster surface to generate a better adhesive for the pigments, incised contour lines, and relief elements that become an integral part of the finished composition (Brysbaert 2002: 96–99; Shaw 2003: 186).

The motifs and styles of the Levantine frescoes are challenging to assess because of their fragmentary nature and the preliminary state of their reconstruction and publication. Yet in general, the motival and stylistic analysis complements the technical evidence that situates these frescoes more closely within an Aegean than a Levantine artistic tradition. Such correspondences reveal themselves in motifs such as sprays of crocuses and a "V-type" iris painted on the Tel Kabri floor, representations of isodomic masonry and round timber beams seen in the Kabri miniature fragments, griffins whose wings display the so-called notched-plume pattern at both Kabri and Alalakh, swaying reed-like plants also found at both Kabri and Alalakh, and running spirals, pinnate foliage, and blue palmate leaves from Qatna. It should be stressed that these parallels may not be exact (for example, the Qatna paintings include unique depictions of crabs and turtles) and that they may not shed light on the identity of the producers of these frescoes (Feldman forthcoming). Rather, the close association of the Levantine frescoes with both a specific Aegean tradition of painted surface decoration and a larger Aegean artistic tradition in toto indicates a strongly rhetorical expression of relatedness between the two. That is, the Levantine frescoes seem to call attention purposely to their "Aegeanness."

I have argued elsewhere that, in opposition to their connections with the Aegean, the features found in the paintings from Alalakh, Qatna, and Tel Kabri would have

Figure 5. Fresco fragments of reeds from the Alalakh palace, Level VII, Ashmolean Museum, Oxford, 1957.35 (reprinted, courtesy of the Ashmolean Museum).

stood out markedly against the broader material cultural landscape of the northern Levant, effectively signaling their "exotic" quality within a northern Levantine milieu (Feldman forthcoming).[8] In particular, the technique of painting without a binding medium on a damp lime plaster is not attested elsewhere in the Near East or Egypt, despite the large number of preserved wall paintings from these areas, including paintings from the roughly contemporary palace at Mari on the Middle Euphrates or the Middle Kingdom tombs at Beni Hasan in Middle Egypt. However, frescoes of this sort seem perfectly at home in the Aegean context, where they correspond to and find parallels with the broader spectrum of material culture, such as ceramics, seals, and even the rare, surviving sculptural monument (Immerwahr 1990).[9]

Distinctions in the architectural contexts of the Levantine and Aegean frescoes indicate an aspect of functional difference between the two corpora, bolstering the

8. See similar arguments put forth by Barbara and Wolf-Dietrich Niemeier (1998: 88–93; 2002: 279–82), who, however, are focused primarily on the national/ethnic identity of the artists. The Niemeiers (1998: 95; 2002: 283) embrace the idea that the frescoes belong to a Mediterranean koiné, an idea that I reject because the frescoes present a stark contrast to other Levantine elite material culture and, as the Niemeiers argue, are best situated within an Aegean tradition. A koiné by definition consists of a shared repertoire such as the repertoire seen in the hybridity of the Late Bronze Age "international style" (see Feldman 2006).

9. Tell ed-Daba seems to fall more into the pattern seen with the Levantine examples; that is, they contrast with surrounding/existing Egyptian material culture in ways that make them stand apart. The Rhodian and Miletian examples, on the other hand, though their contexts are not as well studied, appear to belong to a social environment that embraced Aegean traditions to such a degree that many scholars identify these sites as Minoan colonies (Niemeier 1998).

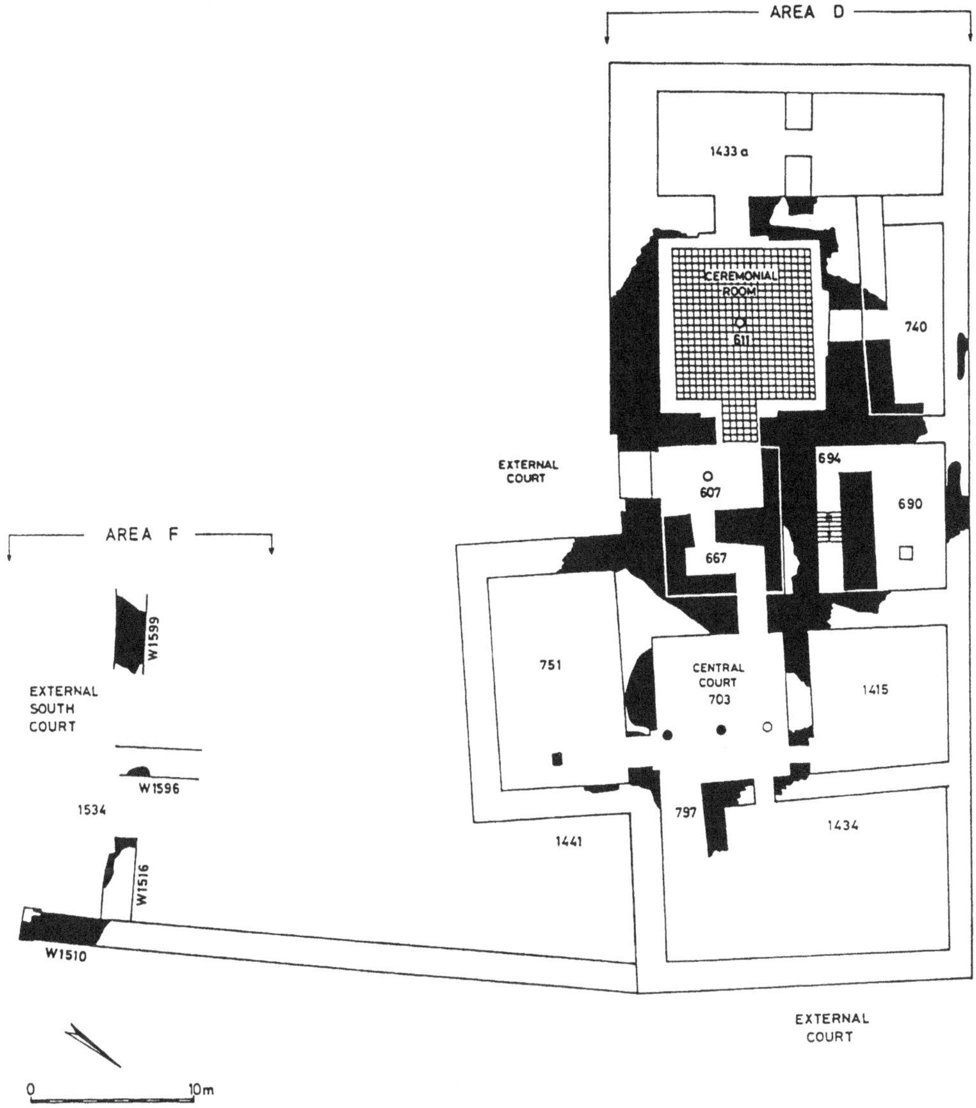

Figure 6. Restored plan of the palace at Tel Kabri, after Kempinski (from Niemeier and Niemeier 2000: fig. 1; reprinted, courtesy of W.-D. Niemeier).

case for understanding the Levantine examples as exotica, and specifically, exotica deployed in conjunction with the ruling elite. Painted frescoes decorate a variety of building types within the Aegean sphere, including palatial, residential, and possibly cultic structures (Blakolmer 2000). For example, at Knossos, most likely the predominant center on Crete, not only is the massive palatial compound filled with frescoes, so too are several of the subsidiary "villas" that surround it, such as the aptly named House of the Frescoes or the Caravanserai (Immerwahr 1990: 42–46,

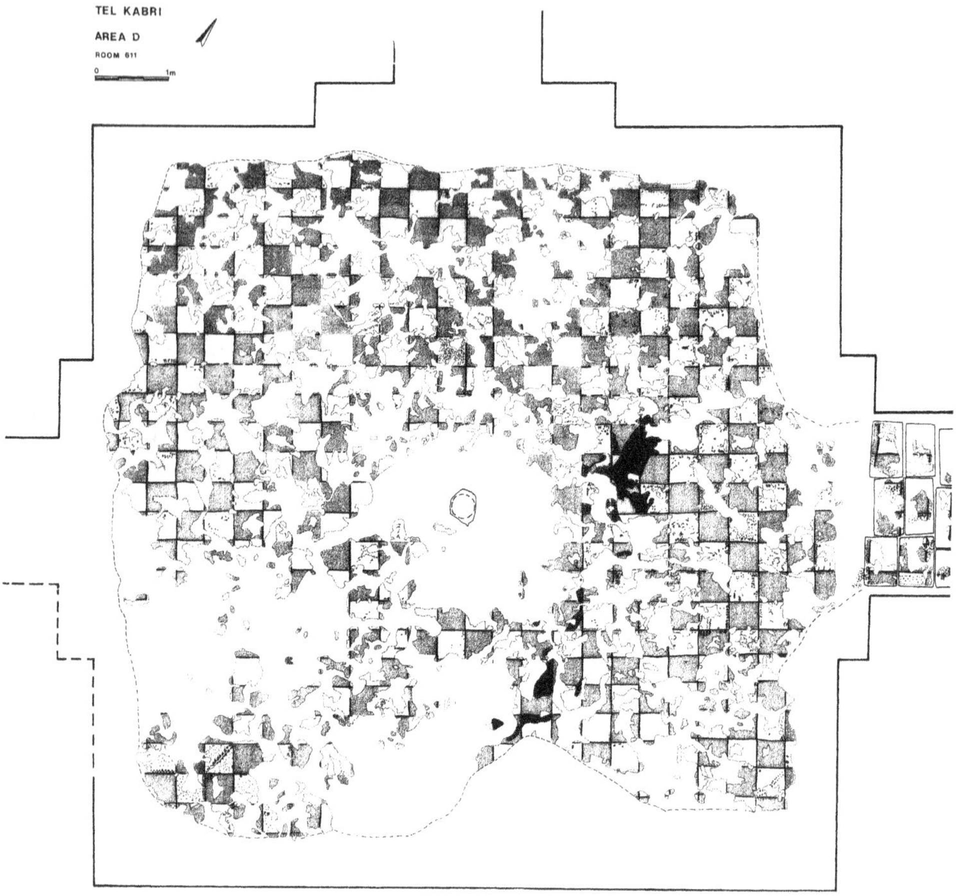

Figure 7. Drawing of painted floor in Room 611, Tel Kabri palace, by B. Neimeier (Niemeier and Niemeier 2000: fig. 2; reprinted, courtesy of W.-D. Niemeier).

78–79). Chronological precedence is extremely difficult to demonstrate given the multiple problems of Middle Bronze Age chronology in both the Levant and the Aegean. Yet, the wealth of frescoes in the Aegean, their relatively widespread architectural distribution, and their intimate formal and stylistic connection with other Aegean artistic production such as pottery all point to these frescoes' being thoroughly at home in the Aegean.

In contrast, in the Middle Bronze Age Levant, frescoes are relatively rare and appear to be restricted to palatial structures (Winter 2000: 747–49). Because excavations in the Levant have focused heavily on palatial structures at the expense of other types of buildings, any architectural comparison between the Aegean and the Levant must proceed with a certain amount of caution. Nonetheless, according to what evidence we do have, a clear pattern emerges. In comparison with the Aegean, the frescoes from the Levant occur only in a single architectural structure at any given site, which can be identified as that site's most important building, typically understood as

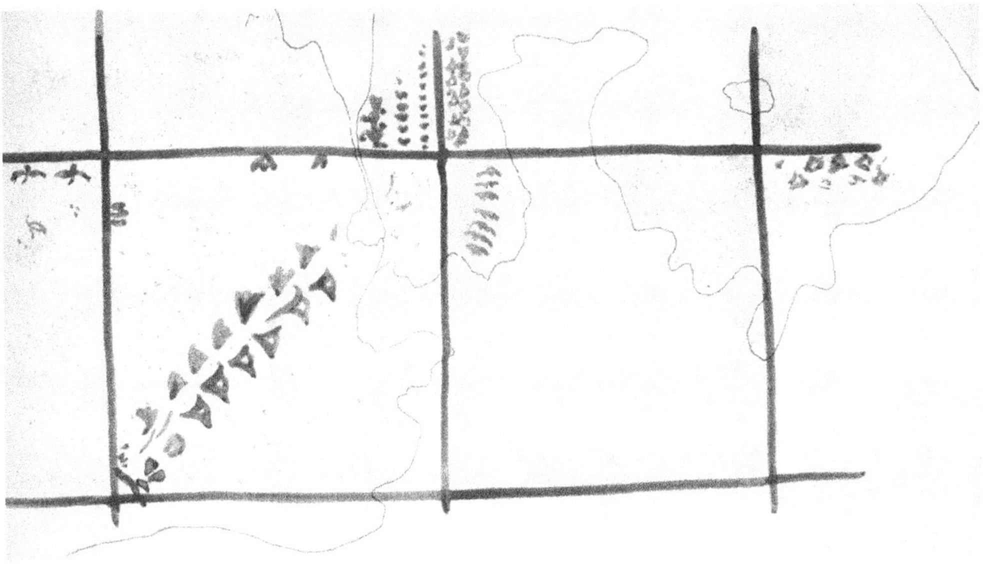

Figure 8. Water-color reconstruction of painted floor in Room 611, Tel Kabri palace, by B. Niemeier (from Niemeier and Niemeier 2000: fig. 8; reprinted courtesy of W.-D. Niemeier).

a palace.[10] This suggests that, not only were they not part of the indigenous tradition, but that their creation and use were tied with the ruling elites, perhaps to be read as one part of an ongoing process of "reinvention" characterizing the Middle (and possibly also the beginning of the Late) Bronze Age (Schwartz 2006).

While on the one hand, the architectural contexts between the Aegean and the Levant appear divergent, on the other hand, a comparison of the architectural contexts among the Levantine buildings produces evidence that points to a certain amount of shared social and political activities within the Levant itself. Although the frescoes themselves stand out in contrast to their surrounding Levantine material culture assemblage, an architectural comparison among the buildings in which they are found presents intriguing similarities of form that suggest that the buildings belong to a broader indigenous tradition and participated in a common sociopolitical environment. The buildings in which the frescoes appear at all three sites (Alalakh, Kabri, and Qatna) share more or less similarly conceived architectural plans: a roughly rectilinear design with irregular arrangements of rooms linked by courts and an emphatic use of columns.

The Yarim-Lim palace at Alalakh is the best preserved of the three (fig. 1).[11] The building rises along three terraces, from north to south, with the principal ceremonial rooms, indicated by their size and basalt orthostat revetment, occupying the lowest

10. Woolley (1955: 231) found fragments of wall paintings in houses from Level IV (Late Bronze Age) but none from Level VII outside the palace.

11. Woolley 1955: 91–110. Nonetheless, the palace was not excavated in its entirety due to overlay from later buildings, leaving Woolley to reconstruct parts of the plan, such as the ramp/stairway in the northeast corner (Room 6).

Figure 9. Detail of single blossom from painted floor in Room 611, Tel Kabri palace (Niemeier and Niemeier 2000: fig. 5; reprinted, courtesy of W.-D. Niemeier).

level (numbered by Woolley, Rooms 1–13). Originally, traffic flowed into the large court (Room 9) that divided the palace into the "public"/"ceremonial" rooms to the north and the "private"/"residential" areas to the south. The only access from the court northward was through Room 8, which led to a staircase to the upper (not preserved) storey and to the main reception suite on the ground floor, what Woolley called the "Chamber of Audience" (Rooms 5 and 5A). At a later period in the building's history (still in the Middle Bronze Age), the palace entrance was shifted from Court 9, where the doorway was blocked up and faced with basalt orthostats, to the room immediately to its north (Room 7), which in turn led into Rooms 5 and 5A. The central reception rooms (5 and 5A) and the large (retiring?) room behind them employed columns to delineate space. The residential section of the palace lay to the south on two rising terraces and presented an array of small rooms, courts and corridors, although Woolley (1955: 94) speculated that the main living areas would have been on the upper storeys that no longer survive. In general, the walls of the palace follow straight lines, which, however, rarely meet at right angles with one another, creating a sense of irregularity. Its overall plan follows a main axis that runs roughly north–south.

The palatial structure at Kabri is quite poorly preserved, with only a few rooms surviving intact and its full plan still uncertain (Oren 2002; fig. 6 here).[12] It has been com-

12. Excavations in the area of the Kabri palace were recommenced in 2005, which has shown that the building occupied a greater extent than previously thought (Yasur-Landau and Cline 2006).

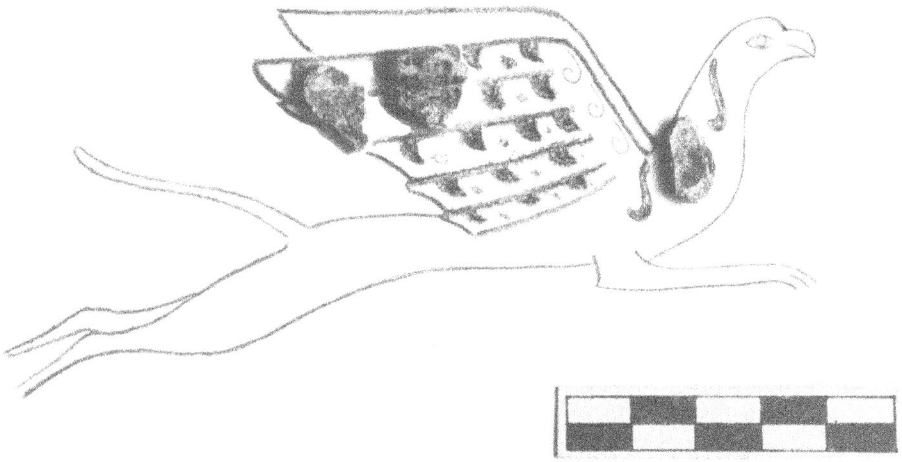

Figure 10. Reconstruction of fresco fragments of griffin from Tel Kabri palace (Niemeier and Niemeier 2000: fig. 13; reprinted, courtesy of W.-D. Niemeier).

pared to the Yarim-Lim palace, and in fact its plan has been heavily reconstructed on the basis of this comparison (Kempinski 1997: 329–30; Oren 2002: 69–70). Justification for this comparison derives from parallels that exist between the two buildings, including the arrangement of a central court (Kabri 703; Alalakh 9) leading to a main ceremonial suite (Kabri 611; Alalakh 5A, 5, and 2) along with a connecting unit (Kabri 690; Alalakh 8) between the ceremonial wing and a staircase. If the Kabri reconstruction can be accepted in general, it too presents a strikingly linear plan with straight edges set slightly askew. Kabri also, like Alalakh, boasts the use of wooden columns to delineate spaces, here seen in Court 703.

This architectural type is seen elsewhere in Levantine palatial buildings—for example, at Ebla in the Western Palace in Area Q (Matthiae 1997: 384–87; fig. 17 here). As at Alalakh and probably at Kabri, the Western Palace sports a mainly rectangular plan, extending along a north–south axis, with straight walls that often join at irregular angles. The whole comprises a series of irregularly formed blocks linked by small courts. If a large court existed, it would have been located in the badly preserved southern extent of the palace. The entrance to the palace probably pierced the southern façade, now mostly destroyed, and was marked by a columned porch. Columns also served to delineate the outer and inner spaces of what has been identified as the main reception room or throne room.

A primary goal of the renewed Qatna excavations has been to reassess and reexcavate the palace structure initially uncovered by Du Mesnil du Buisson in the 1920s.[13] Du Mesnil du Buisson (1935: 71–111) interpreted the remains as three separate units:

With the renewed excavations, our understanding of the Kabri palace architecture might change significantly.

13. For overviews of the ongoing work in the palace, see preliminary excavation reports published in the journals *Mitteilungen der deutschen Orientgesellschaft* and *Akkadica*, and for the 1999 and 2000 seasons, see al-Maqdissi et al. 2002.

Figure 11. Reconstruction of fresco fragments of architecture from Tel Kabri palace (Niemeier and Niemeier 2000: fig. 11; reprinted, courtesy of W.-D. Niemeier).

a unit to the east comprising the palace, an area to the west that he considered a temple to the deity Belet-Ekallim (Nin-Egal) mentioned in inventories found in that location, and the so-called High Place (*Haut-Lieu*) to the north of the temple area. A major result of the new excavations has been to demonstrate that the three units are part of the same palatial structure and that the construction of the palace most likely dates back to the late Middle Bronze Age (al-Maqdissi et al. 2002: 63; Novák 2004; fig. 12 here). Thus stitched together, the plan of Qatna's palace looks somewhat different from the plans of Alalakh, Kabri, and Ebla. Its principal feature is a large, square court (Hall C), about 37 meters × 37 meters, set with four columns on basalt bases in a square in its center. Long, rectangular (broad-room) reception suites lie to the east, while smaller rooms of varying functions (where the wall painting fragments were found) reside to the north.

Unlike the previous three Levantine palaces that we have considered, Qatna presents a more regularized plan based on squares and right angles, reminiscent of Mesopotamian palaces such as Mari, although the use of columns distinguishes it from these (Novák 2004: 305). It does, however, find a parallel (on a smaller scale) at the recently excavated site of Tell Sakka, near Damascus, where wall paintings have also been found, perhaps executed in the fresco technique, but employing clearly Egyp-

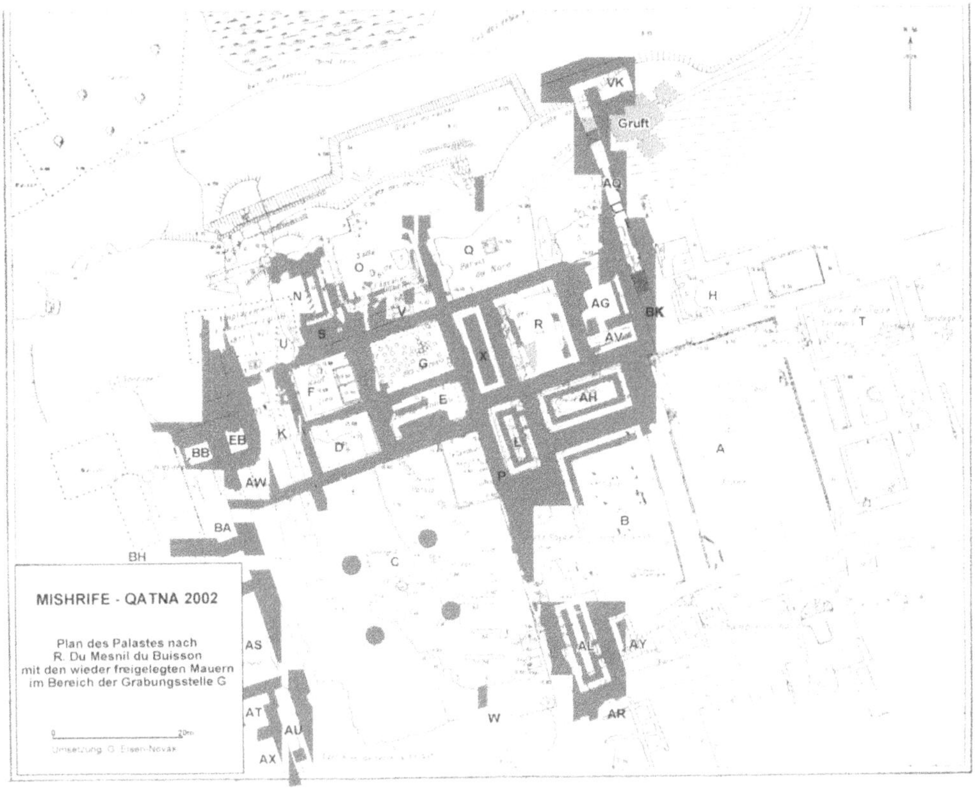

Figure 12. Plan of the palace at Qatna (after Novák 2004: fig. 2; reprinted, courtesy of Dr. M. Novák).

tianizing motifs and style (Taraqji 1999; fig. 18 here).[14] The Middle Bronze Age palatial structure at Tell Sakka features a rectilinear courtyard (close to square in shape, measuring 14.5 × 22.5 meters) with a set of four large columns forming a square in the center and another set of smaller, paired columns marking the southern entrance. The wall paintings were excavated from the walls enclosing the columned courtyard, as well as elsewhere in the building. Adding Tell Sakka to the comparison, though it is not possible to classify its paintings easily, further emphasizes architectural links binding the Levantine corpus together at the same time as setting it apart from the larger corpus of Aegean frescoed buildings.

14. With respect to the Egyptianizing nature of the Sakka wall paintings, it may be noted that Egyptian elements feature as yet another form of foreign, elite material culture deployed in the Middle Bronze Age Levant. For example, Palace P at Ebla contained a series of strongly Egyptianizing cutout ivories, and from Hypogeum C under Palace Q, a mace staff bearing the name of a minor Middle Kingdom ruler was found (Scandone-Matthiae 1997: 417–22); at Qatna, an Egyptian statue of a sphinx bearing an inscription of Princess Ita, daughter of Amenemhet II (ca. 1900) was found in Hall C ("Le Sanctuaire"; Du Mesnil du Buisson 1928: 16, pl. 12). While the use of "Egyptiana" presents a case related to the Aegean-style frescoes, it also entails distinctions, which require more extensive discussion than is possible in this essay.

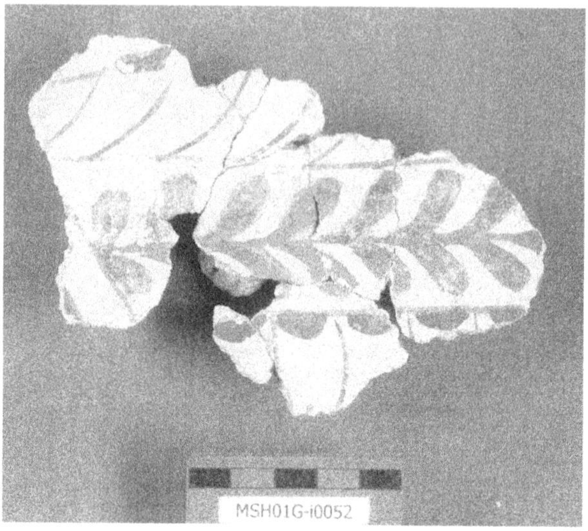

Figure 13. Wall painting fragment with pinnate foliage, Qatna palace (from Novák and Pfälzner 2002: fig. 13; reprinted, courtesy of Dr. P. Pfälzner).

Thus, we can locate these wall paintings within a restricted type of building, namely, palatial structures. The buildings at Qatna and Tell Sakka look remarkably similar, with their main court set round with a four-columned portico. Meanwhile, the structures at Alalakh, Ebla, and Kabri appear comparable, although the Kabri building was poorly preserved and reconstructed in large part through comparison with Alalakh.

One approach to understanding the sociopolitical significance of the frescoes lies in the application of architectural theories relating built environments to social action. According to such theories, highly culture-specific social behavior is conditioned in part by the built environment as a whole (Kent 1990; Rapoport 1990). That is, both architecture and its decoration create, constrain, and prompt social action through their forms and elements, enclosed spaces, patterns of circulation, and embedded cues regarding behavior. In addition, such theories postulate that the paintings themselves might be expected to have had some effect on the social action taking place within the buildings, which raises the question whether these paintings were purposely deployed for the very reason of affecting, changing, or molding social behavior. If we accept that architectural space helped to structure and condition human action, we might propose that the similarity of architectural space found in these buildings indicates a sharing of human behavior at a level much greater than, for example, between these buildings and the much more dissimilar architecture of frescoed buildings from the Aegean. Likewise, the presence of frescoes in these buildings strengthens the theory that they operated within a shared cultural realm and, moreover, that they served similar sociopolitical purposes and were received and deployed within a shared system of values that was, however, distinct from the values of the Aegean. This architectural context is revealing of the role the frescoes played in the Levant; that is, in the Middle Bronze period, they appear in palatial types of buildings, not residential, signaling their intimate association with the group in power and with the establishment of authority in general.

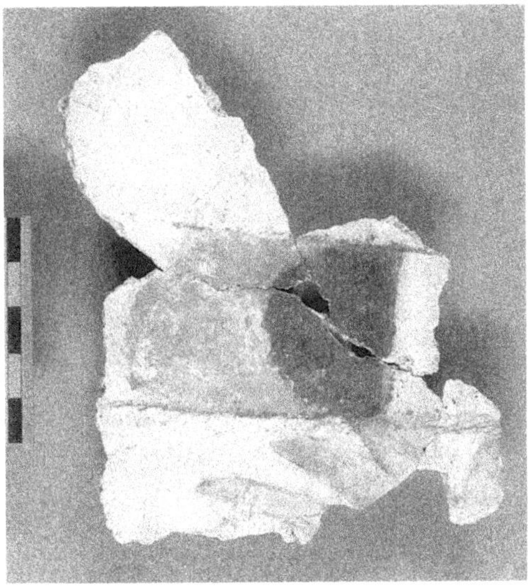

Figure 14. Wall painting fragment with blue palmate leaves, Qatna palace (Novák and Pfälzner 2002: fig. 15; reprinted, courtesy of Dr. P. Pfälzner).

Palaces, as the architectural expression of power par excellence in the Near East and as symbols of a kind of conspicuous consumption, provide one of the richest showcases for asserting, establishing, or negotiating authority (Russell 1998; Winter 1993). Winter (1993: 27) has noted that both the Sumerian and Akkadian words for palace rely on the adjective "great," which implies not just large size but also elevated status. The palace can be understood both as a concrete structure in which numerous activities (administrative, industrial, ceremonial) took place and as abstractly as the institution of rulership. In this sense, form, space, decorative program, and function are all interdependent. Later Assyrian inscriptions describe palaces as awe inspiring and built for the astonishment and wonder of the people, giving them a highly charged rhetorical aspect (Winter 1993: 37–38). The palace would thus be the ideal, perhaps even imperative locus for any "reinvention" processes undertaken by the Middle Bronze Age Levantine rulers.

After the burst of urbanism that characterized the end of the third millennium in the Levant, the region witnessed widespread collapse of city settlements, an event that remains shrouded in obscurity (Cooper 2006; Nichols and Weber 2006). With the revival of urbanism in the second millennium comes the appearance of dynasties bearing new ethnolinguistic names, such as Amorite, suggestive of fundamental changes among the ruling elite. These power shifts seem to correlate with changes in material culture that distinguish the Middle Bronze from the preceding Early Bronze Age.

The chronology of the period in question is fraught with many complications, not least of which is a lack of agreement on the terminology to be used to describe the messy chronological divisions. In general, scholars have concentrated primarily on either the southern or northern Levant, and two distinct scholarly traditions have developed. The northern Levant, including parts of Cilicia, the Amuq plain, western Syria, and Lebanon, presents less dissention, with the Middle Bronze Age more or less bisected into MB I, from around 2000 to 1800, and MB II, from around 1800 to

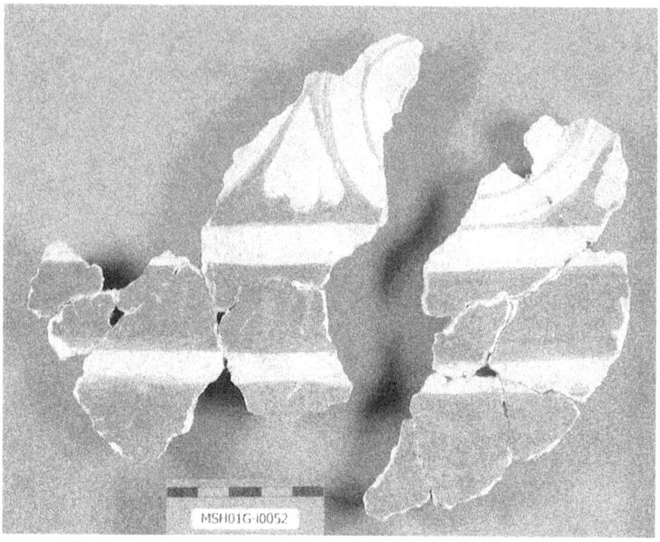

Figure 15. Wall painting fragment with spiral frieze, Qatna palace (Novák and Pfälzner 2002: fig. 14; reprinted, courtesy of Dr. P. Pfälzner).

1600 (Akkermans and Schwartz 2003: 291–92).[15] The southern Levant, however, remains encumbered by several competing dating systems that use variations on the same terminology (for example: EB IV, Intermediate Bronze Age, or MB I; MB I or MB IIA; MB II or MB IIB; and MB III or MB IIC) to designate different assemblages ranging in date from 2300 to 1500 B.C.E. (Dever 2003: 84–85; Ilan 1995: 297; Kempinski 1992; Mazar 1990: 152, 175). While Kabri can be comfortably understood as occupying the southernmost part of the northern Levantine cultural sphere, its geographic position in present-day Israel has meant that southern Levantine chronologies have been applied to its archaeology. It is therefore necessary to tread carefully when comparing chronological aspects of the three Levantine sites.

Regardless of terminology, however, the final centuries of the third millennium and the first centuries of the second millennium are marked by a seemingly cataclysmic collapse of urbanism followed by decentralization and relatively small settlements that display varying degrees of discontinuity in their material culture. By sometime around 1800 or 1700, a vibrant new urbanism appears.[16] This period also witnessed an expansion of regional powers, including the kingdoms of Yamhad in the north centered at Aleppo, Qatna along the middle Orontes River, and Hazor to the south in the Upper Galilee area. Textual evidence, almost entirely lacking for the earlier part of the Middle Bronze Age, becomes relatively more abundant with the sizable archive from Alalakh VII and assorted finds from Ebla, Qatna, and Hazor. The documentation found at Levantine sites is, moreover, amply supplemented by textual

15. The absolute chronology of the Middle Bronze remains very much in debate (for an overview of some of these debates, see Ben-Tor 2004).

16. Recent scholars highlight the fact that both the collapse and subsequent regeneration during this time were not homogeneous across space or time but, rather, witnessed a variety of degrees of collapse as well as a diversity of responses leading to revival (see, for example, Cooper 2006; Nichols and Weber 2006).

Figure 16. Wall painting fragment with landscape, Qatna palace (Novák and Pfälzner 2002: fig. 16; reprinted, courtesy of Dr. P. Pfälzner).

references to the area from other locales, most notably Mari on the Middle Euphrates. Although the exact date of the Levantine frescoes remains elusive, it seems likely that they appeared at the end of the Middle Bronze Age (what might be considered its apogee), perhaps persisting into the early Late Bronze Age, and then fairly quickly disappearing.

The Middle Bronze Age period of the main city of Yamhad, Aleppo, has been little explored archaeologically, given the enormous overlay of later occupations; however, the kingdom itself is relatively well attested in texts from elsewhere (Akkermans and Schwartz 2003: 297; Klengel 1992: 44–64). Archaeologically, Yamhad is best represented by Alalakh to the northwest and Ebla to its south, both cities that eventually came under the political authority of the Yamhad rulers. Alalakh was founded in the Middle Bronze I period (levels XIV–XII), but little is actually known of the city during this early time. Level VII has produced the best evidence in the form of a large archive and substantial architectural remains, although its absolute date remains contested; it should be somewhere in the late eighteenth and/or seventeenth centuries. The archive includes the reigns of Yarim-Lim (probably a son of Hammurapi I of Yamhad), his son Ammitaqum, and Hammurapi. It is also the level from which the fresco fragments derive, found in the so-called palace of Yarim-Lim. Ebla appears to have flourished even during the first centuries of the second millennium (MB I/ Mardikh IIIA), boasting a large earthen rampart and massive stone gateway. The city continued to prosper while under the authority of Aleppo, as indicated by the multiple palaces and their associated finds from the later Middle Bronze (MB II) period.

Qatna, controlling the area immediately to the south of the kingdom of Yamhad, took advantage of its position in the middle Orontes region. Though the recent excavations at the site have discovered a major royal archive (so-called archive of Idanda), it dates to the Late Bronze Age periods of the palace (Richter 2003). Only a few

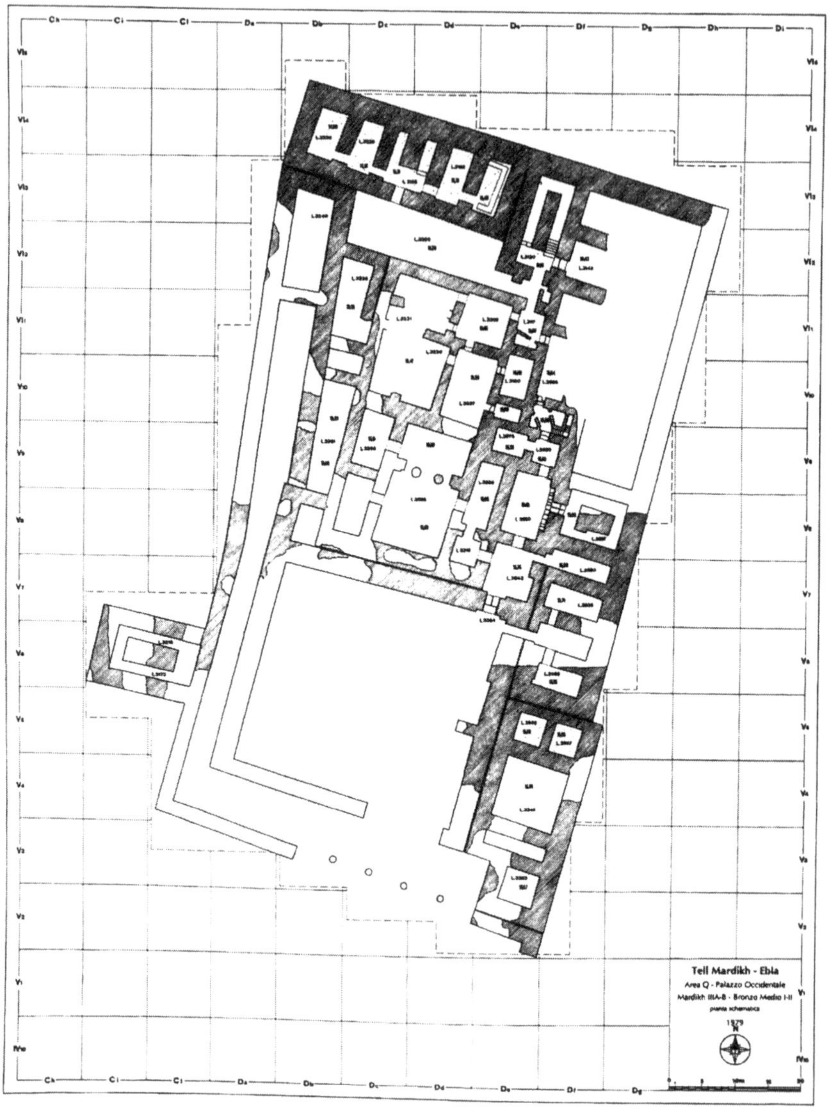

Figure 17. Plan of Western Palace (Q) at Ebla (Akkermans and Schwartz 2003: fig. 9.6; reprinted, courtesy of Paolo Matthiae).

Middle Bronze Age written documents have been discovered at the site (several Old Babylonian school tablets and a couple administrative texts; Richter 2003: 182–83); however, textual information concerning the kingdom also derives from the Mari and Alalakh archives (Klengel 1992: 65–70; 2000). From these sources, it is evident that Qatna was a formidable power, rivaling Yamhad (Klengel 2000). The Middle Bronze Age city covered about 100 hectares and included fortifications. The palace,

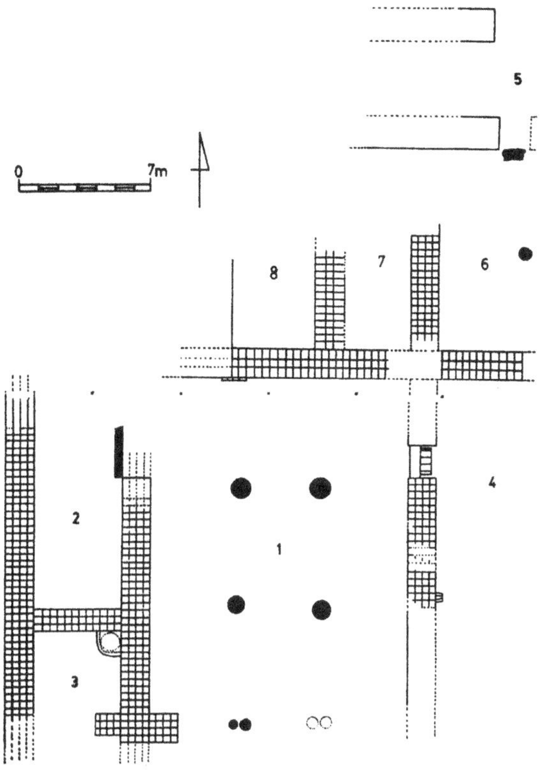

Figure 18. Plan of palace at Tell Sakka (Taraqji 1999: fig. 7; reprinted, courtesy of Dr. A. F. Taraqji and the Direction Générale des Antiquités et des Musées, Ministry of Culture, Syrian Arab Republic).

founded during this period, continued in use down to the Late Bronze Age, sometime in the fourteenth or thirteenth centuries. Recent excavations have discovered a sealed royal tomb beneath the palace, primarily dating to the Late Bronze Age, but with evidence of Middle Bronze Age material as well (al-Maqdissi et al. 2003).

Kabri, in the far north of present-day Israel (commonly referred to in the scholarly literature as Canaan during this period), culturally and in all likelihood politically bridges the northern and southern Levantine regions. It too experienced a period of collapse and reurbanization during the transition from the third to the second millennium (Kempinski 2002: 450–51). There is very little occupational evidence for the period between the Early Bronze Age and the Middle Bronze Age. Then, during the first centuries of the second millennium, Kabri, like many of the other sites in the Levant, displays dramatic changes in its urban character, notably the construction of a rampart and city wall and the reappearance of monumental architecture including the palace in Area D. During the later Middle Bronze period (MB IIB, according to the excavators), Kabri probably served as the commercial and administrative center of the northern part of the Akko Valley with strong ties to the island of Cyprus, a traditional gateway to southwestern Anatolia and the Aegean, evidenced in the numerous Cypriot finds at the site. Like Alalakh, Kabri itself was probably not the capital city of the regional power, which most likely was based at Hazor (Ilan 1995: 306–8;

Kempinski 1997: 327).[17] Rather, Kabri appears to have served as a primary link between the coastal routes and Hazor inland.

Among other factors considered in relation to the reemergence and realignment of urban kingdoms in the Middle Bronze Age is the possible impact of new "ethnic" groups, in particular the Amorites (Akkermans and Schwartz 2003: 288–91). The Amorites, typically identified by the presence in written documents of names in the Semitic Amorite language, remain highly enigmatic with respect to their origins and rise to prominence during the first centuries of the second millennium (Schwartz 1995: 254–55; Whiting 1995).[18] The designation Amorite (martu in Sumerian, *Amurru* in Akkadian) first appears in texts from the mid- and late- third millennium at Ebla and southern Mesopotamia and seems to refer to nomadic pastoralists occupying the area around the Jebel Bishri and the Middle Euphrates such as Emar and Tuttul (Streck 2000: 26–29). After a period at the end of the third millennium with no textual documentation and little archaeological evidence, Amorite dynasties appear in control of major kingdoms in western Syria (Yamhad and Qatna), northern Mesopotamia (Ekallatum-Shubat Enlil), the Middle Euphrates (Mari), and southern Mesopotamia (Babylon, Larsa, Sippar, and elsewhere). Amorite names are also attested at Hazor (Streck 2000: 146).[19]

Despite the strong Amorite link between the kingdoms of Yamhad and Qatna, both of which also boasted palatial structures decorated with Aegean-type frescoes, we cannot equate simplistically the use of frescoes with the Amorites, because there is no evidence for these painting techniques' being employed by Amorite dynasties elsewhere, in particular at Mari, where wall paintings have survived and are all done in the tempera technique. Moreover, Qatna shows a strong Hurrian element in its Late Bronze Age phase, exemplified by the recently excavated royal archive. These observations have significant implications for our assumptions that expect material culture production to map neatly onto ethnolinguistic groups. Indeed, the Middle Bronze Age Levant in general can be characterized as a highly multicultural society, linguistically evident in the presence of other Semitic speaking groups (for example, Akkadian) and Hurrians, in addition to Amorites.[20] This multiculturalism is also evident in syncretisms found in literary and religious texts and in the general heterogeneity of the material culture. Yet even within this diversity, the frescoes stand out forcefully in their "Aegeanness," increasing their quotient of "exoticism."

17. Hazor, with its large city plan and textual associations with Mari, can be considered the southernmost part of the Syro-Mesopotamian sphere (Ben-Tor 2004; Horowitz and Wasserman 2004; Maeir 2000). Current excavations at Hazor are focusing in part on Middle Bronze Age levels. The work has uncovered a late Middle Bronze Age palace complex in Area A-4 that partly underlies a Late Bronze Age palace (http://unixware.mscc.huji.ac.il/~hatsor/hazor.html, accessed 29 December 2005).

18. And see the essay by B. Jahn in this volume, pp. 193–209.

19. The attestation of Amorite names and even ruling dynasties does not demonstrate any direct link, such as invasion, to the processes of collapse and reurbanization, as has been argued in the past for the situation in the southern Levant (contra Kenyon 1966; Mazar 1992: 169–71), though at the very least Amorites benefited from a situation of instability and an absence of any single centralized power (Schwartz 1995: 255; Whiting 1995: 1234–35).

20. For Hurrian names in Middle Bronze Age texts, see Wilhelm 1989: 12–15.

Perhaps counterintuitively, the frescoes in the Levant appear quite late in the Middle Bronze Age and possibly even into the Late Bronze Age, when the new urbanism was fully established. However, if one considers that the process of invention and reinvention of traditions is ongoing (Hobsbawm 1992) and that marshaling the resources and technologies to produce these frescoes required an already powerful and internationally connected community, their late date makes more sense. In this respect, they seem to signal the consolidation of power and the expression of this power at its height; that is, they are the end result of the process of reinvention that began earlier in the second millennium. That this power is not sustained for long and that these frescoes exist in a relatively short chronological horizon pose another set of questions relating to the Middle Bronze–Late Bronze Age transition that fall outside the scope of this study.

A further point of interest with respect to the appearance of frescoes in the Levant is their relative newness at this time in the Aegean as well. Indeed, the near contemporaneity of frescoes in both the Aegean and the Levant (depending, of course, on which chronology one chooses to use and how early one dates the Aegean examples) has suggested to some authors that the "dominant direction of influence" may have been from east to west rather than the reverse (Sherratt 1994: 238). This is, however, a difficult argument to make, given the complete integration of frescoes within an Aegean tradition in contrast to their striking "exoticism" within a Levantine framework (Feldman forthcoming). Nonetheless, the fact that figural frescoes in the Aegean may not significantly predate the examples from the Levant[21] suggests that, if we consider an active deployment of technique, motif, and style by the Levantine elites, then what seems to contribute to the "added value" of the works should be associated with long-distance and exotic associations, as has been proposed by Knapp (1998: 195) and others (for example, Niemeier and Niemeier 1998: 96; 2002: 285). This stands in contrast to the deployment of symbols of Egyptian power, such as are found in Egyptianizing ivories from Ebla and the wall paintings from Tell Sakka, which, although also a major aspect of elite representational strategies in the late Middle Bronze Age, appear to provide legitimation by means of their references to an older and well-established tradition of rulership–namely, Egypt.[22]

In their studies of second-millennium frescoes, both the Niemeiers (1998: 96) and, more extensively, Knapp (1998) invoke Mary Helms's anthropological study that links

21. There is evidence of nonfigural precursors to the fresco tradition in the Early Minoan period at Vasiliki and Myrtos on Crete, where red-painted lime-plastered walls were discovered (Immerwahr 1990: 11). The date of the earliest figural frescoes remains debated due to the poor preservation of architectural evidence from the first palace period (Middle Minoan, ca. 1900–1700 B.C.E.) and the difficulties in determining the chronological sequence of the early frescoes (Immerwahr 1990: 39). This discussion is compounded by the newly proposed higher chronology for Thera that would place the Akrotiri frescoes (and hence Late Minoan IA frescoes in general) in the mid-to-late seventeenth century (Manning 1999).

22. The concept of "age value," that is, a value derived primarily because something is old, has been most commonly associated with the early-twentieth-century scholarship of Riegl (1982: 23–24). However, it is clearly also relevant to the ancient Near East and in particular the second millennium, evident for example in the use of patronymns and the general emphasis in dynastic lineages that in the Late Bronze Age manifests itself in the use of dynastic "heirloom" seals.

power with the acquisition of esoteric knowledge from distant areas. According to this approach, "objects, information, and experiences obtained from afar are imbued with latent power, and have the capacity to increase the prestige and status of those who acquire them" (Knapp 1998: 195). Yet neither addresses the specific motivations or sociopolitical situation of the Levantine rulers who chose to incorporate these frescoes in their palaces.[23] The concept of exoticism, when considered with specific regard to the reemergence and reinvention of an urban-based Levantine elite during the second millennium, can help us better understand the sudden, yet relatively short, appearance of these frescoes at Alalakh, Qatna, and Kabri. Exoticism, as has been discussed for nineteenth-century orientalism, rests more on an apprehension of difference, strangeness, or otherness than on any specific physical attribute (Bohrer 2003: 11). And, similar to proposals made for nineteenth-century European exoticism as a prime participant in the construction and mechanism of power relations (Bohrer 2003: 16; Said 1979)—in concert with the anthropological theories connecting esoterica, knowledge, and power—we might understand the Levantine frescoes as primary players in, not just the display of new authority, but even the accruing of power itself by means of the access and control that these frescoes physically manifest.

Indeed, it is not just the renewal of urban kingdoms that occurs during the Middle Bronze Age; the period also witnesses a complicated kaleidoscope of both competing and shared interests among the kingdoms. Thus, while the architectural comparisons suggest that the Levantine kingdoms engaged in related sociopolitical activities and perhaps shared ideologies, other evidence such as the textual documentation reminds us of the extreme competition that existed between the various dynasties, perhaps most dramatically noted in Hammurapi of Babylon's conquest of Mari. These factional divisions might, in fact, account for the distinctions seen in the architectural configurations between the palaces at Alalakh, Kabri, and Ebla and the palaces at Qatna and Tell Sakka. Given the historically known antagonism between the kingdoms of Qatna and Yamhad (represented here by its dependencies of Alalakh and Ebla) and the geographic proximity of Qatna and Tell Sakka, it is tempting to read these architectural differences as expressive of competition among Levantine elites, while interpreting their shared use of frescoes as expressive of their common needs to establish and maintain regional power bases vis-à-vis other groups.[24] Seen in this light, frescoes, prominently displayed in palatial structures and signaling connections with distant lands and access to esoteric knowledge, would have contributed to an intraregional competitiveness that fostered and helped construct a major reinvention of Levantine society during the Middle Bronze Age.

---

23. Knapp (1998: 205) in fact argues for an "Asiatic origin" of the iconography of both the Levantine and Aegean frescoes and thus analyzes "exotic motifs" within the Aegean from the perspective of Aegean elites who sought to gain "access to the mystical world of Egypt and western Asia, and of creating a dialogue with it."

24. How Kabri fits into this picture remains unclear. Its palace plan appears closer to the plans at Alalakh and Ebla, although its poor preservation leaves these comparisons in some doubt. The current excavation of an MB II palace at Hazor should also contribute to this question when its floor plan is published.

References

Akkermans, Peter M. M. G., and Schwartz, Glenn M.
2003 *The Archaeology of Syria from Complex Hunter-Gatherers to Early Urban Societies (ca. 16,000–300 BC)*. Cambridge: Cambridge University Press.

Ben-Tor, Amnon
2004 Hazor and Chronology. *Ägypten und Levante/Egypt and the Levant* 14: 45–67.

Bietak, Manfred
1996 *Avaris: The Capital of the Hyksos—Recent Excavations at Tell el-Dab'a*. London: British Museum.

Bietak, Manfred, and Marinatos, Nanno
1995 The Minoan Wall Paintings from Avaris. *Ägypten und Levante/Egypt and the Levant* 5: 49–62.

Bietak, Manfred; Marinatos, Nanno; and Palyvou, Clairy
2000 The Maze Tableau from Tell el Dab'a. Pp. 77–90 in vol. 1 of *The Wall Paintings of Thera: Proceedings of the First International Symposium*, ed. S. Sherratt. Athens: Thera Foundation.

Blakolmer, F.
2000 The Function of Wall Painting and Other Forms of Architectural Decoration in the Aegean Bronze Age. Pp. 393–412 in vol. 2 of *The Wall Paintings of Thera: Proceedings of the First International Symposium*, ed. S. Sherratt. Athens: Thera Foundation.

Bohrer, Frederick N.
2003 *Orientalism and Visual Culture: Imagining Mesopotamia in Nineenth-Century Europe*. Cambridge: Cambridge University Press.

Brysbaert, Ann
2002 Common Craftsmanship in the Aegean and East Mediterranean Bronze Age: Preliminary Technological Evidence with Emphasis on the Painted Plaster from Tell el-Dab'a, Egypt. *Ägypten und Levante/Egypt and the Levant* 12: 95–107.

Cooper, Lisa
2006 The Demise and Regeneration of Bronze Age Urban Centers in the Euphrates Valley of Syria. Pp. 18–37 in *After Collapse: The Regeneration of Complex Societies*, ed. Glenn M. Schwartz and John J. Nichols. Tucson: The University of Arizona Press.

Dever, William G.
2003 Chronology of the Southern Levant. Pp. 82–87 in *Near Eastern Archaeology: A Reader*, ed. Suzanne Richard. Winona Lake, IN: Eisenbrauns.

Du Mesnil du Buisson, Robert
1928 L'ancienne Qatna, ou les ruines d'el-Mishrifé au n.-e. de Homs (Émèse): Deuxième campagne de fouilles (1927). *Syria* 9: 6–24.
1935 *La site archéologique de Mishrifé-Qatna*. Paris: de Boccard.

Feldman, Marian H.
2006 *Diplomacy by Design: Luxury Arts and an "International Style" in the Ancient Near East, 1400–1200 BCE*. Chicago: University of Chicago Press.
Forthcoming Knowing the Foreign: Power, Exotica, and Frescoes in the Middle Bronze Age Levant. In *Proceedings of the 51st Rencontre Assyriologique Internationale: Chicago, July 18–22, 2005*. Chicago: Oriental Institute.

Frankfort, Henri
1996 *The Art and Architecture of the Ancient Orient*. Pelican History of Art. 5th rev. ed. New Haven, CT: Yale University Press.

Heinz, Marlies
1992 *Tell Atchana/Alalakh: Die Schicten VII–XVII*. Alter Orient and Altes Testament 41. Neukirchen-Vluyn: Neukirchener Verlag.

Hobsbawm, Eric
1992 Introduction: Inventing Traditions. Pp. 1–14 in *The Invention of Tradition*, ed. Eric Hobsbawm and Terence Ranger. Cambridge: Cambridge University Press. [First published, 1983.]

Horowitz, Wayne, and Wasserman, Nathan
2004 From Hazor to Mari and Ekallatum: A Recently Discovered Old-Babylonian Letter from Hazor. Pp. 335–44 in *Amurru 3: Nomades et sédentaires dans le Proche-Orient ancien, compte rendu de la XLVe Rencontre Assyriologique Internationale (Paris, 10–13 juillet 2000)*, ed. Christophe Nicolle. Paris: Éditions Recherche sur les Civilisations.

Ilan, David
1995 The Dawn of Internationalism: The Middle Bronze Age. Pp. 297–319 in *The Archaeology of Society in the Holy Land*, ed. Thomas E. Levy. London: Leicester University Press.

Immerwahr, Sara
1990 *Aegean Painting in the Bronze Age.* University Park: Pennsylvania State University Press.

Kempinski, Aharon
1992 The Middle Bronze Age. Pp. 159–210 in *The Archaeology of Ancient Israel*, ed. Amnon Ben-Tor. Tel Aviv: Open University of Israel / New Haven, CT: Yale University Press.
1997 The Hyksos: A View from Northern Canaan and Syria. Pp. 327–34 in *The Hyksos: New Historical and Archaeological Perspectives*, ed. Eliezer D. Oren. Philadelphia: University Museum of the University of Pennsylvania.
2002 History of the Site and Its Environs I: The Late Neolithic to the End of the Persian Period. Pp. 449–52 in *Tel Kabri: The 1986–1993 Excavation Seasons*, Aharon Kempinski. Tel Aviv: Tel Aviv University.

Kent, Susan
1990 Activity Areas and Architecture: An Interdisciplinary View of the Relationship between the Use of Space and Domestic Built Environments. Pp. 1–8 in *Domestic Architecture and the Use of Space: An Interdisciplinary Cross-Cultural Study*, ed. Susan Kent. Cambridge: University of Cambridge Press.

Kenyon, K. M.
1966 *Amorites and Canaanites.* London: Oxford University Press.

Klengel, Horst
1992 *Syria, 3000 to 300 B.C.* Berlin: Akademie.
2000 Qatna: Ein historischer Überblick. *Mitteilungen der deutschen Orient-Gesellschaft* 132: 239–52.

Knapp, A. Bernard
1998 Mediterranean Bronze Age Trade: Distance, Power and Place. Pp. 193–207 in *The Aegean and the Orient in the Second Millennium: Proceedings of the 50th Anniversary Symposium, Cincinnati, 18–20 April 1997*, ed. Eric H. Cline and Diane Harris-Cline. Aegaeum 18. Liège: Université de Liège / Austin: University of Texas at Austin.

Maeir, Aren M.
2000 The Political and Economic Status of MB II Hazor and MB II Trade: An Inter- and Intra-Regional View. *Palestine Exploration Quarterly* 132: 37–58.

Manning, Sturt W.
1999 *A Test of Time: The Volcano of Thera and the Chronology and History of the Aegean and East Mediterranean in the Mid Second Millennium BC.* Oxford: Oxbow.

Maqdissi, Michel al-; Luciani, Marta; Morandi Bonacossi, Daniele; Novák, Mirko; and Pfälzner, Peter
2002 *Excavating Qatna.* Berlin: Deutsche Orient-Gesellschaft.

Maqdissi, Michel al-; Dohmann-Pfälzner, Heike; Pfälzner, Peter; and Suleiman, Antoine
2003 Das königliche Hypogäum von Qatna: Bericht über die syrisch-deutsche Ausgrabung im November–Dezember 2002. *Mitteilungen der deutschen Orient-Gesellschaft* 135: 189–218.

Matthiae, Paolo
1997 Ebla and Syria in the Middle Bronze Age. Pp. 379–414 in *The Hyksos: New Historical and Archaeological Perspectives*, ed. Eliezer D. Oren. Philadelphia: University Museum of the University of Pennsylvania.

Mazar, Amihai
1992 *Archaeology of the Land of the Bible, 10,000–586 B.C.E.* New York: Doubleday. [First printed, 1990.]

Mee, Christopher
1982 *Rhodes in the Bronze Age: An Archaeological Survey.* Warminster: Aris & Phillips.

Monaco, Giorgio
1941 Scavi nella zona micenea di Jaliso (1935–1936). *Clara Rhodos* 10: 41–183.

Morandi Bonacossi, Daniele
2006 The Royal Palace of Qatna. Paper presented at the 5th International Congress on the Archaeology of the Ancient Near East: Madrid, Spain, 3–8 April 2006.

Morgan, Lyvia
1995 Minoan Painting and Egypt: The Case of Tell el-Dab'a. Pp. 29–53 in *Egypt, the Aegean and the Levant: Interconnections in the Second Millennium BC*, ed. W. V. Davies and L. Schofield. London: British Museum Press.
2004 Feline Hunters in the Tell el-Dab'a Paintings: Iconography and Dating. *Ägypten und Levante/Egypt and the Levant* 14: 285–98.
2006 Painting and Intercultural Relations. Paper presented at the 107th Annual Meeting of the Archaeological Institute of America: January 5–8, Montreal, Canada.

Nichols, John J., and Weber, Jill A.
2006 Amorites, Onagers, and Social Reorganization in Middle Bronze Age Syria. Pp. 38–57 in *After Collapse: The Regeneration of Complex Societies*, ed. Glenn M. Schwartz and John J. Nichols. Tucson: The University of Arizona Press.

Niemeier, Barbara, and Niemeier, Wolf-Dietrich
1998 Minoan Frescoes in the Eastern Mediterranean. Pp. 69–98 in in *The Aegean and the Orient in the Second Millennium: Proceedings of the 50th Anniversary Symposium, Cincinnati, 18–20 April 1997*, ed. Eric H. Cline and Diane Harris-Cline. Aegaeum 18. Liège: Université de Liège / Austin: University of Texas at Austin.
2000 Aegean Frescoes in Syria–Palestine: Alalakh and Tel Kabri. Pp. 763–802 in vol. 2 of *The Wall Paintings of Thera: Proceedings of the First International Symposium*, ed. S. Sherratt. Athens: Thera Foundation.
2002 The Frescoes in the Middle Bronze Age Palace. Pp. 254–98 in *Tel Kabri: The 1986–1993 Excavation Seasons*, Aharon Kempinski. Tel Aviv: Tel Aviv University.

Niemeier, Wolf-Dietrich
1998 The Minoans in the South-Eastern Aegean and in Cyprus. Pp. 29–47 in *Eastern Mediterranean: Cyprus-Dodecanese-Crete, 16th–6th Cent. B.C.*, ed. Vassos Karageorghis and Nikolaos Stampolidis. Athens: University of Crete and the A. G. Leventis Foundation.

Novák, Mirko
2004 The Chronology of the Royal Palace of Qatna. *Ägypten und Levante/Egypt and the Levant* 14: 299–317.

Novák, Mirko, and Pfälzner, Peter
2002 Ausgrabungen in Tall Misrife-Qatna 2001: Vorbericht der deutschen Komponente des internationalen Kooperationsprojektes. *Mitteilungen der deutschen Orient-Gesellschaft* 134: 207–46.

2003 Ausgrabungen im bronzezeitlichen Palast von Tall Misrife-Qatna 2002: Vorbericht der deutschen Komponente des internationalen Kooperationsprojektes. *Mitteilungen der deutschen Orient-Gesellschaft* 135: 131–65.

Nunn, Astrid
1988 *Die Wandmalerei und der glasierte Wandschmuck im alten Orient.* Leiden: Brill.

Oren, R.
2002 Area D. Pp. 55–72 in *Tel Kabri: The 1986–1993 Excavation Seasons,* Aharon Kempinski. Tel Aviv: Tel Aviv University.

Rapoport, Amos
1990 Systems of Activities and Systems of Settings. Pp. 9–20 in *Domestic Architecture and the Use of Space: An Interdisciplinary Cross-Cultural Study,* ed. Susan Kent. Cambridge: University of Cambridge Press.

Richter, Thomas
2003 Das "Archiv des Idanda": Bericht über Inschriftenfunde der Grabungskampagne 2002 in Misrife/Qatna. *Mitteilungen der deutschen Orient-Gesellschaft* 135: 167–88.

Riegl, Alois
1982 The Modern Cult of Monuments: Its Characteristics and Its Origin. Translated by Kurt W. Forster and Diane Ghirardo. *Oppositions* 25: 21–51. [Originally published in A. Riegl, *Gesammelte Aufsätze,* 1928.]

Rüden, Constance von
2006 The Wall Paintings of Qatna as Evidence of Overseas Communication. Paper presented at the 5th International Congress on the Archaeology of the Ancient Near East: Madrid, Spain, 3–8 April 2006.

Russell, John Malcolm
1998 The Program of the Palace of Assurnasirpal II at Nimrud: Issues in the Research and Presentation of Assyrian Art. *American Journal of Archaeology* 102: 655–715.

Sader, Helen
2006 A Middle Bronze Age Palace with Wall Paintings at Tell el Burak, Lebanon. Paper presented at the 5th International Congress on the Archaeology of the Ancient Near East: Madrid, Spain, 3–8 April 2006.

Said, Edward W.
1979 *Orientalism.* New York: Vintage.

Scandone-Matthiae, Gabriella
1997 The Relations between Ebla and Egypt. Pp. 415–27 in *The Hyksos: New Historical and Archaeological Perspectives,* ed. Eliezer D. Oren. Philadelphia: University Museum of the University of Pennsylvania.

Schwartz, Glenn M.
1995 Pastoral Nomadism in Ancient Western Asia. Pp. 249–58 in *Civilizations of the Ancient Near East,* ed. Jack M. Sasson. New York: Scribner.
2006 From Collapse to Regeneration. Pp. 3–17 in *After Collapse: The Regeneration of Complex Societies,* ed. Glenn M. Schwartz and John J. Nichols. Tucson: The University of Arizona Press.

Shaw, Maria C.
2003 Grids and Other Drafting Devices in Minoan and Other Aegean Wall Painting: A Comparative Analysis Including Egypt. Pp. 179–89 in *METRON: Measuring the Aegean Bronze Age, Proceedings of the 9th International Aegean Conference—New Haven, Yale University, 18–21 April 2002,* ed. Karen Polinger Foster and Robert Laffineur. Aegaeum 24. Liège: Université de Liège / Austin: University of Texas at Austin.

Sherratt, Susan
1994 Comment on Ora Negbi, The 'Libyan Landscape' from Thera: A Review of Aegean Enterprises Overseas in the Late Minoan IA Period. *Journal of Mediterranean Archaeology* 7/2: 237–40.

Streck, Michael P.
2000 *Das amurritische Onomastikon der altbabylonischen Zeit 1: Die Amurriter, die onomastische Forschung, Orthographie und Phonologie, Nominalmorphologie.* Alter Orient and Altes Testament 271/1. Münster: Ugarit-Verlag.

Taraqji, A.
1999 Nouvelles découvertes sur les relations avec l'Égypte à Tell Sakka et à Keswé, dans la region de Damas. *Bulletin de la Société Française d'Egyptologie* 144: 27–43.

Whiting, Robert M.
1995 Amorite Tribes and Nations of Second-Millennium Western Asia. Pp. 1231–42 in *Civilizations of the Ancient Near East,* ed. Jack M. Sasson. New York: Scribner.

Wilhelm, Gernot
1989 *The Hurrians.* Translated by Jennifer Barnes. Warminster: Aris & Pillips.

Winter, Irene J.
1993 "Seat of Kingship"/"A Wonder to Behold": The Palace as Construct in the Ancient Near East. *Ars Orientalis* 23: 27–55.
2000 Thera Paintings and the Ancient Near East: The Private and Public Domains of Wall Decoration. Pp. 745–62 in vol. 2 of *The Wall Paintings of Thera: Proceedings of the First International Symposium,* ed. S. Sherratt. Athens: Thera Foundation.

Woolley, Leonard
1955 *Alalakh: An Account of the Excavations at Tell Atchana in the Hatay, 1937–1949.* Oxford: Society of Antiquaries.

Yasur-Landau, Assaf, and Cline, Eric H.
2006 First Announcement concerning the Results of the 2005 Exploratory Season at Tel Kabri. http://home.gwu.edu/~ehcline/Kabri2005Resultsnew.html (accessed 13 April 2006).

Chapter 3

Sargon of Akkad: Rebel and Usurper in Kish

Marlies Heinz

When Sargon of Akkad (ca. 2340–2280 B.C.) seized power in Kish, it was the beginning of a reign that would restructure the entire political landscape of the Near East. Legend has it that Sargon was the son of a high-ranking priestess who immediately after his birth placed him in a basket and abandoned him to the Euphrates.[1] A man named Aqqi discovered the baby, pulled him out of the river, and adopted him. Sargon became a gardener at his father's estate. It is not known in detail how he ended up at the royal court in Kish. Traditionally it is believed that he was taken there by the town goddess, Ishtar, who had seen him in his father's garden.

Sargon did not belong to the traditional elite of Kish; he did not know anything about his origins. At court he became the king's cupbearer. From this position, he rebelled against the authorities and deprived the legitimate (!) king, Urzababa, of his power with the approval of, and by the will of, the deities An, Enlil, and Ishtar. Sargon became Urzababa's successor and sealed his accession to the throne by taking the title Sharru-kin (= Sargon), which means 'the legitimate king'.

At the beginning of his reign, Sargon changed most of the traditional political structure of Kish. The "old ones" (intimates of the former king?) and the temple priests were deprived of their power, and the palace took over the economic domains of the temples. The economic importance of the temples was thus noticeably marginalized (Steinkeller 1993: 122). Private individuals were now allowed to buy land, including land previously owned by the temples. A number of loyal families became increasingly powerful (Steinkeller 1993: 553ff.), influencing politics, the economy, and the military. Sargon paid special attention to the military, and when he claims in his military reports that he catered to "5,400 men" daily, researchers take this as an indicator of the special attention that Sargon bestowed upon this special unit.[2]

The reforms in personnel structure and the specific development of loyal troops were followed by changes in the organization of the town, its architectural appearance, and the makeup of its population. Kish, according to Sargon's inscriptions, was

---

Author's note: Translated from the German text by Bettina Fest; language editor: Ymke Muler.

1. See Westenholz 1997 and Lewis 1980.
2. See Gelb and Kienast 1990: 167, Text Sargon C1.

remodeled; that is, its urban structure was changed. Reminders of the old were modified if not removed, and the new order was made highly visible. These far-reaching changes culminated in the settling of new citizens in the town, people who were not in any way connected to the original population.[3]

One of the changes Sargon made "at home" was probably both the biggest in terms of organization and the most influential when it came to political importance: Sargon founded Akkad, the new political "capital," the precise location of which remains unknown to this day. Whether this city completely took over the role of the traditional residence of Kish is not known, but its great importance was underscored by Sargon's title "Sargon, King of Akkad." Sargon did not identify with Kish but with Akkad, and it was as king of Akkad that he wanted to be seen and remembered.[4]

Sargon heavily intervened in the existing order "at home" in Kish with his takeover and his political goals. This was also the case in the neighboring countries he attacked: they faced the complete breakdown of their political systems, both locally and regionally, by the end of Sargon's military incursions. Sargon's campaigns into southern Mesopotamia (today southern Iraq)–the region where his most important enemy, Lugalzagesi of Uruk, lived–left behind chaos and destruction.[5]

Uruk, Ur, and Lagash, the big cities of the Sumerian union of cities, were conquered, their walls (city-walls?) demolished, and their elites deprived of power. Lugalzagesi's hometown of Umma also fell into Sargon's hands, and he went on to gain control over Elam in the south of Iran, and Mari, in what is today Syria. Mari, an important harbor and trading center on the Euphrates, was spared destruction by Sargon. Akkadian conquests reached beyond Mari to the northwest and to the Mediterranean Sea. The area of the "Upper Sea," as the Mediterranean was called then, was, by his own account, bestowed on Sargon by the local god Dagan. This area included the region between Mari and Lebanon with its cedar forests, the southwest of Anatolia, and the coast. In the north, the Akkadians progressed as far as the fertile regions of Assyria, where they took over the local agricultural resources as well as the well-developed infrastructure, roads, and communication networks.

From the "Upper Sea" to the "Lower Sea," from the Mediterranean in the west to the Persian Gulf in the southeast, Sargon waged war, conquered cities, plundered and destroyed, robbed local elites of their offices, and replaced them with loyal Akkadian administrators. The economic resources of these regions henceforth primarily increased Akkadian wealth, and by controlling the conquered territories, the Akkadians secured a new distribution system. Sargon established his daughter Enheduanna as EN-priestess in Ur, in what was perhaps the most important strategic step in his political life, thus securing Akkadian control over the spiritual and religious life of the conquered south alongside economic and political dominance.

3. See Gelb and Kienast 1990: 161, Text Sargon C1 and 173, Text Sargon C4.

4. See Franke 1995: 94 and n. 47 for a reference to the Sumerian list of kings, in which Sargon is listed as the founder of Akkad.

5. For the texts of Sargon, see Gelb and Kienast 1990; Westenholz 1997; and Lewis 1980.

The Rebel Seizes Power

As a rebel and usurper, Sargon came to power in a way that could be considered almost classic. In Kish, as in the south of Mesopotamia, established structures were in the process of dissolving. The gods prophesied that the legitimate king of Kish and "lord" of Sargon, Urzababa, would soon lose his power (Cooper and Heimpel 1983; Afanas'eva 1987). Urzababa, who was then still ruling, recognized Sargon as a threat. He unsuccessfully tried to keep him from becoming his successor and to rid himself of the danger to his life and rulership.[6] In the south of the country, Lugalzagesi continued on a grander scale what the rulers of the Sumerian city-states had begun on the local level a generation earlier, from at least the time of Eannatum of Lagash.[7] Eannatum had enlarged the economic sphere of his city as far as Iran by means of warfare and had thus threatened the balance of power among what used to be equally strong city-states. During Lugalzagesi's reign, the union of early dynastic cities had already ceased to exist. The interests of Uruk's ruler lay in the north and thus potentially threatened the realm of Kish as well. The traditional roles in Kish and the surrounding region were destabilized. As cupbearer at court, Sargon was familiar with the politics and personnel there. The problematic situation in the country, the dissolution of the old order, as well as Lugalzagesi's activities presented new opportunities that could not have escaped him. From his privileged position, Sargon took advantage of the situation in order to initiate a takeover in Kish.

Like all rebels, Sargon theoretically had several ways in which he could establish his new position. If he broke all the rules and traditions of the former social community in all domains, a change in the system would be possible as a result of a change in leadership at the top. If he only broke the traditions in select areas of the system, this would lead to changes in broader circles of society and not just the elite and the government apparatus. The system as such and the social, cultural, and economic structure, however, would remain unharmed. Rebellions, according to one common definition, are to a greater or lesser extent the result of hierarchical conflicts in which a group of attackers sees a possible alternative to the ruling system and tries to put this into place by rebelling.[8] Hierarchical conflicts, according to this model, are seldom associated with further consequences to the social system, and usurpation is more or less seen as just a change in leadership at the top of the system, a change that does not necessarily affect the whole community and its concerns. According to Moore (1963: 85), a rebellion is a major change in politics that normally does not result in far-reaching structural changes in the governmental, power, and ruling system. This third type of rebellion would have been a possibility in Kish as well.

Every rebellion causes critical instability in the society concerned. No matter which strategy the rebels choose, they have to succeed in gaining control over the parameters that form the identity and self-definition of the community. In ancient Near

6. Afanas'eva 1987: 244, with a reference to lines 37–48: Urzababa tries to put Sargon into a furnace; and line 53 (p. 245), in which a letter addressed by Urzababa to Lugalzagesi of Uruk is mentioned: the letter suggests that the death of Sargon be arranged; this attempt also fails.

7. For the activities of Eannatum, king of Lagash, see Steible 1982: 143, Text Eannatum 1.

8. See, for example, Giesen 1991: 104ff.

Eastern societies, these parameters were often linked to religion. In addition, the community had to be convinced that only the new order could secure the "good life." Therefore, control over life-sustaining resources was as important as control over the military. The latter formed a guarantee of protection against threats from the outside and in many cases also served as protection for the ruler from internal opposition. Control of religious life and control of economic and military resources provided the means for securing the "superstructure" and the basis for society–that is, provided the connection between symbolic values and real events.

Success, according to the traditional theory of rebellion (Maurer 2004: 107ff.; Eisenstadt 1982), must be achieved quickly in order to demonstrate power while the rebellion is still ongoing. Opposition forces must not only be frightened by threats but must also be confronted with the results of their resistance by actual punishment. Loyal groups and potential supporters, on the other hand, are given material rewards immediately and are promised more in the future in order to secure their support.

With his takeover in Kish, Sargon destroyed the ruling order. With wars against the "others," he destroyed the political system in the south. He disregarded cultural and religious rules and destroyed the organization of the autonomous city-states.

The precise course of Sargon's takeover cannot be gleaned in detail from the written sources. It is only known that the takeover was not desired by the local elites. After the takeover, Sargon's management of the religious traditions of Kish and the surrounding regions became apparent. It was strategically cunning and probably was culturally unavoidable. Taking control of the religious traditions was presumably for the purpose of (and definitely suited for) legitimating his reign, winning supporters, and securing his position.

Rebellion and Religion

The change in the ruling order gained legitimacy by its association with the deities An, Enlil, and Ishtar. According to written sources, these gods had decided on the dethronement of the king. "Not Sargon but the gods are the agents of change" was the ideological message. Sargon did not plan the rebellion; he just benefited from it and at the same time fulfilled the will of the gods–he left his father's house for the court by the will of Ishtar.

The claim that the local deity, in this case Ishtar, clearly welcomed the takeover by a new ruler was part of the tradition of political renewal in the ancient Near East, irrespective of whether the new ruler gained power legitimately or not. The claim that An and Enlil were active in Kish is at first more surprising; their domains should have been in the south and not in northern Babylonia at the beginning of Sargon's rule. This surprise, however, vanishes in light of Sargon's political intentions and gives rise to admiration for his cunning ability to evoke the right gods at the right time and in the right place. He did not just intend to change the system in one city; he planned to change the entire societal system from the "Upper to the Lower Sea" to fit Akkadian ideas. In the third millennium B.C., An was the head of the Sumerian pantheon; he was the father of all the other gods and of all creatures and therefore the ultimate authority in the south. Enlil was not only his son and a second-rank god but also the god responsible for order and royalty in the country. The involvement of these two deities in Kish's political situation was strategically clever in two ways. In order to legitimate his expansionist goals and to secure his hegemonic struggle for power, Sargon needed the support of the gods of the region concerned, just as he had needed Ishtar's support in Kish. If Sargon wanted to legitimate his power in the new areas and find loyal allies among the local people, he needed to offer potential supporters an identification with a new order that appeared attractive. Consequently, Sargon's support by the most powerful deities in the south of Mesopotamia was publicized. Quite rightly one would not choose a city god as partner if one wanted to change the order of the whole country, because a city god's responsibilities were only to the city and did not extend to the country as a whole.

It is doubtful whether Sargon had the support of the religious elites. The propagation of Ishtar's help, which meant the de facto approval of the priests, may just have been a traditional proclamation at the beginning of the reign. This assumption is based on reports on Sargon's treatment of temple property. Land owned by the temples was overtly given to the palace and private individuals, and the priests were thus robbed of their economic base.[9] Trade, which was traditionally an aspect of the economy in which the temples were involved, was now entirely controlled by the palace. The local priests thus appear to have lost rather than profited by the change. By evoking the gods to legitimate his takeover, Sargon showed the priests the limits of their influence in no uncertain terms.

By naming Ishtar as a supporter of the new order, Sargon continued the traditional religious custom and thus evoked a sense of continuity in a time of change. At the same time, he interfered drastically in the local religious organization by marginalizing the priests and by evoking "foreign" deities. Sargon was a master at playing with traditions. Where they furthered his cause, he formally continued them, yet he also deprived them of meaning and subverted them. The management of traditions was crucial for the fate of the whole community as well as the rebel. He had to be wise when deciding what to continue and what to change. How subtle these changes could be is shown by, for example, the religious titles he used to describe his relationship to An, Enlil, and Ishtar (Franke 1995: 96ff.). He appeared as Ishtar's trustee, Enlil's governor, and An's priest, thus assuming roles that were only possible and successful when there was cooperation between humans and gods. In the real world, trustees and governors were installed by kings; in other words, these offices could only be gained by royal approval. Just as the officials were dependent on the king in acquiring a position, the king was dependent on their loyalty in exercising his governance effectually. Only in cooperation with the officials could the reign be successful. Sargon imposed the same relationship on his interaction with the gods. The king was no longer primarily a servant of the divine will but a potentially active and creative part of the divine plan. This new and powerful position of the king, in both the world of humans and the realm of the gods, once again underscored the priests' loss of power and influence.

9. For the Akkadians' treatment of occupied land, see Foster 1993: 25ff.

Rebellion and the Local Political Elite

In the political field, the change in the status quo was much more radical than in the religious sector. The dethronement of Uzarbaba was followed by the impeachment of the "old ones," presumably the counselors of the old king, and their removal from the sphere of the new ruler. When the established elite openly opposed the new order, the most important act of every rebel (once the elite had been removed) must have been the establishment of a new, loyal clientele. These new supporters were not recruited from the religious or the existing political elite of Kish, as has already been demonstrated.

Sargon found a trustworthy and strong clientele within the ranks of the military. According to his own statements, 5,400 men ate with him on a daily basis. The military was an essential and crucial part of his politics and must have worked as a protective force at home, as well as a powerful means of expansion abroad.

Rebellion and the Control of Resources

An important way of demonstrating to a wide audience that the new order had brought the "good life" to the community was to secure its economic needs. In ancient Near Eastern societies, the economy played a crucial part in constructing and sustaining the community, and its representatives were accordingly powerful. The control of resources also meant the far-reaching control of the present and future state of society.

Sargon of Akkad used the field of economics to establish a loyal clientele in Kish. The concentration of control over all resources at the palace made it possible to give temple lands to private individuals. The new landowners who profited from the new order were probably Sargon's first followers. The break in political tradition was followed by a break in the traditional organization of the economy (and later also in the organization of trade). Control over economic aspects of society was especially important to Sargon. Unlike religion, economics was an area in which he broke radically with tradition (just as in the sphere of politics) and distinguished himself with innovations that were probably essential for the approval of the new order by new social groups and were absolutely necessary for the stabilization of his reign.

Rebellion and Structural Change in the Ruling Order

With his interference in the political, religious, and economic order of Kish, with his disposal of the old clientele and establishment of a new clientele, Sargon secured his reign and changed the structures of the political and social community much more profoundly than traditional research into rebellions normally dictates. While most researchers postulate just a change in leadership at the top as the usual result of rebellion, the changes brought by Sargon's takeover went much further and were not limited to the elites. Although one cannot speak of a change in system in Kish itself, the measures taken after the takeover meant profound changes in the cultural and social conditions that were particularly visible to the population of the town.

Giving land to individuals implied that Sargon consciously addressed circles beyond the traditional elites in order to recruit new supporters. In Lagash, the usurper and outsider Urukagina had already pursued this strategy of allowing a wider audience to profit from the new order and thus turning them into its supporters.[10] The structural change in the elites should thus have been enforced by a change in the privileged social groups.

Resettlement as a Political Means of Establishing a Clientele

These measures were seemingly not sufficient in Kish to safely establish the new order in the minds of the people. To achieve this, a new strategy was put into action and a relocation campaign was begun that resulted in the settlement of new groups in Kish.[11]

The relocation of human beings and their integration into a new and strange social system are a huge intervention for all concerned–the old population as well as the newcomers. Relocation means the destruction of established social bonds, not just where people are removed from their familiar environment, but also in the areas where the resettlement takes place. In the new place, the strangers are at first isolated, torn from their familiar relationships and power structures; they have not yet established structures to organize their community. The new settlers are dependent on the protective power of the leaders responsible for their relocation in order to orient themselves. Although the reasons for the resettlements in Kish are not explicitly stated in the sources, one can assume in this particular case that the newcomers (who would have been in need of protection) were established there in order to create a new loyal clientele for Sargon.

The political aims and the impact of resettlement activities on the established population as well as on the resettled population can be seen in the structural changes in Tibet as enforced by the "protective power," China. By relocating and giving preferential treatment to the new population in their new home, the rulers try to establish a stable, long-term, and irreversible basis for their power abroad. This intervention in the status quo is ambivalent and risky for the protective power as well, because the new population might form an alliance with the old one and oppose the new order. Sargon must have been aware of this potential danger; nevertheless, relocation and restructuring of the population in Kish were part of his political program.

Spatial Order as a Visible Sign of the Ruling Order

By the time the resettlements began, the innovations in Kish must have been obvious to everybody. But Sargon did not stop at intervening in the social structures of Kish as a visible sign of his rule. The remodeling of the political and social order was followed by a remodeling of the public space, in order to impose the new order on

10. For those privileged by Urukagina's reforms, see Steible 1982: 311, Text UKG 4–5.

11. For the remodeling and resettlement of the city, see Gelb and Kienast 1990: 161, Text Sargon C1.

the cultural memory of the inhabitants of Kish and surrounding areas. The traces of the old order had to be removed from Kish's appearance. Every ruler in ancient Near Eastern societies used architecture and the design of public space as a political means—as a way of presenting his reign as successful.

Sumerian kings usually dedicated their architectural endeavors to the gods, but this is not something known from Sargon's reign. Designing public space demonstrated both economic power and the power of the ruler over the availability of space—and it allowed the ruler to associate symbols of power with the memory of his particular reign. That this measure was by nature very visible made this strategy just as ambivalent as resettlement was: the construction of representative architecture was a sign of power and was visible to everyone, yet at the same time, its destruction clearly demonstrated political decline and could also be observed by everybody!

It is reported that Kish (as the only place in the region) was remodeled, but we do not know how and to what extent this was done. The officials of Akkad must have known that changes in the spatial order—the concealing of old architectural orders and the destruction of old symbols of power—were an important and powerful strategy in removing the old from memory and postulating the new as relevant. The message of a changed architectural and spatial order was intended to make the new obvious but also to document the economic and political power of the new ruler. This potential was used to transfer the traditional center of political power, Kish, into a place that demonstrated the ideas of a new ruling class. The fact that it was Kish, the capital of the former kings, that underwent a structural remodeling is striking and indicates once more that it was necessary to a establish a highly obvious sign of the new order.

Sargon of Akkad, Founder of a City

Whether the many measures taken to establish Sargon's reign were successful in Kish is not reported explicitly. We do know, however, that Sargon, apart from the reforms already mentioned, intervened profoundly in the existing religious, social, and cultural structures for a second time when he decided to found another political residency alongside Kish and built the city of Akkad.[12] Whether the old networks in Kish remained powerful and obstructive in the establishment of the new order or whether it was politically opportune to place a new city next to the redesigned Kish remains open to debate. The development, however, has to be regarded as a major break with tradition that potentially meant more than just a break in using one place continuously. The traditional places of worship and ritual were located in Kish, as were presumably the cemeteries of the ancestors, and according to the beliefs of the time these could not simply be abandoned and left behind.[13] Sargon, however, saw in this

12. The location of Akkad and its appearance remain unknown. The site of the town has not been identified and excavated. That Sargon founded Akkad is reported in the Sumerian list of kings, which calls Sargon the "King of Akkad, the man who built Akkad" (Franke 1995: 94).

13. The care of the ancestors even after their death was the imperative duty of the living. Neglecting this duty meant bad luck for the dead and the living.

tradition no obstacle to building a new city, a fact that is not really surprising given his biography and the attitude of the traditional elite toward his reign.

The Political Titles of Sargon and Their Identity-Constituting Effects

Whether Sargon considered himself to be within the traditions of Kish at all and identified with them is doubtful. The titles with which he is recorded and with which he wanted to be remembered do not indicate this! Akkad was clearly more important to him as a symbol and as a sign of royal identity than Kish was. Sargon bore the title "King of Akkad." He identified with the new order. The old political order was no longer commemorated with highest priority, while the new order was aggressively promoted and there was a clear break with the old traditions of political order. Whether Sargon's second title was "King of Kish" or "King of the Country" is heavily disputed.[14] It would have been strategically wise to add the new next to the old–King of Akkad and (!) King of Kish–and thus make the new acceptable via the old, to refer back to the old customs of society and to make the new ones appear less threatening. To integrate the new via the old would also fit into the building program for the city: a new city is built in addition to the old center of power.

Conclusion: The Rebellion of Kish and Its Local Consequences

The break with tradition in the political field at first needed a powerful façade that glossed over the break and suggested a continuity of tradition. What would have been more appropriate than the use of religion? This was precisely what the rebel and future king Sargon had in mind when he made the gods responsible for the changes. From a modern perspective, this was a strategically clever move that at the same time obscured the next break with tradition. Referring responsibility and agency to the gods should theoretically strengthen the priesthood after a political rebellion, yet the priests were de facto robbed of their power. The newcomer Sargon cleverly used tradition. The only possible way to gain ultimate legitimacy for the takeover and thus also gain approval for a change in government was by not challenging religious customs openly but continuing them. The subtle measures that initiated the change in religious traditions have already been mentioned.

In politics, however, radical interference with the traditions of cooperation was necessary. The rulers in the south had, according to the rules, acceded to the throne as successors to their fathers, and thus the continuation of tradition had secured success. Sargon, however, could not rely on such a tradition. Instead he challenged this "defect" and created his own tradition. A new clientele was established, and the old networks were broken up. Interventions in the spatial order and the makeup of Kish's population made the change in power in the traditional center visible to everyone, while the founding of the new residence of Akkad and the new ruler's clear identification with this new center emphasized the manifestation of the new far beyond the immediate area. Sargon followed the classic steps to success that a rebel at the center

14. For the reconstruction of the title "King of Kish," see Franke 1995: 95–96.

of a rebellion should take: oppositional forces are heavily punished by the loss of property and responsibilities, while potentially loyal groups are established by bestowing material privileges upon them.

Structural change occurred where Sargon allowed new population groups access to influential positions. He also transferred control over resources and access to resources to new institutions. In particular, he concentrated responsibility for the control of the resources of several institutions in one administrative unit–the palace. The consequences of the rebellion in Kish affected broad circles of society and were not limited to a change at the top of the government, as postulated by some researchers in rebellion theory. Sargon recognized the need to make his political activities visible. By remodeling Kish, relocating new inhabitants there, and founding Akkad, he demonstrated his seemingly unlimited power over space, people, and resources. The building activities could have been read as a sign of political and economic power, but they could also have been intended to gloss over weak spots and to distract the subjects' attention from problems and divert it to prestigious operations of success.

The ambivalence shown by his building activities must have been clear. Architecture is both a witness to and sign of a ruler's power, yet in its decay and destruction it also mirrors the precariousness of the prevailing order.

After his takeover, the rebel and usurper Sargon established unmistakable and highly visible signs that symbolized the new order and gave the old order a new position. The founding of Akkad, the title that emphasized Sargon's connection with Akkad and not Kish, the emphasis on the military and the "5,400 men" he fed daily, as well as the relocation of the population to Kish provided Sargon with a geographical space and a social clientele that expressed the new order, an order that was radically different from the older traditions and customs in Kish. The danger or the goal of this strategy–that it risked, or even intended, a split in society–was inherent to Sargon's activities. He offered opportunities for identification that at first appeared like the establishment of a privileged elite rather than a way of achieving conciliation within a population that was facing the manifold changes brought on by the takeover.

Expansion and Invasion: Sargon the King of Akkad, Sargon the Conqueror

Sargon's rebellion "at home" was followed by "foreign" domination over the south and the expansion of control and dominance over parts of northern Mesopotamia, and over what is today western Syria. The principle of structural change that Sargon applied in Kish was continued "abroad." By removing the local elites in the conquered cities, Sargon secured political control over the occupied territories once his military actions were over.[15] The destruction of cities and the political dethronement of enemies were followed by the next step necessary for securing his rule: establishing control over the losers' economic resources and concentrating the means of survival

15. "From the Lower Sea [the Persian Gulf] citizens of Akkad are governors, even Mari and Elam serve Sargon, the King of the Country" (see Gelb and Kienast 1990: 161, Text Sargon C1).

in the hand of the usurper and foreign ruler. Imports from Tilmun, Maggan, and Meluhha in southern Mesopotamia reached Akkad. This means that the wars in the south had opened up new trading routes to Akkad that transcended regional boarders.[16] Northern Mesopotamia was a transit region for Akkadian trade and also provided Akkad with the necessary agricultural resources. Via the Euphrates, and using Mari as a trading center, the Akkadians reached and controlled the west and from there extended their power to the Levant and Anatolia in order to secure supplies of wood and metal. The direct interventions in the conquered communities' political and military systems were accompanied by more subtle measures, which may not have been immediately visible to everyone but which may have led to profound changes in traditional conditions. Once the Akkadians controlled the politics and the economy of a region, they also took over the cultural realm by dethroning the priests in the most important religious centers and replacing them with intimates of Sargon. In Ur, for example, Sargon's daughter Enheduanna became EN-priestess.[17] By integrating religion into his politics and by using the gods of the conquered to legitimate these events, the Akkadian ruler potentially contributed to a split in the communities concerned, which had to decide whether to remain loyal to their own elite or to embrace Sargon and the new order.

With the restructuring of the old political center of Kish and the founding of Akkad, Sargon made it impossible to overlook the new order "at home" on an architectural level. The interventions in the visible "public" order made Sargon appear as a "constructive" and economically and politically potent ruler. In the occupied regions of the south, to begin with it was the destruction of the cities that made the new order visible,[18] and thus Sargon may have appeared more as a ruthless military leader than a constructive ruler there. With the loss of their architectural environment, these communities also lost the order of their *Lebenswelt*. The razing of city walls documented in equal measure the very obvious defenselessness of the cities and the loss of political autonomy (which, while not directly visible, was certainly discernible to everyone). The loss of order and the symbolic meaning of a destroyed city must have had a deep impact on its citizens' concepts of their own identity. The loss of architectural order was followed by the loss of political order due to the removal of the traditional elites.

Controlling the cities that were most important to the reign of the Akkadians in the occupied areas in the south was the responsibility of trustworthy followers of Sargon. This was a dramatic change in the political tradition of the south, where rulership was traditionally organized dynastically. The dissolution of the autonomy of cities in the south benefited the establishment of a new territorial ruling system based on a concentration of power in Sargon and his political center, Akkad. This was another serious break with tradition, which was begun by Lugalzagesi (Sargon's contemporary and main rival) and completed by Sargon.

16. Gelb and Kienast 1990: 167, Text Sargon C2.
17. See Gelb and Kienast 1990: 64, Text Sargon A1.
18. See Gelb and Kienast 1990: 16, Text Sargon C1: "He has conquered the city and demolished its walls."

Whether the Akkadians conquered the west and the north with their military or whether they "only" controlled it politically and exploited it economically is not reported in the written sources. That access to the resources of both regions was essential for the establishment of an Akkadian realm is shown in the case of the north by archaeological sources. For the west, written documents also exist.

The rebellion in Kish and the reorganization of the political systems in central and southern Mesopotamia had serious and far-reaching consequences. Ebla and Mari were especially affected by the increasing strength of the Akkadian superpower. Located on the Euphrates, Mari had always been an important trading center between the Levant and Mesopotamia and a harbor for the shipping of goods to the south. The Akkadians took advantage of the easily accessible and controllable junction and managed to dominate this place as well.

Ebla was the economic and administrative center of the west, with a focus on wool and textile production as well as the processing of metal, wood, and gemstones. These were imported as raw materials and were then turned into high-quality luxury goods before finally, like the wool and the fabrics, being exported. Highly specialized craftsmanship as well as the import of raw materials and export of finished goods formed the economic bases that guaranteed the city's wealth. A far-reaching network of trade relations (Pettinato 1991: 83) connected the city with autonomous urban centers both near and far, including Tell Brak and Tell Leilan in the northeast and the city of Assur in northern Iraq, and with areas rich in raw materials, such as the Amanus and Taurus Mountains and northern Lebanon, as well as with Palestine and Egypt via Byblos.

The changes in the internal organization of southern and central Mesopotamia were followed by a new direction in foreign politics under Akkadian rule. The far-reaching contact of the formerly independent city-states with more-or-less equal trading partners that extended from Mesopotamia to the Levant was replaced with an aggressive Akkadian policy of territorial expansion through a centralized control of resources.

Tell Leilan and Tell Brak were major trading partners with Ebla. With their fertile hinterlands, they were well suited for agriculture and cattle breeding and were also easily reached and controlled from all directions through the integration of a good road system. In order to enrich the capital, Akkad, the Akkadians placed the fertile agricultural zone around the two cities under their own administration and made them part of their realm. It is not known whether the Akkadians replaced the local elite or just controlled it. Particularism and independence, in any case, gave way to Akkadian centralism. Massive tax duties kept a stranglehold on the cities and made the Akkadian center even richer. The Akkadians controlled the well-developed network of roads that connected the Khabur region with the south and with the neighboring regions in the north and west. They also used the roads for the transport of regional products to the center, Akkad.

The western Levant with its powerful economic and administrative center in Ebla, the Amanus region, northern Lebanon as a provider of cedar wood, and the Taurus with its source of silver were more difficult to access and control than the north and the Euphrates region, but they were very much desired by the Akkadians. Sargon boasts in his inscriptions of not only having seen the west but of having ruled it. A detailed analysis of the reports shows that another scenario was more plausible. By sporadic campaigns directed at the sources of raw material, the Akkadians secured the necessary goods without being constantly present in the west. Both written and archaeological sources document this short-term occupation, control, and plundering of the periphery by the Akkadians. The consequences of their expansive rule, however, went far beyond these activities. They intervened profoundly in the infrastructure that had developed during the second half of the third millennium B.C. in Syria/Lebanon, and eventually caused its destruction. The occupation and control of the north and east resulted in a structural change in the relations of the formerly autonomous cities of the Levant. Trade was now replaced by an exchange of goods between center and periphery that was controlled by the Akkadians and that had only one taker—the Akkadians. Where the well-developed road and communication networks were useful for the foreign occupants, they were maintained; where they could not be controlled, they were destroyed. With the change in the organization of trade, the trade routes also altered. The new routes and the forced structural changes that also took place in the west of the Levant must have robbed Ebla of its economic base. Due to the interregional interventions by the Akkadians, Ebla lost control of the wood and metal sources and thus also lost the ability to provide its own highly specialized artisans with raw materials. At the same time, the formerly independent trading partners and consumers of luxury goods produced in Ebla had vanished due to Akkadian occupation of the north, their control of the city of Mari, and the change in the political organization of Mesopotamia itself. The intervention of the Akkadians in the trade and communication system of the autonomous city-states led to the destruction of this system first in Mesopotamia and later also in Syria/Lebanon. The removal of goods instead of trade and the central political control instead of autonomy of the "Syrian" towns were of greatest benefit to the center of the new order.

The restructuring of the political organization from a decentralized to a centralized system was by necessity followed by a concentration of the control of resources in the center, Akkad. Access to the resources that were not directly available in Akkad and its surrounding area was blatantly put under Akkadian control. The formerly independent and wealthy trading cities of Ebla, Mari, Brak, and Leilan lost their power and autonomy and, just like the regions on the Gulf, came under the domination and control of Akkad. Trade profits were asymmetrical, concentrated entirely on the needs of the political center of Akkad.

Direct and Structural Violence: Politics and Religion

The rebellion of Kish was followed by a drastic change in the political and economic organization from southern Iraq to northern Mesopotamia and the Mediterranean in the west. Interference in the political and economic organization of the conquered region, supported by the military, led to changes in traditional conditions, customs, and rituals. But in the long term, securing Akkadian dominance abroad was not possible by the establishment of military, political, and economic control over the region alone. Cultural integration was essential if Sargon was to find loyal supporters in the conquered population, supporters who would identify with the new order and accept it. However, attempts to gain broad approval of his politics are not immediately discernible in the various forms of Sargon's self-image that have survived. He only provided for certain groups, such as the military, the citizens of Akkad, the clientele that he had established abroad, and possibly the people who had been relocated to Kish.

The image of the "good shepherd" providing the "good life" for all of his subjects was not propagated by Sargon, and in this he differed from the rulers in southern Sumeria before him as well as from the rebel Lugalzagesi, who broke with the political system yet fulfilled traditional cultural and social obligations. The self-representation of Sargon, on the other hand, also showed a break with the traditions of the social community of ruler and population, including–by the removal of the priests in the most important temples of the south–the handling of the conquered people's religious customs and rituals. In order to gain approval and support as the legitimate ruler in spite of these breaks with social and religious rules, Sargon was forced (despite the realities) to present his own actions as beneficial to everyone and to make the changing of traditions and customs appear not only necessary but the only and right way to the "good life." He had to present his attitude as universally valid and as normatively "natural," to harmonize divergent opinions and conditions, and to establish a system of meaning that included the potential of creating a new tradition in which everyone would find his or her place.

One of the most important measures Sargon had to take was to integrate his actions in the realm of the religious. It was culturally essential to secure divine approval. However, this does not mean that the rulers in ancient Near Eastern societies were unaware of the strategic potential of the use of religion in politics. Religion was the major parameter used to legitimate actions in these societies and was probably especially relevant when it came to its fluctuating use by foreign rulers: religion legitimates and stabilizes order and promises security. At the same time, it is a threat to people who do not act according to the divine will. This ambivalence was used by Sargon as legitimation for his actions abroad. Seemingly free of traditional, religious bonds, he also proclaimed at any time the support of the gods who happened to be particularly appropriate for his political needs.

The god An, who resided in Uruk, was, as already mentioned, the head of the Sumerian pantheon, and thus the ultimate authority in the whole country, while his son Enlil was responsible for order in the country. In Kish, according to the legend, both were involved in the divine conspiracy against the ruling king; Enlil bestowed the territory from the Upper to the Lower Sea upon Sargon and made sure that Sargon was not confronted by an equal opponent.

In the western periphery, Sargon used the god Dagan to legitimate his actions. Dagan, the king of the country, leader of the gods, and the highest deity in what is today Syria (his position in the hierarchy of gods is comparable to Enlil) had made the conquest of the foreign territories Armanum and Ebla possible in the first place, according to Sargon's propaganda.

The manipulation of religious responsibilities abroad against the personnel concerned developed into a system of structural and cultural violence, in which the "others" were more or less ideologically defenseless against the Akkadians. With their takeover of the religious system, the Akkadians attacked the most basic religious and political norms and thus also the basis of social community. At the same time, they attacked the conquered elites ideologically in what was politically one of the most powerful fields: religion–which was also the grounds for legitimating their power to their own people.

Only after Enlil pronounced his verdict and gave his order did Sargon conquer Uruk.[19] By showing the conquered that it was their own deities who caused the political change (or at least supported and legitimated it), the Akkadians must have managed to legitimate their victory almost "automatically" even in the eyes of the conquered. The Akkadians therefore put further pressure on the conquered elite and population, who were not only conquered militarily but were also robbed of the divine protection and support of their own gods. Victims were thus turned into perpetrators; the conquered elites were themselves to blame for the violence they had to suffer. This powerful reversal of facts worked well wherever Sargon could demonstrate that the local elites had acted against the will of the local gods, and therefore also against their own culture and society, and had thus lost the support of the gods. The inhabitants of Nippur must have stood by powerless and watched Sargon put his most important opponent, Lugalzagesi, king of Uruk, in the pillory in front of the Enlil Temple, and they must have observed that Enlil did not intervene on Lugalzagesi's behalf.[20] With ideological and propagandistic ruses of this sort, the Akkadians effectively defined war and violence as necessary for reestablishing order in the conquered regions. The legitimacy of the Akkadian actions, according to the ideology of Akkadian propaganda, was not to be questioned because, through the active support of the deities of the conquered societies, the actions of the victors and the new order in the conquered societies could be postulated as happening by the will of the gods. The Akkadian claim to be the legitimate preservers of the traditional order also carried an enormous potential for splitting society. The aim of Akkadian propaganda was to turn the conflict between Akkadians and conquered societies into a conflict within the society and thus destabilize the solidarity that the conquered population felt with their elites.

However, Akkadian ideology went beyond "sowing the seeds of discord amongst their enemies" and thus destroying the solidarity between them. By presenting themselves to the conquered as the preservers of their traditions and values, they pretended to be integrated into the norms and beliefs of the local religious field and in the realm of divine responsibilities. Thus the otherness of the Akkadians was ideologically hidden, and their political dominance was more deeply anchored in the cultural system of the conquered societies. This is a masterful application of the old rule of perfidy, according to which, after a reversal of facts, the victims become the causers of the suffering and the oppressors become the saviors. The appropriation of the

19. Gelb and Kienast 1990: 175, Text Sargon C5.
20. Gelb and Kienast 1990: 171, Text Sargon C4.

local deities by the Akkadians left the conquered population literally "god-forsaken." This transgression of the fundamental pillars of cultural and ideological order was exacerbated by the fact that Sargon replaced not only the political elite in the politically most powerful places but also the leaders responsible for religion and cults and placed the control of matters of cult in the hands of close intimates. He installed his own daughter Enheduanna as EN-priestess in Ur, the most important place of worship in the south, and this symbolic destruction of the old and the traditions was perhaps even more serious than the removal of the worldly elite. Sargon managed to get away with an open break with tradition in politics, yet it was advisable to legitimate it. The political "use" of religious traditions was an influential and powerful tool that was not to be underestimated and a tool that Sargon applied cleverly. He subtly used the tradition of Sumerian religious values that stabilized the community while he destroyed the traditions and propagandized this very destruction as the salvation of the religious, cultural, and social order. All the activities of the Akkadians appeared to be accepted and ordered by the gods who represented law and order in southern Sumeria.

By breaking down the social systems of the conquered–by attacking the spatial order through territorial conquest, by breaking the political order it was connected to, by dethroning the elites, and by interfering with the cultural and religious order and the values and norms of the conquered, which convinced them that they were being punished by their own gods, Sargon had chosen a powerful ideological weapon. He beat the enemy with the enemy's frame of order; he took away the enemy's acknowledged preservers of order and used them against the conquered and showed them how the gods that used to be their own from now on would protect the Akkadian–that is the new, legitimate–order.

The selective and well-aimed interventions of Sargon in the basic, identity-giving cultural and religious parameters of the others–and at the same time their replacement by his own cultural and religious values and norms–were an important part of the ideological manipulation of the conquered nations with which the Akkadians handled conflicts and stabilized and legitimated their power.

Conclusion
Sargon–Ruler and Usurper:
The Ruler Who Caused Disorder and "Globally" Enforced the Establishment of a New Political Order

A revolution (rebellion) can be expected, says Andrea Maurer (2004: 107ff.) in her study of the sociology of governance, "if on the one hand the power of the old rulers dwindles and on the other hand new ideologies, successful isolated actions and an intensive communication make a successful revolution more likely." The initial situation during Sargon's rebellion in Kish may have presented just such a scenario. A rebel has to be able to demonstrate his success quickly (as described above in the classic theory of rebellion)[21] in order to demonstrate his power while the rebellion is still ongoing. The opposition must be punished directly and thus be confronted with the consequences of their subversion, while supporters should be rewarded materially in order to reward and strengthen their loyalty.

A successful rebellion needs organizational skill as well as a subtle ideology, a concept that is based on the hypothesis that the rebellion against the existing order leads to a new and better social order (see Eisenstadt 1982: 16–17). The roots of rebellion often lie in conflicts between different elites; its consequences, however, often go beyond a mere change in leadership at the top. The consequences of Sargon's rebellion seem to reaffirm Eisenstadt's remarks comprehensively (1982: 85ff.).

With Sargon's rebellion in Kish, southern Mesopotamia, and the regions in the north and west, the political system, the basis of legitimating political actions, and the symbols of political power underwent a massive change. The top political positions were filled with new representatives, without any spontaneous coalitions between the old elites and Sargon appearing in Kish or in the conquered cities of the south. In fact, the opposite was true. Old social boundaries dissolved, both in Kish and in the occupied territories, which was especially apparent in the restructuring of the communities of Kish and Akkad. New social groups and lobbies formed or were established through Sargon's measures (new landowners, resettlers) and were integrated into the emerging political system. As a result of the rebellion, it is possible that a broader stratum of society now had an influence on politics (see Eisenstadt 1982: 96).

With the shifting of inner and outer boundaries of the community, the political system changed massively, especially in the conquered regions. The political system of the south disappeared (1982: 96) and was absorbed by the strongly centralized political organization of the Akkadians. At the same time, the economic sector was not exempt from drastic changes. The new landowners mentioned above formed a new economic group and frame of action (1982: 97), while the form and extent of economic distribution also changed. Akkad unremittingly drew resources from the periphery and used them to the benefit of the center. The result of these interventions in the economic maintenance of center and periphery was a break down in working communication and distribution networks, and cities formerly acting as economic centers of what was now the Akkadian periphery lost the basis of their activities. As Eisenstadt (1982) states in his discussion of a model of rebellion, the new center destroyed the established relationships in the periphery.

Sargon's rebellion thus led to a multifaceted, radical break with the social, political, cultural, and religious traditions of the societies in question (1982: 17), symbolized in a highly visible way by the founding of Akkad, the only political center in the new realm. The change from a peer system to a centralized government led to a fundamental redefinition of religious and cultural values as well as basing the different traditions in the realm of Akkad. Along with the control of immediate worldly concerns, the new rulers also aimed for control over the cosmic order. The restructuring by the

21. See also Eisenstadt 1982.

Akkadians seriously limited the authority of local city deities. The autocrat Sargon primarily communicated with the gods who held relevant and far-reaching positions in the pantheon of the conquered community! Thus the Akkadians destroyed the conquered societies' established structures and symbols collective identity and stated collective aims according to the new ruling order (1982: 104).

The center, Akkad, fashioned itself as—and actually became—the guardian of central order, symbolizing the ruling system, monopolizing the symbolization of the relationship between cosmic and social order, and linking these symbols with the political order.

References

Afanas'eva, Veronika K.
1987 Das Sumerische Sargon-Epos: Versuch einer Interpretation. *Altorientalische Forschungen* 14: 237–46.
Althoff, Gerd
2003 *Inszenierte Herrschaft: Geschichtsschreibung und politisches Handeln im Mittelalter.* Darmstadt: Wissenschaftliche Buchgesellschaft.
Assmann, Aleida
1991 Kultur als Lebenswelt und Monument. Pp. 11–25 in *Kultur als Lebenswelt und Monument,* ed. Aleida Assmann and Dietrich Harth. Frankfurt/M.: Fischer Taschenbuch.
Assmann, Aleida, and Harth, Dietrich, eds.
1991 *Kultur als Lebenswelt und Monument.* Frankfurt/M.: Fischer Taschenbuch.
Assmann, Jan
1999 *Das kulturelle Gedächtnis.* 2nd ed. Munich: Beck.
Barlösius, Eva
2002 Die Macht der Repräsentation. Pp. 179–202 in *Gesellschaftsbilder im Umbruch,* ed. Eva Barlösius, Hans-Peter Müller, and Steffen Sigmund. Wiesbaden: VS-Verlag für Sozialwissenschaft.
Behrens, Roger
2002 *Kritische Theorie.* Hamburg: Europäische Verlags-Anstalt.
Ben-Amos, Dan, and Weissberg, Liliane
1999 *Cultural Memory and the Construction of Identity.* Detroit: Wayne State University Press.
Böck, Barbara; Cancik-Kirschbaum, Eva; and Richter, Thomas, eds.
1999 *Munuscula Mesopotamica: Festschrift für Johannes Renger.* Alter Orient und Altes Testament 267. Münster: Ugarit-Verlag.
Bourdieu, Pierre
1992 *Die verborgenen Mechanismen der Macht.* Edited by Margareta Steinrücke. Hamburg: VSA.
2001 *Das politische Feld.* Konstanz: UVK.
Brand Eins: Wirtschaftsmagazin
2005 Macht in Bewegung: Oben ist nicht mehr vorn. Hamburg. April.
Cooper, Jerrold S.
1983 *The Curse of Agade.* Baltimore: The John Hopkins University Press.
Cooper, Jerrold S., and Heimpel, Wolfgang
1983 The Sumerian Sargon Legend. *Journal of the American Oriental Society* 103: 67–82.
Crespi, Franco
1991 Kultur und soziale Praxis: Symbolische und gesellschaftliche Ordnung im Widerspruch. Pp. 112–22 in *Kultur als Lebenswelt und Monument,* ed. Aleida Assmann and Dietrich Harth. Frankfurt/M.: Fischer Taschenbuch.

Dietrich, Manfried, and Loretz, Oswald, eds.
1998 dubsa anta-men: *Festschrift für H. Ph. Römer.* Alter Orient und Altes Testament 253. Münster: Ugarit Verlag.
Dobres, Marcia, and Robb, John
2000 *Agency in Archaeology.* London: Routledge.
Edelman, Murray
1976 *Politik als Ritual.* Frankfurt/M.: Campus Verlag.
Eisenstadt, Shmuel N.
1982 *Revolution und die Transformation von Gesellschaften.* Opladen: Westdeutscher Verlag.
1991 Die Mitwirkung der Intellektuellen an der Konstruktion lebensweltlicher und transzendenter Ordnungen. Pp. 123–34 in *Kultur als Lebenswelt und Monument,* ed. Aleida Assmann and Dietrich Harth. Frankfurt/M.: Fischer Taschenbuch.
Foster, Benjamin R.
1993 Management and Administration in the Sargonic Period. Pp. 11–24 in *Akkad: The First World Empire,* ed. Mario Liverani. Padua: Herder.
Franke, Sabina
1995 *Königsinschriften und Königsideologie: Die Könige von Akkade zwischen Tradition und Neuerung.* Hamburg: LIT Verlag.
Frayne, Douglas R.
1990 *Old Babylonian Period (2003–1595 BC).* The Royal Inscriptions of Mesopotamia: Early Periods 4. Toronto: University of Toronto Press.
Gelb, Ignace J., and Kienast, Burkhart
1990 *Die altakkadischen Königsinschriften des dritten Jahrtausends v. Chr.* Freiburger altorientalische Studien 7. Wiesbaden: Steiner.
Giesen, Bernhard
1991 *Die Entdinglichung des Sozialen.* Frankfurt/M.: Suhrkamp.
Graves-Brown, Paul, and Jones, Sian
1996 *Cultural Identity and Archaeology.* London: Routledge.
Groneberg, Brigitte
2004 *Die Götter des Zweistromlandes: Kulte, Mythen, Epen.* Düsseldorf: Artemis & Winkler.
Haferkamp, Hans
1983 *Soziologie der Herrschaft.* Opladen: Westdeutscher Verlag.
Hall, Stuart
2004 *Ideologie, Identität, Repräsentation.* Hamburg: Argument.
Heimpel, Wolfgang
1992 Herrentum und Königtum im vor- und frühgeschichtlichen Alten Orient. *Zeitschrift für Assyriologie und Vorderasiatische Archäologie* 82: 4–21.
Heinz, Marlies
2002 *Altsyrien und Libanon.* Darmstadt: Wissenschaftliche Buchgesellschaft.
Hoffman, Katherine
1996 *Concepts of Identity.* New York: Icons.
Keith, Michael, and Pile, Steve
1993 Introduction, Part 2: The Place of Politics. Pp. 22–40 in *Place and the Politics of Identity,* ed. Michael Keith and Steve Pile. London: Routledge.
Keith, Michael, and Pile, Steve, eds.
1993 *Place and the Politics of Identity.* London: Routledge.
Kocka, Jürgen
1977 Gesellschaftliche Funktionen der Geschichtswissenschaft. Pp. 11–33 in *Wozu noch Geschichte?* ed. Willi Oelmüller. München: Fink.
Körntgen, Ludger
2003 Repräsentation – Selbstdarstellung – Herrschaftspräsentation. Pp. 85–101 in *Propaganda – Selbstdarstellung – Repräsentation im römischen Kaiserreich des 1. Jhs.n. Chr.,* ed. Gregor Weber and Martin Zimmermann. Stuttgart: Steiner.

Kurtz, Donald V.
2001 *Political Anthropology: Paradigms and Power.* Boulder, CO: Westview.
Lewis, Brian
1980 *The Sargon Legend: A Study of the Akkadian Text and the Tale of the Hero Who Was Exposed at Birth.* American Schools of Oriental Research Dissertation Series 4: Cambridge, MA: American Schools of Oriental Research.
Liverani, Mario, ed.
1993 *Akkad: The First World Empire.* Padua: Herder.
Maurer, Andrea
2004 *Herrschaftssoziologie: Eine Einführung.* Frankfurt/M.: Campus.
Moore, Wilbert E.
1963 *Social Change.* Foundations of Modern Sociology. Englewood Cliffs, NJ: Prentice-Hall.
Morel, Julius, et al., eds.
1997 *Soziologische Theorie.* Munich: Oldenbourg.
Oelmüller, Willi, ed.
1977 *Wozu noch Geschichte?* Munich: Fink.
Pettinato, Giovanni
1991 *Ebla: A New Look at History.* Baltimore: Johns Hopkins University Press.
Preglau, Max
1997 Kritische Theorie: Jürgen Habermas. Pp. 240–64 in *Soziologische Theorie,* ed. Julius Morel et al. Munich: Oldenbourg.
Ragotzky, Hedda, and Wenzel, Horst, eds.
1990 *Höfische Repräsentation: Das Zeremoniell und die Zeichen.* Tübingen: Niemeyer.
Selz, Gebhard
1998 Über Mesopotamische Herrschaftskonzepte: Zu den Ursprüngen mesopotamischer Herrscherideologie im 3. Jahrtausend. Pp. 281–344 in dubsa anta-men: *Festschrift für H. Ph. Römer,* ed. Manfred Dietrich and Oswald Loretz. Alter Orient und Altes Testament 253. Münster: Ugarit-Verlag.
Shils, Edward Albert
1975 Tradition. Pp. 182–218 in *Center and Periphery: Essays in Microsociology.* Chicago: University of Chicago Press.
Soja, Edward W.
2003 *Postmodern Geographies.* 8th ed. London: Verso.
Smith, Monica L.
2003 *The Social Construction of Ancient Cities.* Washington, DC: Smithsonian.
Steible, Horst
1982 *Die Altsumerischen Bau- und Weihinschriften.* Freiburger Altorientalische Studien 5. Wiesbaden.
Steinkeller, Piotr
1993 Early Political Development in Mesopotamia and the Origins of the Sargon Empire. Pp. 107–30 in *Akkad: The First World Empire,* ed. Mario Liverani. Padua: Herder.
1999 Land-Tenure Conditions in Southern Babylonia under the Sargonic Dynasty. Pp. 553–72 in *Munuscula Mesopotamica: Festschrift für Johannes Renger.* Alter Orient und Altes Testament 267. Münster: Ugarit-Verlag.
Van de Mieroop, Marc
1999 *Cuneiform Texts and the Writing of History.* London: Routledge.
Westenholz, Joan Goodnick
1997 *Legends of the Kings of Akkade.* Mesopotamian Civilizations 7. Winona Lake, IN: Eisenbrauns.
Winter, Rainer
2001 *Die Kunst des Eigensinns: Cultural Studies als Kritik der Macht.* Weilerswist: Velbrück Wissenschaft.

Part 2

Changing Order from Within

Chapter 4

The Royal Cemetery of Ur: Ritual, Tradition, and the Creation of Subjects

Susan Pollock

The Royal Cemetery of Ur, excavated by C. Leonard Woolley three-quarters of a century ago, has been famed since its discovery for the lavishness of its burials and in particular for the indications of so-called "human sacrifice" in the 16 Early-Dynastic-IIIa-period (ca. 2600–2450 B.C.E) royal tombs for which the cemetery was named (fig. 1). Woolley distinguished the 16 tombs from the remaining 2,000 or so graves in the cemetery in terms of what he called "peculiarities of structure and ritual" (Woolley 1934: 33). These "peculiarities" included the presence of underground chambers built of brick or stone, evidence for a ritual sequence that occurred in several stages, and multiple simultaneous burials or "human sacrifices" that accompanied the interment of the principal deceased individual. Based on the orderly arrangement of the skeletons in some of the better preserved tombs and the absence of any indication of struggle, Woolley (1934: 41–42) contended that the people who went to their deaths in the tombs did so willingly: "From the first[,] one could not but remark the peacefulness of the bodies; all were in order, not only set out in neat rows but individually peaceful; there was no sign of violence" (1934: 35). Remarkably few scholars have challenged or even seriously reconsidered Woolley's argument that the multiple "attendants" in the tombs went to their deaths willingly, although in a recent treatise on *les morts d'accompagnement* Alain Testart (2004) reaches a related conclusion, arguing that the practice rests on the existence of personal ties of loyalty and dependence.

The general acceptance of Woolley's argument is, on reflection, astonishing. Why and on what basis would people acquiesce in their own (premature) deaths? Bruce

Author's note: I would like to thank Marlies Heinz for the invitation to contribute to this book. Some of the ideas in this essay were presented at the conference (Re-)Sounding Ur: New Perspectives on the Royal Tombs at Harvard University and in a talk at the Department of Near Eastern Studies at Johns Hopkins University. I would like to thank Irene Winter and Glenn Schwartz for the invitations to present those papers and the audiences for their thought-provoking comments. Bruce Dickson and Andrew Cohen kindly made available prepublication versions of their works, for which I am most appreciative. Cohen's book arrived after this essay was finished; if there are obvious places where references to it are omitted, it is due to the unfortunate circumstances of timing. Comments on previous versions of this paper by Reinhard Bernbeck, Scott Beld, Marlies Heinz, and Gebhard Selz were most helpful in clarifying my thinking on many of the issues involved.

Figure 1. Plan of the Royal Cemetery of Ur (after Woolley 1934: pl. 274).

Dickson (2006) has recently argued that the royal tombs might better be viewed as "state-sponsored theaters of cruelty and terror." When one ponders the events that produced the tombs, especially the killing of up to 74 people on the occasion of another person's death, it is hard not to be struck by the sheer enormity of the ideological project that "persuaded" numerous people to lay down their lives, without apparent struggle, upon someone else's death and to do so in a ritual that was staged multiple times over the course of 100 or more years. It hardly seems sufficient to say that people simply fell prey to what James Scott (1990) refers to as the public transcript–that is, that they believed fully in the ideology of the dominant group(s) and thereby endorsed their own subordination. Nor is my own previous instrumental approach to the question adequate–namely, that people's willingness to be killed and buried in a royal tomb might result from "bribery" in the form of promises of a proper funeral and postfunerary rites in return for affiliation with a major institution (Pollock 1991). Rather, in trying to come to grips with the ritual practices for which we have evidence in the royal tombs, it is critical to pose a broader question: how is the consent of state subjects to their own subordination achieved?

Ritual, Ideology, and Consent

One of the significant problems facing people who benefit most from the existence of state structures is how to create bonds of allegiance to the notion of the state (Mitchell 1999) in ways that convince state subjects that they actually share common interests and a common identity (Smith 2004). Benedict Anderson (1991) has referred to this as the creation of an *imagined community*. Perhaps the most stunning feat is to persuade people to consent to give up their lives, either actually or potentially, for an *idea* of the state. To put the point in current terms, we need only think of the ability of modern state actors to convince their young men, and sometimes women, to enroll in an institution–the military–where they may be called upon to fight, to kill others, and possibly lose their own lives for such abstractions as "preserving freedom and our way of life."

In trying to understand how bonds of allegiance to a state are created among its subjects, I have found especially useful the arguments of David Kertzer (1988) and James Scott (1985; 1990) concerning the role of ritual, performance, and legitimacy in politics. Using studies of contemporary as well as historical cases, both scholars have suggested that it is striking how rarely people who are repressed, even to an extraordinary degree, actively rebel against their oppressors; rather, people show a great tendency to conform. Kertzer (1988: 39–40) argues that in stable conditions, people *do* accept the legitimacy of the political system and thereby its ideology. He suggests that people's acceptance of the dominant ideology and thereby the likelihood that they will conform to rather than rebel against their own subordination is enhanced markedly by the use of public ritual. Politics is expressed through ritual and symbolism where ritual is "a potent means of legitimation . . . that . . . offers a way to unite a particular image of the universe with a strong emotional attachment to that image" (1988: 40).

Scott (1985; 1990) takes a rather different position, contending that people generally consent because they see themselves as having no choice, not because they necessarily believe in the system that oppresses them. He (Scott 1990: 4) suggests that "it is in the interest of the subordinate to produce a more or less credible performance, speaking the lines and making the gestures he [*sic*] knows are expected of him." In other contexts or in other manners, "hidden transcripts" are created by subordinated persons to express their dissent and to do so in a way that is hidden from public scrutiny. For Scott, the threat of repression and intimidation is sufficient to explain why people acquiesce in public; indeed, his principal concern is to understand where and how spaces for (public) resistance arise, rather than the reasons why they so often do not.

Based on his survey of archaeological and ethnographic cases in which people went to their death to accompany others, Testart (2004) concludes that the practice rests upon personal ties of loyalty and dependence, which, he suggests, are "naturally" extended beyond life into the realm of death. Importantly, in Testart's argument (2004: 222–31), the people in question are bound by *personal* ties, not by dedication to an abstract cause. His emphasis on the role of personal loyalties has connections to Weber's (1972) concept of charismatic leadership, a point to which I will return later. Testart (2004: 211) claims that an ideology of loyalty and dependence may lead people to go to their deaths unwillingly, but it may also produce acceptance and even valorization of deaths of this sort. In other words, for Testart, consent comes about as a relatively unproblematic result of a particular ideology of social relations.[1]

The work of Louis Althusser (1971; Ricoeur 1994; Lock 1996) on ideology offers another important way of examining how consent is created among subjects—indeed, how subjects are created in such a way that it is difficult for them to question self-evident notions and practices and hence makes it hard to resist them. One of Althusser's most important insights is that ideology is not to be understood as a set of ideas alone but rather as practices. In other words, ideology has a material and an embodied existence in the practices through which people enact it, and thereby live it, on a daily basis. Ideology is inculcated into every state subject, according to Althusser, through what he calls Ideological State Apparatuses, or ISAs. These ISAs consist of multiple institutions or locations through which a dominant ideology is instilled into people from birth onward; examples include the family, religious institutions, and schools. ISAs are especially effective at creating unquestioning subjects, says Althusser, because the various institutions that make them up are both multiple and hence mutually reinforcing and because these institutions *appear* to be dedicated to very different ends, so that people are unaware that they are being molded according to a particular ideology. ISAs instill a dominant ideology not just by promulgating particular ideas about the world (ideological content) but also through particular formalized embodied actions (Bernbeck 2003–4: 279–82): for example, the proper way to behave when in a public library; or, to cite Althusser's famous example, when one performs a ritual action such as kneeling in a church, one *becomes* in some sense a believer. Althusser argues that as a result of internalizing a dominant ideology in these ways, subjects become effectively interpellated by ideology. In other words, each and every person feels directly interpellated, or "hailed," by the dominant ideology and thus conforms to it virtually automatically. Althusser's concern with embodied practices has been echoed in a wide range of literatures, including those concerned with performance (in the sense of Butler [1990; 1993]), tradition (for example, Bourdieu 1999: 69–70; Joyce 2000; Pauketat 2001), and ritual (Bell 1992: 98–101).

Althusser's conception of ideology has its problems: most importantly, the implication that people are unthinkingly duped into acting in accordance with a single dominant ideology, leaving little theoretical space to understand how resistance, change, and withdrawal of consent are possible (Cormack 1992; Žižek 1994; Montag 1996). Nonetheless, his work does help to point the way toward understanding how people's *daily actions*—the most mundane aspects of how they live their lives as well as the unusual and theatrical (the state ritual on which Kertzer focuses)—come together to produce state subjects who often consent, willingly or not, to a dominant ideology. Incorporating Scott's insights allows us to think of this consent not as absolutely unquestioning but as an acquiescence that does not *openly* question, or at least not to

1. On the implications of the concept of loyalty for an understanding of the Royal Cemetery, see Pollock 2007.

the point of refusal to participate. Subordinates go along, at least publicly, because they know they will bear the consequences if they do not. Unlike Scott, who sees this grudging consent prinicipally as a product of actual or threatened repression, Althusser shows how mundane daily practices produce subjects who have imbibed ideological understandings so deeply that, often, little repression is required in order to make them conform. In this way, his insights offer an extension to Kertzer's focus on public ritual.

With these ideas in mind, an understanding of how people in Early Dynastic (ED) Ur were brought to acquiesce to the killing of themselves or others as accompaniments to an important deceased person must come to grips with several issues. These include the practices that formed part of people's daily lives and traditions (Pauketat 2001) and helped to shape their consent to these public transcripts (cf. Walker and Lucero 2000) as well as the form of the spectacular funerary rituals that drew people in through their strong symbolic and emotional elements (Kertzer 1988). An analysis of this sort will need to consider both the content of ideology and the form by which it was inculcated–made into unquestioned, embodied practices, or the production of docile bodies, in Foucault's (1995) terms. To do this involves looking beyond the Royal Cemetery burial practices to consider other constituents of life in the city-states of southern Mesopotamia in the mid-third millennium B.C.E.

Early Dynastic City-States of Southern Mesopotamia

Early Dynastic southern Mesopotamia was a landscape of city-states, each consisting of one or a few major cities surrounded by a rural hinterland (fig. 2). By the middle of the third millennium B.C.E.–around the time of the most spectacular burials in the Royal Cemetery–most of these states were ruled by kings who claimed the right to leadership through a principle of dynastic succession (Gebhard Selz 1998; 2004c).[2] The bulk of the settled population in the alluvial lowlands appears to have lived in urban centers, despite the overwhelming agrarian and pastoral basis of the economy (Pollock 1999).

Although sharing many similarities of culture, religion, and languages, city-states had numerous distinctive characteristics, not least of which were their local gods and associated rituals (Gebhard Selz 1990). City-states engaged in frequent conflicts with one another as well as with lands outside the alluvial lowlands, as each struggled for economic and political advantages. These conflicts occasionally broke out into war, as attested by references in contemporary cuneiform texts, images of violence in various media (especially seals and stelae), and the occurrence of weapons and city walls. City-states formed alliances of convenience to deflect incursions by others or to undertake acts of aggression against their neighbors (for example, Cooper 1983).

Not all of the conflict was external. There are also indications of substantial conflict *within* city-states, often glossed as a struggle between temple and palace. Hans

2. I will return below to a discussion of some of the problems with the use of English terms such as *king* for Mesopotamian concepts.

Figure 2. Map of southern Mesopotamia with some of the principal Early Dynastic urban centers.

Nissen (1988) has suggested that these struggles were principally between local decentralizing elements associated with temples and independent city-states, on the one hand, and the centralizing forces connected to the interests of the palace and attempts to create political alliances that transcended individual city-states, on the other hand (see also Beld 2002). Nonetheless, there was probably not a sharp division between palace and temple in Early Dynastic times. In his consideration of the ritual cycle of the emunusa ('house of the lady') in Lagash, Beld (2002) argues that the temple and the royal economy were deeply interwoven. Members of the royalty exerted substantial control over cult institutions (temples), as can be seen in the "reforms" of Irikagina, one of the last Early Dynastic rulers of the Lagash state. On the surface a sign of Irikagina's piety in the face of corruption, the reforms amount to a redefinition of the property of the ruler's family as belonging to the gods. In this way, Irikagina was made into a more direct representative of the divine world than previous rulers (2002: 80–84), thereby undercutting the power of other elites, perhaps including members of the temple priesthood (for a different interpretation based on changing concepts of leadership, see Gebhard Selz 1998).

Each city-state had one or a small handful of patron deities with whom its well-being was closely connected and to which the principal temple(s) was dedicated. In addition, a host of other gods and goddesses were integrated into a pantheon and worshiped in the numerous other temples and shrines that could be found in each city. Gebhard Selz (1990) has argued that an ongoing process of syncretism encouraged the adoption of deities from other cities and the meshing of different attributes into individual divine figures.

Religion and ritual were an integral part of Mesopotamian life. Most of our knowledge about these matters is confined to elite-sponsored ritual and religion, because these were the practices, beliefs, and ideologies that found their way into the corpus of written texts and inscriptions, and most of the buildings identified archaeologically as loci of religious activities are imposing structures located in major urban centers. The daily beliefs and practices of the bulk of the populace as well as the localities connected with cultic practices in the countryside remain almost unknown and uninvestigated, with the exception of those that have found some echo in the urban-based scribal record or the occasional shrine that has been excavated (1990: 111–12; Cooper 1993; compare with Sallaberger 1993: 264–70).

The picture of ritual that has been formed from the available archaeological and cuneiform sources emphasizes the intricate and locally specific character of the annual ritual cycle in particular city-states. The best documented example is a large corpus of texts belonging to an institution known as the emunusa (= é-mí, the 'house of the lady', or é-^{d}ba-ba$_6$ 'house of the goddess Baba') from the city of Girsu in the state of Lagash (for analyses of the emunusa archive, see Rosengarten 1960; Maekawa 1973–74; Gebhard Selz 1995; Cohen 2001; 2005; Beld 2002). A substantial portion of the texts deals, directly or indirectly, with the rituals in which the queen of Lagash—the earthly head of the emunusa—took part, rituals that were closely connected to the annual agricultural cycle (Beld 2002). In certain months, especially during the growing season, these rituals included offerings of food (bread, flour, oil, fish, fruits, and vegetables), drink (beer and wine), cloth and clothing, and jewelry to dead members of the royal family as well as to the gods (Cohen 2001; Beld 2002: 162–82). Texts as well as image-bearing artifacts make clear the centrality to ritual practices of offerings of food and drink as well as their consumption in feasts (Gudrun Selz 1983; Collon 1992; Pinnock 1994; Schmandt-Besserat 2000; Helwing 2003). Feasts were not confined to agricultural rituals; they also occurred in celebrations of military victories, dedications of new buildings, diplomatic missions, marriages, and funerals (Pinnock 1994; Cohen 2005).

Temples were more than places of worship; some were also institutional landowners and major players in the economic life of the city-state. These and other great households or *oikoi* (including the households of members of the royal family and temples) were large, hierarchically organized socioeconomic units with dependent workforces, managerial personnel, flocks of animals, fields, pastures, orchards, workshops, and artisans' facilities. Members of households were bound to them by ties of dependency rather than by ties of kinship. A household head could be a man, woman, or child; various staff administered the household's day-to-day affairs and oversaw a labor force composed of permanent as well as part-time workers. During the Early Dynastic period, these great households appear to have become increasingly dominant economically. They drew on traditional meanings of the household both linguistically (being designated by the same root word as kin-based households in both Sumerian [é] and Akkadian [*bîtum*]) and socio-functionally, serving as units of production and consumption (Pollock 1999: chap. 5; for discussions of 'houses', see Lévi-Strauss 1987; Carsten and Hugh-Jones 1995; Joyce 2000; Joyce and Gillespie 2000).

Some scholars have suggested that 'kingship' (nam-lugal, in Sumerian) was becoming established as an institution distinct from the temple leadership in the later part of the Early Dynastic period (Frankfort 1978; Heimpel 1992; Gebhard Selz 1998; 2004c; Steinkeller 1999; Cohen 2001; 2005). It should be noted that, although the terms 'king' and 'kingship' are convenient glosses, they carry a conceptual baggage that may hinder understanding more than promote it. The variety of Sumerian terms that connote types of rulers in the first half of the third millennium (including en, ensik, and lugal), the indications for their changing meanings over time, and differences in their semantic range by region all speak to the need for caution when substituting modern terminology. Textual evidence suggests that in southern Mesopotamia prior to the later part of the Early Dynastic period, accession to the position of ruler of a state—mostly designated by the term en—did not follow lines of inheritance but rather was based on appointment by a temple-based elite. In contrast, the position of lugal or ensik—terms that largely supplant en for the designation of a state's leader by ED III in southern Mesopotamia—seems to have been inherited.

Andrew Cohen (2001; 2005) has proposed that, in order for early rulers to establish a notion of rulership that transcended specific persons holding that position, they had to transfer some of their authority as individuals to the office. In a related fashion, Gebhard Selz (2004a: 38) has suggested that institutions and offices, including nam-lugal, were more important than the individuals who filled the positions. Some scholars have viewed the establishment of kingly power as a sign of an increasing separation between a predominantly secular/military and a religious sphere (Steinkeller 1999), although others have questioned whether an attribution of secular power is not anachronistic. Whatever its precise contours, the emergence of a particular notion of rulership at this time is unlikely to have taken place without struggle, whether this struggle was confined to the upper echelons of society or extended beyond them. Like many other political innovations, notions of kingship may have drawn on traditional images and practices as sources of legitimacy; indeed, Weber (1972: 142–44) has argued that, to produce long-term leadership out of a charismatic form, it is necessary to establish the basis of leadership as deriving from tradition or rule-based authority rather than from specific qualities of an individual.

In summary, southern Mesopotamia in late Early Dynastic times was characterized by multiple sources of conflict and considerable social, political, and economic experimentation and change. Under these circumstances, competition among powerful groups ran the risk of spilling out into broader domains and displaying to subordinates the cracks in the edifice of elite domination. To avoid this was in the interests of all powerful groups. Struggles internal to elite groups and institutions likely included attempts to win over supporters through ideological and other means and may have involved the establishment of nam-lugal as a stable and inheritable position. In circumstances such as these, it is hardly surprising to find overt and spectacular public rituals such as the rituals evident in the Royal Cemetery (compare with Geertz 1980), which drew on "traditional" means of claiming legitimacy, such as connections to natural rhythms of the agricultural cycle and the deities who ensured that cycle.

The Royal Cemetery

My argument concerning the Royal Cemetery burials begins with the contention that the cemetery was the burial place for a select group of people from Ur, specifically for the interment of members of great households, with each royal tomb representing one of these households. I suggest that the differences between the ways people in various tombs were prepared for burial as well as the rituals themselves represent distinctions among these households. The killing of household personnel to accompany the head of household upon her or his death along with the elaborate accompanying ritual evident in tomb burial combined to make an ideological statement concerning the supposed demise of the entire household. By drawing parallels between representations of elite feasting and the structure of tomb burial, I suggest that feasting was an important means of inculcating "bodily dispositions," so that, when called upon to do so, selected members of Ur's great households went to their deaths in the tombs.

The Royal Cemetery was excavated during the years 1922 and 1934, as part of the work conducted by C. Leonard Woolley at Ur (Woolley 1934; 1955). Approximately 2,000 graves were recorded, spanning a 500-year period from ED III to the post-Akkadian period (Nissen 1966; Pollock 1985). Woolley made clear that he did not uncover the full extent of the cemetery, and he also remarked that many graves he encountered were so badly preserved that he did not even attempt to record them (Woolley 1934: 16).

As already mentioned, Woolley differentiated 16 of the graves from the remainder, calling them the "royal tombs" and the others "private graves" (fig. 3). He attributed all of the tombs to the earliest phase of the cemetery's use, now referred to as Early Dynastic IIIa (ED IIIa), a period lasting approximately 100 to 150 years. Woolley argued that the people who were privileged to be buried with the pomp and circumstance distinctive of the royal tombs were royalty accompanied to their graves by members of their courts. He based his contention on several lines of reasoning, most

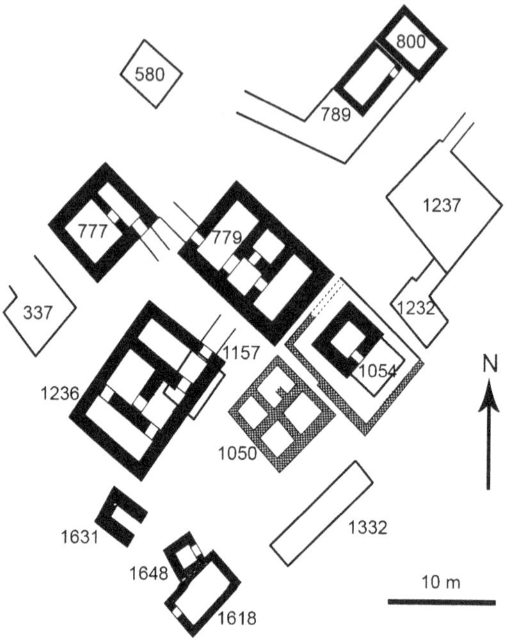

Figure 3. Plan of the royal tombs at Ur (after Woolley 1934: pl. 273).

crucially the occurrence of objects inscribed with royal titles (lugal, nin) in several of the tombs (1934: 37–40); however, very few of these inscribed items were found in direct connection with the principal burials in the tombs. Some scholars have accepted Woolley's interpretation (for example, Reade 2001; Marchesi 2004); others have argued that the tombs' principal occupants were substitute kings, important members of the religious establishment (high priestesses and priests), or unspecifiable powerful and important people (Frankfort 1978: 400–401 n. 12; Moortgat 1949; Moorey 1977; Pollock 1991; Charvát 2002: 224–28; Sürenhagen 2002).

In addition to the 16 royal tombs, 137 of the so-called private graves can be attributed to the ED IIIa period, contemporary with the tombs (Pollock 1985). There are also many graves from the cemetery that cannot be assigned a specific date, so the actual number of non-tomb burials from this period is almost certainly larger. The "private graves" lack built structures, containing instead coffins or mat-wrapped bodies laid in earthen pits. In nearly all cases, they consist of single interments, and although a few contained substantial riches, most were much less lavishly furnished than the royal tombs. Overall, this early phase of the cemetery (to which I confine my discussion here) includes many well-provisioned burials. These burial practices, as well as those from contemporary sites in the alluvial lowlands, represent the culmination of several centuries of increasingly elaborate mortuary patterns in which distinctions among people at death became ever more marked (Pollock 1999: chap. 8).

The Royal Cemetery was apparently reserved for the burial of selected persons (Pollock 1991). I base this argument on two kinds of demographic evidence. First, there are not enough dead in the cemetery to account for the population of the city of Ur during ED IIIa times. At a size of approximately 50 ha, Early Dynastic Ur would have been home to a minimum of 5,000 residents at any one time; quite likely the population was double this, if not higher. Assuming approximately 30 years per generation, a minimum of 15,000 people would have lived and died at Ur during the ED IIIa period. The 509 bodies that can be attributed to the ED IIIa phase of the cemetery clearly do not come close to reaching this number.[3] Even inflating the number of dead by 10 times to account for the undated, unrecorded, and unexcavated burials, the total (5,090) would still be far below the 15,000 necessary to account for the minimum estimated population of the city.

The second part of the demographic argument comes from the remarkable underrepresentation of children in the cemetery. According to Woolley's (1934) records, only 7, or a little more than 1%, of the bodies from this period were bodies of children.[4] This would be an unheard-of child mortality rate for a preindustrial population.

The demographic evidence suggests that the cemetery was reserved primarily for the interment of adults–and only certain adults. On what basis were they selected? I have previously proposed that the dead were members of great households, whether royal or temple-based, a suggestion that receives support from textual references (Cohen 2005: 80) and the absence of burials in any excavated temples or palaces in southern Mesopotamia from this period. People whose ties were principally to their familial households rather than to public institutions may have been buried within their houses, a practice that is well attested at Early-Dynastic-period sites where houses have been excavated, including Abu Salabikh (Martin, Moon, and Postgate 1985; Steele 1990), Fara (Martin 1988), and Khafajah (Delougaz, Hill, and Lloyd 1967).

Royal Cemetery burial was confined to members of great households, but more specifically, I suggest, to adults who held ritual/cultic or managerial posts within these institutions. The royal tombs were clearly not burial places for families, as indicated by the presence of a single principal occupant in each tomb (where information about the primary burial can be ascertained) and the virtual absence of children. Grave goods accompanying the deceased–principally elaborate forms of dress, symbols of officialdom (such as seals), and weaponry–point to their identities as cultic or managerial personnel. This argument receives some circumstantial support from Beld's (2002: 137–40) analysis of the Lagash e m u n u s a. Upon Irikagina's ascent to power, there was a significant reorganization of household personnel with a portion of the staff removed and replaced by outsiders. Although not conclusive evidence, this shift in personnel offers a provocative indication that some household members might "disappear" upon the decease of the head of household under whom they had worked.

Significant differences exist among the tombs, which may be indicative of differences among the households from which they were derived (Pollock 2007). These include architectural variability (multichambered and single-chambered examples as well as others with little evidence of architectural construction); marked differences

3. The number of 509 bodies is based on the 137 private graves plus 372 bodies in the 16 Royal Tombs.

4. Although neither Woolley nor any of his team members was a trained osteologist, he was a careful observer and is unlikely to have neglected noting the skeletons of young children.

in sequences of ritual activities, including tombs that exhibit complex vertical depositional sequences (for example, tombs 1050 and 1054) and others consisting of more or less simultaneous depositional events (for example, tombs 789 and 800); number of interments per tomb; and striking variations in the kinds and quantities of grave goods. These distinctions are not only those of preservation, nor do they seem to be solely a product of variable individual wealth or social standing. Rather, I suggest that differences among households (between temples and royal households, for example, but also between particular temples or particular royal households) were carried over into burial practices, which emphasized similarities in the styles of costume and adornment of persons buried in a single tomb and their differences from others.

This argument for the household affiliations of tombs can be taken a step further to suggest that they marked the *metaphorical* death of these households, coinciding with the death of the head of household. The ritual "killing" of households is widely attested in ethnographic and archaeological literature (Hill 1995; Stevanović 1997; Walker and Lucero 2000). In the case of the royal tombs, a notion that the household was supposed to have died might help account for the presence of people representing a relatively stereotyped set of roles, such as guards and attendants. The metaphorical killing of a household may have been part of an ideological denial of the heritability of the resources and wealth of the great households, akin to the principle that lands held by state officials were not to be inherited (Gelb 1976: 196). Alternatively, if (some of) the tombs held the interments of kings (or queens), the "death" of the royal household may have been an expression of the fragility of kingship at the time (Pollock 2007). If tomb burials were metaphorical deaths of households, valuables found in the tombs may have been the property of the household, not the personal possessions of individual household members (Gebhard Selz 2004b: 203–4).[5]

Although households may have metaphorically died (and along with them a not-insignificant number of household members), other personnel remained alive. An examination of what was and was not buried in the tombs suggests that the fundamental economic basis of the household remained intact. Children (the next generation of administrators and/or workers), laborers, and most tools used in agricultural, domestic, and ordinary artisanal pursuits were not buried in the tombs. Overall, there is a near absence of anything that would indicate the occupations or economic roles of the deceased.[6] Rather, the material accompaniments of the dead seem to have accentuated ritual, class, gender, and household affiliations.

It is now possible to ask the principal question of this essay with more precision: how were certain members of great households in Early Dynastic Ur convinced to go to their deaths in the royal tombs as an accompaniment to someone else? Following

5. For an attempt to categorize grave goods by their meanings to and possession by the living, see Meyer 2000.

6. Although there are tools in some of the graves (for example, chisels, awls, fishhooks, saws, and whetstones), many of these are made of metal or semiprecious stones, and they occur in very small quantities in comparison with the items of personal adornment and vessels that predominate in the graves. Numerous kinds of tools (for example, tools associated with agricultural tasks, such as sickles) are entirely absent.

the ideas of Weber and Testart, one might postulate that personal loyalties bound subjects to a charismatic leader. Yet this does not in itself explain why this loyalty extended beyond life into death (contra Testart 2004), because the practice was of quite limited temporal duration. A further exploration of this question requires an examination of the formal aspects of the burial ritual and the parallels between these elements and contexts of daily life.

Connections between mundane practices and the formalized actions of ritual performances have been characterized "as a form of repeated *citation* of a disciplinary norm" (Joyce 2000: 187, emphasis in original). In a related vein, a number of scholars have emphasized that "successful" changes (those that are accepted and adopted) often begin from familiar practices or traditions (Walker and Lucero 2000: 133; Alt 2001; Pauketat 2001). What kinds of mundane practices might have prepared members of Ur's great households to acquiesce to their own early death? Drawing on the earlier discussion of ritual and ideology, those practices may have been the sort that incorporated specific embodied routines that "naturalized" them and helped to ensure their proper performance, not just in daily activities but also on spectacular and unusual ritual occasions. One of the practices that bridged the mundane and the spectacular was feasting and the closely associated practices of making food and drink offerings to the gods and to the dead.

The importance of feasting in Early Dynastic Mesopotamia has already been noted. In addition to the connections of feasts to the annual ritual cycles of city-states, an emphasis on the consumption of food, drink, and libation-pouring in the context of funerals has been frequently remarked upon (Wright 1969: 83; Forest 1983: 136; Winter 1999) and most recently has been the subject of an extended analysis by Cohen (2005).[7] Texts mention the distribution of bread and beer to mourners and singers at royal funerals (Bauer 1998: 558–59; Beld 2002: 173, 212). The offering of food and drink to the dead was an important obligation of the living and formed one of the primary points of contact between the dead and the living (Heimpel 1987–90; Cohen 2005). Votive offerings that included food and drink formed central parts of what Beld (2002) refers to as the ritual economy, which involved obligations such as maš-da-ri-a offerings from elite members of temples and the royal family to other temple institutions (Rosengarten 1960; Beld 2002) and deliveries of produce by the people working in temple properties (Bauer 1998: 522). Images of banquet scenes on seals, votive plaques, and inlaid musical instruments portray people (most commonly in pairs) drinking together in a formalized scene that occasionally includes food as well (fig. 4; Amiet 1980; Gudrun Selz 1983; Schmandt-Besserat 2000; Pollock 2003). Seals with banquet scenes are especially common at Ur (Amiet 1980: 123).

The centrality of feasting and offerings of drink and food in the regular ritual life of members of the elite in Mesopotamia in the mid-third millennium would have

7. Cohen argues that the kinds of vessels present in the tombs and graves, as well as the kinds that are absent, indicate that they were used in graveside feasts rather than being equipment for preparing food in the afterlife. I am not convinced by this argument, because the lack of vessels used to prepare food may be another part of the general absence in the graves of tools used in productive enterprises.

Figure 4. A banquet scene on a seal from tomb 1237, body 7 (U. 12374) (reprinted by permission of the University of Pennsylvania Museum, Philadelphia).

helped to inculcate correct etiquette, procedures, and unquestioning obedience to the rules of the feast, thereby creating "docile bodies" (Foucault 1995). I should emphasize that I am speaking here specifically about *elite* participation in feasting; neither the images nor the texts at our disposal tell us much about feasting among the masses of people.[8] Similarly, the feasts associated with royal tomb burial must be understood as involving people of the highest standing–those who were buried as principal occupants of the tombs–plus the persons "privileged" to share their last earthly feast or the feasts of which they would partake in the netherworld. Through the inculcation of the practical knowledge of the appropriate decorum of elite feasting–the bodily positions, gestures, protocol–to the point that participants performed their parts without reflecting on how or why they acted as they did, subjects were prepared in a formal sense to partake in the ultimate feast leading to death. Beyond formalities there must also have been notions of *why* it was appropriate for certain people to accompany certain others to their deaths, perhaps following ties of loyalty (see Testart 2004; Pollock 2007). For present purposes, I concentrate on the ideological *form*, as expressed through participation in feasts.

The evidence from the royal tombs points clearly to the importance of the burial feast, regardless of whether the accompanying persons in the tombs actually partook in a ritual meal before going to their death or if the provisions were intended for use in the netherworld or for the journey there (Cohen 2005). I base this argument on the numerous similarities in details between the ways feasts and votive offerings are portrayed among the living (in texts and images) and the material remains of the royal tombs.

(1) The presence of vessels in graves, principally ceramic but also stone and metal examples, was part of a tradition that had existed for centuries, in which the deceased were interred with various kinds and quantities of containers (Pollock 1999: chap. 8). It is not just a matter of the number or type of vessels present but the fact that many of the dead in the royal tombs held a cup in one hand, raised in front of their chest

8. As I have suggested here, most of the people interred in the royal tombs probably belonged to middle or upper social echelons (contra Pollock 1991). The near absence of information on feasting and other ritual practices among the laboring classes that formed the bulk of the population is due not just to problems of sources but also to the limited research that has been addressed to these issues.

or toward their mouths (fig. 5; Woolley 1934: 35–36). This gesture is the same as the gesture seen in depictions of feasts on seals and other image-bearing artifacts. Even where no cup was present, the dead were in many cases buried with their hands in front of their chest, in a gesture very similar to the drinking pose. Although less common than drinking cups, large jars are also present in some of the tombs, and Puabi's tomb (800) included several examples of drinking tubes that parallel the tubes used by banqueters in seal scenes to drink out of jars.

Figure 5. Skeleton of Meskalamdug, the person buried in grave 755, with a gold bowl in his hands (after Woolley 1934: fig. 35).

(2) Feasting scenes on seals, plaques, and inlaid items depict people bringing animals, loads on their heads, and jars presumably filled with foodstuffs or drink, all seemingly to be understood as votive offerings and/or provisions for feasts, as indicated in texts. Graves often contained an abundance of jars and bowls, some with remnants of foodstuffs, including wheat, barley, peas, chickpeas, apples, dates, bread, meat of sheep or goat, fish, and perhaps pig and birds (Ellison et al. 1978). The similarities between this food in the graves and the food mentioned in texts concerning votive offerings and feasts are striking (for example, Beld 2002: 108, 164, 174).

(3) In some of the tombs, there is evidence for the pouring of liquids that may be an indication of libation-pouring known from texts and images (Heimpel 1987–90; Winter 1999). These include drains (tomb 1054), holes in the floor that may have served as conduits for liquids (in 789 and 800), and "offering tables" (in 337 and 1237) as well as long-necked spouted metal jars and ceramic "lamps," which Winter (1999) has suggested may have been used in making liquid offerings.

(4) Depictions of feasts often feature musicians playing lyres or harps, instruments that are present in several of the royal tombs and in only one other contemporary grave in the cemetery. The inlays on some of the lyres depict feasting scenes, a kind of double referent in which scenes of feasting are present on objects used in the feasts. They are similar in this regard to banquet seals found commonly in the royal tombs (fig. 6).

Figure 6. Depiction of a feasting scene on a lyre found in tomb 789, with animals and half human–half animal figures as the musicians, dancers, and servers (U. 10556) (reprinted by permission of the University of Pennsylvania Museum, Philadelphia).

(5) Several of the tombs contain wagons or sledges drawn by animals, similar to the wagons that can occasionally be found in scenes of feasts (Gudrun Selz 1983: 332–36, 470–71; Jans and Bretschneider 1998: 161, pl. 2). Wheeled vehicles, including wagons and chariots, were commonly connected to war (Jans and Bretschneider 1998: 165), suggesting that associated banquets may have been victory celebrations or may have made reference to them, in addition to connections between wagons and transportation of the dead to the underworld (Meyer 2000).

(6) Some tombs include model boats of bitumen, silver, or copper that evoke images and textual mentions of boat processions to cultic destinations where offerings and feasts took place (Gudrun Selz 1983: 469–70; Beld 2002).

(7) Iconographic representations of feasts frequently portray individuals with elaborate hairdos and, where there is sufficient detail to discern it, elaborate clothing. The tomb occupants, both the principal burial as well as most of the "attendants," were dressed in elaborate jewelry, much of it emphasizing the head and perhaps the hair.

(8) There are also parallels in terms of what is *not* found in the tombs and the connections of these absences to text- and image-based portrayals of feasts and votive offerings. Most striking is the almost total absence of anything in the burials that refers directly to the economic roles and activities of the deceased. As already mentioned, the graves contain few tools, and especially notable by their absence are implements that would have been used in agrarian pursuits or in textile production, which together formed the backbone of the Mesopotamian economy. These absences closely parallel Early Dynastic images of feasting and offerings, which also focus on end products—the ritual occasions themselves and not the ways the provisions were acquired and produced (contra

Schmandt-Besserat 2000: 396).[9] Texts concerned with festivals and offerings also tend to ignore the productive dimensions behind these activities, focusing instead on the allocation of raw materials and end products.

Feasting and related offerings cannot alone account for all elements of the mortuary rituals evident in the royal tombs or for the coerced consent that led nearly 350 people to give up their lives in these ceremonies. Some of the tombs were the product of a rather different set of ritual actions; for example, tomb 1054 includes a lengthy sequence of depositional acts, and there is also much more emphasis on men than women among the dead in this tomb, in contrast to many of the others, and on weaponry among the material accompaniments (Pollock 1983). Nonetheless, the preponderance of similarities between elements of tomb burial and feasts, many of them associated with religious ceremonies, points to practices of elite feasting as one of the ways in which residents of Ur were persuaded to participate in funerary feasts that led in many cases to their own deaths.

Conclusion

The crux of my argument for why several hundred people in Ur acquiesced to their own premature deaths on the occasion of the death of another person rests on the importance of (invented) tradition, routine practices, and the establishment of a notion of kingship that transcended individual holders of that office. In particular, I have highlighted the embodied practices–involving feasting and offerings of drink and food–that contributed to the formation of "disciplined bodies" that were prone to perform appropriately because they had internalized the scripts for doing so, along with a sense of loyalty and lack of alternatives should they "choose" to live on (Scott 1985; Wagner 2002; Testart 2004). The public and spectacular character of Royal Cemetery funerals likely played a significant part in the process (Cohen 2005), adding to the emotional weight of the events and to widespread knowledge of each person's role as participant.

Some 100 to 150 years after they began, the royal tombs and the practices they incorporated came to an end. Although it is tempting to view the cessation of tomb burial as a sign of resistance and refusal on the part of the people of Ur, it is perhaps more likely that the reasons lie elsewhere. Borrowing from Testart's (2004) arguments, I argue that the end of tomb burial may have been part of a process by which the ties between leaders and subjects became increasingly formalized and bureaucratized. In the case of Ur, this transition may have been linked to the establishment of a tradition of kingship that was increasingly based on a formal office with specific rules of inheritance. With a growing acceptance of a hereditary institution of kingship, an ideology that incorporated the notion of the "death" of a royal household upon the death of the king or queen would cease to make sense (Pollock 2007).

9. This forms a distinct contrast to many Late Uruk seal images that depict what appear to be mundane activities, including textile production, care of animals, filling of storehouses, and tasks involving vessels.

In this essay I have proposed a way to understand burial practices in the royal tombs at Ur.[10] Moving beyond the Royal Cemetery, these thoughts may point the way toward understanding not just how people in Early Dynastic Ur were persuaded to participate in these death rituals but also how we today continue to be drawn into the ideologies of the powerful against our interests and perhaps even against our better judgment.

10. For a discussion of the relationship between the tombs and the "private graves," see Pollock 2007.

References

Alt, Susan

2001 Cahokian Change and the Authority of Tradition. Pp. 141–56 in *The Archaeology of Traditions: Agency and History before and after Columbus*, ed. Timothy Pauketat. Gainesville: University Press of Florida.

Althusser, Louis

1971 Ideology and Ideological State Apparatuses (Notes towards an Investigation). Pp. 127–88 in *Lenin and Philosophy and Other Essays*. Translated by Ben Brewster. New York: Monthly Review Press.

Amiet, Pierre

1980 *La glyptique mésopotamienne archaïque*. Paris: Centre National de la Recherche Scientifique.

Anderson, Benedict

1991 *Imagined Communities: Reflections on the Origin and Spread of Nationalism*. 2nd ed. London: Verso.

Bauer, Josef

1998 Der vorsargonische Abschnitt der Mesopotamichen Geschichte. Pp. 431–585 in *Mesopotamien: Späturuk-Zeit und Frühdynastische Zeit*, by Josef Bauer, Robert Englund, and Manfred Krebernik. Edited by Pascal Attinger and Markus Wäfler. Freiburg: Universitätsverlag.

Beld, Scott

2002 *The Queen of Lagash: Ritual Economy in a Sumerian State*. Ph.D. diss., University of Michigan.

Bell, Catherine

1992 *Ritual Theory, Ritual Practice*. Oxford: Oxford University Press.

Bernbeck, Reinhard

2003–4 Politische Struktur und Ideologie in Urartu. *Archäologische Mitteilungen aus Iran und Turan* 35–36: 267–312.

Bourdieu, Pierre

1999 Rethinking the State: Genesis and Structure of the Bureaucratic Field. Pp. 53–75 in *State/Culture: State-Formation after the Cultural Turn*, ed. George Steinmetz. Ithaca, NY: Cornell University Press.

Butler, Judith

1990 *Gender Trouble: Feminism and the Subversion of Identity*. London: Routledge.

1993 *Bodies That Matter: On the Discursive Limits of "Sex."* London: Routledge.

Carsten, Janet, and Hugh-Jones, Stephen, eds.

1995 *About the House: Lévi-Strauss and Beyond*. Cambridge: Cambridge University Press.

Charvát, Petr

2002 *Mesopotamia before History*. London: Routledge.

Cohen, Andrew
2001 Dehistoricizing Strategies in Third-Millennium B.C.E. Royal Inscriptions and Rituals. Pp. 99–111 in *Historiography in the Cuneiform World*, ed. Tzvi Abusch et al. Proceedings of the XLVe Recontre Assyriologique Internationale. Bethesda, MD: CDL.
2005 *Death Rituals, Ideology, and the Development of Early Mesopotamian Kingship: Towards a New Understanding of Iraq's Royal Cemetery of Ur.* Leiden: Brill.

Collon, Dominique
1992 Banquets in the Art of the Ancient Near East. Pp. 23–30 in *Banquets d'Orient*, ed. R. Gyselen. Bures-sur-Yvette: Groupe pour l'étude de la civilisation du Moyen-Orient.

Cooper, Jerrold
1983 *Reconstructing History from Ancient Inscriptions: The Lagash-Umma Border Conflict.* Sources from the Ancient Near East 2/1. Malibu, CA: Undena.
1993 Sacred Marriage and Popular Cult in Early Mesopotamia. Pp. 81–96 in *Official Cult and Popular Religion in the Ancient Near East*, ed. Eiko Matsushima. Heidelberg: Carl Winter.

Cormack, Mike
1992 *Ideology.* Ann Arbor: University of Michigan Press.

Delougaz, Pinhas; Hill, Harold; and Lloyd, Seton
1967 *Private Houses and Graves in the Diyala Region.* Oriental Institute Publications 88. Chicago: University of Chicago Press.

Dickson, Bruce
2006 Public Transcripts Expressed in Theaters of Cruelty: The Royal Graves at Ur in Mesopotamia. *Cambridge Archaeological Journal* 16/2: 123–44.

Ellison, Rosemary, et al.
1978 Some Food Offerings from Ur, Excavated by Sir Leonard Woolley, and Previously Unpublished. *Journal of Archaeological Science* 5: 167–77.

Forest, Jean-Daniel
1983 *Les pratiques funéraires en Mésopotamie du cinquième millénaire au début du troisième: Étude de cas.* Paris: Éditions Recherche sur les Civilisations.

Foucault, Michel
1995 *Discipline and Punish: The Birth of the Prison.* Translated by Alan Sheridan. New York: Vintage. [Original pub., 1975]

Frankfort, Henri
1978 *Kingship and the Gods.* Chicago: University of Chicago Press.

Geertz, Clifford
1980 *Negara: The Theater State in Nineteenth-Century Bali.* Princeton: Princeton University Press.

Gelb, Ignace
1976 Quantitative Evaluation of Slavery and Serfdom. Pp. 195–207 in *Kramer Anniversary Volume: Cuneiform Studies in Honor of Samuel Noah Kramer*, ed. Barry Eichler. Alter Orient und Altes Testament 25. Kevelaer: Butzon & Bercker / Neukirchen-Vluyn: Neukirchener Verlag.

Heimpel, Wolfgang
1987–90 Libation. Pp. 1-5 in vol. 7 of *Reallexikon der Assyriologie und vorderasiatischen Archäologie.* Berlin: de Gruyter.
1992 Herrentum und Königtum im vor- und frühgeschichtlichen Alten Orient. *Zeitschrift für Assyriologie und vorderasiatische Archäologie* 82: 4–21.

Helwing, Barbara
2003 Feasts as a Social Dynamic in Prehistoric Western Asia: Three Case Studies from Syria and Anatolia. *Paléorient* 29/2: 63–86.

Hill, J. D.
1995 *Ritual and Rubbish in the Iron Age of Wessex: A Study on the Formation of a Specific Archaeological Record.* British Archaeological Reports, British Series 242. Oxford: Tempus Reparatum.

Jans, Greta, and Bretschneider, Joachim, with a contribution by Walther Sallaberger
1998 Wagon and Chariot Representations in the Early Dynastic Glyptic: "They Came to Tell Beydar with Wagon and Equid." Pp. 155–94 in *Subartu IV: About Subartu. Studies Devoted to Upper Mesopotamia, Vol. 2: Culture, Society, Image,* ed. Marc Lebeau. Turnhout: Brepols.
Joyce, Rosemary
2000 *Gender and Power in Prehispanic Mesoamerica.* Austin: University of Texas Press.
Joyce, Rosemary, and Gillespie, Susan, eds.
2000 *Beyond Kinship: Social and Material Reproduction in House Societies.* Philadelphia: University of Pennsylvania Press.
Kertzer, David
1988 *Ritual, Politics, and Power.* New Haven, CT: Yale University Press.
Lévi-Strauss, Claude
1987 *Anthropology and Myth: Lectures, 1951–1982.* Translated by Roy Willis. Oxford: Blackwell.
Lock, Grahame
1996 Subject, Interpellation, and Ideology. Pp. 69–90 in *Postmodern Materialism and the Future of Marxist Theory: Essays in the Althusserian Tradition,* ed. Antonio Callari and David Ruccio. Hanover, NH: Wesleyan University Press.
Maekawa, Kazuya
1973–74 The Development of the É-MÍ in Lagash during the Early Dynastic III. *Mesopotamia* 8–9: 77–144.
Marchesi, Gianni
2004 Who Was Buried in the Royal Tombs of Ur? The Epigraphic and Textual Data. *Orientalia* 73: 153–97.
Martin, Harriet
1988 *Fara: A Reconstruction of the Ancient Mesopotamian City of Shuruppak.* Birmingham: Chris Martin.
Martin, Harriet; Moon, Jane; and Postgate, J. Nicholas
1985 *Graves 1 to 99.* Abu Salabikh Excavations 2. London: British School of Archaeology in Iraq.
Meyer, Jan-Waalke
2000 Zur Möglichkeit einer kulturhistorischen Einordnung von Grabfunden. *Altorientalische Forschungen* 27: 21–37.
Mitchell, Timothy
1999 Society, Economy, and the State Effect. Pp. 76–97 in *State/Culture: State-Formation after the Cultural Turn,* ed. George Steinmetz. Ithaca, NY: Cornell University Press.
Montag, Warren
1996 Beyond Force and Consent: Althusser, Spinoza, Hobbes. Pp. 91–106 in *Postmodern Materialism and the Future of Marxist Theory: Essays in the Althusserian Tradition,* ed. Antonio Callari and David Ruccio. Hanover, NH: Wesleyan University Press.
Moorey, P. R. S.
1977 What Do We Know about the People Buried in the Royal Cemetery of Ur? *Expedition* 20/1: 24–40.
Moortgat, Anton
1949 *Tammuz: Der Unsterblichkeitsglaube in der altorientalischen Bildkunst.* Berlin: de Gruyter.
Nissen, Hans
1966 *Zur Datierung des Königsfriedhofes von Ur.* Bonn: Rudolf Habelt.
1988 *The Early History of the Ancient Near East, 9000–2000 B.C.* Translated by Elizabeth Lutzeier, with Kenneth Northcott. Chicago: University of Chicago Press.
Pauketat, Timothy, ed.
2001 *The Archaeology of Traditions: Agency and History before and after Columbus.* Gainesville: University of Florida Press.

Pinnock, Frances
1994 Considerations on the "Banquet Theme" in the Figurative Art of Mesopotamia and Syria. Pp. 15–26 in *Drinking in Ancient Societies: History and Culture of Drinks in the Ancient Near East,* ed. Lucio Milano. Padua: Sargon srl.

Pollock, Susan
1983 *The Symbolism of Prestige: An Archaeological Example from the Royal Cemetery of Ur.* Ph.D. diss., University of Michigan.
1985 Chronology of the Royal Cemetery of Ur. *Iraq* 47: 129–58.
1991 Of Priestesses, Princes and Poor Relations: The Dead in the Royal Cemetery of Ur. *Cambridge Archaeological Journal* 1: 171–89.
1999 *Ancient Mesopotamia: The Eden That Never Was.* Cambridge: Cambridge University Press.
2003 Feasts, Funerals, and Fast Food in Early Mesopotamian States. Pp. 17–38 in *The Archaeology and Politics of Food and Feasting in Early States and Empires,* ed. Tamara Bray. New York: Kluwer Academic Press.
2007 Death of a Household. In *Performing Death: Social Analyses of Funerary Traditions in the Ancient Mediterranean,* ed. Nicola Laneri. Oriental Institute Seminars 3. Chicago: Oriental Institute, University of Chicago.

Reade, Julian
2001 Assyrian King-Lists, The Royal Tombs of Ur, and Indus Origins. *Journal of Near Eastern Studies* 60: 1–29.

Ricoeur, Paul
1994 Althusser's Theory of Ideology. Pp. 44–72 in *Althusser: A Critical Reader,* ed. Gregory Elliott. Oxford: Blackwell.

Rosengarten, Yvonne
1960 *Le régime des offrandes dans la société sumerienne d'après les textes présargoniques de Lagaš.* Paris: de Boccard.

Sallaberger, Walther
1993 *Der kultische Kalender der Ur III-Zeit.* Berlin: de Gruyter.

Schmandt-Besserat, Denise
2000 Feasting in the Ancient Near East. Pp. 391–403 in *Feasts: Archaeological and Ethnographic Perspectives on Food, Politics, and Power,* ed. Michael Dietler and Brian Hayden. Washington, DC: Smithsonian Institution Press.

Scott, James
1985 *Weapons of the Weak: Everyday Forms of Peasant Resistance.* New Haven, CT: Yale University Press.
1990 *Domination and the Arts of Resistance: Hidden Transcripts.* New Haven, CT: Yale University Press.

Selz, Gebhard
1990 Studies in Early Syncretism: The Development of the Pantheon in Lagaš: Examples for Inner-Sumerian Syncretism. *Acta Sumerologica* 12: 111–42.
1995 *Untersuchungen zur Götterwelt des altsumerischen Stadtstaates von Lagaš.* Occasional Publications of the Samuel Noah Kramer Fund 13. Philadelphia: University of Pennsylvania Museum.
1998 Über mesopotamische Herrschaftskonzepte: Zu den Ursprüngen mesopotamischer Herrscherideologie im 3. Jahrtausend. Pp. 281–344 in dubsar anta-men: *Studien zur Altorientalistik. Festschrift für Willem H. Ph. Römer zur Vollendung seines 70. Lebensjahres mit Beiträgen von Freunden, Schülern und Kollegen,* ed. Manfried Dietrich and Oswald Loretz. Münster: Ugarit-Verlag.
2004a Composite Beings: Of Individualization and Objectification in Third Millennium Mesopotamia. *Archiv Orientální* 72: 33–53.
2004b Early Dynastic Vessels in 'Ritual' Contexts. *Wiener Zeitschrift für die Kunde des Morgenlandes* 94: 185–223.

2004c "Wer sah je eine königliche Dynastie (für immer) in Führung!": Thronwechsel und gesellschaftlicher Wandel im frühen Mesopotamien als Nahtstelle von *microstoria* und *longue durée*. Pp. 157–214 in *Macht und Herrschaft*, ed. Christian Sigrist. Münster: Ugarit-Verlag.

Selz, Gudrun

1983 *Die Bankettszene: Entwicklung eines "überzeitlichen" Bildmotivs in Mesopotamien von der frühdynastischen bis zur Akkad-Zeit.* Wiesbaden: Franz Steiner.

Smith, Adam

2004 The End of the Essential Archaeological Subject. *Archaeological Dialogues* 11: 1–35.

Steele, Caroline

1990 *Living with the Dead: House Burial at Abu Salabikh, Iraq.* Ph.D. diss., State University of New York at Binghamton.

Steinkeller, Piotr

1999 On Rulers, Priests and Sacred Marriage: Tracing the Evolution of Early Sumerian Kingship. Pp. 103–37 in *Priests and Officials in the Ancient Near East*, ed. Kazuko Watanabe. Heidelberg: Carl Winter.

Stevanović, Mirjana

1997 The Age of Clay: The Social Dynamics of House Destruction. *Journal of Anthropological Archaeology* 16: 334–95.

Sürenhagen, Dietrich

2002 Death in Mesopotamia: The 'Royal Tombs' of Ur Revisited. Pp. 324–38 in *Of Pots and Plans: Papers on the Archaeology and History of Mesopotamia and Syria Presented to David Oates in Honour of His 75th Birthday*, ed. Lamia al-Gailani Werr et al. London: Nabu.

Testart, Alain

2004 *Les morts d'accompagnement: La servitude volontaire I.* Paris: Errance.

Wagner, Elisabeth

2002 Die Gefolgschaftsbestattungen im Königsfriedhof von Ur: Ein "Soziales Drama"? Pp. 88–94 in *Der "Garten Eden" im dritten Jahrtausend: Einblicke in das Leben städtischer Gesellschaften in Südmesopotamien zur frühdynastischen Zeit (ca. 2850–2350 v. Chr.)*, ed. Marlies Heinz and Dominik Bonatz. *Freiburger Universitätsblätter* 156. Freiburg: Rombach.

Walker, William, and Lucero, Lisa

2000 The Depositional History of Ritual and Power. Pp. 130–47 in *Agency in Archaeology*, ed. Marcia-Anne Dobres and John Robb. London: Routledge.

Weber, Max

1972 *Wirtschaft und Gesellschaft: Grundriss der verstehenden Soziologie.* 5th ed. Tübingen: Mohr Siebeck.

Winter, Irene

1999 Reading Ritual in the Archaeological Record: Deposition Pattern and Function of Two Artifact Types from the Royal Cemetery of Ur. Pp. 229–56 in *Fluchtpunkt Uruk: Archäologische Einheit aus methodischer Vielfalt. Schriften für Hans Jörg Nissen*, ed. Hartmut Kühne, Reinhard Bernbeck, and Karin Bartl. Rahden: Marie Leidorf.

Woolley, C. Leonard

1934 *Ur Excavations II: The Royal Cemetery.* London: The British Museum.

1955 *Ur Excavations IV: The Early Periods.* London: The British Museum.

Wright, Henry

1969 *The Administration of Rural Production in an Early Mesopotamian Town.* Anthropological Papers 38. Ann Arbor: University of Michigan Museum of Anthropology.

Žižek, Slavoj

1994 How Did Marx Invent the Symptom? Pp. 296–331 in *Mapping Ideology*, ed. Slavoj Žižek. London: Verso.

Chapter 5

The Divine Image of the King: Religious Representation of Political Power in the Hittite Empire

Dominik Bonatz

Introduction

This essay aims to scrutinize the use and function of religious images during the Hittite Empire period (ca. 1350–1200 B.C.E.). It is, however, not concerned with images of divinities as such but, rather, with secular rulers, insofar as their images fulfill clear religious functions. That is, components of political iconography can be compared with aspects of attested religious iconography. It will be seen that within this network of relationships, habitual patterns associated with early state society—in this case Hittite—can be detected, patterns that help in the reconstruction of visual praxis as mirrored in both politics and religion. Before I embark on this undertaking, however, to put the chosen material to the test, I must briefly discuss what is meant by *visual praxis* and indeed how the terms *religion* and *politics* may be defined within the context of this praxis.

David Morgan in his book *The Sacred Gaze* (2005: 55) has provided a very usable typology of the functions of religious visual culture. He writes that religious images accomplish one or more of the following aims for the people who cherish und use them: (a) they order space and time, (b) they "imagine" community, (c) they communicate with the divine or transcendent, (d) they embody forms of communion with the divine, (e) they collaborate with other forms of representation, (f) they influence thought and behavior by persuasion or magic, and (g) they displace rival images and ideologies. This typology of functions is, for our purposes, pertinent in almost every case and not only offers a meaningful list of ready-made questions but also helps to clarify a few ideas vis-à-vis the differences between religion and politics. Were "divine" in (c) and (d) above, for example, to be replaced with "tradition," "civilization," or "nation," would the same functions also be found to apply to nonreligious images Morgan 2005: 55), especially to political images? Religion and politics both serve in the structuralization of social order. As is commonly made manifest in the ancient Near East, the very slight difference between the two depends on the form of the forces or powers to which they appeal. Whereas in the case of religion one would claim these powers to be "supernatural" or "transcendent," in the case of politics they are human. Catherine Albanese (1999: 11), however, in her definition of religion speaks similarly of "ordinary and extraordinary powers, meanings, and values" that permit a religious orientation; this indirectly underlines the fact that often no great difference exists between what people consider to be religiously motivated and what they consider to be politically motivated. My treatment of the historical material is based on this assessment. On the one hand, it serves in defining religion and politics based not on their institutional characters but on their praxis. On the other, it facilitates the investigation of the phenomenon of the interaction of religious and political praxis as symbolized by the visual practices of their respective cultural communities.

Before I begin in this essay to speak of the Hittites, a cultural community that passed long ago into history, I must clarify methodologically what we mean by the expression *visual praxis*. A technical definition of visual culture would be, for example, "the analysis and interpretation of images and the ways of seeing (or gazes) that configure the agents' practices, conceptualities, and institutions that put images to work" (Morgan 2005: 33). It is clear, though, that the second aspect of visual culture–namely, the ways of seeing–can only be discussed very superficially in the context of the ancient Near East. We lack the sources to answer how the images were viewed, what emotions they elicited in those who gazed upon them then, and who within the restricted circles of the elites had access to the images.[1] Indeed, it is hard to speak of a visual *culture* at all, for various reasons, but we may, nevertheless, begin with the concept of visual *praxis*. The images have survived the millennia, physical manifestations of the acts of visual praxis. They outlasted their creators and, frequently, on this basis have become endowed with meaning. As instances of the construction of reality, they mirror the various ways of thinking and behaving of past cultures. From each image emerges a timeless agency, whose message it is possible both to preserve and transform.[2] It is this agency that should stand at the center of any consideration of visual praxis in Hittite times.

The Hittite Royal Couple as Bound to the Gods

In Hittite religion, the king and the queen were the principal servants of the gods. They were responsible for tending to the well-being of all the deities within the realm of their dominion and represented the central figures responsible for binding the empire into a single unified entity. We can deduce this role from numerous ritual texts and visual representations, such as the relief from Alaca Höyük, in which king and queen stand worshiping the statue of a god represented by a bull (fig. 1). It seems that the libation ritual, in particular, functioned as a motif of the closeness of the royals to the gods. On the Boston Silver Rython, it is the king alone who is depicted pouring out water in front of the Storm-god, who is driving his chariot (Emre 2002: 230–32,

1. Very few sources, and then mainly sources from the Neo-Assyrian areas, provide information regarding the esthetic function of the images and of the reactions they were supposed to provoke in the contemporaries who gazed upon them; on this, see Cancik-Kirschbaum 1999: 112–15; Winter 1997. A study of the visual experience articulated in earlier Mesopotamian texts has been presented by Winter 2000. With regard to Hittite areas, there have so far been no investigations that have addressed the issues of seeing and the esthetic function of images.
2. On image agencies in the ancient Near East, see Bonatz 2002.

Figure 1. Orthostats from Alaca Höyük representing Hittite queen and king, ca. 1300–1200 (drawing by Ulrike Zurkinden-Kolberg after Bittel 1976: fig. 214).

fig. 15). The most monumental example of a libation scene can be found on the rock relief of Fraktın, which depicts Hattushili III and Puduheba: he is in front of the standing Storm-god, unusually represented shouldering a crook and therefore alternatively interpreted as a hunting-god (van Loon 1985: 15) or a tutelary god of the fields (Mayer-Opificius 1993: 361); and she is before the enthroned Sun-goddess, who holds a bowl in her right hand (fig. 2). What we see in the visual representations, then, is a privilege exclusively ascribed to the king and the queen. In Hittite visual practice, performing in honor of the gods was represented as being more than a matter of religious ritual. It was a matter of divine destiny.

From these images, we may conclude that the "body politic" of the king was deeply connected with the sphere of supernatural powers to which Hittite religion appealed.[3] As a consequence, the death of a king (and a queen) was thought not only to create a politically unstable situation but to be highly disconcerting from a religious point of view. To put it in a formula that was current then, kings and queens who died "became gods." *Expressis verbis*, from the first lines of the rituals for cremation and burial of deceased Hittite kings and queens, the disaster that the disturbance of the political and religious order announced is evoked: "If a great disaster or disturbance

3. Following Louis Marin's fundamental study on the portraiture of Louis XVI, scholars of the ancient Near East have begun to discuss the concept of the multifaceted nature of the king (Bahrani 2003: 138–45; Winter 1997: 374). They claim that in the images of kings in the ancient Near East we also often recognize different embodiments: first, the specific, historical personage; second, the exemplar of the institution of kingship; and third, the sacred person sanctioned by the gods. The "body politic" thus exemplifies the institution of kingship, deeply intertwined with the "sacred body," the expression of the king's religious status. For Hittite kings, a similar approach has been taken by van den Hout (1994: 38, 52).

Figure 2. Rock relief of Fraktın representing Puduheba and Hattushili III, ca. 1270–1250 (Ehringhaus 2005: fig. 112; photo reprinted courtesy of Prof. Horst Ehringhaus).

occurs in Hattusha, in that a king or queen has become a god . . ." (KUB XXX 16+ vs. I 1–2; after Otten 1958: 20–21; compare Haas 1994: 216). In order to overcome this disaster and in order to deal with the threat to social order that the death has brought about, not least emotionally, a 14-day ritual of the dead is held, the central aspect of which is the transference of the royal corpse together with its paraphenalia to the underworld. To this end, the deceased is accompanied to the hereafter by cattle, horses, mules, and sheep, a piece of turf as *pars pro toto* for the pastureland, as well as picks and spades, broken into pieces (KUB XXX 24a+ vs. I 1–26, vs. II 1–6; Otten 1958: 58–61; Haas 1994: 224). The image of the deceased king as farmer and livestock holder in the underworld corresponds to the significance of the agrarian economy in Hittite society and the role that the royal pair played in guaranteeing agricultural production.[4] The royal ancestors (Hittite: *karuilies* LUGAL^{meš}) existed in the hereafter among the divine ancestors (Hittite: *karuilies* DINGIR^{meš}), who were also known as

4. As is made most clear in the function the king and queen played in the ritual for the great spring festival AN.TAḪ.ŠUM^{SAR} in Hattusha and in other parts of the realm (Haas 1994: 772–826). The function of the king as "shepherd" in the Hittite ritual for the dead is particularly clear at the point of transference of the turf as *pars pro toto* for the pasturelands. It takes place at the point of appeal to the Sun-god and ends with the words: "Now, Sungod, take this as legitimately dedicated pasture/meadow-land! And none shall snatch it away from him (or) contest it legally! There shall pasture cattle, sheep, horses and mules for him on this pasture/meadow-land!" (KUB XXX 24 vs. II 1–4; after Haas 1994: 224–25; compare Otten 1958: 60–61).

the gods of 'below' (*katteres* Dingir^{meš}), that is, subterranean divinities led by the goddess of the dead, Lelwani. They all influenced growth on earth—which is one reason why the agrarian cult was so closely linked to the ancestor cult (Gonnet 1995: 192–93). It was also a reason why an effective afterlife was conjured up for the deceased kings and queens—a continued existence in the hereafter, which at the same time guaranteed the survival and prosperity of the ruling dynasty. The various forms of Hittite ancestor cult (see Haas 1994: 243–48; van den Hout 1995: 45–46; Gonnet 1995) served the purpose of securing the maintenance of this existence and thereby of counteracting one of the possible crises that the Hittite dynasty believed itself to be exposed to through the absence of divine assistance. It was, indeed, possible to turn the disaster evoked by a death in the royal family into a positive sign by means of the "becoming-a-god" notion, what van den Hout (1994: 38) referred to as a "privilege of death," from which those who remained should also be able to profit.

The creation of the rock reliefs at Fraktın may have been stimulated by the status of the royal ancestors as divine powers in the life hereafter who were capable of effecting change. Closer analysis reveals that the ritual behavior represented there took place less in this sphere than in a transcendent sphere. The robe and headgear of the royal pair are conspicuously similar to the attire worn by the divine pair before them; this is the main reason that it has been suggested that the scene depicts Hattushili and Puduheba in the afterlife (Hawkins 1990: 311 n. 48; Mayer-Opificius 1993: 361–63). The bond between humankind and the gods that the king and queen sealed while alive, they obviously continued to maintain after death—the representation of which this appears to verify.

The libation scene conveys the basic religious ideas that lie behind the pictorial representation of the royal pair. Aside from the examples cited in this context, however, royal females are rarely portrayed in the art.[5] The king shown alone is the focus of many more representations within the realm of the divine than is the queen. As will be shown, iconographic forms are evident here that make no reference to known canonical textual material, simply because the message they convey has little to do with religious conventions and more to do with political aims.

Visualizing the Divine Ancestor

The pictorial decoration of the rock sanctuary Yazılıkaya, which lies near Hattusha, dates back essentially to Tuthaliya IV (ca. 1240–1215). In the main Chamber A of the

5. Danuheba, for example, Muwatalli II's spouse, indeed possessed her own seal, upon which an image of a female personage appears dressed in a veiled gown (Neve 1993: fig. 157). However, it is not likely that the seal owner is depicted here but, rather, the Sun-goddess of Arinna, just as is the case with the representation on Tuthaliya IV's seal (fig. 9 here). More commonly, the queens' or kings' mothers share one or more seals with their spouses or sons, as do Hinti und Malnigal, the wives of Shuppiluliuma I, and Malnigal again in her role as the mother of Murshili II (Neve 1993: figs. 147, 153); Danuheba and Puduheba as the spouses of Muwatali II (Neve 1993: fig. 155) and Hattushili III (Neve 1993: figs. 152, 158), respectively; and Danuheba as Urhi-Teshub's mother (Neve 1993: fig. 147). In the middle of these seals, there are no anthropomorphic forms to be seen but merely the hieroglyphic inscription of the names of both seal owners.

Figure 3. Relief no. 64 of Yazılıkaya representing Tuthaliya IV, ca. 1230 (Bittel et al. 1975: pl. 39.2; photo reprinted courtesy of Gebr. Mann Verlag, Berlin).

cult complex, there are 65 reliefs still surviving in which a procession of the gods of the Hurrian pantheon is represented that leads toward the highest gods of the pantheon, Teshub and Hebat (Bittel et al. 1975: pls. 12–38; Seeher 2002: figs. 1–8). The image of the complex's founder, Tuthaliya IV (fig. 3 here), appears on a rock face in a position that overlooks the entire procession and makes direct eye contact with the pair of chief gods on relief nos. 42–43. In general, the function of Chamber A is to be connected with the New Year and Spring festival AN.TAḪ.ŠUM (Otten 1956: 101–2; van Loon 1985: 19–20; Macqueen 1999: 128; Seeher 2002: 113), although Haas (1994: 639), in view of the image of Tuthaliya there, suggests that the chamber was the location of the coronation ceremony.

The adjoining Chamber B houses further representations of Tuthaliya IV. On relief no. 81, he appears being embraced and led by his protective deity, Sharruma (Bittel et al. 1975: pls. 48–49). In addition to this, however, a colossal statue of the king stood within the chamber (Neve 1989: 350–51, figs. 2–3). The limestone base of the statue is still *in situ* at the northern end of the chamber. A basalt panel found in the village of Yekbaz, not far from Yazılıkaya, which preserves the remains of two feet obviously clad in pointed shoes with turned-up toes, fits the base exactly (Neve 1989: 351 n. 51). On the basis of the size of the feet, it can be estimated that the statue had an original height of some 3.8 meters. Its attribution to a standing image of Tuthaliya

IV is based on the cartouche (relief no. 83) on the rock wall to the right of the statue's pedestal, in which the name Tuthaliya is written in Hittite hieroglyphs.

When one examines the colossal standing image of Tuthaliya IV in the context of the other images in Chamber B, it becomes clear that we are dealing here with a complex linked to the death cult of this king (compare Neve 1989: 349). In front of the image in which Sharruma leads the king is the relief (no. 82) of the underworld-god Ner(i)gal in the form of a colossal sword (Bittel et al. 1975: pl. 51). Opposite him appear 12 marching gods, armed with scimitars (nos. 69–80), probably an anonymous group of underworld-gods (Güterbock 1965: 198; Bittel et al. 1975: 117, 124, 256, pls. 44–46). Tuthaliya's statue is located, therefore, among (indeed amid) a row of representations of divinities drawn from the hereafter. It must have been installed here after the death of the ruler, to which an inscription in the name of Shuppiluliuma II, Tuthaliya's son and successor, bears witness (KBo XII 38):

> But this image [of my father] Tuthaliya was (still) n[ot made]. Thus, I, Shuppiluliuma, [the Great King], King of Hatti, son of Tuthaliya, the Great King, grandson of Hattushili, the Great King, and descendant of Murshili, the Great King, made it. As my father, the Great King Tuthaliya, was a veritable King, just so I drew the veritable manly deeds. (In this way) I ensured nothing was missing (and) I withheld nothing. I erected a constant/eternal rock-hekur (and) I made an image; this I brought into the constant/eternal rock-hekur, I decorated it and pacified him (the spirit of the dead King).[6]

The "rock-hekur," one of the places consecrated by the gods for the worship of the ancestors of the dynasty, is probably referring to chamber B in Yazılıkaya, in the case of Shuppiluliuma's inscription, although I recognize that places of this sort may have existed elsewhere in the realm (Otten 1963: 22; Haas 1994: 245–46). The erection of a memorial statue for the dead father obviously coheres with the reference to the rebuilding measures that Shuppiluliuma II had undertaken there (Neve 1989: 349). The enthroning of the dead ruler as a divine(?) ancestor in the underworld would probably have taken place simultaneously with or shortly after Shuppiluliuma II's enthronement as the new ruler.[7]

Shuppiluliuma built his father a monument at a time when the Hittite Kingdom found itself in serious difficulty with regard to foreign policy. Besides a growing loss of state authority on the borders of the realm, a new problem in the shape of pirates had come to the fore–the so-called Sea Peoples. Shuppiluliuma was compelled to pursue a military operation against Alashiya (Cyprus) and fight there against the ever-approaching foe of the sea. The very same text that mentions the erection of the statue for Tuthaliya reports on these events (KBo XII 38 RS III; Otten 1963: 20–21), and although it is admittedly fragmentary, it does appear that Shuppiluliuma is thereby drawing a direct connection between the erection of the *hekur*-cultic location

6. After Haas 1994: 639; compare Otten 1963: 16–17.

7. Arnuwanda III, who was regent for a brief time in between, does not alter the picture here. He obviously failed to erect a memorial to the deceased Tuthaliya, which Shuppiluliuma II, with proper self-interest, now takes responsibility to do.

Figure 4. Relief block from Temple 5, House A in the upper town of Boğazköy representing Tuthaliya (probably I), ca. 1240–1215 (Neve 1993: fig. 100; photo reprinted courtesy of Dr. Peter Neve).

in Yazılıkaya and his own victorious deeds in Alashiya. Shuppiluliuma allows himself to be guided by the manly deeds of Tuthaliya, who had previously defeated Alashiya, establishing a memorial in the hekur through the erection of the statue. The composition must originally have been inscribed on the statue in monumental script, as another or similar version of it that is attested as a rock inscription at Nişantepe in Hattusha suggests (Neve 1989: 63, fig. 124). This was a political statement that was promulgated during the time of crisis shortly before the fall of the Hittite Kingdom, and Shuppiluliuma sought to circumvent the crisis through reenacting the deeds of his father. In accordance with Hittite traditions of belief, a deceased father takes up a protective function as an ancestor virtually automatically and thus receives the necessary care devoted to the dead. The spatial and pictorial production by Shuppiluliuma in memory of the dead paternal ancestor was supposed to lend this function a special and hopefully long-lasting expression. It aimed at establishing communion with the divine for the strengthening of both political and religious power.

We can only speculate about the exact appearance of Tuthaliya's statue. On the basis of the torso of a monumental statue from Alaca Höyük, Neve reconstructed the image of a standing man, dressed in a long robe, with his hands crossed over his breast (Neve 1989: 351, fig. 3). Mind you, the head is also missing from the statue from Alaca Höyük (Koçay 1973: pls. 40–41). One may imagine that it was adorned with a horned headdress, given that the figure represented a deified personage, and on the basis of representations of other deified rulers. The same thing is to be found on a relief block set in the wall as a pilaster from the "Chapel" (House A) in Temple 5 in the upper town of Hattusha, for example (fig. 4; see also Neve 1987: 63–64, figs. 16–17). The figure is turned to the right. It is clad in a short skirt, pointed shoes with turned-up toes, and a pointed hat with four pairs of horns representing divinity, and a large earring. A spear, poised over the right shoulder in attacking pose, underlines the martial aspect of the man—the ruler Tuthaliya, according to the hieroglyphs on the outstretched fist. In contrast to the names of the ruling monarchs, this name is supplied with the epithet "Great King" alone. The signs for "Tabarna" and "My Sun" are missing. The image thus represents one of Tuthaliya IV's similarly named predecessors and not the man himself, seeing that he should be regarded as the architect of the structural ensemble at Temple 5 and therefore as donor of the reliefs in House A.[8] Most likely we have here an image of Tuthaliya I, to whom Tuthaliya IV refers before referring to his father, Hattushili (III), and grandfather, Murshili (II), in his geneaology.[9]

We may judge the psychological reasons behind the allusion to a forefather of almost 200 years earlier[10] in the context of the entire Temple 5 complex and the enclosed Houses A–C (Neve 1987: fig. 14). The temple has at its disposal, in its northwestern corner, an annex, similar to a house, which on the grounds of its architectural peculiarities likely represents a combination in form between a cult location and a residence for the royal family (compare Neve 1987: 66). While members of the ruling house were able to conduct their private cult for the highest gods—that is, Teshub and Hebat—in this place, the cult of the dynastic ancestors was pursued in the connecting area of the chapel-like Houses A–D, an area surrounded by Temenos walls.[11] We may assume that Houses B and C, in the same complex and virtually identical to house A, were dedicated to the other two regents named in Tuthaliyas IV's genealogy, Hattushili III and Murshili II, given the particular circumstances of their rule (compare Neve 1987: 68). Worked pilasters were found here that were similar to the relief block from House A; they had no images but nevertheless could have fulfilled a cultic function (Neve 1987: 64–65, fig. 15). The cult of the royal ancestors that would have been enacted in this area stretched therefore beyond the immediate forefathers of the ruling dynasty back to the period before the foundation of the great kingdom. It shows the extent of the effort made to maintain continuity within this dynasty and the strength of the desire to secure a political inheritance through the conscious evocation of the ancestors. The architecture of the building ensemble bears witness to this as occurring in close correlation with the cult for the highest gods—a cult that was performed in a way analogous to the cult of the ancestors, because these too had become gods.

8. Neve 1987: 68; 1993: 36; see, however, van den Hout (1995: 548), who on unconvincing grounds sees it as the image of the incumbent ruler and founder, Tuthaliya IV.

9. Gonnet in Neve 1987: 70. Besides that, Shuppilulima (I) is named first in the list of Tuthaliya IV's predecessors, albeit not frequently (van den Hout 1995: 557).

10. Tuthaliya I's dates of rule may be taken to be ca. 1420–1400 B.C.E.

11. Another complex, named House D, was interpreted by the excavator as a podium altar, which could have served the cultic function of both temple and ancestor chapel (Neve 1987: 66, 68).

Figure 5. Relief block from Chamber 2 on the "Südburg" of Boğazköy representing Shuppiluliuma (probably I), ca. 1200 (Neve 1993: fig. 214; photo reprinted courtesy of Dr. Peter Neve).

The Image of the Divine Warrior

The iconography of the ruler in the relief from House A is that of a martial god. He is dressed in a tall, pointed hat adorned with many horns, the symbol of a god. With his attacking posture and shouldered lance in the right hand, he resembles the image of the Storm-god with lance from Çağdin (near Gaziantep; Bittel 1976: fig. 207). The hand-held lance corresponds to hieroglyph L. 28 for 'strong'/'powerful' (*muwatalli*; Laroche 1960: 21), a common epithet of the Storm-god. The similarity between the two images is indeed not a matter of mere chance but serves to emphasize the supernatural power of the divinized royal ancestor. That this power is now pictorially associated with the character of a martial god does not necessarily correspond to the image of the dead ruler as agriculturalist and husbandman of livestock in the afterlife that the Hittite ritual of the dead evokes. The martial components obviously counted for more in the pictorial world, because, being expressions of the power of the Hittite royal house, they served to underline the latter's political ambitions.

The image of Shuppiluliuma, on a relief block inserted into the wall of Chamber 2 on the "Südburg" of Boğazköy, is similar (fig. 5). The Great King appears as a divinized warrior with a horned, pointed hat, with a lance in one outstretched hand and the other holding a bow slung over his shoulder. At the end of the chamber, a relief with the representation of the Sun-god is displayed (Neve 1993: fig. 211). To the side is an inscription of Shuppiluliuma II, in which the function of the chamber as a "divine earth road" (that is, a route to the underworld) is described (Hawkins 1995: 44–45, fig. 15). Based on the perceptions of the afterlife of the Chamber 2 complex, it seems unlikely that Shuppiluliuma II is represented here, especially because he was the last known ruler of the Hittite realm, and a posthumous construction is hardly probable.[12] It is far more likely that the image represents Shuppiluliuma I, who as an ancestor guarded the entry to the afterlife. It is not at all surprising that Shuppiluliuma II chose the image of this patron, who as founder of the great regime embodied the strength and power that Shuppiluliuma II himself craved in the face of the destruction that threatened it.

Protecting the Kingdom: The Divine Image of Kings and Princes on Hittite Rock Reliefs

In contrast to the "private" sphere of the temple and cult buildings in Hattusha, Hittite kings and princes in the iconography of divine warriors are portrayed on public monuments–the rock reliefs. The figures in question on the rock reliefs from Imamkulu, Hanyeri, and Hamide/Hemite[13] all hold a spear in an outstretched hand, wear a sword hung from a belt, and shoulder a bow with the other hand. Each has a round cap, upon the forehead side of which a single horn is portrayed. The head-high captions identify the persons represented as princes.[14] Their supernatural status is underlined on the one hand by their closeness to the images of gods, and on the other hand by the proximity of the Storm-god, who is portrayed in front of the princes in the rock reliefs at Imamkulu and Hanyeri (here symbolized as a bull).

Among the rock reliefs at Karabel A and Karabel B are royal figures in the guise of god-warriors,[15] and there are similar figures on the newly discovered rock reliefs at the Hatip Springs as well (fig. 6). Just like the princes, these figures carry a sword, spear, and bow; but based on the horned, pointed hats that they wear, they were personages of a higher rank.[16] A caption appears in front of the head of the relief at

12. For alternative views, see Neve 1993: 72, 80; and van den Hout 1995: 558.

13. Börker-Klähn 1982: 258–60, nos. 314–16; Kohlmeyer 1983: 80–95, figs. 33, 36, 39, pls. 22, 23.4, 32, 33.2, 34, 36.1; Ehringhaus 2005: 70–80, 107–12, figs. 133–35, 142–45, 193–95.

14. Thus, in general, the identity of the represented person is considered to be accounted for (thus Börker-Klähn 1982: 258–59; Kohlmeyer 1983: 83, 90, 93; Beyer 2001: 351; Ehringhaus 2005: 72–73, 80, 108). Only Herbordt (2005: 58), in the context of her study of the prince and official seals from Hattusha, doubts that the bow-carrying figure in the rock reliefs can be indisputably identified as a prince.

15. Börker-Klähn 1982: 255–257, nos. 311–12; Kohlmeyer 1983: 12–28, 25–28, figs. 2, 5, pls. 2–4, 6; Ehringhaus 2005: 87–91, figs. 161–62.

16. It remains unclear whether both figures on the rock reliefs in Gavurkalesi, presented in adoration pose before an enthroned goddess and armed with a sword are gods or rulers (Börker-Klähn 1982: 257–58, no. 313; Kohlmeyer 1983: 43–48, fig. 16, pls. 19–20). Their existence will thus be mentioned here only in passing.

Figure 6. Rock relief of Hatip representing Kurunta, ca. 1220 (Ehringhaus 2005: fig. 186; drawing reprinted courtesy of Prof. Horst Ehringhaus).

Karabel A that refers to King Tarkasnawa of Mira (Hawkins 1998: 4, fig. 3). In Hatip, the caption reads: "Kurunta, the Great King, [. . . .], son of Muwatalli, the Great King, the hero" (Dinçol 1998: 161, fig. 1).

Without doubt, the creation of the images as rock reliefs and their geographical locations indicate that these pictorial messages should be understood within a geopolitical context.[17] Imamkulu lies southeast of Kayseri on the western side of the Bey Dağ, at the beginning of one of the roads leading over the Gezbel Pass and at the border of the land of Kizzuwatna. At the other end of the pass route, that is, on the eastern side of the Bey Dağ, there is a relief from Hanyeri. Both reliefs fulfilled a cultic function and assisted the traffic between differing geographical areas, as indicated by their presence at exposed locations, in each case near a mountain and a spring, and by the fact that the Storm-god was presented at the center of the reliefs (Kohlmeyer 1983: 86, 90; Ehringhaus 2005: 76).

Farther south, on the way to Cilicia, where the Ceyhan emerges from the mountains, the Hamide relief was produced. The view from here stretches as far as the Misis

17. For maps with details about the geographical location of the rock reliefs, see Kohlmeyer 1983: 153; and Ehringhaus 2005, endnote at the back; and see both for a comprehensive description of the location. For the location of the reliefs lying to the west, see also the map in Hawkins 1998: fig. 11.

Mountains in the Cilician Plateau, where the rock relief at Sirkeli representing Muwatallis II may be found. Only Tarhundapiya, the name of the father of the donor of the Hamide relief, is preserved, but Kohlmeyer (1983: 94–95) argues that the relief was an expression of the ambitions of some prince at a strategically important location to rule in that area at the moment of the fall of the great Hittite Kingdom, following Tuthaliya IV's death.

At another geographical location, to the west, we have the reliefs at Karabel Pass. They are at an exposed point along an important route across the Boz Dağları (the Tmolos range in classical antiquity), linking the valleys of the Gediz (Hermos) and the Küçük Menderes (Cayster) rivers, and thus leading from the region of Sardis to the region of Ephesus, to be identified with the Late Bronze Age Apasa. The reliefs and their inscriptions demonstrate that Tarkasnawa, king of Mira (one of the lands of Arzawa) and a contemporary of Tuthaliya IV, sought to secure his area of rule toward the west as far as the coast and the Meander Valley (Hawkins 1998: 21–31).

Kurunta's relief at the Hatip Springs is 17 km south of Konya, thus within former Ikuwaniya and the Hittite realm. Its donor, the reasonably well-known king of Tarhuntassa, has most recently come to light as a result of the discovery of a bronze tablet in Boğazköy (Otten 1988). As the son of Muwatalli II, Kurunta was installed as king in Tarhuntassa by Hattushili III and consequently ruled there as a vassal of Tuthaliya IV. At the end of his career, however, he appears to have harbored ambitions for the Hittite throne itself. This, at least, makes sense of the discovery of seal impressions from Boğazköy in which he is described as the "Great King" in Hattusha (Otten 1998: 4–6, figs. 1–2). He also takes the title "Great King" in the rock relief at the Hatip Springs (fig. 6), which suggests that the monument was erected on Hittite soil as an expression of his new demands for power (compare Dinçol 1998: 163).

The rock reliefs mentioned may be connected above all with the expression of clear political statements aimed at the Hittite Empire at the moment of its greatest crisis, if we follow the aforementioned interpretations of the rock reliefs from Hamide, Karabel, and Hatip. The donors of the reliefs pursued their geopolitical aims using pictorial propaganda with iconography taken entirely from the Hittite repertoire. The choice of a divine warrior as the central motif in the majority of the rock reliefs, however, poses the question whether the donor had arranged to present an image of himself with divine attributes or an image of a deceased ruler, turned god, as an ancestor. Dinçol (1998: 162–63) does not opt for either of these interpretations. He prefers to see the representations of the divine warrior (such as the one at Hatip) not as the depiction of the ruler as donor of the image but as a god with an apotropaic function to protect the image and inscription. Herbordt (2005: 57–58, fig. 39a–f) expressed similar reservations in her study of the motif of the bow-carrier on clay bullas in the Nişantepe archive in Hattusha. The motif is identical to the representation of the princes on the rock reliefs. As a motif on the seals of princes and high officials (scribes and priests), it obviously enjoyed substantial popularity at the time of the Empire. Whether the seal owner intended it as a reproduction of his own image or the image of his protective god is, according to Herbordt (2005), impossible to determine.

The Contingent Nature of Hittite Art

Any discussion of the divinization of Hittite rulers obviously suffers from our not knowing *when* a Hittite ruler was able to adopt the attributes of a god in pictorial art and what these attributes actually said about the divine status of the ruler. As was made clear above, it is possible to see deceased rulers who have become divinized ancestors in some of the representations in question, which reflect the expression "king-becomes-god" found in the texts. However, anyone who sees in this possibility a Hittite *doxa*—a convention regarding divination that required that all pictorial representations of it were also reflected in the written record—must also question whether representations of living rulers with divine attributes were even possible. Development of the images certainly must have followed some rules but this development was not necessarily paralleled in the texts. Therefore, the unfolding of Hittite visual art may be more accurately described as contingent.

According to one of the essential realizations of Bourdieu's theory of praxis, each form of praxis is contingent.[18] There is no culture in which the forms of life-praxis can be predicted with certainty. The location of an individual within society is indeed a consequence of an understandable (insofar as it follows from society's rules—the *doxa*) but nevertheless contingent praxis. This applies as much to individuals at the pinnacle of Hittite society as elsewhere and, therefore, to the images through which they function in the field of visual praxis. As Bourdieu explains, the style of a society continually redefines and alters itself anew; this can be called "evolving meaning" (Bourdieu 1994: 152). Hittite works of pictorial art are also linked to each other through a chain of significant relationships that together constitute a unique Hittite style. These relationships, however, were not carved in stone but were interconnections that formed a composite system made up of rules and exceptions (compare Bourdieu 1994: 153). Of particular interest to our analysis are the exceptions that led to changes in the norms. These exceptions are evidence of broader political events and instances of individual political fates set against the wider historical backdrop. These exert influence on the so-called *habitus*[19] as embodied by the system of Hittite society: the king and his family. Thus, the system of images alters itself just as does the *habitus* of the high-ranking personalities under the influence of unpredictable eventualities. The world of images, on the constant lookout for what was new, absorbed whatever political stimulation it found while remaining within the preestablished religious forms—without there necessarily being any textual reflection of this alteration. Thus it becomes clear that the formula "if a king becomes a god" was able to escape its ritual and textual confines and, via the production of new forms of images, became linked with notions other than those for which there is textual attestation.

Anthropomorphic representations of kings appear late in Hittite art, from the time of Muwatalli II (ca. 1290–1272) on. From the beginning, the royal image took on

18. Saake (2004: 96–99), for example, adopts a contingency-theoretical approach in his reflection on Bourdieu's work.

19. In the terminology of Noam Chomsky's generative grammar, the *habitus* may be defined as a system of internalized, "deep-structure" forms that lead to all typical thoughts, perceptions, and actions of a culture (Bourdieu 1994: 143).

Figure 7. Seal impression of Murshili III, ca. 1270–1260 (drawing by Ulrike Zurkinden-Kolberg after Neve 1993: cover photograph).

the traits of a god in such a way that the differences between the images of king and god were commonly very slight. Van den Hout (1995) describes this process in some detail as part of his investigation into the iconography of the Hittite Great Kings and attempts to explain it. He makes reference to the numerous pictorial similarities between ruler and god that significantly altered the image of the Hittite king. He distinguishes formally between a pictorial group A, in which the king carries the *lituus* and wears the long robe and rounded skull cap that are associated with the image of the Sun-god,[20] and a group B, in which the king wears a horned, pointed cap and is mostly presented in warrior-like aspect.[21] With respect to group A, it is not hard to find an explanation for the similarity of the images with those of the Sun-god, for at least from the time of Hattushili on, the Hittite kings used the title 'My Sun', ^{d}UTU^{ši} (Fauth 1979: 229–30), thereby presenting themselves as the Sun-god's representative on earth, which also eventually resulted in a pictorial expression of this idea. There is no reason to assume that in this case the image and ruler were not contemporary. It is, however, harder to account for the images in which the king wears the horned, pointed hat, the unmistakable symbol of divinity. In contrast to the conventional view, a view also supported here so far as some of the images are concerned (namely, the images in which royal ancestors are presented), van den Hout (1995: 559–60) has postulated that these images are representations of living rulers. The earliest attestation of this phenomenon to which he refers is the seal bearing the name Murshili (III).

20. Van den Hout 1995: 551–53; see, for example, the image of Muwatalli II on the rock relief in Sirkeli (Bittel 1976: fig. 195) and on seals of the same ruler (Beran 1967: pl. 12.250–252); furthermore, the image of a king on a relief from Alaca Höyük (fig. 1) and the representation of Tuthaliya on relief nos. 64 (fig. 3) and 81 in Yazılıkaya.

21. Van den Hout 1995: 553–61; in essence, the images from Hattusha already treated here are to be counted among these.

Here, the figure of the divine warrior with lance, sword, and bow stands behind the Storm-god steering a wagon led by bulls (fig. 7). According to van den Hout (1995: 559), the king is being portrayed in this image of the god.[22] In accordance with Hittite seal practices, the use of a dynastic seal is excluded, which would mean that this seal must represent the ruler, namely, Murshili III/Urhi-Teshub (ca. 1272–1265).[23] It may follow, then, that the same applies to the seals of princes and officials from Hattusha mentioned above. Although these images use round hats and not the horned, pointed ones, given the lower status of the seal owners, the figures represented could be deified self-portraits (Herbordt 2005: 57–58, fig. 39a–f). The impressions of two seals of Urhi-Teshub as crown prince (*tuḫkanti-*) recently found in the Nişantepe archive have provided the first clear evidence for the use of divine features in the images of living individuals, for there the seal owner is represented as a god with a pointed hat in the embrace of the god Sharruma (fig. 8; see also Herbordt 2005: 69–71, fig. 46a–d, cat. nos. 504, 505, 507). This cannot be an image of the deceased Urhi-Teshub, for we know that he followed his father, Muwatalli II, as Great King, with the throne name Murshili (III). Van den Hout's (1995: 559) thesis that rulers from Murshili III on were able to appropriate the iconography of gods while still alive has thus been confirmed retrospectively through the discovery of Urhi-Teshub's crown-prince seals. Perhaps, this extraordinary step in the development of the representation of kings occurred in connection with the difficult state in which Urhi-Teshub found himself as he succeeded his father to the throne and used this form of representation to legitimate his claims in the face of the demands for the throne made by his uncle, Hattushili (III) (Herbordt 2005: 71; 2006: 31).

After Urhi-Teshub, Tuthaliya IV has himself represented twice as a god with a horned crown in the embrace of the Storm-god. One is the image of a stamp seal impression on a tablet (RS 17.159) from Ugarit (fig. 9); the other is the recently published impression of a cylinder seal, the use of which by a Hittite king is unique. It was found among the sealed bullas from the royal archive of Nişantepe in Hattusha (Herbordt 2006: figs. 130–31). In both cases, the image only superficially resembles relief no. 81 in Yazılıkaya. On the seals, the god doing the embracing is not Tuthaliya's personal protective god, Sharruma, but the Storm-god Tarhunta (on the stamp seal) or Kummani (on the cylinder seal), and the ruler does not don the simple round cap but the many-horned, pointed hat, just as does the Storm-god. Unlike the Yazılıkaya relief, which may be accounted for within the context of the religious rock sanctuary in which it is found, the seal evokes a political demand that is manifested by the image's closeness to the Storm-god, the highest god of the empire.

It is thus clear, that beginning in the thirteenth century, Hittite rulers, princes, and probably even high officials as well began to use divine iconography for their pictorial self-representations. This does not mean that they claimed divine status during their

22. Dinçol (2002: 91) sees here instead the image of the protective deity ^{DINGIR}LAMMA, while Hawkins (2006: 50) favors the Stag-god.

23. Schaeffer (1956: 16–17) had already pointed out that the well-known seal impression of Tuthaliya IV on tablet RS 17.159 from Ugarit (fig. 9) must have depicted the ruling monarch because the tablet records the king's verdict (compare also Hawkins 1990: 311–12 n. 48).

Figure 8. Seal impression of Urhi-Teshub, ca. 1275 (drawing by Ulrike Zurkinden-Kolberg after Herbordt 2005: pl. 40:504.2a).

lifetimes (as noted also by van den Hout 1995: 559). The self-portrait as a god is, rather, an expression of an increasing awareness of the need for legitimation and should be evaluated as a common reaction to difficult outside circumstances. The images of rulers and other highly ranked individuals as gods were thereby able to serve the purpose of underpinning personal claims to power and offering protection through the proximity of the supernatural, just as did the images of the ancestors among the ranks of the gods.

International Politics and the Persuasive Function of Religious Images

The representations on seal images therefore had a special meaning, for seals ensured that the message could be spread over great distances and also ensured the repeated validation of this message. The above-mentioned seal impression of Tuthaliya IV from Ugarit (fig. 9) is relatively well known. The king is represented to the right, in the Storm-god's embrace,[24] while to the left stands the Sun-goddess. In the middle of the image, Tuthaliya's cartouche is presented twice, crowned by the winged Sun. As in heraldry, the seal image unites essential aspects of Hittite rule in which the king is the protégé of the highest gods. The message appears, on the basis of the pictographic character of both image and script, to have been generally understandable, even for those who lived far from central Hittite areas. The document from Ugarit with Tuthaliya's seal dealt with the divorce of Ammishtamru, king of Ugarit, from the princess of Amurru. It is indicative of the powerful influence that he sought to exercise over the political (marriage) alliances of his vassals that Tuthaliya sanctioned this

24. For a discussion as to whether it is, in fact, Tuthaliya and not a god who is represented here, see the note above as well as van den Hout 1995: 558 n. 63.

Figure 9. Seal impression of Tuthaliya IV, ca. 1240–1215 (Bittel 1976: fig. 192; photo reprinted courtesy of Editions Gallimard).

divorce. This was one instance in which the royal seal fulfilled its restricting foreign policy objectives.

However, it was not only the message of the Great King that was successfully broadcast in this way within the north Syrian area. The strong presence of seal images with representations of kings, princes, and high officials in the guise of divine warriors is particularly noticeable in the north Syrian area.[25] In places such as Emar that were under the control of the Hittite kingdom based in Carchemish, images such as these functioned more than ever as proof of central state authority. The power of the custodian of the Hittite Empire was obviously strengthened by using an image of himself with supernatural and militaristic attributes on the seals. The custodians used this image to project themselves as powerful figures, who toward the end of the thirteenth century were striving for ever greater independence.

Documents from Ugarit (Schaeffer 1956: 20–29, figs. 27–35) and Emar (Beyer 2001: 47–49, A2a-b, A3) have been found with the seal of Ini-Teshub (ca. 1270–1220), the Hittite viceroy in Carchemish, for example, and bear witness to his unlimited authority.[26] On two of the three attested types of seal, only the name and royal

25. Beyer 2001: 347–53, figs. 65–67. According to the seal inscription, leading private individuals are the owners of the seals, sometimes described as scribes, and on this basis to be understood as referring to high officials in the local administration (for example, Beyer 2001: 106–7, A101–A103). If the captions with the names were to be interpreted similarly to the captions on the royal seals (which are taken to refer to the figure of the divine warrior beside which they are placed), then it follows that these officials would also be presenting images of themselves in this way.

26. On this, see Klengel 1992: 124–26. Ini-Teshub, who had occupied the post of viceroy at Carchemish beginning with the days of Hattushili III, later acquired the title "Great King" from Tuthaliya IV himself (Klengel 1992: 124–25 n. 197).

Figure 10. Seal impression of Ini-Teshub, ca. 1270–1220 (Schaeffer 1956: fig. 34; drawing reprinted courtesy of Mission archéologique des Ras Shamra–Ougarit).

titulary of this ruler appear, without mention of his genealogy (figs. 10, 11).[27] Ini-Teshub is represented on both seals as a god with a club on his shoulder, greeting the Storm-god, who stands in front of him on a bull, with his right hand raised. Two differences in the otherwise identical seal images are informative, because they may indicate a change in the status of the seal owner. In one, the ruler has a round hat with a horn, and in the other, he wears a horned, pointed hat. In the first case (fig. 10), the so-called solar figure makes an appearance as a third form in the image. This figure wears a long robe, carries a *lituus*, is supported by a bull man, and has the winged Sun attached to its head. Differing opinions exist as to the identity of this figure, though Beyer (2001: 341–47) has argued plausibly on the basis of material in Emar that the motif parallels the royal Hittite title dUTU^{ši} 'My Sun' and may have been created in northern Syria to evoke the image of the Hittite "Great King." The particular dialect of the glyptic workshop in Carchemish is expressed in this "solar figure." Here a "supernatural image" that was allegedly capable of symbolizing the umbrella-like rule and protective power of the Hittite Great King is shown off to advantage. The identical figures are also found, for example, on the seal of one Shahurunuwas (Beyer 2001: A1), the father of Ini-Teshub and his predecessor on the Carchemish throne, and on the seal of Prince Heshmi-Teshub (2002: A4a–b), Ini-Teshub's brother. It is missing from Ini-Teshub's seal, in which he represents himself as a god with a horned, pointed cap (fig. 11). Instead, a male figure standing on a bull and marked as a god by wearing a round horned hat appears with a raised spear attacking an upright lion. The motif of the lion-conquerer has a secure place within the iconography of the ancient Near East, on the basis of which Beyer (2001: 49) suggests that we also see Ini-Teshub, king of Carchemish, as being represented in this figure. Ini-Teshub would thus be represented twice on this seal: once as a divine adorant of the Storm-god and once as a heroic lion-hunter. This composition makes it quite clear that Ini-Teshub

27. The inscription alone claims: "seal of Ini-Teshub, king of Carcemish." In contrast, the first of Ini-Teshub's well-known seals has a longer inscription (see Beyer 2001: 47, A2a) in which he describes himself as the servant of Kubaba, the son of Shahurunuwa, the grandson of Sharri-Kushuh and great-grandson of the Hittite Great King Shuppiluliuma. This is the only seal on which a god is represented with a double axe and a club, who according to the caption is Sharruma.

Figure 11. Seal impression of Ini-Teshub, ca. 1230 (Schaeffer 1956: fig. 32; drawing reprinted courtesy of Mission archéologique des Ras Shamra–Ougarit).

feels himself to be subordinate not to the political protective power but to the highest god, the Storm-god. His own status is emphasized in the image by means of the pointed, horned hat and club, and by placing himself opposite the symbol of the highest ranking god, with whom he obviously compares himself.

As the use of this seal on a tablet found in Ugarit shows,[28] it is to be dated to a later period of Tuthaliya IV's reign and may be readily understood to be the last in a series of Ini-Teshub's royal seals. It demonstrates the means by which the viceroy of Carchemish employed iconography to project a supernatural image of himself, one that lent expression to his elevated claims to power, which on the one hand raised his image to the level of the Hittite Great Kings but on the other hand differentiated him from the deified self-representations used by the elite who surrounded him. The choice and assemblage of motifs on Ini-Teshub's seal were therefore deliberate, original, and exemplary of the Carchemish style. Only the religious aspects of the seal iconography remains within the tradition of Hittite royal art, an art that constantly used pictorial religious language.

The connection between the religious context and the political meaningfulness of the images will be demonstrated here with a final example, Tuthaliya's relief in Alalakh. The representation is found on a basalt orthostat, uncovered in the level I temple that was also used in a secondary context as a step between the lion sculptures (fig. 12). Woolley (1955: 241–42) dated the original presentation of the reliefs to level III of the temple; however, this is not possible on historical grounds, because level III bears all the hallmarks of Mitannian dominance over Alalakh (compare Heinz 2002: 164). Only with Shuppiluliuma I, at the end of level II (around 1340), can we be certain of a Hittite presence and therefore be able to explain the existence of Hittite monuments. The ruler, who is named Tuthaliya on the monument, must therefore be Tuthaliya IV (ca. 1240–1215). His relief was obviously erected in level IA and, after the destruction of the building by fire, was purloined along with other orthostats (Woolley 1955: 85) and used in the new building of level IB as a step in the temple entrance. In this way, the inhabitants of Alalakh toward the end of the twelfth century discharged their duty vis-à-vis a symbol of Hittite dominance.

28. RS 17.59; Schaeffer 1956: 28–29. The content of the tablet deals with the conflict between Tuthaliya and the strengthened Assyrian Empire in which Ugarit sought to remain neutral, but as compensation for which Ugarit had to pay the Hittite king a considerable amount of gold. Ini-Teshub was the intermediary in this transaction.

Figure 12. Orthostat from the temple in Alalakh representing a royal family and inscribed with the name Tuthaliya, ca. 1240–1215 (Woolley 1955: pl. 48a; photo reprinted courtesy of the Society of Antiquaries of London).

The form of the representation and the identity of the person depicted have drawn little attention so far. Woolley (1955: 241) saw there a Hittite king (Tuthaliya IV) followed by his spouse and an "attendant." The identitification of the person as Tuthaliya, however, appears to me to be problematic for various reasons. The figure is wrapped in a long cloak that is open at the front, revealing a short skirt. The headwear consists of a round cap with a single horn at the front. On the basis of all the images cited thus far, this is a divine attribute used in the representations of viceroys, princes, and high officials, but not the Hittite Great King. He dons either the pointed, horned cap or appears in the guise of the Sun-god with *lituus* in hand, as in Muwatalli's rock relief in Sirkeli (Bittel 1976: fig. 195) and an orthostat from Alaca Höyük (fig. 1). From an iconographic viewpoint, the main figure in the Alalakh relief cannot represent the Hittite Great King. Its gesture with raised fist with thumb forward is nevertheless identical with the gesture of the Hittite kings represented in the reliefs at Sirkeli and Alaca Höyük. The latter reveal the meaning of the gesture. It constitutes a form of greeting to the gods or divine symbols. In Alaca Höyük, for example, it is directed toward an altar, behind which stands a podium with a bull on it, the symbol of the Storm-god (fig. 1). In Alalakh, in contrast, the greeting gesture is directed toward the over-large hieroglyphs of the name Tuthaliya.[29] The Hittite king is thus

29. On the reading, see Güterbock in Woolley 1955: 241.

not presented pictorially but pictographically in the form of the hieroglyphs of his name. This interpretation makes sense, because it explains why the figure standing to the left of the hieroglyphs is not the Hittite king but a vassal who in reverential mode turns toward the name of his master. Behind his neck, a second hieroglyph caption was inscribed, of which only the title, "the king's son," can still be read. I do not hesitate to read this as the designation of a person from the family of the local regency and thus of the king of Alalakh, serving under Tuthaliya.[30] The woman who follows him is wearing a long, floor-length, closed gown similar to the gown worn by the woman following the king in the relief from Alaca Hüyük. Other details cannot be discerned; even the long object in her outstretched hand cannot be identified. Behind, worked onto the surface of the small side of the basalt block is the figure of a male, virtually identical to the main figure, only smaller.[31] In summary, we see here the family of the local regent of Alalakh bearing witness to their respect for Hittite sovereignty.

We know from the texts of the Emirgazi altars that a cult dedicated to Tuthaliya was introduced during his lifetime (Hawkins 1995: 86–102; 2006: 54–65). This cult also involved the erection of a stele to the Hittite king. Thus, one may assume that the Alalakh relief was also related to the concept of a political theology during the reign of Tuthaliya IV. It is one of the (no doubt forced) pictorial evocations of loyalty to the Hittite Great King made at a time when Alalakh was still under Hittite domination. The context in which this loyalty was expressed, on the other hand, is revealing. It took place within the context of a treatment that may be described as religious, given that the location was the temple in Alalakh. The protagonists are themselves designated with divine symbols. Their cultic treatment, however, did not address a godhead but the Hittite Great King, whose name alone suffices as an object of "supernatural power" worthy of devotion. The image shows that there is barely any discernible difference between the appearance of the transcendant divine and the appearance of a living ruler. The particular form by which religious imagery expresses Hittite power eliminates this difference.

Concluding Remarks

The late appearance in Hittite pictorial art of the representation of the ruler occurs within the context of a visual culture, which is almost without exception determined by religious motivation. The iconographic phenotype of the king integrates

30. Unfortunately, the absence of textual sources from Alalakh dating to level I at the end of the thirteenth century means that we are unable to reconstruct the history of the period or the names of the rulers. However, in the annex to the level IB temple, a white steatite bulla seal was found with the following hieroglyphic inscription: "Pa-lu-wa, son of the king, lord of the land" (Woolley 1955: 266, pl. 67, no. 155). Given that the object found was a seal and not a seal impression, it is probable that this Paluwa was resident in Alalakh and was likely regent there. It is thus also possible that he is represented on the relief.

31. This figure does not hold a spear in his outstretched hand as Woolley (1955: 141) writes. The straight line running from the elbow of his raised arm is instead the braid trim of a cloak of the same length as the cloak worn by the main figure.

itself seamlessly with this world of religious imagery because it bears the characteristics of the gods. His representation as a god or as godlike is not necessarily evidence of the supposed divine existence of the ruler, whether in this life or the next. It shows, rather, the supernatural powers with which he was believed to interact, either while alive or dead. It was precisely because of the possibilities afforded by the medium of an image in overcoming the physical boundaries of interaction and in presenting the ruler as one with the gods that the images could function as propaganda. Via this unity with the divine, the Hittite royal house was able to cultivate the notion of a world of rule for itself and its ancestors reaching out over time and space.

As an icon of universal power, the divine image of the ruler enjoyed an exclusive status and was first and foremost an instrument of political interest. As a religious representation, however, it remained part of a system that sought to derive its power from communion with the divine, and this consequently led to a very unique religious form of political representation. The Hittite image of rule embodied both political and religious aspects, taken together; it was a fiction of power that was neither historically typological nor explicable by reference to a canonical text but was unique to the historical moment.

Appendix

Approximately one hundred years after the fall of the Hittite Empire, a ruler called Taitas in Halab (Aleppo) reworked the Hittite tradition of propaganda through religious imagery. On a central relief on the eastern wall of the cella of the temple on the citadel at Aleppo, he is presented opposite the Storm-god of Aleppo with fist raised in greeting (Gonella, Khayyata, and Kohlmeyer 2005: figs. 124–26).[32] No sacrificial table or other object separates the two similarly sized figures. This opposition of god and ruler brings a far greater sense of unity to the composition, in which the boundaries between worldly and religious power have been comprehensively removed. In order to round off this unit, a procession of regional and interregional deities moves from the left hand side, along the north wall of the cella, toward the main image of the Storm-god and the king facing him (Gonella, Khayyata, and Kohlmeyer 2005: figs. 157, 159). It is as if at a time in history shaped by the struggle of Hittite successor states in north Syria to survive, the spatial and pictorial production in the temple at Aleppo is recording the emigration of supernatural powers charged with representing the interests of the state in a new area of rule.

32. On the dating and more detailed description of this and the other reliefs from the Aleppo temple, see Gonella, Khayyata, and Kohlmeyer 2005: 90–111.

References

Albanese, C. L.
1999 *America: Religions and Religion.* 3rd ed. Belmont, CA: Wadsworth.
Bahrani, Z.
2003 *The Graven Image: Representation in Babylonia and Assyria.* Philadelphia: University of Pennsylvania Press.
Beran, T.
1967 *Die Hethitische Glyptik von Boğazköy.* Wissenschaftliche Veröffentlichungen der Deutschen Orientgesellschaft 76. Berlin: Mann.
Beyer, D.
2001 *Emar IV: Les sceaux.* Orbis biblicus et orientalis: Series Archaeologica 20. Fribourg: Editions Universitaires / Göttingen: Vandenhoeck and Ruprecht.
Bittel, K.
1976 *Die Hethiter.* Munich: Beck.
Bittel, K., et al.
1975 *Das hethitische Felsheiligtum Yazilikaya.* Berlin: Mann.
Bonatz, D.
2002 Agens Bild: Handlungszusammenhänge altorientalischer Bildwerke. Pp. 53–70 in *Bild-Macht-Geschichte: Visuelle Kommunikation im Alten Orient,* ed. M. Heinz and D. Bonatz. Berlin: Reimer.
Börker-Klähn, J.
1982 *Altvorderasiatische Bildstelen und vergleichbare Felsreliefs.* Baghdader Forschungen 4. Mainz: von Zabern.
Bourdieu, P.
1994 Der Habitus als Vermittlung zwischen Struktur und Praxis. Pp. 125–58 in *Zur Soziologie der symbolischen Formen.* 5th ed. Frankfurt am Main: Suhrkamp.
Cancik-Kirschbaum, E.
1999 Religionsgeschichte oder Kulturgeschichte? Über das Verhältnis von Kunst und Religion im Alten Orient. Pp. 101–18 in *Kunst und Religion,* ed. R. Faber and V. Krech. Würzburg: Königshausen and Neumann.
Dinçol, A.
1998 The Rock Monument of the Great King Kurunta. Pp. 159–66 in *Acts of the IIIrd International Congress of Hittitology, Çorum, September 16–22, 1996.* Ankara.
2002 'Tabarna' und 'Ädikula'-Siegel: Die Siegel hethitischer Großkönige und Großköniginnen. Pp. 88–93 in *Die Hethiter und ihr Reich: Das Volk der 1000 Götter.* Catalog of an exhibition held in the Kunst- und Ausstellungshalle der Bundesrepublik Deutschland, Bonn. Stuttgart: Theiss.
Ehringhaus, H.
2005 *Götter, Herrscher, Inschriften: Die Felsreliefs der hethitischen Großreichszeit in der Türkei.* Mainz: von Zabern.
Emre, K.
2002 Felsreliefs, Stelen, Orthostaten: Großplastik als monumentale Form staatlicher und religiöser Repräsentation. Pp. 218–33 in *Die Hethiter und ihr Reich: Das Volk der 1000 Götter.* Catalog of an exhibition held in the Kunst- und Ausstellungshalle der Bundesrepublik Deutschland, Bonn. Stuttgart: Theiss.
Fauth, W.
1979 Sonnengottheit (^{d}UTU) und 'Königliche Sonne' (^{d}UTU^{ši}) bei den Hethitern. *Ugarit Forschungen* 11: 227–63.
Gonella, J.; Khayyata, W.; and Kohlmeyer, K.
2005 *Die Zitadelle von Aleppo und der Tempel des Wettergottes.* Münster: Rhema.

Gonnet, H.
1995 Le culte des ancêtres en Anatolie hittite au IIe mill. avant notre ère. *Anatolica* 21: 189–95.
Güterbock, H. G.
1965 A Votive Sword with Old Assyrian Inscription. Pp. 197–98 in *Studies in Honor of Benno Landsberger on His Seventy-Fifth Birthday*, ed. H. G. Güterbock. Assyriological Studies 16. Chicago: University of Chicago Press.
Haas, V.
1994 *Geschichte der hethitischen Religion*. Handbuch der Orientalistik 1/15. Leiden: Brill.
Hawkins, J. D.
1990 The New Inscription from the Südburg of Boğazköy-Ḫattuša. *Archäologischer Anzeiger* 1990: 305–14.
1995 *The Hieroglyphic Inscription of the Sacred Pool Complex at Hattusa (SÜDBURG)*. Studien zu den Boğazköy-Texten, Supplement 3. Wiesbaden: Harrassowitz.
1998 Tarkanaswa King of Mira: 'Tarkondemos', Boğazköy Sealings and Karabel. *Anatolian Studies* 48: 1–31.
2006 Tudḫaliya the Hunter. Pp 49–76 in *The Life and Times of Ḫattušili III and Tutḫaliya IV*, ed. T. P. J. van den Hout. Leiden: Nederlands Instituut voor het Nabije Oosten.
Heinz, M.
2002 *Altsyrien und Libanon: Geschichte, Wirtschaft und Kultur vom Neolithikum bis Nebukadnezar*. Darmstadt: Wissenschaftliche Buchgesellschaft.
Herbordt, S.
2005 *Die Prinzen und Beamtensiegel der hethitischen Grossreichszeit auf Tonbullen aus dem Nişantepe-Archiv in Hattusa*. Boğazköy-Hattuša Ergebnisse der Ausgrabungen 19. Mainz: von Zabern.
Hout, T. P. J. van den
1994 Death as a Privilege: The Hittite Royal Funerary Ritual. Pp. 37–75 in *Hidden Futures: Death and Immortality in Ancient Egypt, Anatolia, the Classical, Biblical and Arabic-Islamic World*, ed. J. M. Bremmer, T. P. J. van den Hout, and R. Peters. Amsterdam: Amsterdam University Press.
1995 Tuthaliya und die Ikonographie hethitischer Großkönige des 13. Jhs. *Bibliotheca Orientalis* 52: 545–73.
Klengel, H.
1992 *Syria, 3000 to 300 B.C.: A Handbook of Political History*. Berlin: Akademie.
Koçay, H. Z.
1973 *Alaca Höyük Kazisi*. Türk Tarih Kurumu Tarafindan Yayinlarindan 5/28. Ankara: Türk Tarih Kuruma Basımevi.
Kohlmeyer, K.
1983 *Felsbilder der hethitischen Großreichszeit*. Acta praehistorica et archaeologica 15. Berlin: Staatliche Museen zu Berlin.
Laroche, E.
1960 *Les Hiéroglyphes Hittites*. Première partie: L'écriture. Paris: Centre Nationale de la Recherche Scientifique.
Loon, M. N. van
1985 *Anatolia in the Second Millennium B.C.* Iconography of Religions 15/12. Leiden: Brill.
Macqueen, J. G.
1999 *The Hittites and Their Contemporaries in Asia Minor*. 2nd ed. London: Thames and Hudson.
Mayer-Opificius, R.
1993 Hethitische Kunstdenkmäler des 13. Jahrhunderts v. Chr. Pp. 357–63 in *Aspects of Art and Iconography: Anatolia and Its Neighbors, Studies in Honor of Nimet Özgüç*, ed. M. J. Mellink et al. Ankara: Türk Tarih Kuruma Basımevi.

Morgan, D.

2005 *The Sacred Gaze: Religious Visual Culture in Theory and Practice.* Berkeley: University of California Press.

Neve, P.

1987 Boğazköy-Hattuša: Ausgrabungen in der Oberstadt. *Anatolica* 14: 41–88.

1989 Einige Bemerkungen zur Kammer B in Yazilikaya. Pp. 345–55 in *Anatolia and the Ancient Near East: Studies in Honor of Tahsin Özgüç*, ed. K. Emre et al. Ankara: Türk Tarih Kuruma Basımevi.

1993 *Hattuša: Stadt der Götter und Tempel.* Mainz: von Zabern.

Otten, H.

1956 Ein Text zum Neujahrsfest aus Boğazköy. *Orientalistische Literaturzeitung* 51: 101–5.

1958 *Hethitische Totenrituale.* Berlin: Akademie.

1963 Neue Quellen zum Ausgang des hethitischen Reiches. *Mitteilungen der Deutschen Orientgesellschaft* 94: 1–23.

1988 *Die Bronzetafel aus Boğazköy.* Studien zu den Boğazköy-Texten, Supplement 1. Wiesbaden: Harrassowitz.

Saake, I.

2004 Theorie der Empirie: Zur Spiegelbildlichkeit der Bourdieuschen Theorie der Praxis und der Luhmannschen Systemtheorie. Pp. 85–117 in *Bourdieu und Luhmann*, ed. A. Nassehi and G. Nollmann. Frankfurt am Main: Suhrkamp.

Schaeffer, C. F.-A.

1956 *Ugaritica III: Sceaux et cylindres Hittites, épée gravée du cartouche de Mineptah, tablettes Chypro-Minoennes et autres découvertes nouvelles de Ras Shamra.* Mission archéologique de Ras Shamra 8. Paris: Geuthner.

Seeher J.

2002 Ein Blick in das Reichspantheon: Das Felsheiligtum von Yazilikaya. Pp. 112–17 in *Die Hethiter: Das Volk der 1000 Gotter.* Catalog of an exhibition held in the Kunst- und Ausstellungshalle der Bundesrepublik Deutschland, Bonn. Stuttgart: Theiss.

Winter, I. J.

1997 Art *in* Empire: The Royal Image and the Visual Dimensions of Assyrian Ideology. Pp. 359–81 in *Assyria 1995: Proceedings of the 10th Anniversary Symposium of the Neo-Assyrian Text Corpus Project*, ed. S. Parpola and R. M. Whiting. Helsinki: Neo-Assyrian Text Corpus Project.

2000 The Eyes Have It: Votive Statuary, Gilgamesh's Axe, and Cathected Viewing in the Ancient Near East. Pp. 22–44 in *Visuality before and beyond the Renaissance*, ed. R. S. Nelson. Cambridge: Cambridge University Press.

Woolley, L.

1955 *Alalakh: An Account of the Excavations at Tell Atchana in the Hatay, 1937–1949.* London: Oxford University Press.

Chapter 6

Nabonidus the Mad King: A Reconsideration of His Steles from Harran and Babylon

Paul-Alain Beaulieu

The legend of the madness of Nabonidus, Babylon's last king (556–539 B.C.), has haunted the literature and historiography of Babylonia, ancient Judaism, and the Western world for more than 25 centuries. The version of this legend most familiar to us is the fourth chapter of the book of Daniel, where the madness is reattributed to another king of Babylon, Nebuchadnezzar II (605–562 B.C.). Yet the number of ancient sources alluding to other versions of the story points to the existence of a once richer tradition, of which only scattered elements have survived. This makes the task of disentangling the web of legend that grew around the life and personality of Nabonidus fraught with difficulties. Even among our relatively small body of sources, one can recognize conflicting points of view. In cuneiform sources the theme of the king's eccentric behavior appears mainly in the Verse Account of Nabonidus (Schaudig 2001: 563–78). This text probably originates in the period shortly after the conquest of the Babylonian Empire by Cyrus in 539 B.C., although it is known only from a single later copy. The Verse Account harshly censures the deeds of the fallen king, depicting the capture of Babylon by Cyrus the Great as an act of liberation. It remains to this day one of the few truly polemical documents from ancient Mesopotamia. The Verse Account voices no direct claim that Nabonidus was insane. Of course, madness is a culturally bound notion, one that would be very difficult to define for an ancient society. Nevertheless, none of the few Akkadian words and expressions that might suggest madness occurs in the Verse Account to describe Nabonidus. The text presents itself as a criticism of policies more than personality–that is to say, the intimation of madness, if any, stems from the allegedly unusual nature of the decisions made by the king, not from a diagnosis of his mental state.

Other cuneiform sources offer negative accounts of the king. The Cyrus Cylinder depicts Cyrus as emancipator and severely condemns Nabonidus, yet makes no allusion to his madness (Schaudig 2001: 550–56). The same is true of the Dynastic Prophecy, a document stemming from the clerical environment of the Esagil temple in Babylon in the latter part of the fourth century B.C. (Grayson 1975b: 24–37). This is presumably the same milieu that had generated much hostility to the religious ideas of Nabonidus 200 years earlier, and not surprisingly the Prophecy contains an account of his reign that is almost entirely disapproving. Yet the motif of madness is also absent from it. Other sources are more neutral. The Babylonian Chronicle records year after year the king's absence from Babylon and his cancellation of the New Year's Festival yet expresses no specific outrage at this behavior (Grayson 1975a: 104–11). It also reports other events of his reign in typically dispassionate tone. Berossus in his Babyloniaca also refuses to embark on a wholesale condemnation of Nabonidus. While he presents him as a usurper, a fact that Nabonidus himself admitted openly, nothing else he reports in his succinct account of the king's reign can be construed as an element in the dark legend of a mad ruler (Verbrugghe and Wickersham 1996: 60–61). Thus, the memory of Nabonidus was not unanimously negative after all. This is perhaps how we should explain the fact that the two usurpers who arose in Babylon at the beginning of the reign of Darius I and took Nebuchadnezzar (III and IV) as throne names both claimed to be sons of Nabonidus (Streck 2001a). The transmission of the memory of Babylon's last king during the first two centuries after his downfall appears as a complex issue, with impartial chronographers, opponents, and possibly even supporters leaving traces of their narratives in the tradition. Still, however, one cannot find a source that raises the issue of Nabonidus's mental or physical health to explain his behavior.

The picture changes, however, as we move into the Hellenistic period and shift the focus of our attention to the Jewish tradition. The discovery of the Aramaic *Prayer of Nabonidus* among the Qumran manuscripts has provided the missing link proving that the figure of Nebuchadnezzar in the book of Daniel resulted from a conflation of two traditions, one about Nebuchadnezzar, the other about Nabonidus (Collins 1996). This had been suspected long before the discovery of the *Prayer*, for there are several clues as to the presence of a Nabonidus tradition in the book of Daniel. The most obvious one is the fact that Belshazzar, who was in reality the son of Nabonidus (Bēl-šar-uṣur), appears in the book as a son of Nebuchadnezzar. But the crucial aspect of the Daniel and Qumran traditions is the transformation of the king's legend of erratic rule into one of disease and insanity. The motif of Nebuchadnezzar's sudden madness in Daniel 4, of his beastly behavior and removal from human society, obviously finds its origin in Nabonidus's ten-year-long sojourn in the northern Arabian oasis of Teima. Here the *Prayer of Nabonidus* has proved crucial because it provides a bridge between the Jewish stories and their Babylonian sources. The *Prayer* claims that Nabonidus, afflicted with a grievous skin disease for seven years, was cured after praying to the god of the Jews. The rest is fragmentary but appears to reproduce an encyclical letter, written by the king at the behest of a Jewish diviner, acknowledging the superiority of the Most High God over Babylonian idols.

Some have noted the analogy between these claims of a skin disease that forced the king into isolation and a standard curse formula found in cuneiform sources of the second and first millennium calling for the moon-god Sîn to inflict on the transgressor the skin disease *saḫaršubbû* and send him roaming the arid steppe like a wild ass (Watanabe 1984; Grelot 1994). As recently pointed out by Cavigneaux (2005), a cuneiform chronicle from Uruk dated to the Hellenistic period associates a similar curse with Šulgi, the second and most successful ruler of the Third Dynasty of Ur. In this chronicle, Šulgi is accused of desecrating the cult of Marduk and favoring Ur, the city of the moon-god Sîn and historically the capital of Šulgi's kingdom. As punishment, he is afflicted with a skin disease that covers his body. The chronicle belongs to an apocryphal tradition that attributed to Šulgi various sacrileges against the cult of Marduk. There is little doubt that this tradition was eventually conflated with elements of the legend of Nabonidus, who was also guilty of neglecting the cult of Marduk in favor of the moon-god Sîn of Ur and Harran. The entire story was probably picked up by Babylonian Jews, who reformulated it, associating mental illness with skin disease, and the forced quarantine in the desert imposed on the king with his withdrawal to the oasis of Teima. All this eventually found its way into the Qumran corpus and the book of Daniel. The legend of the mad king of Babylon had reached maturity. Of course, one can argue that these motifs already circulated during the lifetime of Nabonidus to resurface in writing only later due to accidents of preservation. This may well be the case. Nevertheless, considering the fairly large corpus of sources dating from the Neo-Babylonian, Achaemenid, and Hellenistic periods, it seems more reasonable to assume that the legend of the madness of Nabonidus crystallized at a later date, outgrowing a dominant strain in the cuneiform tradition that remembered him as unorthodox and misguided, though not necessarily as insane.

If Nabonidus's madness was a secondary motif, should we still believe the more mundane claims of malfeasance and impiety voiced in the Verse Account? While this text is a piece of propaganda, it is remarkable that sources dated to the reign of Nabonidus often corroborate its claims. For instance, it decries Nabonidus for his pretensions to literacy, knowledge, and wisdom, and indeed one can find claims of this sort in the building inscriptions of the king and other writings commissioned by him. Similarly, it accuses Nabonidus of various crimes of impiety, asserting that he made a horrifying new image of the moon-god of Harran and even tried to convince the clerics of the Esagil temple in Babylon that their sanctuary belonged to the moon-god Sîn because of its symbol in the shape of a lunar crescent. These accusations do not seem so excessive in the light of the king's own inscriptions, which provide direct evidence for the making of a new statue of Sîn for Harran, for the notion that the Esagil temple belonged to the moon-god, and even for the association of the lunar crescent with the city of Babylon. The list could go on. The real question is: to what extent did any of the claims made by Nabonidus and denounced in the Verse Account reflect actions that were illegitimate for a king? Previous Mesopotamian kings boasted of literacy, knowledge, and wisdom. In the previous century, Ashurbanipal had laid the very same claims. Even Nabonidus's attempts to syncretize Marduk with the moon-god Sîn and prove the latter's superiority plunge their roots very deep in the history of Mesopotamian thought. They also stand in remarkable continuity with some religious developments of the late Assyrian period. Lewy (1948) demonstrated long ago that the rise of the moon-god Sîn of Harran began in the late Assyrian period and was particularly favored by the monarchs of the Sargonid dynasty, in particular Esarhaddon and Ashurbanipal. Recently Schaudig (2002) has discussed additional evidence for this process. Official texts of seventh-century Assyria promote the syncretism between the gods Aššur and Sîn, and even in Babylonia the inscriptions of Sîn-balāssu-iqbi, who was governor of Ur during the early years of the reign of Ashurbanipal, raise Sîn to the position of supreme leader of the gods, equating him with the god Enlil.

The Verse Account even extends its wholesale condemnation of Nabonidus to his military conquests and alleged oppression of subjected peoples. One can hardly think of another case where adding new conquests became ground for criticism of a Mesopotamian ruler by his own constituency. Is the Verse Account, by satirically mirroring the king's own claims, not simply trying to delegitimize actions that in other contexts would seem perfectly acceptable? It seems essential to take a fresh approach to the question and consider the inscriptions of Nabonidus from another angle. How did Nabonidus choose to represent his own power? In the context of what type of legitimacy did he strive to convey his religious ideas and political designs to his subjects? In considering these questions, I will concentrate mostly on inscriptions that were intended to be in public view and conveyed an image of his regal power that was likely to reach a wider audience. Among these inscriptions, the Harran Stele (Schaudig 2001: 486–99) and the Babylon Stele (Schaudig 2001: 530–32, as Tarif-Stele) stand out as the most important monuments.

The Neo-Babylonian Figure of the Ideal King

Royal inscriptions were most likely composed by scribes in the central administration. We can assume that scribes always worked under close royal supervision, but the degree of involvement on the part of the sovereign must have varied considerably. Nabonidus, who claimed to know the art of writing, probably exercised even tighter control of the official scriptorium. We know almost nothing about the process of composing and editing royal inscriptions other than what we can infer from the texts themselves. However, some interesting evidence has recently been adduced by Gesche (2000) in her doctoral dissertation on the late Babylonian school curriculum. She has demonstrated that, after a basic introduction to cuneiform (*Elementarunterricht*), the curriculum was broadly divided into two branches: the first level of training (*Erste Schulstufe*) and the second level (*Zweite Schulstufe).* In the first level, students copied a basic canonical corpus of syllabaries, vocabularies, and lexical lists (Syllabary S^a, Vocabularies S^{b}A and S^{b}B, Ḫar-ra = *ḫubullu* I–III and the Weidner god list) and a corpus of noncanonical lists devised in the late periods specifically for student training (a list of male and female personal names, acrographic lists of verbal paradigms, LÚ lists, list ummia = *ummânu*, basic arithmetical and metrological lists, lists of month names, lists of geographical names, and excerpts from administrative and legal texts). At this level of education, few literary texts were copied except proverbs and a group of five compositions that all portrayed the king as protagonist. These included the Weidner Chronicle (Al-Rawi 1990), the Letter of Samsuiluna to Enlil-nādin-šumi (Al-Rawi and George 1994), the Standard Babylonian Recension of the Cuthean Legend of Narām-Sîn (Westenholz 1997: 294–368), the Birth Legend of Sargon (Westenholz 1997: 36–49), and the Standard Babylonian *Epic of Gilgamesh* (George 2003: 379–741). Miscellaneous excerpts from historical inscriptions completed this corpus. The prominence of the royal ideology in texts studied in the first level of the schools has led Gesche to postulate that most students who completed it were initially destined to pursue careers in the royal administration. Students who graduated into the second level of training, on the other hand, probably planned to embrace one of the higher intellectual disciplines of the scribal craft. This stage included advanced study of the lexical corpus and texts that belonged to the *āšipūtu*. Texts propagating the mystique of the monarchy were largely absent from this curriculum. These students probably continued their training in the temple or under the supervision of senior exorcists (*āšipu*), lamentation singers (*kalû*), or diviners (*bārû*), who were often members of their extended families.

Scribes in the royal administration who composed official inscriptions must have found inspiration in the texts they studied in school, in particular the works of literature that centered on the figure of the king. The most conspicuous case of this sort of influence is the Cuthean Legend, which bears striking affinities to the inscriptions of Nabopolassar recording his expulsion of the Assyrians from Babylonia. The figure of Narām-Sîn, who enjoins future kings to avoid war, remain passive, and trust in the providential guidance of the gods, provided an illustrious model for Nabopolassar who, in a similar address, presents himself as a contemplative ruler who remained faithful to the gods Marduk and Nabû in times of adversity and requited brutality with kindness (Beaulieu 2003). One can also point to an interesting parallel between the Weidner Chronicle and the Istanbul Stele of Nabonidus (Schaudig 2001: 514–29, as Babylon-Stele). We now know that the chronographic portions of the Weidner Chronicle belong to an apocryphal letter of Damiq-ilišu, king of Isin, to another ruler who is probably Apil-Sîn, king of Babylon. Damiq-ilišu relates to his correspondent his experience of an incubation dream, in which the goddess of Isin, Ninkarrak (= Ninisinna = Gula), revealed to him that the gods Ea and Marduk would raise Babylon to the status of cosmological and political capital. This bears an intriguing resemblance to a passage of the Istanbul Stele in which Nabonidus seeks a confirmation of his rule from the goddess Nintinugga (= Gula) during an incubation dream. After a favorable omen from the goddess, Nabonidus proceeds to be confirmed king in the temple E-niggidrikalamma-summu. There he receives the scepter from Nabû and beholds the seat of his wife Tašmētu, who is equated with Gula in the inscription. Then Nabonidus seeks approval of his rule from Marduk and bestows gifts on Ea and other gods of Babylon. One could argue that the resemblance with the Weidner Chronicle is coincidental. However, these are the only two reports of actual incubation dreams involving the goddess Gula in the entire cuneiform record, and they both involve legitimation of kingship and the recognition of Babylon as political center and Marduk as its main god (Butler 1998: 233–35).

It is also significant that, of the five educational compositions that centered on the figure of the king, no fewer than four belong to the genre of *narû* literature. *Narû* compositions were fictional accounts of the deeds of famous kings allegedly inscribed on steles (*narûs*) to instruct present and future generations. The Cuthean Legend of Narām-Sîn is the archetypal *narû* composition. The text of the Legend was purportedly copied from a genuine stele onto a tablet, and the opening lines of the composition even invite the reader to open the tablet-box that contains the copy and read from it. The same motif appears in the *Epic of Gilgamesh* (Westenholz 1997: 300). The *Epic* claims that Gilgamesh inscribed all his travails on a stele. The text of this stele, which is identical with the text of the *Epic*, was allegedly copied on tablets and buried under the walls of Uruk as a foundation deposit to be retrieved by future generations. Hardly could the analogy with building inscriptions have been conveyed in more elegant fashion. The Birth Legend of Sargon also belongs to the same genre, even though the word *narû* does not appear in the preserved portions of the text. Finally, the Letter of Samsuiluna specifies that its content must be inscribed on a stele, this being indicated by the formula *umma ana narê* ('thus for the stele'). Of the five compositions outlined above, only the Weidner Chronicle lacks an explicit connection to *narû* literature. However, it displays another fundamental feature shared by all five compositions. All of them portray kings addressing other kings, officials, or a larger audience of their subjects, always with the purpose of giving instructions for proper guidance and government. In this sense, *Gilgamesh* also belongs to this category, because *Gilgamesh* addresses not only his contemporaries but also future generations, kings, and commoners alike. Finally, and this is probably the most important thread that unites our five compositions, it is noteworthy that they present a consistent and distinctive image of the monarchy. They depict the king always in the same role; not as conqueror, administrator, or provider of social justice but as religious leader and teacher of wisdom. This, no doubt, corresponded to the ideal figure of the king promoted by official circles in the time of the Babylonian Empire.

This last point is important to understand the ancient polemic around the figure of Nabonidus, because professing to be a religious leader and teacher of wisdom is precisely the main charge brought against him in the Verse Account and is also the guise under which Nabonidus chose to present himself to his subjects. The evidence obtained from Gesche's reconstruction of the school curriculum shows that the claims laid by Nabonidus, far from embodying the fantasies of an eccentric, stemmed from the mainstream tradition of cuneiform learning. The possibility that Nabonidus was a court official before his accession to the throne should also be considered, because his status as royal functionary would have made him familiar with the corpus studied in the first level of scribal training, in which all the texts propagating the royal ideology were studied (Beaulieu 1989: 79). This particular construct of the role of the monarchy would have been deeply imbedded in his consciousness long before his elevation to kingship. We must therefore conclude that on this particular issue the Verse Account attempts to delegitimize acts that belonged to the realm of royal prerogatives. As far as representations of his own power and role as king are concerned, Nabonidus was acting within the recognized and legitimate parameters of late Babylonian civilization.

The Letter of Samsuiluna as Model for the Harran Stele

The Letter of Samsuiluna presents an interesting example of the sources of Nabonidus's self-representation as king. This text reproduces a letter allegedly sent by the Old Babylonian king Samsuiluna to a certain Enlil-nādin-šumi, governor of the land (*šākin ṭēm māti*). Enlil-nādin-šumi is ordered to inscribe on a stele the text of a royal proclamation chastising temple administrators and the priesthood of the cult centers of Akkad for lying, committing abominations, desecrating the rites of their gods, and altering divine commands. The proclamation then reviews the correct state of affairs mandated by Marduk in primeval times and extends an invitation to the sinful priests to acknowledge the contents of the stele and speak to Samsuiluna, presumably as an indication of their repentance and willingness to learn the correct ways. Al-Rawi and George propose to seek the historical setting of this text in the time of Nebuchadnezzar I (1125–1104 B.C.). This is supported by the occurrence in it of the formula *umma ana narê*, which is also found in a historical-literary text relating to Nebuchadnezzar I's campaign against Elam, the Letter of Nebuchadnezzar I to the Babylonians (Frame 1995: 21–23). They also argue that the religious reforms that crystallized during his reign and resulted in the consecration of Marduk as king of the gods and the displacement of Enlil must have provoked widespread anger among the traditional priesthood of cities such as Nippur and Uruk. The composer of the text would have served the royal purpose in asserting the duty of the priests to submit to the authority of the king in these matters. Why was Samsuiluna chosen to illustrate this point? The question is impossible to answer. We know that some religious upheavals occurred during his reign, notably in the wake of the abandonment of southern cities and the migration of their cults to northern Babylonia (Charpin 2004: 342–46). But this in no way suffices to explain the origin of the letter. Its apocryphal nature seems, at any rate, quite obvious. However, an inscription of king Ipiq-Eštar of Malgium demonstrates that the ideology propagated by the letter was already in existence during the Old Babylonian period. In this inscription, Ipiq-Ištar accuses the people of his country (*mātum in napḫari kalûšu*) of having committed a sacrilege by destroying the temple and cult of the goddess Bēlet-ilī and then proceeds to restore them in their original form (Frayne 1990: 669–70). The inscription does not specifically charge temple officials and the priesthood with the crime, yet the substance of the message is quite similar to the Letter of Samsuiluna. It also proclaims that the duty of the king is to safeguard ritual prescriptions in his realm and restore them when his own subjects rebel and commit sacrileges.

The Letter of Samsuiluna instructs the recipient to record the accusation of sacrilege on a stele (*umma ana narê*). Similar accusations leveled by a Babylonian king at his subjects are otherwise attested only in two inscriptions of Nabonidus, and significantly these two inscriptions also happen to be recorded on Steles. The first accusation occurs in the Istanbul Stele. There, Nabonidus blames the people of Uruk for having removed the image of Ištar from the Eanna temple during the reign of Eriba-Marduk in the eighth century and replacing it with an improper representation of the goddess. The stele then recalls the return of the proper image to Uruk, which we know to have taken place under Nebuchadnezzar II, who was probably mentioned in the break at the beginning of column III. Two later sources from Uruk, the Uruk Prophecy and the Crimes and Sacrileges of Nabû-šuma-iškun, ascribe the very same misdeeds to this eighth-century king, thus indirectly exonerating the inhabitants of Uruk (Beaulieu 2001). The second accusation appears in the Harran Stele. This inscription certainly dates to the period after the return of the king from his sojourn in Teima and commemorates the rebuilding of the Eḫulḫul temple in Harran. The opening segment of the inscription recalls how intimately the order to rebuild Eḫulḫul was tied to Nabonidus's call to kingship by the patron deity of the temple, the moon-god Sîn. Yet, after reporting that the moon-god had sent him a dream ordering the rebuilding of his sanctuary, Nabonidus goes on, accusing the inhabitants of the cities of Babylonia of rebellion, sacrilege, sinful behavior, and, above all, of disregarding the great godhead of Sîn and forgetting the proper rituals of their cult places. This, claims Nabonidus, forced him into exile. Only after a ten-year-long sojourn in Arabia did the propitious time arrive for returning to Babylonia and rebuilding the Eḫulḫul, thus fulfilling the divine command. It may be instructive here to compare the Letter of Samsuiluna with the Harran Stele.

Letter of Samsuiluna

1. *a-na* ^{Id}*en-líl-na-din*-MU ^{lú}GAR-UŠ$_4$ KUR [o o] ⸢x x⸣ [o]-⸢x⸣-*bit-tu*$_4$
2. *a-pil su-ú-nu ru-bu-tu* ^{lú}GÌR.NÍTA ⸢x⸣ [*ma-ḫa-zi*? *a*]*k-ka-di-i*
3. *ma-la ba-šu-ú qí-bi-ma um-ma* [^{I}*sa-am-su-i-lu-n*]*a* LUGAL *kiš-šat* [o o o]-⸢x-*ma*!⸣
4. *um-ma a-na na-re-e gi-mir ma-ḫa-*⸢*zi* KUR URI⸣[^{ki} *šá*?]
5. *ul-tu ṣi-it* ^{d}UTU-*ši a-di e-reb* ^{d}UTU-*ši* [o]
6. *nap-ḫar-šú-nu a-na* ŠU.MIN-*ka uš-tag-m*[*i*?-*ru*?]
7. *áš-me-e-ma* ^{lú}KU$_4$-É! *ki-na-al-tu* $^{lú!}$NU.ÈŠ ^{lú}*pa-ši-š*[*i*? o]
8. *ù* ^{lú}DINGIR.GUB.BA.MEŠ *šá ma-ḫa-zu* KUR URI^{ki} *ma-la* ⸢GAL⸣-[*ú*?]
9. *sar*!?-*ra-a-tu*$_4$ *i-ta*!-*ḫaz an-zil*!-*lu*$_4$ *ik-tab-su da-me il-*⸢*tap-tu*⸣
10. *la šal-ma-a-tu*$_4$ *i-ta*!-*mu-ú šap-la-nu* DINGIR.MEŠ-*šú-nu ú-ḫa-an-na-pu*!?
11. *ú-šá-an-na*!-*pu i-ṣab-bu-ru i-sur*!-*ru a-mat* DINGIR.MEŠ-*šú-nu la iq-bu-ú*
12. *a-na* UGU DINGIR.MEŠ-*šú-nu šak-nu*

To Enlil-nādin-šumi, governor of the land, x x x x x x x, son of the loins of princeship, superintendent of all [the cult centers of A]kkad, speak, thus [Samsuilun]a, king of the world, [o o o o] x, thus for the stele: "(Concerning) all the cult centers of the land of Akkad, all of those from east to west [which] I have given entirely into your control, I have heard (reports) that the temple officials, the collegium, the *nešakku*-priests, the *pašīšu*-priests, and the *dingirgubbû*-priests of the cult centers of the land of Akkad, as many as there are, have taken to falsehood, committed an abomination, been stained with blood, spoken untruths. Inwardly they profane and desecrate their gods, they prattle and cavort about. Things that their gods did not command they establish for their gods."

Harran Stele

1. *i-piš-ti* ^{d}30 GAL-*ti šá* DINGIR.MEŠ *ù* ^{d}*iš-tar*
2. *ma-am-ma-an* NU ZU-*šú šá ul-tu u*$_4$-*mu ru-qu-tu*
3. *a-na* KUR *la tu-ri-du u* UN.MEŠ KUR ⟨*la*⟩ *ip-pal-su-ma*
4. *ina ṭup-pi la iš-ṭu-ru-ma la iš-tak-ka-nu*
5. *a-na u*$_4$-*mu ṣa-a-ti* ^{d}30 EN DINGIR.MEŠ *u* ^{d}INNIN *a-ši-bu-tú*
6. *šá* AN-*e šá ina pa-ni* ^{Id}PA-NÍ.TUK LUGAL TIN.TIR^{ki}
7. *ul-tu* AN-*e tal-li-ku a-na-ku* ^{Id}PA-I

8. DUMU *e-du šá mam-ma-an la i-šu-ú šá* LUGAL-*u-tú*
9. *ina lìb-bi-ia la tab-šu-ú* DINGIR.MEŠ *u* ^{d}INNIN *a-na* UGU-
10. -[*i*]*a ú-ṣal-lu-ú ù* ^{d}30 *ana* LUGAL-*ú-ti*
11. [*i*]*m-ba-an-ni ina šá-at mu-ši* MÁŠ.GE$_{6}$ *ú-šab-ra-an*
12. *um-ma* É.ḪÚL.ḪÚL É ^{d}30 *šá* ^{uru}KASKAL *ḫa-an-ṭiš*
13. *e-pu-uš* KUR.KUR.MEŠ *ka-la-ši-na a-na* ŠU.MIN-*ka*
14. *lu-mál-la* UN.MEŠ DUMU.MEŠ TIN.TIR^{KI} BÁR.SIP^{ki}
15. EN.LÍL^{KI} ŠEŠ.UNUG^{KI} UNUG^{KI} UD.UNUG^{KI} ^{LÚ}SANGA.MEŠ
16. UN.MEŠ *ma-ḫa-zi* KUR URI^{ki} *a-na* DINGIR-*ú-ti-šu*
17. GAL-*ti iḫ-ṭu-ʾi-i-ma i-še-ti u ú-gal-li-lu*
18. *la i-du-u e-ze-ez-su* ⟨GAL-*tú*⟩ *šá* LUGAL DINGIR.MEŠ ^{d}NANNA-*ri*
19. *par-ṣi-šú-nu im-šu-ʾi-i-ma i-dab-bu-bu sur-ra-a-tú*
20. *u la ki-na-a-tú ki-ma* UR.GI$_{7}$ *it-ta-nak-ka-lu*
21. *a-ḫa-miš di-ʾu u* SU.GU$_{7}$-*ú ina* ŠÀ-*bi-šú-nu*
22. *ú-šab-šu-ú ú-ṣa-aḫ-ḫi-ir* UN.MEŠ KUR

The great deed of Sîn, which nobody among the gods and goddesses knew, which since distant days had not come down to the land, and (which) the people had ⟨not⟩ seen and not recorded on tablets for eternity, (that) you Sîn, lord of the gods and goddesses residing in heaven, have come down from heaven in the time of Nabonidus, (and) I, Nabonidus, the only son who has nobody, in whose hearth was no (thought of) kingship, the gods and goddesses prayed on my behalf to Sîn and he called me to kingship. He revealed to me in a night dream (what follows): "Build quickly Eḫulḫul, the temple of Sîn in Harran, and I will deliver all lands into your hands." (But) the people, the citizens of Babylon, Borsippa, Nippur, Ur, Uruk, (and) Larsa, the temple administrators (and) the people of the cult centers of the land of Akkad, offended his (Sîn's) great godhead and they misbehaved and sinned, (for) they did not know the great wrath of the king of the gods, Nannar. They forgot their rites and would speak slanders and lies, devouring each other like dogs. (Thus) pestilence and famine appeared among them,[1] and he (the moon-god) reduced the people of the land.

The two texts formulate in a similar way the failure of the inhabitants of Babylonia to carry on the old rites of their cult centers. Given the extreme rarity of these accusations, it seems likely that the motif was borrowed from the Letter of Samsuiluna into the Harran Stele, thus providing one more example of the influence of the school curriculum on official inscriptions. However, the Harran Stele contains one additional motif that is not present in the letter, the motif of divine abandonment. The preamble of the stele declares in cryptic terms that Sîn, after a long absence, finally came down from heaven to the land in the reign of Nabonidus. The funerary stele of Adad-guppi, the mother of Nabonidus, which was also found at Harran, provides a precise chronology for the duration of the god's absence (Schaudig 2001: 500–513).

1. I understand the verb *ušabšû* to be an impersonal 3rd-person plural, and the subject of *uṣaḫḫir* to be the moon-god Sîn.

The inscription states that in the 16th year of Nabopolassar (610–609 B.C.) Sîn became angry with his city and temple and went up to heaven. As a result, the people of Harran and their city turned into ruins.

Funerary Stele of Adad-guppi

1. *a-na-ku* ^{fd}IM-*gu-up-pi-i*ʾ AMA
2. ^{Id}*na-bi-um-na-*ʾ*i-id* LUGAL TIN.TIR^{ki}
3. *pa-li-iḫ-tu* ^{d}30 ^{d}NIN.GAL ^{d}NUSKU
4. *ù* ^{d}*sa-dàr-nun-na* DINGIR.MEŠ-*e-a*
5. *šá ul-tu mé-eṣ-ḫe-ru-ti-ia áš-te-*ʾ*u-u*
6. DINGIR-*ú-ut-su-un šá ina* MU 16-KAM ^{Id}PA-A-ÙRI
7. LUGAL TIN.TIR^{ki} ^{d}30 LUGAL DINGIR.MEŠ *it-ti* URU-*šu*
8. *ù* É-*šú iz-nu-ú i-lu-ú šá-ma-míš* URU *ù*
9. UN.MEŠ *šá ina* ŠÀ-*bi-šú il-li-ku*! *kar*!-*mu-ti*
10. *ina* ŠÀ-*bi šá aš-ra-a-tú* ^{d}30 ^{d}NIN.GAL ^{d}NUSKU
11. *u* ^{d}*sa-dàr-nun-na áš-te-*ʾ*u-u pal-ḫa-ku* DINGIR-*ut-su-un*
12. *šá* ^{d}30 LUGAL DINGIR TÚG.SÍG-*šú aṣ-bat-ma mu-ši u ur-ra*
13. *áš-te-né-*ʾ*a-a* DINGIR-*ut-su* GAL-*ti*

> I am Adad-guppi, mother of Nabonidus, king of Babylon, worshiper of Sîn, Ningal, Nusku and Sadarnunna, my gods whose divinity I have sought since my childhood. Because in the 16th year of Nabopolassar, king of Babylon, Sîn, the king of the gods, became angry with his city and temple and went up to heaven, the city and the people inside it became ruins. On account of the fact that I had (always) sought the sanctuaries of Sîn, Ningal, Nusku and Sadarnunna, worshiping their great divinity, I took hold of the hem of the garment of Sîn, king of the gods, and day and night I besought his great divinity.

The Harran Stele does not openly state that the sinful behavior of the people resulted from the absence of Sîn from his sanctuary of Harran, yet the two motifs are juxtaposed in a manner that suggests a causal relation between the two facts. The Stele of Adad-guppi contains no accusation of sacrilege, yet it clearly attributes the derelict state of Harran and its inhabitants to the absence of the god Sîn. The two monuments espouse a doctrine that views divine abandonment as the direct cause of the devolution of a human community from a blessed state to one of sinfulness and decrepitude. This doctrine was not new. It is already formulated in Seed of Kingship, a historical-literary text concerning the reign of Nebuchadnezzar I (Frame 1995: 23–28). After a long introduction celebrating the mystical ancestry of Nebuchadnezzar, the text states that in the reign of a former king Marduk became angry and full of wrath, ordering that the land be abandoned by its gods. As a consequence, the people lost their minds, becoming treacherous and godless. Demons filled the land and even entered the cult centers, and in the end the population diminished, presumably because of diseases. Finally the Elamites came in and plundered the land, carrying off its gods.

Seed of Kingship is one of several texts that celebrate Nebuchadnezzar's victory over Elam and his return of the statue of Marduk to Babylon. These texts all explain these events in light of the theology of divine abandonment. The Letter of Nebuchadnezzar I to the Babylonians, which contains a message allegedly sent by Nebuchadnezzar to the people of Babylon during his campaign against Elam, belongs to this group. Al-Rawi and George pointed out that the Letter of Nebuchadnezzar and the Letter of Samsuiluna display the same general structure, beginning with an address of the king followed by the substance of his message to be inscribed on a stele, the message proper being introduced by the formula *umma ana narê*. The Letter of Nebuchadnezzar describes how Marduk finally relented from his anger at all the cult centers and commissioned Nebuchadnezzar to declare war on Elam and bring back his statue to the Esagil temple. Here also we find suggestive resemblances with the Harran Stele. The medium for the two texts is a stele (*narû*). They share the motif of the return of the absent deity to its city, Marduk to Babylon in the time of Nebuchadnezzar I, and Sîn to Harran in the time of Nabonidus. Finally, in both cases the king must leave his country for some time and lead a military campaign in order to return the god to his abode. It seems as if the king must undergo the same ordeal of absence and exile experienced by the god, to earn the privilege of taking his hand and restoring him to his sanctuary.

To sum up, the dramatic regression of a human community into sin appears in two different contexts. In Seed of Kingship, the devolution is caused solely by divine abandonment. In the Letter of Samsuiluna, the cause is not stated; it merely provides ground for the reigning king to lecture his subjects and pose as supreme leader in religious matters. The Harran Stele combines the two motifs. The passage describing the disobedience and sinfulness of the people does not appear immediately after the statement that Sîn had been absent from the land a long time. Between these two statements is inserted the report on the dream sent by the god Sîn to Nabonidus, in which he promises to deliver all the countries into his hands and orders him to rebuild his temple. Yet, in spite of this propitious omen of divine return and reconciliation, which no doubt was widely publicized by the king, his subjects broke out in rebellion and disregarded their rites. There is a very distinct reason why the two motifs were joined in the Harran Stele. The god who is about to return to the Eḫulḫul temple is not the same as the one who left it when Harran was sacked by the Medes in 609 B.C. It is, in a sense, a new deity, and this, I believe, explains the cryptic formulation of the preamble of the Harran Stele. An aura of mystery must surround the epiphany of the deity whose wondrous deeds had never come down to the land and never been recorded for posterity. To be sure, the deity about to take up residence in the restored Eḫulḫul is a deity with the same name as the old one but with a different theology and a different appearance. For the new deity to be accepted, Nabonidus must emphasize his role as religious leader, as teacher of rituals and cultic prescriptions. Therefore, the sacrilegious behavior of his subjects must not only be attributed to the long absence of Sîn from his temple, which in itself would be a sufficient cause, but also, and especially, to their inherent shortcomings in religious matters, especially when it comes to the god Nannar (Sîn), and this is perhaps why the stele specifies that the people "did not know the great wrath of the king of the gods, Nannar." The land will return to a harmonious state only when the people learn the proper rituals and behavior from their king and when the new representation of the god Sîn that has been revealed to him comes down from heaven and takes up residence in the Ehulhul temple. Nabonidus relied on a solid tradition to make these claims, a tradition that was still very alive in Babylonia. The Letter of Samsuiluna belonged to the school curriculum, and such texts as the Letter of Nebuchadnezzar and Seed of Kingship are known from Neo-Babylonian manuscripts and were therefore in circulation in the time of Nabonidus.

The Theology of the Moon

One dissonance must be emphasized, however. All these texts from the stream of cuneiform tradition propagate a vision of Babylon as a cosmological and political capital, with Marduk at the core and the king as his representative and alter ego. The theology of Nabonidus, centered on Harran and the moon-god Sîn, seems at odds with these principles. Because our effort to understand Nabonidus's theology depends largely on the Harran Stele, it is essential to investigate the details of this monument in greater depth. One important feature of the Harran Stele that has not been satisfactorily commented upon is the iconography of the relief on its rounded top. There we see Nabonidus carrying a long staff and paying heed to the symbols of the moon (Sîn), the sun (Šamaš), and Venus (Ištar). The staff is surmounted with the wedge-shaped symbol of the god Nabû representing the stylus of the scribe, the *qāntuppu* (Gadd 1958: 40). The presence of Nabû's symbol on the staff was motivated by the fact that the investiture of the king in that period took place in the Temple of Nabû in Babylon, where the new monarch received the scepter. This scepter is certainly the long staff carried by Nabonidus on the relief of the Harran Stele. The ceremonial name of the Temple of Nabû in Babylon was E-niggidri-kalamma-summu 'House that bestows the scepter of the land' (George 1993: no. 878) and, as mentioned earlier, Nabonidus reports on his enthronement there in the Istanbul Stele.

The full significance of this relief emerges only as we compare the Harran Stele with the Babylon Stele, its counterpart from Babylon. This monument was discovered early in the nineteenth century and is now in the British Museum (BM 90837). The portion of the inscription that is still preserved does not duplicate the Harran Stele. However, the occurrence in it of the phrase *ipišti Sîn ippalsū* 'they (the people of Akkad) saw the deed of Sîn' is an obvious reflex of the opening lines of the Harran Stele. It seems therefore that the Babylon Stele was a local adaptation of the Harran Stele. A stele with an almost identical inscription to that of the Harran Stele was also found at Larsa (Schaudig 2001: 532–34), and additional fragments of steles that might be ascribed to Nabonidus and represent additional local versions of the Harran Stele were discovered in Uruk and Babylon (Schaudig 2001: 535–43).

The relief on top of the Babylon Stele is nearly identical with the one found on the Harran Stele but with one notable exception. The staff carried by Nabonidus on the Babylon Stele is not surmounted with the symbol of Nabû but with the lunar crescent of the god Sîn, the *uskaru* (Gadd 1958: 41). One would normally expect the symbol of Nabû to appear in Babylon and the symbol of Sîn to be displayed at Harran. Obviously, the swapping of symbols carried a specific intent. The closest parallel I can think of is the swapping of names between the walls of Babylon and Nippur in the wake of the consolidation of the Marduk theology under the Second Dynasty of Isin. At that time, the inner and outer walls of Babylon, the city of Marduk, came to be known as Imgur-Enlil and Nēmetti-Enlil, and the inner and outer walls of Nippur, the city of Enlil, as Imgur-Marduk and Nēmetti-Marduk (George 1992: 344–51). This was a means of proclaiming the identity of Marduk and Enlil and, by the same token, that of Babylon and Nippur. However, the swapping of symbols on the Harran and Babylon Steles lacked this perfect symmetry. Indeed, although Sîn was the main god of Harran, Nabû was not the main god of Babylon. Theological arguments could be invoked to propel Nabû to that position, yet the tradition unanimously ascribed the role of chief god of Babylon to Marduk. However, there is one way in which the swapping makes more immediate sense. It equates the two gods who bestow kingship. Nabû filled this role in Babylon, and we know from Neo-Assyrian sources that Sîn performed the same deed in Harran, which functioned almost as a western capital of the empire under the Sargonids and was the last capital of Assyria from 612 to 609.

The swapping also implies that Harran and Babylon are one and the same city, the city of kingship. One finds a distant echo of this notion in the Dynastic Prophecy, which alludes to Nabonidus as the king who '[will establish] the dynasty of Harran' (*palê Ḫarran* [*išakkan*]). Another implication of the swapping is that it proposes a syncretism between the gods Sîn and Nabû. As will be discussed below, this notion finds support in late religious and theological texts that equate Nabû with the god Sîn. This syncretism was reinforced by other scholastic texts and rituals equating Nabû with the god Anu or explaining Anu as the crescent of the new moon, the *uskaru*. This implied a triple syncretism among Nabû, Sîn, and Anu. The most important complex of traditions to elucidate these theological speculations is the Theology of the Moon.[2] It is quoted as follows in the Harran Stele (Exemplar 2, col. II)

22. ^{d}30 EN DINGIR *šá ina* U$_4$ 1-KAM TUKUL^{d}*a-nù*
23. *zi-kìr-šú* AN-*e ta-lap-pa-tú u* KI-*tì*
24. *ta-ḫe-ep-pu-u ḫa-mi-im* GARZA ^{d}*a-nù-*
25. *tú mu-gam-mi-ru pa-ra-aṣ* ^{d}EN.LÍL-*ú-tú*
26. *le-qu-u* GARZA ^{d}IDIM-*ú-tú*
27. *šá nap-ḫar gi-mi-ir* GARZA AN-*e*
28. *ina qa-ti-šú tam-ḫu* ^{d}EN.LÍL DINGIR.MEŠ
29. LUGAL LUGAL.LUGAL EN EN.EN

O Sîn, lord of the god(s), whose name on the first day (of the month) is "weapon of Anu," (insofar as) you touch (or strike) heaven and smash the earth, who gathers the rites of Anūtu, completes the rites of Enlilūtu, (and) grasps the rites of Eaʾūtu, who grabs in his hands the totality of the rites of heaven, Enlil of the gods, king of kings, lord of lords.

2. The denomination "Theology of the Moon" does not refer to one specific text but to a tradition reflected in a number of theological and religious texts from the late periods.

This is an incomplete version of the Theology of the Moon, which focuses largely on the first day of the month and the *uskaru*, here reinterpreted as a weapon. More-detailed versions can be found in the esoteric series i-NAM-giš-ḫur-an-ki-a (i-NAM) and a late astrological compendium that reads as follows (Livingstone 1986: 47):

1. DIŠ 30 *ina* IGI.LÁ-*šú* TA U$_4$ 1-KAM EN U$_4$ 5-KAM 5 *u$_4$-mi* U$_4$.SAKAR ^{d}*a-nù*
2. TA U$_4$ 6-KAM EN U$_4$ 10-KAM 5 U$_4$.MEŠ *ka-li-ti* ^{d}*é-a*
3. TA U$_4$ 11-KAM EN U$_4$ 15-KAM 5 *u$_4$-mi* AGA *taš-ri-iḫ-ti ip-pi-ir-ma* ^{d}*en-líl*
4. ^{d}30 ^{d}*a-nù* ^{d}*en-líl u* ^{d}*é-a par-ṣu-šu*

1. The moon, in its appearance, from the 1st to the 5th day, for 5 days, is the crescent, the god Anu.
2. From the 6th to the 10th day, for 5 days, it is the kidney, the god Ea.
3. From the 11th to the 15th day, for 5 days, it dons a tiara of glory, the god Enlil.
4. (This is why) the rites of the god Sîn are (those of) Anu, Enlil, and Ea.

Similar details are recorded in the fourth division of i-NAM (Livingstone 1986: 28–33). There we read that the moon's 'appearance on the 1st day (of the month is) a crescent, the god Anu' (1. IGI.DU$_8$.A U$_4$ 1-KAM U$_4$.SAKAR ^{d}*a-nù*); that it becomes 'a half crown on the 7th day (in) a kidney shape, the god Ea' (2. *maš-lu$_4$* AGA U$_4$ 7-KAM *ka$_{15}$-lit* ^{d}*é-a*); and finally that it waxes 'to wear a crown on the 15th day (in the shape of) a circle, the god Enlil' (3. *a-pa-ru* AGA U$_4$ 15-KAM BÙR ^{d}*en-líl*). The series records additional information, including the important heading to the effect that '[Fruit is (the name of) S]în because the god Anu called [it]s name' (1. [DIŠ GURUN ^{d}3]0 MU ^{d}*a-nù im-bu-ú* MU.N[I]). After this short exposition, the fourth division continues with a well-known type of henotheistic exegesis that explains the names of many gods as names of Sîn, including not only Anu, Enlil, and Ea but also Šamaš, Adad, Bēl and Marduk, Ištar, Ninurta, Nergal, Šakkan, Gibil, Nusku, and even Uraš and Ki (heaven and earth).

These theological texts do not propose a syncretism between Sîn and Nabû. Nor do they advance the notion that Nabû and Anu are one and the same god. In fact, they do not mention Nabû at all. Yet this omission is only apparent. The first words of the 4th division of i-NAM yield the key to the solution of this double theological equation: *Inbu Sîn aššu Anu imbû šumšu* 'Fruit is (the name of) Sîn because Anu called its name'. The phrase is construed as a pun on the word *inbu* 'fruit' and the 3rd-person preterite of the verb 'to call', *ibbû*, which is *inbû* in its morphographemic form, and *imbû* with dissimilation. The appellation *Inbu* for the moon-god Sîn occurs in other sources. We find it in the inscription of Nabonidus recording the elevation of his daughter to high priestess of Sîn in Ur (Schaudig 2001: 373). The assonance between *Inbu* and *Nabû* must have induced the identification of Sîn, the Divine Fruit, with Nabû. The entry could also be invoked to support the triple identification of Sîn, Nabû, and Anu with one another. The god Anu, by calling (*imbû*) the Divine Fruit (*Inbu* = Sîn = Nabû), became the 'caller' (*nābû*), the word 'caller' being one of the possible etymologies of the divine name Nabû as participle of the verb *nabû* 'to call'.

It seems difficult to dismiss these resemblances as purely coincidental, especially as they are supported by theological texts that identify Sîn with Nabû and Nabû with

Anu. The identification of Nabû with Anu is proposed in BM 34030, a late Babylonian text of undocumented provenance (Lambert 1997). The obverse consists of five lines, each of which invites a deity to a procession. Each line proposes a syncretism for that deity, first for Marduk who is identified as Enlil, then for Zarpanītu as Bēlet-ili, followed by Tašmētu as Gula, Nanaya as Ištar, and finally Nabû as Anu: obv. 5. *ri-i-di* ^{d}PA ^{d}*a-nù* LUGAL AN-*e* KÙ.MEŠ 'Process, Nabû, Anu, king of the pure heavens'. The reverse, also consisting of five lines, describes the presence of the same deities, in their syncretized forms, taking part in a religious ceremony. The last one is Nabû, who is present as Anu: *a-šib* ^{d}PA *ki-ma* ^{d}*a-nù* 'Nabû is present as Anu'. The origins of this tradition must be sought in Borsippa. The cylinder of Antiochus I commemorating the restoration of Ezida in that city qualifies Nabû's sanctuary as the temple of his Anūtu, his power of Anu: rev. 7. É.ZI.DA É *ki-i-ni* 8. É ^{d}*a-nu-ti-ka šu-bat ṭu-⟨ub⟩ lìb-bi-ka* 'Ezida, the legitimate temple, the temple of your power of Anu, your favorite temple' (Kuhrt and Sherwin-White 1991). But most important is the late ritual SBH 145 VIII, which describes festivals of Nabû in the month Ayaru. The city of origin of the ritual is uncertain, although Borsippa and Babylon are the most obvious candidates.[3] Here Nabû is not only equated with the god Anu but also with the moon-god Sîn (Matsushima 1987):

14. U$_4$ 2-KAM *tar-ba-ṣi u$_4$-mu šá-ḫa-ṭu* ^{d}UTU *qu-ra-du*
15. DINGIR ^{d}NÀ *šá ḫa-da-áš-šu-tú in-na-an-di-iq te-di-*⸢*iq*⸣ ^{d}*a-nu-tú*
16. TA *qé-*⸢*reb*⸣ É.ZI.DA *ina šat mu-ši uš-ta-pa-a na-an-na-ri-iš*
17. *ki-ma* ^{d}30 *ina ni-ip-ḫi-šú ú-nam-mar ik-let*
18. *ina qé-reb* É.UR$_5$.ŠÀ.BA *uš-te-šir i-šad-di-ḫu* ⸢*nam*⸣*-riš*
19. *i-ru-um-ma ana ma-ḫar* ^{d}NIN *ka-li šit-ku-nu ana ḫa-d*[*a-áš-šu-tú*]
20. *ina qé-reb* É.UR$_5$.ŠÀ.BA GIN$_7$ *u$_4$-mu i-šak-kan na-mi*[*r-tú*]

14. On the second day, (in) the courtyard, at the time of the rising ofŠamaš the warrior,
15. the god, Nabû, (as) bridegroom, puts on the garment of the power of Anu (Anūtu).
16. From the midst of Ezida at nighttime he shines forth like the lunar crescent (= Nannar).
17. Like Sîn at his rising he illuminates the darkness.
18. In the midst of Euršaba he marches in procession brightly.
19. He enters into the presence of Bēltu (= Ištar); everything is set up for the wed[ding festival].
20. In the midst of Euršaba, like the day, he establishes the li[ght].

The basic notions expressed in this ritual are identical with the Theology of the Moon for the first six days of the month. The ritual takes place at the beginning of the

3. It is not entirely certain that this ritual took place in Borsippa because Ezida and Euršaba, the temples of Nabû and Ištar (as Nanaya), respectively, in that city were also the names of cellas consecrated to the same deities in the Esagil temple in Babylon (George 1993: s.v. é.ur$_5$.šà.ba and é.zi.da).

month and celebrates the emergence of Nabû as new moon. Nabû is compared to the lunar crescent (*nannariš*) shining forth on the second day, at which point he assumes the identity of the god Anu. This exaltation of Nabû was ritually enacted by the clothing of his image with a special vestment, the garment of the power of Anu. Nabû is further syncretized with the moon-god Sîn. It is even probable that the appellation "the god" that precedes the name of Nabû on the second line should be understood as the common name *ilu* for Sîn. This appellation was favored by Nabonidus, especially in its logographic plural form DINGIR.MEŠ. The appellation *ilu* for the moon-god seems to have been especially popular in Harran. Pagan Syrian inscriptions from this region dated to the first two centuries of our era still address the god of Harran as *ellaha*, echoing the theology favored during the late Assyrian and Babylonian empires (Drijvers 1980: 122–45). At any rate, this ritual provides the background for understanding certain details of the Theology of the Moon. In particular, it enunciates explicitly what is esoterically suggested in the first line of the fourth division of i-NAM. The moon-god Sîn, as *inbu* 'the fruit', as he is called by the god Anu at the beginning of the month, is none other than the god Nabû, who turns out to be Anu himself during the first phase of the moon. Nabonidus, by swapping the symbols of Nabû and Sîn on his staffs depicted on the Harran Stele and the Babylon Stele, clearly followed this tradition.

An Old Myth of Creation

The summary of the Theology of the Moon in the Harran Stele, while being broadly congruent with expositions of the same theology in scholarly texts, introduces new elements in the description of the lunar crescent. The name of the moon-god on the first day of the month in the Harran Stele is not, as we should expect, *uskaru*. It is *kakki Anu* 'weapon of Anu', provided that our reading of the sign KU (TUKUL) as *kakku* is correct.[4] Therefore, the Harran Stele reinterprets the lunar crescent as the weapon of the god Anu. This seems congruent with the rest of the stele, which continues with a praise of the god Sîn that portrays him as the one who touches (or strikes) heaven and smashes the earth with the weapon of Anu when he reappears at the beginning of the month. Is this just a poetic image of the light of the crescent moon radiating in the sky and down to the earth, or should we presume a more meaningful allusion? The verb *lapātu* appears in a number of passages in astrological texts that refer to the shadow of a lunar eclipse touching or covering a particular region of the earth, but this relates to the text of the stele only in a very general way, and the verb *ḫepû* does not to my knowledge occur in any context where it refers to the light of the moon covering the earth or the sky.

4. Another possibility is to read the sign KU as *uskaru*, in which case the name of Sîn at the beginning of the month would be *uskar Anu* 'crescent of Anu'. An echo of this *uskar Anu* appears in the Verse Account, which derides Nabonidus for claiming a wisdom greater than the alleged series *uskar Anu Enlilla* composed by the mythical sage Adapa. However, a reading *uskaru* for the sign KU is not otherwise documented.

The monthly renewal of the moon is a recurrent beginning that may well have denoted the time of creation in the ancient imagination. We should therefore consider the possibility that the Harran Stele alludes here to a myth of creation and organization of the world. Indeed, the Harran Stele alludes to some essential elements of a myth of this sort, such as the weapon wielded by the divine hero (Anu or Nabû as forms of Sîn) and the effect of wielding this weapon on both heaven and earth.[5] Some traditions testify to the existence of a myth involving the god Anu at the time of creation. Recently, Sjöberg (2002) has discussed two short, difficult mythological texts in Sumerian, one dated to the Early Dynastic period (AO 4153) and the other to the Ur III period (NBC 11108). Both texts describe the world just before creation, with the god An, referred to as 'the Lord' (*En*), being the protagonist. In AO 4153, the god An is further described as a 'young hero' *(šul)*, not his habitual portrayal as ancestral figure. The text does not tell us how creation happened. It specifies that in primeval time heaven and earth already existed, though probably in unseparated form, while the other gods did not yet live and the sun and moon had not yet shone. CBS 11108 presents a very similar formulation of the same mythologem but adds one important episode. The first deed of An before creation was to illuminate the sky, while leaving the earth in darkness: 1. a[n e]n-né an mu-zala[g]-⌈ge ki mu⌉-ge_6 'An, the En, illuminated the sky (but) let the earth (still) be dark'. The interpretation of the Theology of the Moon found in the Harran Stele seems to reinstate the god Anu in the same role he held in AO 4153 and CBS 11108. Because of his identification with the new moon, Anu illuminates the world before the beginning of creation in the Harran Stele in a way that is very similar to CBS 11108–touching both heaven and earth with his primeval light in the former, illuminating heaven but leaving earth in darkness in the latter. As seen above, shining forth to illuminate darkness is also the role of Nabû in his incarnation as Anu and as the new moon in the ritual SBH 145 VIII.

The Harran Stele also introduces the concept of the weapon of Anu (TUKUL ^{d}*a-nù*). The reading of the sign KU as TUKUL is uncertain. However, there are reasons to believe that the text refers here to an object reminiscent of the lunar crescent. Indeed, if we rely on other expositions of the Theology of the Moon, the logogram KU in the Harran Stele takes the place normally reserved for the word *uskaru*. Therefore the weapon of the god Anu is likely to be a crescent-shaped object. If we follow the notion that the Harran Stele alludes here to a myth of creation, then this weapon should be the scimitar, scythe, or *harpe* sometimes carried by divine heroes. There is one Babylonian tradition of the primeval combat that agrees remarkably well with the Harran Stele. This is the tradition of the Man in the Moon. Mythological interpretations of the configuration of the surface of the moon seem to be a universal phenomenon. The Babylonians were no exception. They saw on the lunar surface a representation of the divine hero fighting the dragon (Beaulieu 1999). An astrological tablet from Seleucid Uruk bears a drawing of the moon illustrating this belief. Inside the circle of

5. The most intriguing expression in the Harran Stele is *erṣetu taḫeppû* 'you smash the earth'. Significantly, the verb *ḫepû* occurs in *Enuma eliš* to describe Marduk's creative process in splitting (*ḫepû*) Tiamat into two halves and creating heaven out of one half: tablet IV, 137. *iḫ-pi-ši-ma ki-ma nu-un maš-ṭe-e a-na ši-ni-šu* 'He split her into two halves like a dried fish' (Talon 2005: 56).

the moon, we see a male deity holding a lion serpent by the tail and carrying a weapon that is curved at the bottom end. There is no caption identifying the god. However, two late expository texts clearly state that Marduk can be seen in the sun and Nabû in the moon. They also specify that the dragon of chaos, alternatively a lion or Tiamat, can be seen on the lunar surface. Therefore it is probable that the drawing on the Uruk tablet depicts on the lunar surface the god Nabû battling the lion serpent of primeval chaos, thus replacing Marduk in the role of demiurge. This is congruent with the tradition that links Nabû to the moon and syncretizes him with the god Sîn.

This evidence supports the notion that the Harran Stele offers a new interpretation of the traditional theology of the first phase of the moon in the light of old mythologems of the creation of the world. These mythologems may have survived in various forms. Although the traditions recorded in AO 4153 and CBS 11108 probably disappeared from the written record during the second millennium, they may well have continued in oral form. Nabonidus tried to conflate the two traditions just described. The first one viewed the god Anu as demiurge. His first act of creation was to illuminate the sky and the earth in their pristine state. The second act attributed to Nabû the role of divine hero, and possibly also of demiurge, in the cosmological fight against the dragon of chaos. The conflation of the two mythologems presupposed the identity of Anu and Nabû and the belief that both gods were manifestations of the god Sîn as new moon at the beginning of the month. The view of Anu as divine hero appears in AO 4153, which attributes the epithet *šul* 'young hero' to the god. Remembrance of the youthful and heroic character of the god Anu survived into the late periods. The initial verse of the myth of the triumphal return of the god Ninurta to Nippur after his defeat of Asakku, the monster of chaos, compares Ninurta to An: *An-gim dimma* 'shaped like An' (Cooper 1978: 56–57). Ninurta also receives the power of An (*usu an-na*) from his father Enlil in Lugale, another myth that celebrates his victory over Asakku (Annus 2002: 6–7). Like its counterpart, Angim dimma, Lugale is also known from first-millennium manuscripts. Ninurta's assimilation of An's power as divine hero in these myths probably lies at the root of the assumption of the power of Anu by the god Nabû in late theology. Indeed, some theological texts from the first millennium attribute to Nabû the epithets and victories of Ninurta (Pomponio 2001: 21b). This syncretism derived in a large measure from the identification of Marduk with Enlil, which also entailed the identification of their respective sons, Nabû and Ninurta.

A survey of personal names from Harran indicates that Nabû enjoyed some popularity in the area.[6] Yet, he did not belong to the group of major gods worshiped in the Eḫulḫul temple (Sîn, Ningal, Nusku, and Sadarnunna), and indeed the god is present in the Harran Stele only in the guise of his symbol, the *qanṭuppu*. But there is evidence that Nabonidus designed more overt means to signify Nabû's presence. A large

6. Theophoric names honoring Nabû occur several times in the various documents of the Harran Census, dated to the seventh century (Fales and Postgate 1995: 121–45). However, most of the names in the region were West Semitic. In a Neo-Babylonian letter from Sippar published by MacGinnis (1996: 124, no. 28; BM 60105), the administrator of the city of Harran is called Nabû-aḫ-iddin (line 14. ^{Id}NÀ-ŠEŠ-MU, 15. ^{lú}*qí-i-pi šá* ^{uru}*ḫar-ra-nu*).

number of inscribed bricks with the royal titulary of Nabonidus were found at Harran during excavations in the 1980s. Photographs of bricks initially published by Donbaz give the name of the father of Nabonidus as Nabû-balāssu-iqbi, which is the same name found in inscriptions from Babylonia. Subsequently, however, Donbaz published a conflated copy of an additional set of bricks found in the same area. They bear an inscription that is identical with the inscription of the earlier set, with the exception that in most of them the name of Nabonidus's father is spelled Nusku-balāssu-iqbi rather than Nabû-balāssu-iqbi (Donbaz 1991). The difference between the two theophoric elements is slight (^{d}PA for Nabû, ^{d}PA.TÚG for Nusku), and the two gods may have been considered identical in the north (Schaudig 2001: 342–43). At any rate, this intentional double spelling provides one more indication that the centerpiece of the theological program of Nabonidus for Harran was the identification of its patron god Sîn with Nabû. In this case, the equation was reinforced by proclaiming the identity of Nusku, the vizier and son of Sîn of Harran, with Nabû.

The God Lugal-šudu

Nabonidus may have introduced Nabû at Harran in yet another guise, that of the god Lugal-šudu. The Harran Stele commemorates the introduction of a new statue of Sîn to the restored Eḫulḫul temple. Yet it gives no clue as to the features of that cult statue. However, in the Istanbul Stele, Nabonidus mentions an image of Sîn carved on a cylinder seal presented by Ashurbanipal to the Esagil temple in Babylon. This image may well have served as a model for the new statue he introduced into the Eḫulḫul (Lee 1993: 135). This would imply that the statue of Sîn of Harran had been destroyed during the sack of the city by the Medes in 609 B.C. It also means that the necessity of making a new cultic image of Sîn for the city of Harran gave Nabonidus the opportunity to modify it in accordance with his theological views. This is one of the numerous misdeeds laid on him in the Verse Account, which describes the cult statue as follows:

Col. I

21′. [o o o]-*na ib-ta-ni za-qí-qí*
22′. [DINGIR *šá pa-na*]-*ma ina* KUR *la i-mu-ru-uš mam-ma-an*
23′. [o o o]-⸢*ú*⸣ *ki-gal-la ú-šar-me*
24′. [o o o] ^{d}ŠEŠ.KI *it-ta-bi zi-kir-šú*
25′. [*šá* KÙ.GI *u* NA_4] ZA.GÌN *a-pi-ir a-gu-šú*
26′. [o o o] *ši-kin-šú* ^{d}30 AN.MI
27′. [*i-tar-ra*]-*aṣ** ŠU.MIN-*su ki-ma* ^{d}⸢Lugal⸣-šu-du
28′. [o o o] ŠI IS ⸢*pe*⸣-*re-e-tu-uš ki-gal-la*
29′. [*en-du man-za-a*]*s-su a-bu-bu u ri-i-mu*
30′. [o o o] *a-gu-šú i-te-me ši-kin-šú*
31′. [o o o] ⸢x⸣-UD-*šú ut-tak-ki-ir zi-mu-šú*
32′. [o o o *uš*]-*te-lip gat-tu-uš*
33′. [o o o]⸢x⸣ GAL *zi-kir-šú*
34′. [o o o *š*]*á-pal-šú*

21′. [o o o] x he created a phantom,
22′. [a god] whom nobody had seen [previous]ly in the country.
23′. [o o o] x he installed (him) on a pedestal,
24′. [o o o] he called his name Nannar.
25′. His tiara that he dons [is made of gold and lapis] lazuli.
26′. [o o o] his appearance is the god Sîn in eclipse.
27′. [He stret]ches his hand like the god Lugal-šudu
28′. [o o o] x x his hairdo (to?) the pedestal.
29′. [Flanking] his [cult soc]le are a Flood Monster and a Wild Beast.
30′. [o o o] his tiara, his appearance changed,
31′. [o o o] x x he transformed his facial features.
32′. [o o o he] increased his stature.
33′. [o o o] x x his name.
34′. [o o o un]derneath him.

According to the Verse Account, one of the prominent characteristics of the new statue of Sîn of Harran is that it stretches its hand like the god Lugal-šudu. Lee points out that ^{d}Lugal-šu-du is almost certainly a spelling of ^{d}Lugal-šùd-dè, a god who appears as a form of Ninurta in the series An = Anum I and in the Weidner God List (Lee 1994: 34 and 36 n. 18). Indeed, the compound šu-du appears several times in lexical lists as phonetic writing for the sign šùd (KA×SU). He argues that this identification proves that Nabonidus tried to shape the statue of Sîn of Harran into a form of Ninurta in order to reinforce the equation of Sîn with Marduk, who assimilates the attributes of Ninurta in his role as dragon slayer.[7] However, further investigation shows that the question is somewhat more complex.

The main clues to an identification of ^{d}Lugal-šùd-dè are An = Anum I, 218 (^{d}Lugal-šùd-dè = MIN, ^{d}Nin-urta dumu-sag-^{d}BAD-⌜lá⌝-[ke$_4$] 'Lugal-šudde is Ninurta, the first-born son of Enlil'), and the Weidner God List, where he also appears among various forms of Ninurta (Lambert 1987). However, the god surfaces again in An = Anum V, 265, where he is listed with Alla among the retinue of the god Ningišzida, either as herald or vizier (Litke 1998: 193). A similar connection occurs in MVN 13, 17, an Ur III text that associates Lugal-šudde with Alla and places his cult in the city of Gišbanda, which was the center of the cult of Ningišzida (Wiggermann 2001: 369a and 372a). These data firmly anchor Lugal-šudde within the family of chthonic and netherworld deities, of dying and rising gods. These aspects of Lugal-šudde explain why he appears again in An = Anum VI, which is devoted to Nergal and other gods of the netherworld. However, Lugal-šudde appears there as himself (= ŠU), not as a form of Nergal (Litke 1998: 206, l.87). The chthonic connection is also evident in the equation of Dumuzi with the herald Umun-šudde (li-bi-ir ù-mu-un\umun-šùd-dè, without divine determinative) in Emesal litanies (Lambert 1987). Umun-šudde is the Emesal form of Lugal-šudde. One such litany is 4 R 30, 2:11–35 + Sm. 2148, recently edited

7. Similar points are conveyed in column II of the Verse Account. There Nabonidus is accused of having turned Eḫulḫul into a replica of Ekur, the Temple of Enlil in Nippur, and also with setting up guardian spirits at its gates, which are reminiscent of the Esagil temple in Babylon.

by Katz (2003: 318–20). In this litany, Umun-šudde and Alla appear as forms of Dumuzi in his descent to the netherworld. Therefore, if we rely on the evidence from god lists and religious texts, Lugal-šudde was a chthonic and netherworld deity, a dying and rising god, a god of periodic disappearance and renewal. Ninurta also possesses chthonic attributes, and this should probably account for the equation of Lugal-šudde with Ninurta in the Weidner God List and An = Anum I, 218. How then can we relate these aspects of the god to the theology of the moon-god Sîn of Harran, and to Nabonidus's reformulation of that theology? Is the answer really that Lugal-šudde, because of his equation with Ninurta, was thought to be a form of Marduk? The connection of Marduk with the netherworld is not a significant trait of his personality. Therefore, the fashioning of the cult image of Sîn of Harran in the shape of Lugal-šudde would seem a rather unconvincing way of advancing a syncretism between Marduk and Sîn.

The investigation must proceed in another direction. We have recognized earlier the importance of the Theology of the Moon to explain the program of the Harran Stele. In line with this, one may wonder if the chthonic aspect of Lugal-šudde and his identification or association with Dumuzi, Alla, and Ningišzida as god of disappearance and renewal were not understood by Nabonidus and his entourage in light of the mythology of the moon's periodic occultation and reappearance. Some sources support a connection of this sort in an oblique way. The main form of lunar occultation was the *bubbulu*, the period of disappearance of the moon at the end of the month, ideally set on the 29th and 30th days. God lists and rituals associate the *bubbulu* with the god Arabalaḫ. This explanation occurs in An = Anum I, 145, é-bar-ra-la$ḫ_5$ = DUMU U$_4$ 30-KAM U$_4$.NÁ.A 'Abaralaḫ = the son of the 30th day, the day of disappearance of the moon', where Abaralaḫ appears among the seven sons of the god Enmešarra (Litke 1998: 36). A more elaborate explanation occurs in the ritual of the *kalû*, AO 6479, where Abaralaḫ is identified with Nusku: col. III, 13, ^{d}a-bar-ra-la$ḫ_5$ DUMU U$_4$ 30-KAM U$_4$.NÁ.ÀM 14. ^{d}PA.TÚG DUMU *še-la-še-e bu-um-bu-li* 'Abaralaḫ (is) Nusku, the "son" of the 30th day, the day of the disappearance of the moon' (Livingstone 1986: 200). Further details are found in TCL 6, 47, a late commentary from Nippur: obv. 14. ^{d}a-ba-ra-la$ḫ_5$ ^{d}PA.TÚG 15. ^{d}*nin-urta* : ^{d}30 : ^{d}NÀ NU.BÀN.DA DINGIR.GUB.BA.MEŠ *šá ina* IGI ^{d}*da-gan* TA UL.DÙ.A ^{d}*en-me-ša-ra* Ù[RI] 'Abaralaḫ, (who is) Nusku, (is also) Ninurta = Sîn = Nabû, the foreman of the standing gods who have been kee[ping watch] over Enmešarra in the presence of Dagan since time immemorial' (Livingstone 1986: 190–91).

The Theology of the Moon deals only with the first half of the month. Therefore this tradition made up an important addition to it by providing a theological explanation for the last day of the month. It also gave a central role to Nusku, the son of Sîn and the second god in importance at Harran. The identification proposed between Nusku, Ninurta, Sîn, and Nabû in TCL 6, 47 agrees perfectly with a number of theological concepts promoted by Nabonidus in his Harran inscriptions, notably the identification of Sîn and Nusku with Nabû. The introduction of Ninurta in this multiple syncretism is especially interesting. He is often equated with Nabû in late theology, and his equation with Nusku can be justified by the fact that both gods were sons of

Enlil. Therefore the god Lugal-šudde, by virtue of his identification with Ninurta in An = Anum and the Weidner God List, could easily be introduced in this equation. It is also important to note that these gods appear here in their chthonic aspect. They keep watch over Enmešarra, who is imprisoned in the netherworld. This tradition is already present in An = Anum, which lists Abaralaḫ as son of Enmešarra. This evidence provides the best approach to understanding the presence of the god Lugal-šudde in the Verse Account. Lugal-šudde was viewed as a chthonic manifestation of Ninurta, as well as of Nusku, Nabû, and Sîn. He represented the moon in its period of complete occultation, the *bubbulu*.

Finally, we must turn to the form under which Lugal-šudde appears in the Verse Account, Lugal-šudu. On the surface, the spelling ^{d}Lugal-šu-du carries no specific meaning other than being a phonetic rendering of ^{d}Lugal-šùd-dè. Yet, as pointed out by Maul (Schaudig 2001: 566 n. 914), the form seems more purposeful if we understand it as a spelling for a hypothetical ^{d}Lugal-šu-du$_8$ 'The Divine Lord who stretches the hand' (lugal = *bēlu*; šu = *qātu*; du$_8$ = *tarāṣu*). Indeed, the god appears in a verse that, if correctly restored, ascribes this gesture to the god. Some scholars have remarked that the iconography of this region sometimes depicts gods, including probably Sîn of Ḫarran, with the gesture of stretching the hand (Seidl 2000). It is conceivable that, of two possible spellings, the author of the Verse Account adopted ^{d}Lugal-šu-du because it allowed the making of a pun with ^{d}Lugal-šu-du$_8$. The name ^{d}Lugal-šùd-dè means 'The Divine Lord who utters benedictions'. If we understand the divine stretching of the hand (*qāta tarāṣu*) as a gesture of benediction, then the choice of ^{d}Lugal-šùd-dè finds a ready explanation, and so does the oblique pun ^{d}Lugal-šu-du$_8$. The Divine Lord who stretches the hand, the Lord of Harran, is also the Divine Lord who utters benedictions.

I would argue tentatively that the author of the Verse Account, probably reproducing Nabonidus's own speculations, concocted the spelling ^{d}Lugal-šu-du because it conceals an additional pun, this time on the name of the god Nusku. The logogram Lugal in divine names does not mean primarily *šarru* 'king' but *bēlu* 'lord.' Therefore, the meaning 'lord' can be retrojected in these divine names with the more-common logogram for *bēlu*, that is En. This is in a sense what happens in the litanies that equate Dumuzi with Umun/Ù-mu-un-šùd-dè, Umun being the Emesal form of En. Therefore the god ^{d}Lugal-šu-du in the Verse Account could also be understood as ^{d}En-šu-du, and under this form it comes quite close to a reading of the logogram ^{d}Nusku found in late texts, ^{d}Enšada or ^{d}Enšadu (Streck 2001b: 630a). If we rely on the conflated brick inscription published by Donbaz, Nabonidus propagated the notion that Nusku and Nabû were one and the same god. Indeed, because Nusku originated in Nippur as son and vizier of Enlil and only later migrated to Harran to become son of Sîn, he was at an early date equated with Ninurta, Enlil's other son. This explains his later identification with Nabû, who was Ninurta's equivalent. The equation of Ninurta and Nusku with Sîn, found in several texts, including TCL 6, 47, may have ultimately originated during the period of the Third Dynasty of Ur, when the god Nanna of Ur also became a son of Enlil to consolidate the claims of the new dynasty (Klein 2001). The mention of Lugal-šudu and the allusions carried by his name may reflect a dispute over the shape of the features of the statue of Sîn of Harran, which Nabonidus may have intended to look like a form of Nabû or Nusku. The apparent contradiction in having the father (Sîn) borrow the attributes of the son (Nusku = Nabû) was a common phenomenon, and it was specifically vindicated in this case by the textual evidence supporting the identity of Sîn, Nusku, Nabû, and Ninurta.

Why was Nabonidus especially interested in making a new image of the god Sîn of Harran that depicted him stretching his hand like Lugalšudu ([*ittar*]*aṣ qāssu*)? Nabonidus promoted the syncretism beween Sîn and Nabû. Therefore the most likely explanation seems to be that the gesture of stretching the hand is attributed to the god Nabû in the building inscriptions of the Babylonian Empire. Nabû confers kingship and in this role is the god who stretches his hand to the king. Among Neo-Babylonian rulers, only Nabopolassar and Nabonidus employ the standard royal epithet expressing this gesture in their inscriptions, *tiriṣ qāti* DN (Seux 1967: 345). The motif is absent from the inscriptions of Nebuchadnezzar. In the inscriptions of Nabopolassar, we find the formulas *tiriṣ qāti Nabû u Marduk* 'the one to whom Nabû and Marduk stretch their hand' and *tiriṣ qāti Nabû u Tašmētu* 'the one to whom Nabû and Tašmētu stretch their hand'. In the inscriptions of Nabonidus, we find once *tiriṣ qāti Tutu* 'the one to whom Tutu stretches his hand' (Schaudig 2001: 355) and once in a Borsippa inscription *tiriṣ qāti Nisaba* 'the one to whom Nisaba stretches her hand' (Schaudig 2001: 474), with Nabû mentioned in the next line as the god who calls Nabonidus to kingship: [o o *ni-b*]*i-*⌜*it*⌝ ^{d}*na-bi-*⌜*um*⌝ '[the one cal]led by Nabû'. The mention of Tutu seems ambiguous and was perhaps deliberately so. Tutu was a name for both Nabû and Marduk. The mention of Nisaba is significant. She belonged to the circle of Nabû and was identified in late theology with Tašmētu, Gula, and Nanaya. As mentioned earlier, the account of Nabonidus's accession in the Istanbul Stele includes a revelation by incubation dream from Gula, glossed as Tašmētu. The syncretism of Gula with Tašmētu stemmed from the theological equation between their husbands, Ninurta and Nabû. For a king who claimed to have been taught the art of the scribe by the god Nabû himself, what better token of legitimacy than a personal blessing from the old goddess of writing, now become the consort of her old rival? The fact that Nabû conferred kingship in Babylon and possessed a lunar aspect explains why the god occupied an important place in the theological thinking of Nabonidus. After all, Nabonidus's own name, Nabû-naʾid 'Nabû is praised' could not be a better expression of his personal devotion.

A Conflict of Authority and Legitimacy

The theological interpretations of Nabonidus were not accepted by all. This should not surprise us. Interpretation is by nature controversial. Did Nabonidus transgress boundaries? In his defense, one notes that his theological claims can always be supported by textual evidence from the learned tradition of Babylonia. The issue at stake was more likely an issue of authority. Who had the power to sanction an interpretation and validate it? It is important to remember that in late Babylonia both king and scholar claimed to represent this authority. We have examples in the previous history of Mesopotamia in which radical new theological interpretations originated from the monarchy and enjoyed widespread endorsement. The syncretism between Enlil and Marduk, which probably took place during the reign of Nebuchadnezzar I, is one example. Sennacherib's redefinition of the cult and theology of Aššur is another one. Nabonidus provides an example of the contrary. Why? Can it be ascribed solely to external political circumstances? Had the Persians never conquered Babylon, can we speculate that the changes contemplated by Nabonidus would have lasted? Is what we read in sources hostile to him nothing more than the vilification of a fallen regime by collaborationist clerics? Or was the opposition to Nabonidus vocal and active already during his reign? The hints at opposition contained in the Harran Stele seem to suggest the latter option. This induces us to understand the Verse Account not only as a piece of posthumous counterpropaganda but also as a reflection of a conflict of authority within late Babylonian civilization.

To justify his claims, Nabonidus could rely on a tradition that viewed the king as ultimate authority in matters of religion and ritual. One of the most important statements of this tradition occurs in *Gilgamesh*. Gesche has demonstrated that the Epic belonged to the basic core of late Babylonian school texts that served to propagate the ideology of the monarchy. Gilgamesh did not only travel to distant places in search of all wisdom, to learn the secret, and discover the hidden (tablet I, 6–7). After his return, now versed in all antediluvian knowledge, he "restored the cult-centers that the Deluge destroyed, and established the proper rites for the human race" (tablet I, 43–44). The motif of the ideal king as restorer of proper rituals after the Flood was very old (George 1999: xlviii–l). The recently recovered version of the Sumerian tale of The Death of Gilgamesh expresses the same idea in closely identical terms (George 1999: 202). The same motif resurfaces in The Instructions of Ur-Ninurta (Alster 1991). This tradition viewed the postdiluvian monarchy as a restoration of the antediluvian one. The figure of Ziusudra, better known later as Utanapišti, became pivotal as the archetype of the last antediluvian king who transmitted the proper knowledge to humanity that survived the Flood. Indeed, Gilgamesh receives his instructions personally from Ziusudra in The Death of Gilgamesh, in the same way that he is instructed by Utanapišti in the later version of the Epic. In the latter part of the second millennium, King Nebuchadnezzar I of the second dynasty of Isin claimed to have received personal instruction from the god Marduk and to belong to a distant lineage going back to the last antediluvian king who reigned in Sippar, Enmeduranki (Frame 1995: 25). This tradition provides the background for understanding a text such as the Letter of Samsuiluna, which portrays the king overruling the priesthood in religious and cultic matters. As discussed earlier, the same notion was coopted in the Harran Stele.

During the first millennium, however, claims that ran counter to the king's monopoly on the religious and cultic domain began to emerge. Alongside the tradition of antediluvian kings, the learned classes created a parallel tradition of antediluvian sages. Eventually these traditions were merged into parallel lists such as the one compiled by Berossus and its closely related cuneiform counterpart from Hellenistic Uruk (Verbrugghe and Wickersham 1996: 70–71). Parallel lists such as these, which pair each antediluvian king with a sage, must be viewed as retrojections to antediluvian times of the role of scholars, *ummânus*, as royal advisors. A role of this sort is documented in detail by the correspondence of the late Sargonid kings of Assyria. Yet, in spite of the deference shown to the king in this correspondence, it is obvious that all the knowledge resides with scholars. When the latter feel obliged to flatter the king for his scholarship, they do not compare him with Ziusudra, Utanapišti, or any antediluvian king, not even Gilgamesh. They compare him with the antediluvian *apkallu* Adapa (Pongratz-Leisten 1999: 309–19). U'anna-Adapa, known under the form Oannes in Berossus, became the archetype of antediluvian knowledge and wisdom. But he was not a king. He was in a sense the first scholar, the primeval sage instructed by the god Ea personally, and with whom all knowledge originated. The replacement of antediluvian kings by sages in that role reflected the rising claims of the learned elites, especially in Babylonia, to assume the intellectual and religious leadership of their culture. This is the very conflict that is portrayed in the Verse Account, which caricatures Nabonidus as an ignorant man who claims greater knowledge than Adapa himself:

Col. V

8′. GUB-*zu ina* UKKIN *ú-šar-ra-ḫu r*[*a-man-šú*]
9′. *en-qé-ek mu-da-a-ka a-ta-mar k*[*a-ti-im-tú*]
10′. *mi-ḫi-iṣ qan-ṭup-pu ul i-di a-ta-mar n*[*i-ṣir-tú*]
11′. *ú-šab-ra-an* ^{d}*il-te-ri kul-lat ú-ta-*[*ad-da-a*]
12′. U$_4$.SAKAR ^{d}*a-nù* ^{d}*en-líl-lá šá ik-ṣu-ru a-da-p*[*à*]
13′. UGU-*šú šu-tu-qa-ak kal né-me-q*[*u*]
14′. *i-bal-lal par-ṣi i-dal-la-aḫ te-re-e-ti*
15′. *a-na pél-lu-de-e ṣi-ru-ti i-qab-bi ma-ṣi-t*[*ú*]
16′. *ú-ṣu-rat* É.SAG.ÍL ⸢GIŠ⸣.ḪUR.ḪUR *šá ib-ši-mu* ^{d}IDIM *mu-um-mu*
17′. *i-dag-gal ú-ṣu-ra-a-ti i-ta-mi ma-ag-ri-ti*
18′. U$_4$.SAKAR É.SAG.ÍL *iṭ-ṭul-ma i-šal-lal* ŠU.MIN-*šú*
19′. *ú-paḫ-ḫi-ir* DUMU.MEŠ ⸢*um*⸣*-man-nu i-ta-mi it-ti-šú-un*
20′. É *e-pu-uš a-na man-nu an-nu-ú ši-mi-is-su*
21′. *lu-ú šá* ^{d}EN *šu-ú mar-ri še-mi-it-ma*
22′. ^{d}30 U$_4$.SAKAR-*šú il-te-mi-it* É-*su*

8′. He would stand up in the assembly and praise h[imself as follows]:
9′. "I am wise, I am learned, I have seen hid[den things]!
10′. (Although) I do not know the art of the stylus, I have seen sec[ret knowledge]!
11′. The god Saḫar (= Ilteri) has revealed (it) to me (in a dream), he has sh[own me] everything!
12′. As for the Series Uskar Anu Enlil which Adap[a] composed,
13′. I surpass it in all wisdo[m]!"
14′. He would confuse the rites, upset the omens,
15′. speak *what he could* concerning the august cultic prescriptions.
16′. As for the plan of Esagil, the designs which Ea-Mummu (himself) fashioned,

17′. he would look at the plans and utter blasphemy.
18′. (Once) he saw the crescent-shaped symbol of Esagil and took it with his hands.
19′. He gathered the assembly of experts and spoke to them (as follows):
20′. "For whom is the temple built? This is its symbol.
21′. Were it indeed Bēl's, it would be marked with the spade.
22′. (Therefore), Sîn has (indeed) marked his temple with his crescent-shaped symbol!"

This is probably the most significant part of the Verse Account. It contains very explicit allusions to claims aired by Nabonidus in his inscriptions. It also articulates its criticism around the motif of the king's ignorance in an attempt to overturn the notion that royal authority should prevail in religious matters. Indeed, the mention of 'hid[den things]' (= *katimtu*) and 'sec[ret knowledge]' (= *niṣirtu*) in lines 9′–10′, if correctly restored, is possibly a direct allusion to *Gilgamesh* I, 7, where the same two words embody the knowledge that Gilgamesh seeks on his quest for antediluvian wisdom. The alleged royal confession of not knowing the art of cuneiform writing on line 10′ is in flagrant contradiction with the opposite statement of Nabonidus, that he received the scribal craft from the god Nabû himself. With the reference to revelation sent by the god Saḫar on line 11′ begins an enumeration of alleged misdeeds with clearer references to materials found in the Harran Stele. The god Saḫar (written Il-teri) was the West Semitic form of the moon-god worshiped in northern Syria, where theophoric names honoring him are common. The allusion might well be to the dream reported in the Harran Stele, although Nabonidus narrates several dreams sent by Sîn in various inscriptions from Babylonia. In any case, the passage mocks his obsession with these dreams and his urge to publicize them.

Lines 12′–13′ contain a crucial statement that Nabonidus claimed a wisdom greater than Adapa, the first antediluvian sage, especially in relation to the contents of the series Uskar Anu Enlil. The various arguments for the interpretation of this passage have been carefully weighed by Machinist and Tadmor (1993). Two essential points are pressed against Nabonidus. First, his claim to override the wisdom and editorial work of Adapa with his royal authority is void. No reason is given, although the answer is clearly that only scholars–the living *ummânus* who hold their knowledge from antediluvian *apkallus*–have received a mandate to voice authorized interpretations. The second point relates to the name of the series Uskar Anu Enlil. That this is an allusion to Enuma Anu Enlil is obvious. The polemic focuses more specifically on an episode reported in the Royal Chronicle, a historical-literary text praising Nabonidus's achievements (Schaudig 2001: 590–95). The episode in question occurred in the king's second regnal year, when he consecrated his daughter as high priestess of Sîn in Ur on the basis of a lunar eclipse omen recorded in the series Enuma Anu Enlil. The Royal Chronicle offers what is certainly a grossly exaggerated view of Nabonidus's depth of knowledge by claiming that the scholars in charge of interpreting the tablets of Enuma Anu Enlil brought from Babylon could understand the omen properly only after the king had explained it. The crux of the passage is the modified name of the series, Uskar Anu Enlil. This most likely alludes to the designation for the first five days of the month, *uskār Anu* 'crescent of Anu' in the Theology of the

Moon. This satirical pun directed at a king who apparently saw lunar crescents everywhere anticipates the episode related a few lines below. Nabonidus allegedly saw a crescent symbol in the Esagil temple and on that basis claimed that the temple really belonged to Sîn. This finds some confirmation in some of his late inscriptions, which name Esagil and other Babylonian temples as sanctuaries of Sîn's great godhead. Yet the most significant parallel to the crescent symbol episode is probably the relief on top of the Babylon Stele, where Nabonidus carries a staff crowned with the lunar crescent, the *uskar Anu,* instead of the stylus symbol of Nabû that he proudly displays at Harran. Even the sweeping accusations of cultic neglect and ignorance leveled by Nabonidus at the Babylonians in the Harran Stele find an echo in this passage of the Verse Account. Similar accusations are now hurled back at the king, who "would confuse the rites, upset the omens, and *speak what he could* concerning the august cultic prescriptions."

Conclusion

The conflict between king and scholar came to a resolution when the Babylonian monarchy disappeared, leaving the scribal elite solely responsible for the intellectual and religious leadership of their civilization. The Verse Account reflects the views of a segment of this elite who opposed the designs of Nabonidus and were willing to collaborate with the administration imposed by the conquerors. What had they found so objectionable in the theological views of the ousted king? One can detect in the inscriptions of Nabonidus an endeavor to symbolize in religion the cosmopolitan character of the Babylonian Empire. The idea is not new. Lewy theorized more than half a century ago that Nabonidus tried to create an imperial religion centered on the moon-god that would unify the various nations he ruled. The reality was certainly more complex, yet this idea still retains much validity. A similar goal may have been contemplated by the late Sargonid kings of Assyria with the syncretism between Aššur and Sîn of Harran, both equated theologically with Enlil. All this would have implied, however, a decentering of Babylon as cosmological and political capital, a notion that pervaded the intellectual and religious culture of late Babylonia (George 1997). It is this and perhaps only this that may explain the vocal opposition to Nabonidus's religious designs. The loss of centrality by Babylon and its god Marduk reminded the Babylonians of the terrible ordeal their city had suffered under Sennacherib, who brutally stripped the old religious capital of its cosmological role. This was certainly not Nabonidus's intention. However, some of his inscriptions appear to propagate the idea of the subordination of Babylon to a larger political system and of its god Marduk to a new theological expression of this system. Ironically, this is precisely what the Persians achieved. Nabonidus, while appealing to deeply entrenched Babylonian traditions in presenting himself as religious leader and teacher of wisdom, nevertheless failed in his endeavor to create a new theology that would reflect the complex political reality of the Babylonian Empire at the transcendental level. In this respect, he exemplifies the failure of an old monarchy to maintain its legitimacy in times of dissolving order and the incapacity of an ancient but waning civilization to reinvent itself in a world dramatically transformed.

References

Alster, B.

1991 The Instructions of Ur-Ninurta and Related Compositions. *Orientalia* 60: 141–57.

Annus, A.

2002 *The God Ninurta in the Mythology and Royal Ideology of Ancient Mesopotamia.* State Archives of Assyria Studies 14. Helsinki.

Beaulieu, P.-A.

1989 *The Reign of Nabonidus, King of Babylon (556–539 B.C.).* Yale Near Eastern Researches 10. New Haven, CT.

1999 The Babylonian Man in the Moon. *Journal of Cuneiform Studies* 51: 91–99.

2001 The Abduction of Ištar from the Eanna Temple: The Changing Memories of an Event. Pp. 29–40 in *Proceedings of the XLV*[e] *Rencontre Assyriologique Internationale, Part I, Harvard University: Historiography in the Ancient World,* ed. T. Abusch et al. Bethesda, MD.

2003 Nabopolassar and the Antiquity of Babylon. *Eretz-Israel* 12 (*Hayim and Miriam Tadmor Volume*): 1–9.

Butler, S. A. L.

1998 *Mesopotamian Conceptions of Dreams and Dream Rituals.* Alter Orient und Altes Testament 258. Münster.

Cavigneaux, A.

2005 Shulgi, Nabonide, et les Grecs. Pp 63–72 in *An Experienced Scribe Who Neglects Nothing: Ancient Near Eastern Studies in Honor of Jacob Klein,* ed. Y. Sefati et al. Bethesda, MD.

Charpin, D.

2004 Histoire politique du Proche-Orient Amorrite (2002–1595). Pp. 25–480 in *Mesopotamien: Die altbabylonische Zeit,* D. Charpin, D. O. Edzard, and M. Stol. Orbis Biblicus et Orientalis 160/4. Fribourg.

Collins, J. J.

1996 4Q Prayer of Nabonidus ar. Pp 83–93 in *Qumran Cave 4, vol. XVII: Parabiblical Texts, Part 3,* ed. G. Brooke et al. Discoveries in the Judaean Desert 22. Oxford.

Cooper, J. S.

1978 *The Return of Ninurta to Nippur.* Analecta Orientalia 52. Rome.

Donbaz, V.

1991 A Brick Inscription of Nabonidus from Harran. *Annual Review of the Royal Inscriptions of Mesopotamia Project* 9: 11–12.

Drijvers, H. J. W.

1980 *Cults and Beliefs at Edessa.* Etudes préliminaires aux religions orientales dans l'empire romain 82. Leiden.

Fales, F. M., and Postgate, J. N.

1995 *Imperial Administrative Records, Part II: Provincial and Military Administration.* State Archives of Assyria 11. Helsinki.

Frame, G.

1995 *Rulers of Babylonia: From the Second Dynasty of Isin to the End of Assyrian Domination (1157–612 B.C.).* The Royal Inscriptions of Mesopotamia: Babylonian Periods 2. Toronto.

Frayne, D. R.

1990 *Old Babylonian Period (2003–1595 B.C.).* The Royal Inscriptions of Mesopotamia: Early Periods 4. Toronto.

Gadd, C. J.

1958 The Harran Inscriptions of Nabonidus. *Anatolian Studies* 8: 35–92.

George, A. R.

1992 *Babylonian Topographical Texts.* Orientalia Lovaniensia Analecta 40. Leuven.

1993 *House Most High: The Temples of Ancient Mesopotamia.* Mesopotamian Civilizations 5. Winona Lake, IN.
1997 'Bond of the Lands': Babylon, the Cosmic Capital. Pp 135–45 in *Die Orientalische Stadt: Kontinuität, Wandel, Bruch,* ed. G. Wilhelm. Colloquien der deutschen Orient-gesellschaft 1. Berlin.
1999 *The Epic of Gilgamesh: A New Translation.* New York.
2003 *The Standard Babylonian Gilgamesh Epic.* 2 vols. Oxford.

Gesche, P. D.
2000 *Schulunterricht in Babylonien im ersten Jahrtausend v. Chr.* Alter Orient und Altes Testament 275. Münster.

Grayson, A. K.
1975a *Assyrian and Babylonian Chronicles.* Texts from Cuneiform Sources 5. Locust Valley, NY. Reprinted, Winona Lake, IN, 2000.
1975b *Babylonian Historical-Literary Texts.* Toronto.

Grelot, G.
1994 Nabuchodonosor changé en bête. *Vetus Testamentum* 44: 10–17.

Katz, D.
2003 *The Image of the Netherworld in the Sumerian Sources.* Bethesda, MD.

Klein, J.
2001 The Genealogy of Nanna-Suen and Its Historical Background. Pp 279–301 in *Historiography in the Cuneiform World. Proceedings of the XLVe RAI, Vol. 1: Harvard University, 1998,* ed. T. Abusch et al. Bethesda, MD.

Kuhrt, A., and Sherwin-White, S.
1991 Aspects of Seleucid Royal Ideology: The Cylinder of Antiochus I from Borsippa. *Journal of Hellenic Studies* 111: 71–86.

Lambert, W. G.
1987 Lugal-šudde. P. 152 in vol. 7 of *Reallexikon der Assyriologie.*
1997 Syncretism and Religious Controversy in Babylonia. *Altorientalische Forschungen* 24: 158–62.

Lee, T. G.
1993 The Jasper Cylinder Seal of Aššurbanipal and Nabonidus' Making of Sîn's Statue. *Revue d'assyriologie et d'archéologie orientale* 87: 131–36.
1994 Propaganda and the Verse Account of Nabonidus' Reign. *Bulletin of the Canadian Society for Mesopotamian Studies* 28: 31–36.

Lewy, J.
1948 The Late Assyro-Babylonian Cult of the Moon and Its Culminations at the Time of Nabonidus. *Hebrew Union College Annual* 19: 405–89.

Litke, R. L.
1998 *A Reconstruction of the Assyro-Babylonian God-Lists, An = ᵈA-nu-um and An: Anu ša amēli.* Texts from the Babylonian Collection 3. New Haven, CT.

Livingstone, A.
1986 *Mystical and Mythological Explanatory Works of Assyrian and Babylonian Scholars.* Oxford.

MacGinnis, J.
1996 Letters from the Neo-Babylonian Ebabbara. *Mesopotamia* 31: 99–159.

Machinist, P., and Tadmor, H.
1993 Heavenly Wisdom. Pp 146–51 in *The Tablet and the Scroll: Near Eastern Studies in Honor of William W. Hallo,* ed. M. E. Cohen et al. Bethesda, MD.

Matsushima, E.
1987 Le rituel hiérogamique de Nabû. *Acta Sumerologica* 9: 158–61.

Pomponio, F.
2001 Nabû. A: Philologisch. Pp. 16–24 in vol. 9 of *Reallexikon der Assyriologie.*

Pongratz-Leisten, B.
1999 *Herrschaftswissen in Mesopotamien.* State Archives of Assyria Studies 10. Helsinki.
R = Rawlinson, H. C. 1861–91
The Cuneiform Inscriptions of Western Asia. London.
Rawi, F. N. H. Al-
1990 Tablets from the Sippar Library, I. The 'Weidner Chronicle': A Supposititious Royal Letter concerning a Vision. *Iraq* 52: 1–13.
Rawi, F. N. H. Al-, and George, A. R.
1994 Tablets from the Sippar Library III: Two Royal Counterfeits. *Iraq* 56: 135–48.
SBH = Oberhuber, Karl
1990 *Sumerisches Lexicon zu "George Reisner Sumerisch-babylonische Hymnen nach Thontafeln griechischer Zeit (Berlin 1896)."* Innsbruck: Institut für Sprachwissenschaft der Universität Innsbruck.
Schaudig, H.-P.
2001 *Die Inschriften Nabonids von Babylon und Kyros' der Großen.* Alter Orient und Altes Testament 256. Münster.
2002 Nabonid, der 'Gelehrte auf dem Königsthron': Omina, Synkretismen und die Ausdeutung von Tempel- und Götternamen als Mittel zur Wahrheitsfindung spätbabylonischer Religionspolitik. Pp. 619–45 in *Ex Mesopotamia et Syria Lux: Festschrift für Manfried Dietrich zu seinem 65. Geburtstag,* ed. O. Loretz et al. Alter Orient und Altes Testament 281. Münster.
Seidl, U.
2000 Babylonische und assyrische Kultbilder in den Massenmedien des 1. Jahrtausends v. Chr. Pp. 89–114 in *Images as Media: Sources for the Cultural History of the Near East and the Eastern Mediterranean (1st Millennium* B.C.E.), ed. C. Uehlinger. Orbis Bibilicus et Orientalis 175. Freiburg/Göttingen.
Seux, M.-J.
1967 *Epithètes royales akkadiennes et sumériennes.* Paris.
Sjöberg, Å. W.
2002 In the Beginning. Pp. 229–47 in *Riches Hidden in Secret Places: Ancient Near Eastern Studies in Memory of Thorkild Jacobsen,* ed. T. Abusch. Winona Lake, IN.
Streck, M. P.
2001a Nebukadnezzar III. und IV. P. 206 in vol. 9 of *Reallexikon der Assyriologie.*
2001b Nusku. Pp. 629–33 in vol. 9 of *Reallexikon der Assyriologie.*
Talon, P.
2005 *The Standard Babylonian Creation Myth Enma Eliš.* State Archives of Assyria Cuneiform Texts 4. Helsinki.
Verbrugghe, G. P., and Wickersham, J. M.
1996 *Berossos and Manetho, Introduced and Translated: Native Traditions in Ancient Mesopotamia and Egypt.* Ann Arbor, MI.
Watanabe, K.
1984 Die literarische Überlieferung eines babylonisch-assyrischen Fluchthemas mit Anrufung des Mongottes Sîn. *Acta Sumerologica* 6: 99–119.
Westenholz, J. G.
1997 *Legends of the Kings of Akkade: The Texts.* Mesopotamian Civilizations 7. Winona Lake, IN.
Wiggermann, F. A. M.
2001 Nin-ĝišzida. Pp. 368–73 in vol. 9 of *Reallexikon der Assyriologie.*

Part 3

Perceptions of a New Order

Chapter 7

Cyrus the Great of Persia: Images and Realities

Amélie Kuhrt

Introduction

Cyrus the Great of Parsa (modern Fars in southwestern Iran) founded the great Achaemenid Persian Empire, which stretched from the Indus Valley to the Aegean and lasted well over two hundred years (550–330 B.C.). The name of the Empire derives from the eponymous ancestor of the royal line, first cited as such by the fourth ruler (and usurper) of the Empire, Darius I (DB §2: Kent 1953; Schmitt 1991). It was the largest empire the world had yet seen and had no rivals for most of its existence.[1] Its administrative structure, embracing an enormous number of very different cultures, peoples, languages, was remarkably effective in holding this enormous territory together. Elements of the Achaemenid system were adopted and adapted by its conqueror, Alexander the Great (336–323), and the successor kingdoms established on its former terrain after his death (see, for example, Briant 1990; Sherwin-White and Kuhrt 1993).

The diverse pieces of evidence, when combined, yield the following picture of Cyrus. Although a Persian, Cyrus had close links to the Median king Astyages. Median power, based in Ecbatana (modern Hamadan in northwest Iran), included Fars, parts of Central Asia to the east, and reached westward as far as the Halys River in Anatolia. Cyrus led a successful Persian revolt against his Median overlord in 550, took over the larger part of his dominions, and extended them by conquering adjoining areas: the Lydian Kingdom, including the Greek cities of the Aegean seaboard in the 540s, and the Neo-Babylonian Empire, which embraced the entire Fertile Crescent (from the Persian Gulf to the Egyptian frontier) in 539. He rounded off these successes by mounting a campaign of conquest against tribes living beyond the Jaxartes River (modern Syr Darya) in northeastern Central Asia. Here he met his death in 530, and the region remained outside direct Persian control. Egypt, too, had not been conquered by the time he died, but his son and successor, Cambyses (530–522), added this important territory in the 520s. Darius I (522–486) subsequently added northwestern India and consolidated frontiers in the west, involving a temporary expansion

1. The most up-to-date, detailed study of the Empire is Briant 1996 [2002]; see also his critical bibliographical updates: Briant 1997; 2001. A brief introduction can be found in Kuhrt 1995: chap. 13; excellent longer discussions are Wiesehöfer 1993 [1996] and Allen 2005, the latter beautifully illustrated.

into Europe. After this, the Empire broadly stabilized inside its frontiers. Cyrus was thus responsible for about 90% of Persia's territorial conquests, achieved within the remarkably short time of 20 years. With the exception of his last unsuccessful venture, Cyrus's progress was marked throughout by the generosity with which he treated his defeated opponents, the respect he showed to local cultures, and his support for local cults. These policies laid the foundations for the Empire's remarkable success. The Persians celebrated his achievements in song and story, and his tomb was the object of a centrally funded cult down to the last days of the Empire.

Evidence Shaping the Traditional Image of Cyrus

That is the picture we have of Cyrus, based on very disparate material, which has been read selectively and fitted together to provide this attractive, heroic image. It has dominated modern European perceptions of Cyrus as the model of the enlightened and tolerant ruler from the fifteenth century to the present.[2] What are its constituent elements?

First, there is the evidence contained in the Old Testament. Isaiah 44–55 ("Deutero-Isaiah") hails him as Yahweh's anointed, chosen and named by Israel's god to destroy Babylon. This will deliver his people, the Jews, from their captivity in the land of Nebuchadnezzar, the hated king who had deported the population of Judah and destroyed Jerusalem together with its temple between 597/6 and 582. This, in turn, will allow the restoration of the Jewish community and its central cult. Ezra 1 and 5–6 offer two versions (in Hebrew and Aramaic, respectively) of an edict issued by Cyrus after his Babylonian victory. According to this, he ordered the Jews to rebuild their temple with moneys from the royal treasury and reactivate its cult. The account of Jerusalem's restoration is elaborated by the first-century A.D. Jewish historian Josephus (*Ant.* 11.1–18).

Second, we have the fifth- and fourth-century B.C. Greek writers, on whom later visions of Cyrus and the Persian Empire (in Greek and Latin) were generally based.[3] The first to make a lasting impact on Western scholars and create the normative picture of Cyrus as a ruler and conqueror of unparalleled wisdom, competence, justice, generosity, and piety is the work of the Athenian soldier-philosopher Xenophon, *Education of Cyrus*, translated into Latin in the 1440s.[4] Herodotus's *Histories*, written several decades earlier, trace the rise of the Persian Empire to the point where its seemingly unstoppable expansion was brought to a halt by the Greeks of Europe in 480 and 479. His account of the heroic founder is less idealized than Xenophon's and

2. See the articles by Lewis, Brosius, and Sancisi-Weerdenburg in Sancisi-Weerdenburg and Drijvers, eds. 1990.

3. There *are* occasional divergences in later classical writers, suggesting divergent or additional stories told about Cyrus; for example, Strabo 15.3, 6, who says that Cyrus took his name from the Cyrus River near Pasargadae, his birth-name being Agradates (Henkelman 2003a: 195–96). But the outlines of Cyrus's character and progress generally follow the earlier writers.

4. Xenophon lived in the later-fifth and well into the fourth century. See Sancisi-Weerdenburg 1990 for the reception of his work and its wide circulation in fifteenth-century Italy.

diverges considerably on many points of fact, but the generally positive impression of Cyrus that readers draw from Herodotus is solid. A full translation (into Latin) of Herodotus was first published in 1474, and his account gradually gained in popularity, although it was not necessarily always trusted.[5] A third important writer, whose work certainly originally contained a long and detailed story of Cyrus's origins and rise to power, is Ctesias, the composition of whose *Persica* only just predated Xenophon. Apart from substantial selections of his work in later writers,[6] his Persian history is known primarily from a summary made by the ninth-century Byzantine patriarch Photius–the original is lost. This became known in the West in the middle of the sixteenth century and was often published as an appendix to Herodotus, whose version of events it frequently contradicts. It has for long been considered an inferior, unreliable, gossipy work, although its value, at least as a source for Persian traditions about the past, is now being more and more appreciated.[7] The heroic nature of Cyrus and his triumphs against all odds emerge clearly in what we have of Ctesias. The differences in his story do not undermine a modern reader's favorable impression of the Persian king.

These then were the prevailing images of the Achaemenid Empire's founder in the minds of scholars before the decipherment of the Old Persian and Mesopotamian cuneiform scripts in the 1850s. Not a single one of these works was written less than a 100 years after Cyrus's death, and not one emanated from his homeland. Archaeological exploration in the nineteenth century changed this situation to some extent by adding material from Persia itself, as well as texts from the time of Cyrus. Most important was the discovery in 1879 of a clay foundation cylinder in the area of the Marduk Temple in Babylon.[8] Although damaged, it presents Cyrus, after his victory over the Babylonian king Nabonidus, proclaiming the restoration of sanctuaries and the return of deportees. This seems to harmonize perfectly with the Old Testament texts: the decree reverses the destructive, intolerant policies of earlier Assyrian and Babylonian regimes and proves Cyrus to have been an active supporter, even promoter, of local cults. Not only captive Jews but the Babylonians themselves can be seen in this document (as well as a Babylonian literary text published in 1924)[9] to have rejoiced at their liberation. Sadly, no informative texts in Cyrus's name have ever been found in Fars. But his new royal city of Pasargadae, first studied by Ernst Herzfeld in 1908,[10] bears witness to the regime's new spirit. Its fine stone structures and airy, columned

5. Contrast Xenophon's *Cyropaedia*, a translation of which *into French* already existed in 1470, possibly even earlier (see Sancisi-Weerdenburg 1990: 43). For the transmission and translation of Herodotus's Greek text, see Rollinger in Bichler and Rollinger 2000: 122–29.

6. Most important is the lengthy paraphrasing of the rise of Assyria and its fall to the Medes by Diodorus (see Lenfant 2004: F1b) and the extensive use made of him by Plutarch for his *Life of Artaxerxes* (II).

7. See the detailed reassessment by Lenfant 2004.

8. BM 90920; Weissbach 1911: XI; 2–9.

9. The "Persian Verse Account," first published by Smith (1924: 27–97, pls. 5–10).

10. The fundamental work on Pasargadae is Stronach 1978. For the history of exploration and excavation at Pasargadae, with full references, see Boucharlat 2005. The brief inscriptions in Cyrus's name at Pasargadae were (almost certainly) added later by Darius I; see, for example, Stronach 1997.

pavilions were dotted over an area of 5 square kilometers, set in gardens, with no sign of any permanent habitation.[11] It had no fixed defenses and had a free-standing gate building, in contrast to the enclosed, inward looking, heavily fortified palaces of Nineveh and Babylon.[12]

A Critical Reasessment

By tracing the accumulation of these very different pieces of evidence over time, one piled on top of the other, we can see how they might be fitted together to reinforce the prevailing image of Cyrus, the wise and tolerant statesman. It explains how the very positive reputation he enjoys came into being, was reinforced over the centuries, and has scarcely ever been challenged.[13] But it is important to realize that this reputation is the result of selective and/or uncritical reading. In order to assess the complexities of the figure of Cyrus and get closer to some of the historical realities, we need to consider each testimony critically and assess it within its proper context.

The biblical material is exceptionally complex, and there is no agreement among biblical scholars as to when Isaiah 44–55 or the book of Ezra was written or compiled. There is also no agreement on what kind of material underlies these presentations or how historically reliable it might be. Opinions vary so hugely that neither text can be treated as providing independently trustworthy evidence.[14] Certainly, the Jerusalem community within the tiny province of Yehud was reconstituted at some point after the Babylonian depredations within the period of Persian rule; certainly, there was a restoration of the Jerusalem temple and its cult. But exactly when this happened remains obscure. For the idea that it occurred under Cyrus or that he played a decisive role in this reconstruction, there is no supporting evidence. The earliest hints at a possible rebuilding do not occur until the reign of Darius I (522/1–486) and make no reference to Cyrus.[15] Moreover, it is quite unclear how or why this rebuilding was undertaken, and the evidence for any Persian royal involvement is extremely shaky. A further, at present insoluble, problem is knowing how extensive Nebuchadnezzar's destruction in Judah was, so that it is hard to evaluate the impact and scope that any restoration might have had.[16] So, while we can see that Cyrus came to be *credited* with this reversal in Judah's fortunes and thus came to occupy a favorable place in Jewish (and, indeed, Christian) visions of the past, this may well have been a retrospective honor bestowed upon him as the emblematic Persian king rather than a reflection of a historical event. Whatever one's position in the debate, it must be admitted that the

11. For the idea, still much in vogue, that, apart from the stone buildings, Pasargadae only ever housed temporary nomadic encampments, see Hansman 1972.

12. See the lyrical evocation of Stronach 2001a: 96–97.

13. A rare exception is D. W. Griffith's great silent screen epic *Intolerance*, of 1916, which portrays Cyrus as a bigot, crushing the free and easy life enjoyed by the Babylonians under a pleasure-loving Belshezzar and the kindly dreamer Nabonidus.

14. See Ackroyd 1990; Bedford 2001; Grabbe 2004.

15. Haggai and Zechariah 1–8; see the detailed discussion by Bedford (2001), who argues that the initiative to rebuild the temple came from the Jews who had remained in Jerusalem and was not inspired or ordered by any of the Persian kings.

16. See particularly the perhaps slightly overstated arguments of Barstad 1996.

biblical evidence, echoed by Josephus, has no independent value with respect to the nature of Cyrus's policy toward his new subjects.

The defining classical accounts present by no means a uniformly consistent picture of Cyrus as particularly "good" as opposed to a generally successful conqueror. Xenophon's *Education of Cyrus* is the exception, but it is clear that this work is more in the nature of a philosophical novel on the ideal ruler than a history founded on facts. It fits into contemporary Greek political debates about kingship and, where his account can be tested against hard and fast evidence, is plainly ahistorical.[17] Herodotus presents Cyrus as the grandson of the Median king Astyages, who attempts unsuccessfully to have him killed at birth because of a dream prophesying his future power. Foiled in this, Cyrus defeats the Medes and liberates the Persians from Median servitude. In response to a challenge from the Lydian king Croesus, he victoriously defeats him and is only stopped from executing him by divine intervention. Only when frustrated by this miracle does Cyrus decide to take Croesus into his entourage as a valued adviser. His generals are ordered to bring the Aegean coastal regions to heel, which is achieved by exceptionally brutal means (enslavement, massacre, and wholesale destruction; see Hdt. 1.153–76). The Persian conquest of Babylon is preceded by the anecdote of an enraged Cyrus, "punishing" a river for causing the death of one of the sacred white horses (Hdt. 1.189). Cyrus's bloody end in the land of the Massagetae is a textbook example of what befalls the greedy expansionist whose ambitions know no bounds (Hdt. 1.201–14).[18] Ctesias's Cyrus hails from the poorest of pastoral tribes and the most ignoble parentage but manages to work his way up to an honored position in the Median court (Lenfant 2004: F8d* [1–7]). His defeat of Astyages involves the torture of his children and grandchildren, followed by the execution of his son-in-law, and ultimately Astyages' death (*FGrH* 688 F9 [1–3; 6]). In the course of the Lydian war, Cyrus executes Croesus's son, resulting in the suicide of Croesus's wife. Only after repeated attempts to chain up Croesus are divinely frustrated[19] does Cyrus relent and treat him with honor (*FGrH* 688 F 9 [4; 5]). The stories show a man of great ability in the field, a brilliant tactician, ready to deploy whatever measures necessary to achieve his ends.

What about the Cyrus Cylinder (for the text, see appendix no. 1 below), which has played such a prominent part in confirming Cyrus's unprecedented humaneness?[20] The first point to note is that the cylinder is a document commemorating Cyrus's building work, which was placed in the foundations of the Marduk sanctuary in

17. See the useful discussion in Sancisi-Weerdenburg 1993.

18. See Sancisi-Weerdenburg (1990: 33–35) on this as the dominant and defining feature of Cyrus for Dante (in both *Purgatorio* and *De Monarchia*), Bocaccio, and Petrarch, before the arrival of Greek texts from Byzantium, the most decisive of which in revolutionizing his reputation being Xenophon's *Cyropaedia*. Until then, Cyrus was put on a par with Xerxes as an exemplar of vice and tyrannical rule. Note also the important discussion by Wiesehöfer (1993: 71–89), showing how the popular images of Cyrus and Xerxes can be reversed.

19. Note that at one point in this episode, Croesus's guards were beheaded.

20. Note the much-repeated statement that it is the "First Declaration of Human Rights"; see particularly some of the contributions to the volume celebrating the 2,500th commemoration held by the Shah of Iran in 1971 ("Homage Universel," *Acta Iranica* 1st series [1974]). A notice on the Circle of Ancient Iranian Studies (www.cais-soas.com) electronic bulletin board in January 2006, reporting on the loan of the cylinder to Tehran, described the document in the same words.

Babylon, the Esagila. Place and function inevitably help to determine its message. Thus it is, inevitably, Babylon's patron god Marduk who appears as the chief protagonist, personally engineering Cyrus's triumph.[21] Because it is by his will that Cyrus becomes the new king, it is inescapable that the preceding ruler's reign must have run counter to the divine order. This is the standard way in which Babylonians dealt with the problem they had faced repeatedly in the preceding two centuries, when they had had to submit to the rule of a series of usurpers and Assyrian conquerors (Kuhrt 1987). Closer examination of the text and comparison with earlier material shows, indeed, that each motif in the Cyrus Cylinder was drawn from a repertoire of traditional Mesopotamian themes, used by earlier claimants to the Babylonian throne to legitimize their rule. One such example is the commemorative cylinder of the Chaldean leader Marduk-apla-iddina II (the biblical Merodach-baladan, 721–710), who had no rightful claim to the Babylonian throne but seized it by force during the uncertain period that followed Sargon II's usurpation of the Assyrian kingship in 722/1 (see appendix, no. 2).[22] If we compare this text with the Cyrus Cylinder, we find many of the elements that appear there being deployed by Marduk-apla-iddina in order to strengthen his grip on the throne. Thus, he has been personally chosen for kingship by the head of the Babylonian pantheon, who has ensured his victory over the previous Assyrian rulers. In response, Marduk-apla-iddina performs the sacred rites and restores the sacred shrines. The confirmation that he is acting correctly and piously is that he finds a royal inscription placed in the temple foundations by an earlier, legitimate Babylonian king. This he honors by leaving it undisturbed and placing his own memorial document next to it. Cyrus, it should be noted (appendix, end of no. 1), acted in precisely the same way, reverently acknowledging the Assyrian king, Ashurbanipal, as an earlier, revered predecessor, whose pious work on the temple's fabric is marked and honored (see further, Kuhrt 1983).[23]

---

21. A fragmentary cylinder from Sin's (the moon-god) Temple in Ur (UET I, no. 307) is normally attributed to Cyrus, because its wording resembles the wording of the Cyrus Cylinder from Babylon:

> [. . .] and over the people joyfully named my name, Sin, [the lamp] of heaven and earth, with his favorable omen filled my hands with the four quarters of the world. I returned the gods to their shrines [. . .] let them dwell. [. . .] life of long days, a firm throne, an everlasting reign and kingship without equal, grant me as a gift.

But the argument is not watertight. As is clear (see below), the wording of the Cyrus Cylinder is standard Babylonian for texts and situations of this sort. So Schaudig's contention (2001: 480–81) that it could well refer to Nabonidus (himself a usurper of the Babylonian throne; see Beaulieu 1989) carries considerable weight. But this also must of course remain hypothetical. If it *should* eventually be found to relate to Cyrus, then it would reflect the fact that, when carrying out work in Sin's city and on his house, the Persian king would have presented his achievements as due to Ur's patron god.

22. Further motifs comparable to the Cyrus Cylinder (divine abandonment in response to the plight of inhabitants, gathering the scattered peoples, etc.) are inscribed in the introduction to the land-gift bestowed by Marduk-apla-iddina II on Bel-ahhe-eriba, the governor of Babylon. The donation is commemorated on an exceptionally fine boundary stone (Akk. *kudurru*, VS I 37, esp. i 17–42; ii 28–29), now in the Vorderasiatisches Museum, Berlin (see Leemans 1944–48: §7). The image of the king making the grant to Bel-ahhe-eriba is often reproduced (see, for example, the cover of Kuhrt 1995, vol. 2).

23. Note that the section mentioning Ashurbanipal at the end of the text is a fragment originally in the Yale Collection, now joined to the Cyrus Cylinder. The fact that it belongs to the Cyrus Cylinder was only recognized in the early 1970s (see Walker 1972: 158–59) and has had an important effect

Interestingly, the annals of Sargon II (722–705) present the Assyrian king's own defeat of Marduk-apla-iddina, 12 years later, in very similar terms to the words used by his enemy earlier (appendix, no. 3). What this text adds, significantly, is that, after triumphing over the current ruler, the new claimant to the Babylonian throne enters into negotiations with representatives of the Babylonian citizen body (appendix no. 3, section iii). Their successful conclusion is signified, in Sargon's case, by the community leaders' formally offering the 'left-overs' (Akk. *riḫate*) from the divine meals, which were regularly presented to the acknowledged king of Babylon (see Fuchs 1994: 332 n. 349). In accepting these, the new aspirant also accepted the duties that went with being a Babylonian sovereign: to respect and uphold the privileges of the urban elite and care for divine and civic dwellings. Work on sanctuaries and urban buildings was not something that could be undertaken at will; it required consultation with the gods (through divination) to see whether the proposed work was in line with divine plans. Approval of the plan to build, through the proclamation of positive omens, in turn demonstrated that the gods favored the new ruler. And this favor was reconfirmed by the new king, who traditionally formed and brought the first building brick, finding the inscription of a pious earlier ruler who had performed work that was similarly blessed.[24]

These comparisons must make it plain that the Cyrus Cylinder fits perfectly with established *Babylonian* traditions for coping with the serious disruptions created by war and conquest. This, of course, has important implications for the historical conclusions we can draw from it. Thus, nothing in it signals the introduction of a new Persian (as against Assyro-Babylonian) policy. All references to the "restoration" of shrines and their staffs are part of a familiar rhetoric deployed by conquerors and would-be kings, ready to accept the duties incumbent on them in their new position as rulers in Babylon. In fact, it reflects the pressure that Babylonian citizens were able to bring to bear on the new royal claimant more than it casts light on the character of the potential king-to-be. In this context, the reign of the defeated predecessor was automatically described as bad and against the divine will—how else could he have been defeated? By implication, of course, all his acts became, inevitably and retrospectively, tainted.

This is also, perhaps, how we should understand the so-called "Persian Verse Account."[25] The composition, which may have been publicly sung,[26] is a litany of crimes that slander Nabonidus mercilessly and end with a veritable paean of praise for Cyrus. It repeats and elaborates some of the themes found in the introductory passage of the Cyrus Cylinder, echoes of which appear in Deutero-Isaiah's vision of Cyrus as the anointed of Yahweh, the chosen tool to deliver his people from oppression and usher in a Judean renaissance. Getting at the complex historical realities that lie behind

in clarifying our understanding of the text. The new version of the text, including the Yale fragment, was first edited by Berger (1975).

24. On the elaborate rituals of building in Mesopotamia, see Kuhrt and Sherwin-White 1991; Bedford 2001: 157–80; Fried 2003.

25. See above, n. 9. Schaudig 2001: 563–78 is the most recent edition, with a new translation.

26. The suggestion was made by Von Voigtlander 1963.

these standardized proclamations propounded in the name of and in support of a victor *after* his triumph is virtually impossible. But one thing must be clear: neither text can be used to support the idea that Cyrus introduced radical new policies of religious tolerance, including the unprecedented return of deportees to their former homes.

Historical Realities

Let me now turn to a text that gives us a clearer sense of Cyrus and confirms some of the conclusions already drawn. It still inevitably provides only a partial picture, but what we have is revealing. This is a Babylonian chronicle (the "Nabonidus Chronicle"; see appendix, no. 4). It covers (with breaks) the reign of Nabonidus (556–539), including his defeat and Cyrus's conquest. The chronicle is part of the Babylonian chronicle series, which begins in the middle of the eighth century and continues into the second century B.C. The texts were (almost certainly) compiled on the basis of contemporary notations relating to astronomical observations—part of a kind of database correlating planetary movements, weather, prices, and political events.[27] Their exact purpose is not known, but it is probable that they were linked to attempts to manage the future. Important for the historian is the fact that the chronicles, based on material of this sort, were not written at the behest or in the interests of any political agency. The chronicles are scrupulous in noting defeats suffered by Babylonian kings, the kings' failure to arrive on time in the military arena, or the fact that the text being used by the writer is damaged or has omitted information and his compilation is thus incomplete.[28] The chronicle's dispassionate statements (terse as they may be) are, where we have them, extremely reliable.

What emerges from this particular chronicle? First, and valuably, it gives us a virtually certain date for Cyrus's defeat of the Median king Astyages (550) and a very precise chronology for his conquest of Babylon itself (October 539). From the moment of Cyrus's victory, the Babylonian business community dated its transactions by him as ruler, which thus provide us with a date for his death: between the 12th and 31st of August, 530. Herodotus's curiously precise figure of 29 years for Cyrus's length of reign may well be right (Hdt. 1.214), which would place Cyrus's accession to the Persian throne in 559. These are the *only* chronologically fixable points of Cyrus's career. Apart from this, the chronicle has a (now unfortunately fragmentary) account of the struggle between Cyrus and Astyages. It states clearly that the conflict was provoked by the Median king, whose expansion plans included the conquest of Persia. This contradicts the still-widespread and reiterated notion that Persia was subject to the Medes.[29] Conversely, it agrees with Herodotus's account that the Median army mutinied and handed Astyages over to Cyrus (Hdt. 1.127–30).

The chronicle contains a further mention of Cyrus in 547/6, which is usually taken to be a reference to Cyrus's conquest of Lydia (see appendix, no. 4 ii 15–18). But, it

27. This has been contested by Brinkman (1990) but is defended by van der Spek (2003) and Kuhrt (2000).
28. See, for example, ABC 1, i 6–8, 36–37; 3, line 28.
29. See on this the discussion by Rollinger 1999.

is worth emphasizing yet again that, however attractive this is, the traces in the tablet do *not* make this reading possible, so we do not know the object of Cyrus's campaign in that year. Neither Herodotus nor Ctesias has a precise, reliable chronology for the sequence of events, and we know very little in detail of Cyrus's other activities, so we should resist the temptation to force the chronicle entry to fit in with what we should like it to say.[30]

Most important, and largely preserved, is the chronicle's account of Cyrus's confrontation with Nabonidus. It is possible that tension between the two powers had been growing for some time—certainly there is *a* reference to Persia in a very broken context in the chronicle's entry for 540. This may explain Nabonidus's action in collecting the divine statues of several cities in Babylon for (one assumes) safety in the face of the expected Persian attack (Beaulieu 1993). In late September 539, the Babylonian army led by its king faced the Persian troops on the Tigris, near Opis. The battle was won by Cyrus, who followed up his victory by plundering the city and massacring its inhabitants. Shortly after this, Sippar, which was next in line of attack, surrendered, perhaps in order to avoid sharing the fate of Opis.[31] From what follows, it is clear that Cyrus halted there but sent his general (Gubaru/Gobryas) with an army ahead to invest Babylon and take the defeated Babylonian king prisoner. Only *after* Babylon had been secured (three weeks later) did Cyrus himself enter the city, which was now prepared to receive him as its new ruler (see Pongratz-Leisten 1993: chap. 5; Kessler 2002), almost certainly as a result of negotiation with representatives of the Babylonian citizenry.[32] Cyrus made the appropriate royal gestures in response—that is, initiating the "restoration" of order following the disruptions of war. After making arrangements for the administration of the country, which (as we know from Babylonian documents) continued to rely heavily on the existing Babylonian framework and personnel, he installed his son, Cambyses, as king of Babylon. The formal occasion for this was the Babylonian New Year Festival, celebrated in late March 538. This was a lengthy ceremony (two weeks) during which the king's contract with the Babylonian gods and citizens was publicly reaffirmed. The festival had grown in importance during Babylonia's disturbed history in the immediately preceding centuries,[33] and its correct celebration by Assyrian kings had been carefully noted by Babylonian chroniclers. An important phase in the festival was the point where the king led the image of the god Nabu from the "Sceptre House" in procession into the main temple courtyard. Because Cambyses had already been formally installed as king of Babylon in Nabu's cella (confirmed by the local dated documents), he would have been expected to enact this phase of the ceremony. But a recent restudy of the last lines of the chronicle (George 1996: 379–81) suggests strongly that it was Cyrus who took the lead in

30. This problem was trenchantly analyzed by Cargill (1977), and the position has not changed since, although it continues to be asserted that the chronicle provides a precise date for Cyrus's conquest of Lydia. For a full reexamination, see Rollinger in press.

31. Note Tolini's discussion (2005) of Babylonian evidence indicating a longer, planned, concerted resistance by Nabonidus and his army *after* the Battle of Opis.

32. See the passage in Sargon's Annals (see appendix, no. 3 [iii]), and compare with Babylon's surrender to Alexander (Kuhrt 1990; van der Spek 2003).

33. See Kuhrt 1987; Pongratz-Leisten 1993 and the comments and corrections in George 1996.

this–but robed, as the chronicle observes, in Persian ("Elamite") dress. The political message of this action, in the context of this very traditional Babylonian ceremony, must be that there was a clear limit to how far Cyrus was prepared to fall in with Babylonian custom. Instead, the Babylonians were made to recognize, unmistakably, that they were now subjects of a foreign ruler.

In trying to trace something of Cyrus's background, we find that the Babylonian material is again revealing. With one exception, Cyrus's title in the chronicle is "King of Anshan." Until perhaps the early seventh century, the region of Fars in southwest Iran and its main city, Anshan, formed a significant part of the old kingdom of Elam.[34] It is now generally accepted that, by at least the late second millennium, Iranian pastoralists (that is, Persians) had moved into this territory and mingled with the local population.[35] From the late eighth century onward, Elam experienced political problems as a result of conflict with Assyria. In the course of this, its kings had lost control of the Fars region, certainly by the middle of the seventh century, if not earlier. One outcome was the emergence of a new, small kingdom there, ruled by a Persian dynasty, whose members took the ancient and sonorous *Elamite* title "King of Anshan." Cyrus, whose name may itself be Elamite (Henkelman 2006: 32), proudly traces their genealogy in the Cyrus Cylinder: "Son of Cambyses, great king, king of Anshan, grandson of Cyrus, great king, king of Anshan, great-grandson of Teispes, great king, king of Anshan" (see appendix, no. 1 [iv]). The historical reality of this claim is confirmed by the Elamite legend on an heirloom seal impressed on five of the published Persepolis Fortification tablets, which reads: "Cyrus, the Anshanite, son of Teispes," that is, Cyrus's grandfather.[36] So this "Persian" dynasty perceived itself to be ruling part of the old Elamite realm, using a venerable Elamite title. Further, it had clearly held this position for about a century before Cyrus's reign. And the archaeological evidence from Fars suggests that, from around the time of the dynasty's formation, the region became much more densely settled (de Miroschedji 1985). This evidence contradicts the later traditions found in Herodotus, Ctesias, and Xenophon, according to whom Cyrus's family was not royal, with the Persian dynasty only beginning with him. Instead, we now need to see him as fourth in a line of "great kings" who had begun to lay the groundwork on which the Persian Empire was built. It is quite possible that Astyages' attack on Cyrus was a move to try and contain the growth of this threatening power.

Although it is possible to see something of this development, it still remains rather shadowy, and nothing prepares one for Cyrus's immense achievements. It is only with him that the landscape of Fars was transformed by the creation of the great royal residence at Pasargadae, which was a name taken from Cyrus's tribe (Hdt. 1.125). It contained a series of substantial stone buildings, using novel architectural forms and layouts. Elaborately columned buildings took their inspiration from a building tradi-

34. Anshan (modern Tal-i Malyan) is located 48 km west-northeast of later Persepolis.
35. See the thorough and very clear analysis in Henkelman 2003a; 2003b.
36. PFS 93* impressed on PF 692–5, 2033, dating between 503/2 and 500/499 (see Hallock 1977: 127–28, fig. E5; Garrison and Root 1996/1998, figs. 2a–c).

tion used in previous centuries and on a smaller scale for palatial residences in the northern and middle Zagros.[37] A series of palaces (or pavilions) was set around an artificially irrigated formal garden.[38] The magnetic surveys recently conducted by French and Iranian archaeologists show that the seemingly isolated stone structures were surrounded by mud-brick buildings and walls; thus, the urban nature of Pasargadae can no longer be denied (Boucharlat and Benech 2002; Boucharlat 2003). Parts of the palaces (P and S) were decorated with reliefs clearly derived from the Assyrian iconographic repertoire, although one, the winged genie on Gate R, combines Elamite and Egyptian features. A large structure, the Zendan, possibly associated with royal ceremonies (Sancisi-Weerdenburg 1983), displays features found in a seventh-century temple in the central Zagros (Tepe Nush-i Jan, Stronach 2001b: 624–25, figs. 1–3). A substantial and well-fortified citadel dominates the site. Particularly intriguing is a great precinct containing a stepped altar set on a platform; a similar platform with stair access faces it.[39] It reminds one, inevitably, of what was to become the standard image of the king on the facade of the rock-cut royal tombs from Darius I on: the king with the tip of his bow resting on his foot, stands on a stepped podium facing a fire altar on an identical podium; he raises his hand in a gesture of salutation to a figure in a winged disc, with hand outstretched in the same manner; the whole scene is set on a throne-like structure borne aloft by labeled representatives of the imperial subjects (Schmidt 1970). The tomb of Cyrus himself,[40] which was the focus of a royally funded cult until the last days of the Empire, sits high on a stepped base. This evokes a ziggurat, perhaps the great Elamite ziggurat at Chogha Zanbil (Khuzestan), which was certainly still visible. Its gabled roof is reminiscent of the architectural traditions of western Anatolia. The masonry techniques, indeed, confirm that people from that part of the world were engaged in the construction work at Pasargadae (Nylander 1970; Boardman 2000: 53–62). The creation and building of the city (5 km sq.) was an immense undertaking that implies the existence of a developed administrative structure to deal with the logistics of so large an enterprise. It not only drew manpower from the newly conquered territories but also selected motifs, techniques, and layouts from the new imperial lands to create a spectacular setting in which Cyrus's vision of his kingship could be celebrated in an appropriate ceremonial setting (Root 1979). It remained an important center in the region throughout the Empire's existence and was the locus for the initiation of each new king, who was ritually associated with the founder of the Persian Empire there before being crowned (Plutarch,

37. The main sites are Hasanlu IV (Dyson 1965; 1989; Young 2002), Tepe Nush-i Jan (Stronach 2001b; see now Stronach and Roaf 2007), Baba Jan (Goff 1969, 1970, 1977, 1978, 1985), Godin Tepe (Young 1969; Young and Levine 1974).

38. Stronach 1989. The recent French-Iranian research on the site indicates that more sections of the city were laid out as parkland than previously thought (Boucharlat and Benech 2002).

39. It was thought that associated with the precinct was a structure intended to accommodate an audience. But the French survey (above, n. 37) has established that this terrace and the walls are later in date.

40. See Arrian's description, *Anabasis* VI 29.4–7, derived from Alexander the Great's companion, Aristobulus, which suggests that the tomb was set within a garden, although this could be a misreading (see Henkelman 2006: chap. 5.7.4).

Artaxerxes 3.1–2). The combination of motifs from earlier, now-subject polities and the use of a mixed labor force tangibly reflect Persian claims to world dominion—an ideology fully developed by Cyrus's successors.

Conclusions

Although the evidence is not immense, it is sufficient to counter the image of the Cyrus of modern European and Judeo-Christian tradition. Instead of a young idealistic liberator with a new vision for ruling the world, we can begin to define a king, heir to an already fairly significant realm, who deployed both brutal and placatory gestures in a calculated and effective manner. Evidence for his treatment of defeated enemies is not unequivocal. While Ctesias and Herodotus both have him treating Croesus kindly, the lyric poet Bacchylides has Croesus and his family vanish from the face of the earth, suggesting that, according to some traditions, he was killed.[41] For Nabonidus's fate, we have the statements of the early-third-century B.C. Babylonian scholar Berossus (*FGrH* 680 F10a) and the hellenistic Babylonian "Dynastic Prophecy,"[42] according to both of which he survived. But both are late, and Xenophon has him killed in battle, a fate that is not confirmed by the reliable "Nabonidus Chronicle" (see appendix, no. 4); it reveals no more than that he was taken prisoner, with his ultimate fate being unknown. It would not, of course, be unprecedented for defeated kings to be taken into the victor's court and provided with resources: the ration texts from Nebuchadnezzar's palace illustrate precisely this practice (Weidner 1939). Building on the local infrastructure in order to administer newly conquered territory was a standard and logical interim measure for any conqueror.[43] In terms of religious tolerance, too, it is hard to define the difference between Assyrian and Achaemenid practices. The Assyrians acknowledged the potency of local deities.[44] Imposing the "yoke of Assur" on or setting up "the weapon of Assur" in conquered territory symbolized incorporation into the empire and the duties that this entailed, not the forcible imposition of a new religion (Holloway 2002: 158–77). This is comparable to the ideology propagated by Darius I and his successors: Auramazda was the god of the king, most clearly expressed in one of Darius's inscriptions from Susa:

---

41. Bacchylides of Keos lived ca. 520–450 and thus represents an earlier tradition than Herodotus (see Maehler 1982: F3, for the relevant poem).

42. Grayson 1975: 32–33, ii 20–21, which reads "The king of Elam [i.e., Persia] will change his place[. . .]. He will settle him in another place[. . .]. He will settle him in another land[. . .]." For a detailed discussion of this text, arguing against Grayson's interpretation that it shows Cyrus in a poor light, see van der Spek 2003: 319–20.

43. The example of Judah under Babylonian rule between 597/6 and 582 is a rather obvious example of this.

44. Some may be reluctant to accept the speech of the Assyrian commander at the siege of Jerusalem in 701 (2 Kgs 18:19–25) or the story of the Assyrian king responding to a request to send an expert to instruct the new inhabitants of Samaria about Yahweh (2 Kgs 17:25–28) as evidence of the fact that the Assyrian regime acknowledged the power of local gods and may even have supported their cult. It nevertheless seems to me revealing that these stories were included in the biblical narrative. In addition, there is the material from elsewhere presented and discussed by Cogan 1974.

1 I (am) Darius, the great king, king of kings, king of countries, son of Hystaspes, the Achaemenid.
2 King Darius proclaims: Auramazda is mine; I am Auramazda's; I worshipped Auramazda; may Auramazda bear me aid. (Kent 1953: DSk)

The king's deity, who had created the universe and placed it under the care of the Persian ruler, encapsulated the ideals of Persian imperial order, which it was the duty of all subjects to obey and uphold.

Finally, political considerations motivated Cyrus's actions at every step. In order to establish and consolidate control as firmly as possible, he needed to woo the support of local elites, something best done by accommodating himself to local norms whenever possible. But this was preceded by victory in battle and a definitive show of force, followed by no uncertain reminders to new subjects of their subservient position. What we can define of his career fits smoothly with the behavior of his imperial predecessors and successors.

Cyrus was a remarkable soldier and was politically pragmatic. The explosion in size of the tiny Persian Kingdom during his reign remains astonishing.[45] His rapid conquests of vastly dispersed territories not previously united under one political umbrella are easily comparable with, possibly greater in their breath-taking scope and scale than Alexander the Great's epic achievements. This, together with the widely diffused messages of his piety and statesmanship derived from Ezra, Isaiah, and Xenophon, combined with heroic stories of his rise to power help to explain the continued persistence of his reputation as a uniquely able and merciful ruler. It is hard for the less-immediately-attractive, down-to-earth evidence with its gaps and uncertainties to compete with, let alone displace them. Legend and tradition have the power to create their own persistent truths.[46]

Appendix

1. Cyrus Cylinder[47]

(i) vilification of predecessor:

An imitation of Esagila he made [. . . .] to Ur and the other cult centers. A cult order that was unsuitable [. . .] he spoke daily, and, an evil thing, he stopped the regular offerings [. . .] he placed in the cult centres. The worship of Marduk, king of the gods, he removed from his mind. He repeatedly did that which was bad for his city. Daily [. . .] he destroyed all his [subjects] with an unending yoke. In response to their

45. The importance of the Elamite element in the "ethnogenesis" of the Persians is emerging ever more clearly: bureaucratic practice (Cameron 1948; Hallock 1969); iconography (Alvarez-Mon 2004); cult (Henkelman 2006). The political significance of the Elamite Kingdom and its survival into the sixth century have been stressed by several scholars recently (Potts 1999; 2005; Waters 2000; Henkelman 2003a; 2003b; 2006: 1–38). All this illuminates an important aspect of the Persian Empire's prehistory but still leaves the development of the kingdom of Anshan/Persia up through the reign of Cyrus II largely in the dark.

46. For a striking example of this, see Kuhrt 2003.

47. Text edition: Berger 1975: 192ff.; Schaudig 2001: 550–56. English translation is my own.

lament the Enlil of the gods grew very angry [. . . .] their territory. The gods who lived in them left their dwelling-places, despite his anger (?) he brought them into Babylon.

(ii) a good, new ruler is personally picked by Babylon's god:

Marduk [. . . .], to all the places, whose dwelling-places were in ruins, and to the inhabitants of Sumer and Akkad, who had become like corpses, he turned his mind, he became merciful. He searched through all the countries, examined (them), he sought a just ruler to suit his heart, he took him by the hand: Cyrus, king of Anshan (= Parsa/Fars), he called, for the dominion over the totality he named his name. Gutium and all the Ummanmanda (= Media) he made subject to him. The black-headed people, whom he allowed his hands to overcome, he protected in justice and righteousness. Marduk, the great lord, who cares for his people, looked with pleasure at his good deeds and his righteous heart. He ordered him to go to Babylon, and let him take the road to Babylon. Like a friend and companion he went by his side. His massive troops, whose number was immeasurable like the water of a river, marched with their arms at their side.

(iii) the new ruler enters in triumph amid public rejoicing:

Without battle and fighting he let him enter his city Babylon. He saved Babylon from its oppression. Nabonidus, the king who did not honor him, he handed over to him. All the inhabitants of Babylon, the whole of the land of Sumer and Akkad, princes and governors knelt before him, kissed his feet, rejoiced at his kingship; their faces shone. 'The lord, who through his help has brought the dead to life, who in (a time of) disaster and oppression has benefitted all'—thus they joyfully celebrated him, honoured his name.

(iv) genealogy and titles:

I, Cyrus, king of the universe, mighty king, king of Babylon, king of Sumer and Akkad, king of the four quarters, son of Cambyses, great king, king of Anshan, grandson of Cyrus, great king, king of Anshan, great-grandson of Teispes, great king, king of Anshan, eternal seed of kingship, whose reign was loved by Bel and Nabu and whose kingship they wanted to please their hearts—when I had entered Babylon peacefully, I set up, with acclamation and rejoicing, the seat of lordship in the palace of the ruler.

(v) the new ruler cares for city and cults:

Marduk, the great lord, [. . . .] me the great heart, [. . .] of Babylon, daily I cared for his worship. My numerous troops marched peacefully through Babylon. I did not allow any troublemaker to arise in the whole land of Sumer and Akkad. The city of Babylon and all its cult centres I maintained in well-being. The inhabitants of Babylon, [who] against the will [of the gods . . . .] a yoke unsuitable for them, I allowed them to find rest from their exhaustion, their servitude I relieved.

(vi) divine blessings provoke the homage of rulers further afield:

Marduk, the great lord, rejoiced at my [good] deeds. Me, Cyrus, the king, who worships him, and Cambyses, my very own son, as well as all my troops he blessed mercifully. In well-being we [walk] happily before him. [At his] great [command] all the kings, who sit on thrones, from all parts of the world, from the Upper Sea to the Lower Sea, who dwell [in distant regions], all the kings of Amurru, who dwell in tents, brought their heavy tribute to me and kissed my feet in Babylon.

(vii) Return of cult statues and their staffs:

From [. . . .], Ashur and Susa, Agade, Eshnunna, Zamban, Meturnu and Der as far as the territory of Gutium, the cities on the other side of the Tigris, whose dwelling-places had [of o]ld fallen into ruin–the gods who dwelt there I returned to their home and let them move into an eternal dwelling. All their people I collected and brought them back to their homes. And the gods of Sumer and Akkad, which Nabonidus to the fury of the lord of the gods had brought into Babylon, at the order of Marduk, the great lord, in well-being I caused them to move into a dwelling-place pleasing to their hearts in their sanctuaries. May all the gods, whom I have brought into their cities, ask before Bel and Nabu for the lengthening of my life, say words in my favour and speak to Marduk, my lord: 'For Cyrus, the king, who honors you, and Cambyses, his son, [. . . .] the kingship.' The lands in their totality I caused to dwell in a peaceful abode.

(viii) increased offerings and repair/completion of buildings in Babylon:

. . .] goose, 2 ducks and 10 wild doves, over and above the goose, ducks and wild doves [. . .] I supplied in plenty. To stengthen the wall Imgur-Enlil, the great wall of Babylon [. . . .], I took action. [. . .] The quay-wall of brick on the bank of the moat, which an earlier king had built, without completing the work. [. . .] on the outer side, what no other king had done, his craftsmen (?), the levy [. . .] in Babylon [. . . with] asphalt and bricks I built anew and [completed the work on it (?)]. [. . .] with bronze bands, thresholds and *nukuse* (door-posts) [. . . in] their [gates]

(ix) reference to act of pious earlier ruler:

[. . . An inscription] with the name of Ashurbanipal, a king who preceded me [. . .] I found [. . .]

2. Cylinder of Marduk-apla-iddina II, Chaldean King of Babylon (721–710)[48]

(i) a good, new ruler is personally picked by Babylon's god:

He (Marduk) looked (with favor) upon Marduk-apla-iddina, king of Babylon, the prince who reveres him, to whom he (Marduk) stretched out his hand [. . .] The king of the gods [. . .] duly named him to the shepherdship of the land of Sumer and Akkad, personally said: 'This is indeed the shepherd who will gather the scattered (people).'

(ii) Marduk causes the Assyrians to be defeated:

With the power of the great lord, the god Marduk, and of the hero of the gods, the god Utulu, he defeated the widespread army of Subartu (i.e., Assyria) and shattered their weapons. He brought about their overthrow and prevented them from treading on the territory of the land of Akkad.

48. Text and English translation: Frame 1995: B.6.21.1.

(iii) Maruk-apla-iddina performs the divine rituals and restores shrines:

With the excellent understanding which the god Ea, the creator, maker of all things, had bestowed upon him, (and with) the extensive knowledge which the god Ninsiku had granted him, he directed his attention to performing the rites, to administering correctly(?) the rituals, and to renovating the cult centres and the sanctuaries of the divine residences of the great gods of the land of Akkad.

[. . .]

(iv) reference to act of pious earlier ruler:

I saw the royal inscription of a king who had preceded me (and) who had built that temple. I did not alter his inscription, but (rather) I placed (it) with my own inscription. [. . .]

3. Annals of Sargon II of Assyria (722–705) *(defeated Marduk-apla-iddina II, 710–709)*[49]

(i) reviling of previous ruler:

He (Marduk-apla-iddina, the Chaldaean) entered the land of Sumer and Akkad, dominated (it) and ruled Babylon, the city of the lord of the gods, 12 years against the will of the gods.

(ii) Marduk picks Sargon as king:

But Marduk the great lord, saw the evil deed of the land Kaldu, which he hates, and on his lips was (the command) to remove sceptre and throne of his kingship from him. Me, Sargon, the reverent king, he chose definitively from among all the kings and raised my head (i.e., elevated me to this role). In order to block the path of the Kaldu, the evil enemy, into the land of Sumer and Akkad, he made my weapons strong.

(iii) After Sargon's victories in Babylonia, Marduk-apla-iddina flees to his homeland; Sargon waits in the Assyrian fortress of Dur-Ladinnu, north of Babylon:

The citizens of Babylon and Borsippa, the *erib-biti,* the *ummâne,* those skilled in workmanship (and) who go before and direct the land, who had been subject to him (i.e., Marduk-apla-iddina), brought the 'remnant' (of the divine meals) of Bel and Sarpanitum, of Nabu and Tashmetum to Dur-Ladinnu into my presence, invited me to enter Babylon and made glad my soul. Babylon, the city of the lord of the gods, I entered amidst rejoicing, stood before the gods, who dwell in Esagil and Ezida, and made pure, additional offerings before them.

4. Cyrus's Defeat of the Medes and His Conquest of Babylonia *(The Nabonidus Chronicle)*[50]

(*col. ii*) 1. (550/49) (Astyages) mustered (his army) and marched against Cyrus, king of Anshan, for conquest [. . .]

49. Text edition: Fuchs 1994: lines 260–63; 311–14. English translation is my own.

50. Text edition: Smith 1924: 98–123; *ABC* no. 7; Glassner 2004: no. 26. English translation is my own.

2. The army rebelled against Astyages (*Ishtumegu*) and he was taken prisoner. They handed him over to Cyrus [. . .]

3. Cyrus marched to Ecbatana ((kur)*Agamtanu*), the royal city. The silver, gold, goods, property [. . .]

4. which he carried off as booty (from) Ecbatana he took to Anshan. The goods (and) property of the army of [. . .]

(ii 5–12: report on Nabonidus's activities and events in Babylonia, 549–547 B.C.; then:)

13. (547/6) On the fifth day of the month Nisanu (6 April) the queen mother died in Durkarashu which (is on) the bank of the Euphrates upstream from Sippar.

14. The prince and his army were in mourning for three days (and) there was (an official) mourning period. In the month Simanu (June)

15. there was an official mourning period for the queen mother in Akkad. In the month Nisanu (April) Cyrus, king of Parsu, mustered his army

16. and crossed the Tigris below Arbailu (= mod. Erbil). In the month Ayyaru (May) [he marched] to [. . . .]

17. He defeated its king, took its possessions, (and) stationed his own garrison (there) [. . . .]

18. Afterwards the king and his garrison was in it [. . . .]

(ii 19–end of column: primarily internal Babylonian affairs)

(col. iii; beginning broken)

1. (540/539) [. . .] killed(?)/defeated(?). The river . . . [. . .]

2. [. . .] . . . Ishtar of Uruk [. . .]

3. [. . .] of Per[sia(?) . . . .]

4. [. . . . .]

([539/8] iii 5–10: description of New Year festival performed by Nabonidus and his measures to protect divine statues)

10. Until the end of the month Ululu (ended 26 September) the gods of Akkad [. . .]

11. which are above the . . . and below the . . . . were entering Babylon. The gods of Borsippa, Cutha,

12. and Sippar did not enter. In the month Tashritu (27 September–27 October) when Cyrus did battle at Opis on the [bank of]

13. the Tigris against the army of Akkad, the people of Akkad

14. retreated. He carried off the plunder (and) slaughtered the people. On the fourteenth day (6 October) Sippar was captured without battle.

15. Nabonidus fled. On the sixteenth day (8 October) Ug/Gubaru, governor of Gutium, and the army of Cyrus without a battle

16. entered Babylon. Afterwards, after Nabonidus returned, he was captured in Babylon. Until the end of the month the shield

17. of the Guti (i.e., troops) surrounded the gates of Esagila. Interruption (of rites/cult) in Esagila or the temples

18. there was none, and no date was missed. On the third day of the month Arahshamnu (29 October), Cyrus entered Babylon.

19. They filled the *haru*-vessels in his presence. Peace was imposed on the city, the proclamation of Cyrus was read to all of Babylon.

20. He appointed Gubaru, his governor, over the local governors of Babylon.

21. From the month Kislimu (25 November–24 December) to the month Adaru (22 February–24 March 538) the gods of Akkad which Nabonidus had brought down to Babylon

22. returned to their places. On the night of the eleventh of the month Arahshamnu (6 November 539) Ug/Gubaru died. In the month [. . .]

23. the king's wife died. From 27 Adaru (20 March) to 3 Nisanu (26 March) [there was] mourning in Akkad.

24. All of the people bared(?)/shaved(?) their heads. When on the 4th day (of Nisanu = 27 March 538), Cambyses, the son of Cyrus,

25. went to E-ningidar-kalamma-summu (= temple of Nabu *ša hare* in Babylon), the official of the sceptre-house of Nabu [gave him(?)] the sceptre of the land.

26. When [Cyrus(?)] came, in Elamite attire, he [took] the hands of Nabu [. . .]

27. lances and quivers he picked [up, and(?)] with the crown-prince [he came down(?)] into the courtyard.

28. He (or: they) went back [from the temple(?)] of Nabu to E-sagila. [He/they libated] ale before Bel and the Son of [. . .]

References

ABC = Grayson, A. K.

2000 *Assyrian and Babylonian Chronicles.* Reprinted, Winona Lake, IN.

Ackroyd, P.

1990 The Biblical Portrayal of Achaemenid Rulers. Pp. 1–16 in *The Roots of the European Tradition,* ed. H. Sancisi-Weerdenburg and H. J. W. Drijvers. Achaemenid History 5. Leiden.

Allen, L.

2005 *The Persian Empire: A History.* London.

Alvarez-Mon, J.

2004 Imago Mundi: Cosmological and Ideological Aspects of the Arjan Bowl. *Iranica Antiqua* 39: 203–32.

Barstad, H. M.

1996 *The Myth of the Empty Land: A Study in the History and Archaeology of Judah during the "Exilic" Period.* Symbolae Osloenses Fasc. Suppl. 28. Oslo.

Beaulieu, P.-A.

1989 *The Reign of Nabonidus, King of Babylon 556–539 B.C.* Yale Near Eastern Researches 10. New Haven, CT.

1993 An Episode in the Fall of Babylon. *Journal of Near Eastern Studies* 52: 241–61.

Bedford, P.

2001 *Temple Restoration in Early Achaemenid Judah.* Supplements to Journal for the Study of Judaism 65. Leiden.

Berger, P.-R.
1975 Der Kyros-Zylinder mit dem Zusatzfragment BIN II Nr. 32 und die akkadischen Personennamen im Danielbuch. *Zeitschrift für Assyriologie* 64: 192–234.
Bichler, R., and Rollinger, R.
2000 *Herodot.* Studienbücher Antike 3. Hildesheim.
Boardman, J.
2000 *Persia and the West: An Archaeological Investigation of the Genesis of Achaemenid Art.* London.
Boucharlat, R.
2003 Le Zendan de Pasargades: De la tour "solitaire" à un ensemble architectural. Données archéologiques récentes. Pp. 79–99 in *A Persian Perspective: Essays in Memory of Heleen Sancisi-Weerdenburg*, ed. W. Henkelman and A. Kuhrt. Achaemenid History 13. Leiden.
2005 Pasargadai. Pp. 1351–63 in vol. 10 of *Reallexikon der Assyriologie*, ed. D. O. Edzard and M. P. Streck. Berlin.
Boucharlat, R., and Benech, C.
2002 Organisation et aménagement de l'espace à Pasargades: Reconnaissances archéologiques de surface, 1999–2002. *Achaemenid Research on Texts and Archaeology* note 1. http://www.achemenet.com/ressources/enligne.
Briant, P.
1990 The Seleucid Kingdom, the Achaemenid Empire and the History of the Near East in the First Millennium B.C. Pp 40–65 in *Religion and Religious Practice in the Seleucid Kingdom*, ed. P. Bilde et al. Studies in Hellenistic Civilization 1. Aarhus.
1996 *Histoire de l'empire perse: De Cyrus à Alexandre.* Paris. [= *From Cyrus to Alexander: A History of the Persian Empire*, trans., P. T. Daniels. Winona Lake IN, 2002.]
1997 *Bulletin d'histoire achéménide I. Topoi* Supplement 1: 5–127.
2001 *Bulletin d'histoire achéménide II.* Persika 1. Paris.
Brinkman, J. A.
1990 The Babylonian Chronicle Revisited. Pp. 73–104 in *Lingering over Words: Studies in Ancient Near Eastern Literature in Honor of William L. Moran*, ed. T. Abusch, J. Huehnergard, and P. Steinkeller. Atlanta.
Cameron, G. G.
1948 *Persepolis Treasury Tablets.* Oriental Institute Publication 65. Chicago.
Cargill, J.
1977 The Nabonidus Chronicle and the Fall of Lydia: Consensus with Feet of Clay. *American Journal of Ancient History* 2: 97–116.
Cogan, M.
1974 *Imperialism and Religion: Assyria, Judah and Israel in the Eighth and Seventh Centuries B.C.E.* Society of Biblical Literature Monograph 19. Missoula, MT.
Dyson, R.
1965 Problems of Proto-historic Iran as Seen from Hasanlu. *Journal of Near Eastern Studies* 24: 193–217.
1989 Rediscovering Hasanlu. *Expedition* 31/2–3: 3–11.
FGrH = Jacoby, F.
1923–58 *Die Fragmente der griechischen Historiker.* Berlin.
Frame, G.
1995 *Rulers of Babylonia from the Second Dynasty of Isin to the End of Assyrian Domination (1157–612 B.C.).* Royal Inscriptions of Mesopotamia, Babylonian Periods, 2. Toronto.
Fried, L.
2003 The Land Lay Desolate: Conquest and Restoration in the Ancient Near East. Pp. 21–54 in *Judah and the Judeans in the Neo-Babylonian Period*, ed. O. Lipschits and J. Blenkinsopp. Winona Lake, IN.

Fuchs, A.
1994 *Die Inschriften Sargons II. aus Khorsabad.* Göttingen.

Garrison, M. B., and Root, M. C.
1996/1998 *Persepolis Seal Studies: An Introduction with Provisional Concordances of Seal Numbers and Associated Documents on Fortification Tablets 1–2087.* Achaemenid History 9. Leiden.

George, A.
1996 Studies in Cultic Topography and Ideology. *Bibliotheca Orientalis* 53: 365–95.

Glassner, J.-J.
1993 *Chroniques Mésopotamiennes.* La roue à livres. Paris. [= *Mesopotamian Chronicles*, ed. B. R. Foster. Writings from the Ancient World 19. Atlanta, 2004.]

Goff, C.
1968 Luristan in the First Half of the First Millennium B.C.: A Preliminary Report on the First Season's Excavations at Baba Jan, and Associated Surveys in the Eastern Pish-i Kuh. *Iran* 6: 105–34.
1969 Excavations at Baba Jan, 1967: Second Preliminary Report. *Iran* 7: 115–30.
1970 Excavations at Baba Jan, 1968: Third Preliminary Report. *Iran* 8: 141–56.
1977 Excavations at Baba Jan: The Architecture of the East Mound, Levels II and III. *Iran* 15: 103–40.
1978 Excavations at Baba Jan, 1967: The Pottery and Metals from Levels III and II. *Iran* 16: 29–65.
1985 Excavations at Baba Jan, 1967: The Architecture and Pottery of Level I. *Iran* 22: 1–20.

Grabbe, L. L.
2004 *A History of the Jews and Judaism in the Second Temple Period*, vol. 1: *Yehud: A History of the Persian Province of Judah.* London.

Grayson, A. K.
1975 *Babylonian Historical-Literary Texts.* Toronto.

Hallock, R. T.
1969 *Persepolis Fortification Tablets.* Oriental Institute Publication 92. Chicago.
1977 The Use of Seals on the Persepolis Fortification Tablets. Pp. 127–33 in *Seals and Sealing in the Ancient Near East*, ed. McG. Gibson and R. D. Biggs. Bibliotheca Mesopotamica 6. Malibu, CA.

Hansman, J.
1972 Elamites, Achaemenians and Anshan. *Iran* 10: 101–25.

Henkelman, W.
2003a Persians, Medes and Elamites: Acculturation in the Neo-Elamite Period. Pp. 181–231 in *Continuity of Empire(?): Assyria, Media, Persia*, ed. G. B. Lanfranchi, M. Roaf, and R. Rollinger. History of the Ancient Near East Monograph 5. Padua.
2003b Defining Neo-Elamite History. *Bibliotheca Orientalis* 60: 251–64.
2006 *The Other Gods Who Are: Studies in Elamite-Iranian Acculturation Based on the Persepolis Fortification Texts.* Ph.D. diss., Leiden.

Holloway, S. W.
2002 *'Assur Is King! Assur Is King!': Religion in the Exercise of Power in the Neo-Assyrian Empire.* Culture and History of the Ancient Near East 10. Leiden.

Kent, R. G.
1953 *Old Persian: Grammar, Texts, Lexicon.* 2nd ed. New Haven, CT.

Kessler, K.-H.
2002 *harinê*: Zu einer problematischen Passage der Nabonid-Chronik. Pp. 389–93 in *'Sprich doch mit deinen Knechten aramäisch, wir verstehen es!' 60 Beiträge zur Semitistik: Festschrift für Otto Jastrow zum 60. Geburtstag*, ed. W. Arnold and H. Bobzin. Wiesbaden.

Kuhrt, A.

1983 The Cyrus Cylinder and Achaemenid Imperial Policy. *Journal for the Study of the Old Testament* 25: 83–97.

1987 Usurpation, Conquest and Ceremonial: From Babylonia to Persia. Pp. 20–55 in *Rituals of Royalty: Power and Ceremonial in Traditional Societies*, ed. D. Cannadine and S. Price. Past and Present. Cambridge.

1990 Alexander and Babylon. Pp. 121–30 in *The Roots of the European Tradition*, ed. H. Sancisi-Weerdenburg and H. J. W. Drijvers. Achaemenid History 5. Leiden.

1995 *The Ancient Near East, c. 3000–330* B.C. 2 vols. London.

2000 Israelite and Near Eastern Historiography. Pp. 257–79 in *Congress Volume: Oslo 1998*, ed. A. Lemaire and M. Saebø. Vetus Testamentum Supplement 80. Leiden.

2003 Making History: Sargon of Agade and Cyrus the Great of Persia. Pp. 347–61 in *A Persian Perspective: Essays in Memory of Heleen Sancisi-Weerdenburg*, ed. W. Henkelman and A. Kuhrt. Achaemenid History 13. Leiden.

Kuhrt, A., and Sherwin-White, S.

1991 Aspects of Seleucid Royal Ideology: The Cylinder of Antiochus I from Borsippa. *Journal of Hellenic Studies* 111: 71–86.

Leemans, W. F.

1944–48 Marduk-apal-iddina II, zijn tijd en zijn geslacht. *Jaarberich van hel Vooraziatisch-Egyptisch Genootschap: Ex Oriente Lux* 3/9–10: 432–55.

Lenfant, D.

2004 *Ctésias de Cnide: La Perse; L'Inde; Autres Fragments.* Coll. des Universités de France/ Association Guillaume Budé. Texte établi, traduit et commenté. Paris.

Maehler, H.

1982 *Die Lieder des Bakchylides, Teil 1: Die Siegeslieder: Edition, Übersetzung, Kommentar.* Leiden.

Miroschedji, P. de

1985 La fin du royaume d'Anshan et de Suse et la naissance de l'empire perse. *Zeitschrift für Assyriologie* 75: 265–306.

Nylander, C.

1970 *Ionians at Pasargadae: Studies in Old Persian Architecture.* Boreas: Uppsala Studies in Ancient Mediterranean and Near Eastern Civilizations 1. Uppsala.

Pongratz-Leisten, B.

1993 Ina Šulmi Irub: *Die kulttopographische Programmatik der* akitu-*Prozession in Babylonien und Assyrien im 1. Jahrtausend v.Chr.* Baghdader Forschungen 16. Mainz.

Potts, D.

1999 *The Archaeology of Elam: Formation and Transformation of an Ancient Iranian State.* Cambridge World Archaeology. Cambridge.

2005 Cyrus the Great and the Kingdom of Anshan. Pp. 7–28 in *Birth of the Persian Empire*, ed. V. S. Curtis and S. Stewart. London.

Rollinger, R.

1999 Zur Lokalisation von Parsu(m)a(š) in der Fars und zu einigen Fragen der frühen persischen Geschichte. *Zeitschrift für Assyriologie* 89: 115–39.

in press The Median "Empire": The End of Urartu and Cyrus the Great's Campaign in 547 B.C. (Nabonidus Chronicle II 16). In *Ancient West and East* 6.

Root, M. C.

1979 *The King and Kingship in Achaemenid Art: Essays on the Creation of an Iconography of Empire.* Acta Iranica 19. Leiden.

Sancisi-Weerdenburg, H.

1983 The Zendan and the Kabah. Pp. 145–51 in *Kunst, Kultur und Geschichte der Achämenidenzeit und ihr Fortleben*, ed. H. Koch and D. N. Mackenzie. Archäologische Mitteilungen aus Iran Supplement 10. Berlin.

1990 Cyrus in Italy: From Dante to Machiavelli, Some Explorations of the Reception of Xenophon's *Cyropaedia*. Pp. 31–52 in *The Roots of the European Tradition*, ed. H. Sancisi-Weerdenburg and H. J. W. Drijvers. Achaemenid History 5. Leiden.

1993 Cyropaedia. Pp. 571–72 in vol. 6 of *Encyclopaedia Iranica*. New York.

Sancisi-Weerdenburg, H., and Drijvers, H. J. W., eds.

1990 *The Roots of the European Tradition*. Achaemenid History 5. Leiden.

Schaudig, H.

2001 *Die Inscriften Nabonids von Babylon und Kyros' des Grossen samt den in ihrem Umfeld entstandenen Tendenzschriften: Textausgabe und Grammatik*. Alter Orient und Altes Testament 256. Münster.

Schmidt, E. F.

1970 *Persepolis III: The Royal Tombs and Other Monuments*. Oriental Institute Publication 70. Chicago.

Schmitt, R.

1991 *The Bisitun Inscription of Darius the Great: Old Persian Text*. Corpus Inscriptionum Iranicarum 1/1/1. London.

Seidl, U.

2003 Wie waren die achaimenidischen Doppelprotomen-Kapitelle ausgerichtet? Pp. 67–77 in *A Persian Perspective: Essays in Memory of Heleen Sancisi-Weerdenburg*, ed. W. Henkelmann and A. Kuhrt. Achaemenid History 13. Leiden.

Sherwin-White, S., and Kuhrt, A.

1993 *From Samarkhand to Sardis: A New Approach to the Seleucid Empire*. Hellenistic Culture and Society 13: Berkeley, CA.

Smith, S.

1924 *Babylonian Historical Texts relating to the Capture and Downfall of Babylon*. London.

Spek, R. van der

2003 Darius III, Alexander the Great and Babylonian Scholarship. Pp. 289–346 in *A Persian Perspective: Essays in Memory of Heleen Sancisi-Weerdenburg*, ed. W. Henkelmann and A. Kuhrt. Achaemenid History 13. Leiden.

Stronach, D.

1978 *Pasargadae*. Oxford.

1989 The Royal Garden at Pasargadae: Evolution and Legacy. Pp. 475–502 in *Archeologia Iranica et Orientalis: Miscellanea in honorem Louis Vanden Berghe*, ed. L. Meyer and E. Haerinck. Ghent.

1997 Darius at Pasargadae: A Neglected Source for the History of Early Persia. *Topoi* Supplement 1: 351–63.

2001a From Cyrus to Darius: Notes on Art and Architecture in Early Achaemenid Palaces. Pp. 95–111 in *The Royal Palace Institution in the first Millennium* B.C., ed. I. Nielsen. Monographs of the Danish Institute at Athens 4. Aarhus.

2001b Nush-i Jan. Pp. 624–29 in vol. 9 of *Reallexikon der Assyriologie*, ed. E. Ebeling et al. Berlin.

Stronach, D., and Roaf, M.

2007 *Nush-i Jan*, vol. 1: *The Major Buildings of the Median Settlement*. Leuven.

Tolini, G.

2005 Quelques éléments concernant la prise de Babylone par Cyrus. Note 3 of *Achaemenid Research on Texts and Archaeology*. http://www.achemenent.com/ressources/Publications en ligne/Arta.

Von Voigtlander, E. N.

1963 *A Survey of Neo-Babylonian History*. Ph.D. diss, University of Michigan.

Walker, C. B. F.

1972 A Recently Identified Fragment of the Cyrus Cylinder. *Iran* 10: 158–59.

Waters, M.
2000 *A Survey of Neo-Elamite History.* State Archives of of Assyria Study 12. Helsinki.
Weidner, E. F.
1939 Jojachin, König von Juda, in babylonischen Keilschrifttexten. Pp. 923–35 in *Mélanges Syriens offerts à Monsieur René Dussaud.* Bibliothèque Archéologique et Historique 30. Paris.
Weissbach, F. H.
1911 *Die Keilinschriften der Achämeniden.* Vorderasiatische Bibliothek 3. Leipzig.
Wiesehöfer, J.
1993 *Das Antike Persien: Von 550 v.Chr. bis 650 n.Chr.* Zurich. [= *Ancient Persia,* trans. A. Azodi. London 1996.]
Young, T. C.
1969 *Excavations at Godin Tepe: First Progress Report.* Toronto.
2002 Syria and Iran: Further Thoughts on the Architecture of Hasanlu. Pp. 386–98 in *Of Pots and Plans: Papers on the Archaeology and History of Mesopotamia and Syria Presented to David Oates in Honour of His 75th Birthday,* ed. Lamia Al-Gailani Werr et al. London.
Young, T. C., and Levine, L. D.
1974 *Excavations of the Godin Tepe Project: Second Progress Report.* Toronto.

Chapter 8

The Migration and Sedentarization of the Amorites from the Point of View of the Settled Babylonian Population

Brit Jahn

Introduction

Cuneiform Texts and the Ethnicity of the Amorites

The Amorites have left no written documents in the Amorite language, or if Amorite documents ever existed, they have not survived. Thus, we must rely on Sumerian and Akkadian cuneiform texts for information about the migration and sedentarization of the Amorites in the ancient Near East. But how are we to identify the Amorites in the cuneiform texts? The clearest reference is found in texts in which people are referred to as Amorites (Sumerian = martu, Akkadian = *amurrû*).[1] However, by the end of the Ur III period (2111–2003 B.C.), the martu/*amurrû* designation had disappeared, because of the assimilation and integration of the Amorites.[2] From then on, it is hardly possible to differentiate between the Amorites and the older, established population of Babylonia.

A linguistic analysis of personal names is a second way to distinguish Amorites from other peoples. Amorite personal names appear mostly in a Northwest Semitic dialect that can be differentiated from Akkadian, and they seem to characterize an ethnic group (see also Streck 2004a: 318). Nevertheless, we must be cautious in using this method because of the possibility that names were changed during the process of acculturation and integration into Babylonian culture. Traditions or memories of personal ancestors could also influence name choice. Last but not least, the choice of names was surely influenced by passing fashion. However, one must assume that the Amorites would have taken on Akkadian names due to the higher prestige of the Sumero-Babylonian culture, rather than the other way round. The use of Amorite names in the heartland of Babylonia decreased during the reign of Śamśu-ʾiluna,

1. The terms martu and *amurrû* are mostly collective terms for nomads from the point of view of Babylonians, but this does not imply that the nomads belonged to only one tribe. We have to reckon with the possibility that the name of a single tribe was used to refer to all nomads. See also Streck 2000: 26–29.

2. Some texts from Tell Asmar (ancient Ešnunna) speak of persons described as martu only in the Old Babylonian period (see Gelb 1968).

which may have been due to the increasing integration of the Amorites and their adoption of the Babylonian social and cultural way of life.[3]

The Amorites from the Fāra Period to the Ur III Period

Cuneiform texts from Šuruppag (ancient Fāra, about 2550 B.C.) and Ebla (about 2300 B.C.) provide the first evidence of a hitherto unknown ethnic group (Edzard, Farber, and Sollberger 1977; Bonechi 1993; Archi 1985). This population is called *mar-du/tu/tum*, marking them as strangers and non-Babylonians. The Amorites are also attested in cuneiform texts from the Akkad period (about 2340–2198 B.C.).

An inscription of Narām-Suʾen, the fourth king of the Akkad dynasty, recounts his military victory on the Amorite mountain of Bašar (Ğebel Bišrī; Frayne 1993: 90–94).[4]

Col. ii 16–20: ^{16}*a-na* ^{17}*ba-sa-ar* ^{18}sa.dú-*ì* ^{19}mar-tu^{ki} ^{20}. . .

. . . to Bašar, the Amorite mountain.[5]

Col. iii 1–24: *na-⟨ra-am⟩-/*^{d}*s[uʾen]* ^{2}*da-núm* ^{3}buranun/^{íd}*-tám* ^{4}*a-na* ^{5}*ba-śa-ar* ^{6}śa.dú-*ì* ^{7}mar-tu^{ki} ^{8}*ik-śu-ud/-su$_{4}$-ma* ^{9}šudul ^{10}*is-{ku$_{8}$}-ni$^{!}$-a-ma* ^{11}*iś-ku$_{8}$-na/-ma* ^{12}*i-tá-aḫ-za-ma* ^{13}*in* di.ku$_{5}$ ^{14}*an-nu-ni-[t]im* ^{15}⌜*ù*⌝ ^{16}*e[n-lí]l* ^{17}*na-⟨ra-am⟩/-*^{d}*⟨suʾen⟩* ^{18}*da-[núm]* ^{19}*in* kaskal[+()] ^{20}*in ba-śa-a[r]* ^{21}śa.dú-*ì* ^{22}mar-tu$^{[k]i}$ ^{23}unu^{ki}-*[a]*m ^{24}*iš$_{11}$-*⌜*ar*⌝

Narām-Suʾen, the mighty, (crossed) the Euphrates River in the direction of Bašar, the Amorite mountain, reached him (Amar-girid), and they joined battle and fought one another. By the verdict of the goddess Annunītum and the god Enlil, Narām-Suʾen, the mighty, was victorious over the Urukean at Bašar, the Amorite mountain.

Although this text gives an account of a military campaign of Narām-Suʾen against Amar-girid, the king of Uruk, without mentioning the Amorite population, the year-name of Šar-kali-šarrī, the last king of the Akkadian Empire, shows that war was also waged against the Amorites in Ğebel Bišrī (Gelb 1952: 139, no. 268; Thureau-Dangin 1898: pl. 6, no. 17; 1903: 57, no. 124):

in 1 mu *šar-kà-lí-*lugal*-rí* mar.tu*-am in ba-sa-ar*^{kur} *iš$_{11}$-a-ru*

In the year in which Šar-kali-šarrī defeated the Amorites at Basar.

The main reason for these battles was surely the rulers' expansionist desires, and closely connected with this was the procurement of important resources, especially wood and stone, which were in insufficient supply in Babylonia. It is known that, for example, Gudea received NA-stones and alabaster for his buildings from Ğebel Bišrī.

Gudea Statue B (Edzard 1997: 30–38)

Col. vi ^{3}*ù-ma-núm* ^{4}ḫur-sag me-nu-a-ta ^{5}ba$_{11}$-sal-la ^{6}ḫur-sag mar-tu-ta ^{7} $^{na_{4}}$na-gal ^{8}im-ta-e$_{11}$ $^{9–12}$. . . ^{13}*ti-da-núm* ^{14}ḫur-sag mar-tu-ta ^{15}nu$_{11}$-gal lagab-bé-a ^{16}mi-ni-túm . . .

---

3. In this regard, Streck (2004a: 335–42) has examined and evaluated the personal names of the Old Babylonian period.

4. For the connection of *basalla* and *basar* with Ğebel Bišrī, see Edzard 1957: 35.

5. Wilcke (1997: 23) reads *e-il$^{?}$-lí-a-[a]m* 'war dabei hinaufzusteigen', and Sommerfeld (2000: 423) reads ŠU.DU$_{8}$.A 'hielt er (den Weg) ein (?)'. For a summary, see Streck 2000: 32 n. 1.

> [3-12]He brought down large NA-stones from Umānum, the mountain of Menua, and from Basalla, the Amorite mountain [9-12]. . . [13-16]He brought alabaster blocks from Tidanum, the Amorite mountain. . . .

Apart from the campaigns of the rulers of Akkad and Gudea, it is impossible to identify Amorites within the Babylonian heartland at this time. It seems that the Amorites were exclusively associated with the region of the Middle Euphrates.[6]

Migration into Babylonian Territory during the Ur III Period

I understand the term *migration* to mean a unique, directed movement. In contrast to this, *transhumance* (often called seasonal migration) characterizes seasonal pastoral mobility, which will not be taken into consideration in this essay.

From the Ur III period on, the pressure of Amorite migration into Babylonia increased, for some unknown reason. The "dimorphic oscillations" that have been defined by Rowton probably played an important role. A sudden change in climate, illnesses and epidemics, famines, population growth, or political changes–any of these could be the catalyst for a shift in the balance of settled people and nomads (Rowton 1976: 24–30; also Schwartz 1995: 255a–b). Attempts to keep these people out of Babylonia culminated in the building of a fortification wall, the existence of which is recorded, although no ruins have yet been located. The wall was begun under Šulgi, the second king of the Ur III Dynasty, and finished by the fourth king of this dynasty, Šū-Suʾen, in his fourth year of reign. This event was recorded as a year- name:[7]

> mu ^{d}*šu*-^{d}*suʾen* lugal-urí^{ki} bàd-mar-tu *mu-ri-iq ti-id-nim* mu-dù
>
> Year: Šū-suʾen, the king of Ur, has built the Martu-wall, which keeps away the Tidnum.

Nevertheless, letters by Ibbi-Suʾen, Šū-Suʾens's successor and the last king of the Ur III period, refer to attacks by Amorites, demonstrating that the Amorites' migration into Babylonia was not substantially affected by the construction of this wall (see pp. 196–97).

The massive penetration of Amorites into Babylonia at this time, however, does not mean that there were no Amorites in southern Mesopotamia previously. One must assume that they gradually infiltrated Babylonia, conformed to urban life, and became integrated into the social and cultural structures of the settled population (Wilcke 1969–70: 16; Lemche 1995: 1201a; Schwartz 1995: 254b). This may explain the considerable increase of towns under Amorite influence immediately after the collapse of Ur.[8]

---

6. For a summary of this conclusion, see Streck 2000: 31–36.
7. For the building of the wall and its possible location, see Wilcke 1969–70: 2–12.
8. Whiting (1995: 1234–36) explains the rise of Amorite dynasties as resulting from a prior dependence on Amorite mercenaries: "Amorites simply took over cities they were once hired to protect, cities that were weakened by long years of dominance by a central, though no longer effective, authority."

The Threat to Babylonian Towns in the Ur III Period

Although the increasing number of Amorites in Babylonia was already perceptible during the reign of Šulgi, it was Ibbi-Suʾen, the last king of Ur, who was especially threatened by Amorites on several different fronts (see below). The secession of the urban centers of Ešnunna, Susa, Umma, Lagaš, and Nippur further weakened the kingdom.[9] A famine in Ur was probably the reason that Išbi-Erra,[10] governor of Isin, abandoned Ibbi-Suʾen, keeping back the necessary grain.

In an apparently fictitious letter to Ibbi-Suʾen, Išbi-Erra writes:[11]

> 7inim mar-tu (lú)kúr-ra šà ma-da-zu(-šè) ku_4(var. kur)-ra giš (ì; var. bí)-tuku-(àm)
> 8144,000 še gur še-dù-a-bi šà ì-si-in-na(-šè; var. ke_4) ba-an-ku_4-ur (var. re-en)
> 9a-da-al-la-bi mar-tu dù-dù-a-bi sà kalam-ma (var. mu)-šè (ba-an/ni)-ku_4-(re-en)
> 10bàd-gal-gal-bi im-mi-in-dab_5
> 11mu mar-tu še-ba sìg-ge(-d[è) nu-mu-e-da-sum-mu (var.]-un-da-ak-e)
> 12ugu-mu mu-ta-ni(-ib)-KAL ba-dab_5-en
>
> One heard information that hostile Amorites penetrated the interior of your country. I took 144,000 kor barley, all of the grain, into the town of Isin. Now, all of the Amorites have penetrated the interior of the country. They have occupied all large fortresses. Because of the Amorites, I cannot give the barley rations for supplies. They are stronger than I. I could be taken prisoner.[12]

Although Išbi-Erra is surely exaggerating, it is clear that the invasion of the Amorites was a factor that needed to be taken seriously and that the Martu-wall was ultimately ineffective.[13] Unfortunately, specifics regarding the duration of the Amorite migration process are lacking.

---

9. The absence of year-names under Ibbi-Suʾen and the use of localized year-names is conclusive evidence of the independence of these towns (Sallaberger and Westenholz 1999: 174–78).

10. Ibbi-Suʾen called Išbi-Erra the "man from Mari" and made a point of noting that he was not of Sumerian descent.

> Letter to Puzur-Numušda from Ibbi-Suʾen (see Falkenstein 1950: 61; see also Edzard 1964: 150):
> 19 Iiš-bi-dèr-ra numun-ke-en-ge-ra nu-me-a . . . 34lú má-ríki-ke_4 . . .
> Išbi-Erra, who isn't of Sumerian stock . . . the man from Mari . . .

11. Text publication: Legrain 1922: 33 and pl. 4, no. 9; transliteration and translation by Jacobsen 1953: 39–40; Wilcke 1969–70: 12–13. Summary of the letter by Edzard 1957: 45–46. The Ibbi-Suʾen texts are not original compositions. Based on linguistic and historical criteria, we believe that these texts were later scribal-exercise copies of previously composed literature. Thereforer, these texts cannot be entirely trusted (see Streck 2000: 36–37 and comment 1).

12. In the following part of this letter, Išbi-Erra asked Ibbi-Suʾen to send 600 ships so that he could transport barley. But Ibbi-Suʾen was not in a position to send the ships. Instead of turning to the governors who were allied with Ibbi-Suʾen for help, Išbi-Erra took advantage of the crisis to become the independent ruler of Isin.

13. In his reply, Ibbi-Suʾen accused Išbi-Erra of not having stopped the Amorite invasion (Gurney and Kramer 1976: 15–16, copy p. 83; Wilcke 1970: 55):

> 14$puzur_4$-nu-muš-da šagin bàd-igi-ḫur-sag-gá 15mar-tu lúkúr-ra šà kalam-mu-šè
> 16a-gin_7 im-da-an-ku_4-ré-en
> How can you permit that Puzur-Numušda, the governor of Badigiḫursaĝ, to let the hostile Amorites penetrate the interior of my country?

The threat to the urban centers by the Amorites in the Ur III period stands in contrast to the subjugation of the Amorites under Ibbi-Suʾen, which is evident in two documents (see below). Unfortunately, it is impossible to determine the reasons for this change during the reign of Ibbi-Suʾen.

> Year-name of Ibbi-Suʾen (the 17th year of reign; see *RlA* 2:146):
>
> mu ^{d}i-bí-^{d}suʾen lugal uri^{ki}-ma-ra mar-tu á im-ùlu-ul-ta uru^{ki} nu-zu gú im-ma-an-ga$_{2}$-ar
>
> Year: Ibbi-Suʾen, king of Ur, subjected the Amorites, the strength of the southern storm, who do not know towns.

The subjugation of the Amorites is also mentioned in a letter from Ibbi-Suʾen to Puzurnumušda (Falkenstein 1950: 62–63):

> ^{35}ì-ne-šè mar-tu kur-bi-ta ^{d}en-líl á-daḫ-mu im-ma-zi
>
> Now, Enlil, my helper, has mobilized the Amorites from the mountain.

However, it seems as though Ibbi-Suʾen succeeded in controlling the Amorites only during the 17th year of his reign and then only by forming an alliance with them. This year-name also supplies evidence that the Amorites made troops available to the king.[14] Because only important incidents appear in year-names, which is typical of the Sumero-Babylonian tradition, it is particularly significant that a year-name includes a reference to the subjugation of the Amorites.

A military conflict between Išbi-Erra and the Amorites can be dated to the time of the alliance between Ibbi-Suʾen and the Amorites. It is likely that the expulsion of the Amorites from Babylonia was not as much the primary motivation as the destruction of Ibbi-Suʾen's ally.

> Year-name of Išbi-Erra (8th year of reign; Sigrist 1988: 13–14):
>
> mu uru^{ki} mar-tu ba-ḫul
>
> Year: the towns of Amorites were destroyed.

This year-name also shows that the Amorites were not exclusively transhumant pastoral nomads, but also settled in one way or another.[15] This evidence suggests that their settlement was a long-term process of infiltration rather than a single mass migration.

Finally, we should mention that, in addition to military conflicts inside Babylonia, economic interactions between Išbi-Erra and Amorites outside Babylonia are well known.[16]

> ^{18}a-gin$_{7}$ mar-tu-e an-ta nam-mu-ši-in-gi
>
> How can it be that you did not go into action against the Amorites?

14. The Amorites in the Kingdom of Mari also had to perform military service in the regiments of the Mari king or his vassals, as indicated in numerous documents.

15. The cuneiform tablets from Mari often mention *alānū* 'settlements' of the Amorites on which they farmed and to which they returned after transhumance in the spring (see Streck 2002: 169–70).

16. See Buccellati 1966: 238–39 and references to Amorites named *Šamānum* (Išbi-Erra 21 and 25) and *Usî* (Išbi-Erra 13–15, 26) on pp. 116–17 and 119.

Sedentarization and Striving for Power

The processes of Amorite sedentarization cannot be precisely determined for Babylonia. Rowton describes sedentarization as a normal process of nomadism that primarily affected the richest and the poorest within a tribe and was caused by the attraction of nearby urban centers (Rowton 1973: 254). Weak strata of the population tended to become sedentary if their herds were reduced because of unfavorable events such as drought, disease, and so forth, so that they could not ensure food for their families. During the reign of Ibbi-Su'en, a letter from Išbi-Erra speaks of a lack of barley; administrative and economic documents from this time also show a drastic rise in the price of barley and cattle, a shift in cattle feed from barley to reeds, and a change from wages paid in barley to wages paid in dates and oil.[17] These difficulties would have affected the Amorite nomads as well and may have been one reason that they became sedentary. The economically and socially privileged strata, however, especially the tribal elite, were lured by the advantages of a sedentary life. Their comparatively quick integration into the political apparatus of a state without losing influence in the tribe was one important factor. In this way, these Amorite groups served as mediators between tribe and state. Simultaneously, the state gained opportunities to control nomadic activities. This process must have taken place even before we find evidence for rulers bearing Amorite names. An external attack and takeover by the Amorites can probably be excluded because there is no record of such an event whatsoever in the cuneiform texts (except for the letters of Išbi-Erra and Ibbi-Su'en), which we would expect to find for an incidence of such importance.[18] Considering Rowton's thesis, we may tentatively conclude that the Amorite usurpers already held influential positions in the urban centers before they came to power and that they had gradually become assimilated into urban life.[19]

With the fall of Ur at the end of third millennium B.C., numerous small city-states developed that were not united under a central power again until the reign of ʿAmmu-rāpiʾ of Babylon. During these 200 years, approximately, the Amorites assumed political leadership of many Babylonian towns. At the same time, the Sumerian culture was nearly replaced by the culture of the Akkadians.[20]

Traditions, Reflections, and Perceptions

Royal Titles

Royal titles are found in royal and votive inscriptions as well as on seals in the ancient Near East and were an expression of a king's influence and power. Which titles

17. Sallaberger (Sallaberger and Westenholz 1999: 177) proposes that an important reason for the decrease in the production of cereals lies in a change of the river, but he does not exclude oversalinization of the soil, the decreasing size of fields, or the emigration of the population.

18. The Sumerian text of the Lamentation of Ur does not mention the m a r t u, while in contrast, the people of Šimaški and Elam are explicitly mentioned as the lú-ḫa-lam-ma 'destroyer' of Ur (see Römer 2004: 1 and 57).

19. See n. 8 above.

20. For a summary, see Streck 2000: 37–38.

did the autonomous Amorite rulers assume after the fall of Ur? Did they have any of their own epithets for referring to kings?

A comparison of royal titles shows interestingly enough that Amorite rulers assumed the titles of Sumerian kings. The titles used most often were:

1. lugal kala-ga 'mighty king' or nita-kala-ga 'mighty man' and the Akkadian equivalents *da-núm* and *dan-nu* 'the mighty';
2. lugal of GN 'king of GN';[21]
3. lugal ki-en-gi-ki-uri and lugal kalam *šu-me-ri-im ù ak-ka-di-im* 'king (of the land) of Sumer and Akkad'.

Other titles were introduced by the Amorite rulers and hint at Amorite descent, but not every Amorite ruler used these new titles. It may be that personal preferences and awareness of one's own descent or traditions played an important role.

One of these titles was *ra-bí-an-(nu-um)* mar-tu 'chief of the Amorites',[22] which was used by Zabāya and Abī-sarē, both kings from the Larsa dynasty. In inscriptions of Warad-Sîn, he calls his father Kudur-Mabuk ad-da kur mar-tu 'father of the Amorite land', whereas inscriptions of Kudur-Mabuk himself use the title *a-bu*/ad-da *e-mu-ut-ba-la* 'father of the Emutbala', the name of an Amorite tribe. An inscription of Itūr-Šamaš, governor of Kisurra, mentions the title *ra-bí-an ra-ba-bi-ma* 'chief of Rabbeans', also an Amorite tribe.[23] The title lugal (da-ga-an kur) mar-tu^{ki} 'king of (all lands of the) Amorites', which is introduced by ʿAmmu-rāpiʾ and otherwise used only by ʿAmmī-ditāna, is similarly novel.

Although royal titles appear that may have referred to a king's Amorite descent, they are very rare. The use of an Amorite personal name was another indicator of a king's descent.[24] Royal titles that followed the Sumerian or Akkadian tradition appear much more frequently. The adoption of Sumerian and Akkadian royal titles may be another indication that the Amorite kings were assimilated before they became kings and probably held important offices in towns.[25] Because the Amorites were a minority in comparison with the Babylonian population, we can also assume that the influence of the Sumero-Babylonian culture was great enough that the Amorites continued to use well-known Babylonian traditions.

It is also worth looking at Syria, an area that can rightly be called the heartland of the Amorites, and from which various Amorite tribes maintained close contact with the urban centers. In this region, an Amorite dynasty was established at Mari almost 200 years after the fall of Ur and was destroyed by ʿAmmu-rāpiʾ of Babylon about 60 years later.[26] There were no Amorite royal titles used by the Mari kings,

21. GN is an abbreviation for "Geographical Name."

22. For other evidence for the title *rabiānum martu*, see Seri 2005: 55–60.

23. See Seri 2005: 60–61.

24. For example, ʾAbī-ḏāryī (*a-bi-sa-ri-e*), Śumu-ʾel (*su-mu-el*) of the Larsa dynasty; Śumu-ʾabum (*su-mu-a-bu-um*), Śumu-laʾel (*su-mu-la*-dingir) and ʿAmmu-rāpiʾ (*ḫa-am-mu-ra-bi*) of the First Dynasty of Babylon, and so on. For the reading and translation of these personal names, see Streck 2000.

25. See p. 195 above and n. 8.

26. Perhaps for reasons of dimorphic oscillations (see p. 195 above), Yaggid-lîm succeeded to the throne of Mari (ca. 1825+X B.C.), founding the so-called Lîm Dynasty (1825+X–1760/1 B.C.). This

although we have to take into consideration the fact that royal titles are only known for Yaʿdun-lîm and D̲imrī-lîm. These two kings called themselves:

1. lugal *ma-ri*[ki] *tu-ut-tu-ul*[ki] *ù ma-at ḫa-na* 'king of Mari, Tuttul and the land of Ḫana',
2. lugal kala-ga or lugal *da-[núm]* (only D̲imrī-lîm) 'mighty king',
3. lugal *ga-aš-ru-um* 'powerful king',
4. *ri-im šar-ri* (only Yaʿdun-lîm) 'wild bull of the king', and
5. *na-ra-am* [d]da-gan (only D̲imrī-lîm) 'beloved of the god Dagan'.

All these titles are linguistically well within the Akkadian tradition. Akkadian was also the official language there, as the corpus of Mari texts shows.[27] Thus it is not surprising that royal titles were also written in Akkadian. The reasons that Akkadian was preferred at Mari can only be speculated. Perhaps even then, international relations rendered the use of Akkadian necessary, considering that Akkadian became the lingua franca of the ancient Near East after the fall of Ur, as we all know.

This section on Mari and the royal titles of its rulers shows that no titles that are obviously Amonite can be found and that, instead, the titles are completely consistent with the Sumero-Babylonian tradition. Thus, the royal titles do not provide much information about Amorite traditions. Perhaps the use of titles in the Babylonian tradition is an indication that the Amorites appropriated the Babylonian principle of genealogical rights to the throne.

Perception of the Amorites by the Settled Population

In various cuneiform literary texts (myths, epics, hymns, royal inscriptions, proverbs), there are allusions to the strangeness of the Amorites, primarily in the representation of their way of life and their lack of what were considered essential customs.

Myths and Epics

There are five myths and epics that refer to the Amorites (a–e):

a. *Enki and the World Order* (Benito 1969: 99; also Kramer and Maier 1989: 43)

> 248 uru nu-tuku é nu-tuku-ra 249 [d]en-ki-ke$_4$ mar-tu máš-anše saĝ-e-eš mu-ni-ri[g$_7$]

> To those who know no towns, who know no houses, to the Amorites did Enki give animal herds.

---

dynasty ruled during the heyday of Mari, when the city enjoyed international renown. Originally peaceful relations with ʿAmmu-rāpiʾ of Babylon were severed, because the Mari king entered into an alliance with the king of Ešnunna, who made an enemy of ʿAmmu-rāpiʾ of Babylon. This ultimately led to the destruction of Mari by ʿAmmu-rāpiʾ (ca. 1761/60), based on his year-names. However, it remains uncertain whether the last king of the Lîm Dynasty, D̲imrī-lîm, was able to escape or was killed in the encounter. After the destruction, Mari became an insignificant town, never again to attain prominence.

27. Some letters use Northwest Semitic terms that are not attested in Babylonia: For example: *qaṭālum* 'kill, slaughter' instead of the usual Akkadian verb *dâkum* 'kill'; *ḫārum* 'donkey stallion' instead of *imērum* 'donkey, donkey stallion'; and *ḫazzum* 'goat' instead of *enzum* 'goat'.

b. *Curse of Akkad* (Cooper 1983: 52–53)

[46]mar-tu kur-ra lú še nu-zu [47]gu$_4$ du$_7$ máš du$_7$-da mu-un-na-da-an-ku$_4$-ku$_4$

The Amorites from the mountains, people who know no barley, offered her (Inanna) perfect cattle and perfect goats.

c. *Enmerkar and the Lord of Aratta* (Cohen 1973: 70, 119)

[144]kur-mar-tu ú-sal-la ná-a

The land of Amorites lies in the pasture.

d. *Lugalbanda and Enmerkar* (Wilcke 1969: 118–19 and 124–25)

[303/369]ke-en-gi ki-uri nigín-na-a-ba [304/370]mar-tu lú še nu-zu ḫu-mu-zi

In the whole land of Sumer and Akkad, the Amorites, people who know no barley, revolted.

e. *Marriage of Martu* (Klein 1997)

The best-known reference to the strangeness and barbarity of the Amorites appears in the myth called the "Marriage of Martu."[28] The leading person is the god Martu, who was the *theos eponymos* of the Amorites. He was not worshiped by the Amorites, but he was already integrated into the Mesopotamian pantheon as early as the Old Akkadian period. He reflected characteristics and way of life of the nomadic population, which from the point of view of the sedentary population were strange and uncivilized.

[127]á-še šu-bi ḫa-lam úlutim ^{u}[^{gu}ugu$_4$-bi] [128]an-zil-gu$_7$ ^{d}nanna-[kam] ní nu-[tuku] [129]šu dag-dag-ge-bi x[. . .] [130][níĝ-gi]g é dingir-re-e-ne-[kam] [131][ĝalga-b]i mu-un-lù-lù šu [sùḫ-a dug$_4$-ga] [132]l[ú ^{k}]^{uš}lu-úb mu$_4$-a [. . .] [133]za-lam-ĝar ti im im-šèĝ-[ĝá . . .] sizkur [nu-mu-un-dug$_4$-ga] [134]ḫur-saĝ-ĝá tuš-e ki [dingir-re-ne nu-zu-a] [135]lú u[z]u-dirig kur-da mu-un-ba-al-la dùg gam nu-zu-àm [136]uzu nu-šeĝ-ĝá al-gu$_7$-ze [137]u$_4$-tìl-la-na é nu-tuku-a [138]u$_4$ ba-ug$_7$-a-na ki nu-túm-mu-dam

[127]Lo, their hands are destructive, (their) features (are those of) [monkeys]. [128]They are those who eat what is taboo to the god Nanna, [they have] no reverence. [129]In their roaming around. [. . .] [130]They are an abomination [to] the temples of the gods. [131]Their [counsel] is confused. They are those [who cause] (only) dis[turbance]. [132]A m[an] who is clothed in leather-sac [. . .] [133]A tent-dweller, [in] wind and

28. This myth deals with the dissatisfied Martu, who does not yet have a wife and children, although he is a very successful hunter. Therefore, he asks his mother to let him marry. With her consent, a festival is held in the town of Inab, to which Numušda, the god of the town of Kazulla, together with his wife and daughter and others are invited. Martu, who is an excellent athlete, excels in the war game taking place there. Consequently, he gains the favor of Numušda, who wants to reward him with gifts. Martu, however, does not want the awards but instead asks for the hand of Numušda's daughter. Finally (the text is not extant or is only fragmentary at this point), Numušda agrees. The bride's friend warns her about marrying a god because of his rough behavior; however, the bride does not change her mind.

rain [. . .] [who offers no] prayer, [134]who lives in the mountains, [who knows not] the places [of the gods]. [135]A man who digs up truffles near the mountains, who knows no submission (lit., bending of the knees), [136]who eats meat that is uncooked, [137]who has no house in his lifetime, [138](and) on the day on which he dies, he will not be brought to a (burial) place.

Proverb

To date, only one proverb is known that refers to the Amorites.

f. *Proverb* (Alster 1997: 107, 3.140)

gig-gú-nida làl-gin$_7$ íb-ak mar-tu ì-gu$_7$-a níĝ-šà-bi nu-un-zu

Gunida-wheat was made instead of honey.[29] The Amorites who ate it did not recognize what was in it.

Royal Inscriptions and Hymns

g. *Inscription of Šū-Su'en* (Frayne 1997: 299, lines 24–29):

[24]u$_4$-bi-t[a] [25]mar-tu lú ḫa-lam-m[a] [26]dím-ma-ur-ra-gin$_7$ [27]ur-bar-ra-gin$_7$ [28]tùr x [x] x [29]lú še nu]-zu

Since these times, the Amorites, the destroyers, who are created like dogs, like wolves, [. . .] the hurdle. A person who knows [no barley].

h. *"Hymn of Išme-Dagan"* (= Išme-Dagan A+V, Römer 1989: 53; see also ETCSL: c.2.5.4.01, "A praise poem of Išme-Dagan [Išme-Dagan A+V]," with bibliography)

[266]mar-tu é nu-zu uru$^{ki!}$ nu-zu [267] ^{lú}líl-la ḫur-saĝ-gá tuš-a

The Amorites, who know no houses, who know no towns, . . . [30]who live in the mountains.

An allusions to problems with the Amorites in foreign policy appears in the lamentation of Nippur, which dates to the reign of Išme-Dagan of Isin (Tinney 1996: 114–15):[31]

[231]ugu-bi-ta *ti-id-nu-um* nu-gar-ra íb-ta-an-zi-ge$_4$-eš-àm

They have removed the treacherous Tidnum from upon it!

29. Alster completes: "(A cake) was made of Gunida-wheat instead of honey. . . ."

30. The translation of lú líl-la by Edzard 1957: 32 and Römer 1965: 54, line 272 is *lillu* 'Tölpel'. The translation by the ETCSL as 'primitives' also goes back to the equation lú líl-la = *lillu*. For líl, see Edzard 2003: 180: "Der Kontext legt eine Übersetzung 'der aus der windigen (Zone)' oder 'der aus der Leere' nahe, was eine passende Beschreibung des Nomaden wäre." This opinion is based on the equation lú líl-la = *a-wi-il zi-qi-qí-*[*im*] (MSL 12: 186, lines 27–33), known from the Babylonian Lu-series, which, interestingly, was followed in the list by various groups of the population (Suteans, Amorites, Assyrians, mountain-dwellers, and Elamites). Streck (2000: 75) translates 'Leute des Windes', where líl = *zāqāqum* 'wind, breath, spirit' is also associated with the idea of a deserted and barren place. This association is also shown in the reading líl^{æērum} = 'steppe' in the Old Babylonian series proto-Lu (MSL 12:63, line 824).

31. For a short summary of the historical background of the Isin I Dynasty, see Tinney 1996: 2–6.

Interpretation

Texts a, b, d, (g), and h stereotype the Amorites as "not knowing" towns, houses, or grain, which must have seemed uncivilized from the point of view of the Babylonian population.[32] However, these clichés have nothing in common with the real life of the Amorites, and various statements—that (1) the god Enki offered cattle to the Amorites, (2) the Amorites offered perfect cattle and goats to the goddess Inanna, and (3) they lie in the pasture—are not negative. These statements describe typical Amorites as cattle-breeders who originally lived near the mountains and hills, which they used for the pasture during their transhumance.

Although literary texts do not necessarily reflect real historical situations, I would nevertheless like to consider their references to the presence of the Amorites in Sumer and Akkad. The written version of the *Lugalbanda Epic* (d), which originated in the Ur III period,[33] proves indirectly that the Amorites had already infiltrated Babylonia but had not been completely integrated at the time of its writing.[34] Perhaps the date of origin can be more precisely pinpointed if one takes the construction of the Martu wall into consideration. Because this wall was supposed to keep away the Amorites, its completion should certainly be dated to a point in time when the majority of the Amorites were not yet present in Babylonia. Accordingly, this epic can be dated to sometime after the construction of the wall at the earliest, when the Amorites had already infiltrated the Babylonian heartland in large numbers.

The *Marriage of Martu* (e) provides the best insight into a nomadic way of life, especially aspects of nomadism as perceived by the sedentary population. Thus, the Amorites are called "tent-dwellers who dig for truffles and eat uncooked meat." We learn from Old Babylonian Mari correspondence that the nomads used tents during transhumance and dug for truffles.[35] Perhaps there is some truth to the idea of eating

32. In spite of this, the Guteans are depicted much more negatively in the *Curse of Akkad*:

^{155}gu-ti-um^{ki} un kéš-da nu-zu ^{156}dím-ma lú-ùlu^{lu} galga ur-ra SIG$_7$.ALAN ^{ugu}ugu$_4$-bi

Gutium, a person who knows no inhibitions, with human instincts, but of canine intelligence and monkey's features.

33. For the time of origin of Sumerian literary texts, see Wilcke 1969: 1 with bibliography.

34. This is also shown by the economic and administrative texts that single out Amorite differences. Research is currently being done at the Institute of Ancient Near Eastern Studies in Leipzig, where Constance Dittrich addresses questions concerning the social and cultural integration of the Amorites in the Ur III period in the Collaborative Research Centre: "Difference and Integration: Interactions between Nomadic and Settled Forms of Life in the Civilisations of the Old World" (see http://www.nomadsed.de/) as part of the German Research Foundation. Ur III–period economic, administrative, and legal texts from Puzriš-Dagan, Girsu, Umma, Nippur, Ur, and Isin as well as letters from Ešnunna are the focus of the research (forthcoming).

35. For example, ARM 26/1, 115 n. 70: A.3200

$^{13'}$*i-nu-ma im-me-er-tum ša* ^{lú}*ḫa-na*^{meš} $^{14'}$*i-na ma-ti-ma ir-te-ú mi-im-ma a-na im-me-er-ti-š[u]* $^{15'}$*ù a-na ku-uš-ta-ra-ti-šu tu-ga-al-la-al-ma* $^{16'}$*it-ti-ka a-na-ak-ki-ir*

If, when the cattle of the Ḫaneans are being pastured in the country, you should cause any damage to their cattle or their tents, I will become hostile to you.

FM 2 68: 34 [M.6006]

^{22}[x] ^{lú}*aw-na-na-i ša* ⸢*a*⸣*-na kam-a-tim* ^{23}*[a-na na-we-em]* ⸢*il-li*⸣*-ku-[nim]* ⸢*ṭe*$_4$*-ma-am*⸣ ^{24}*[ú-te-ru-nim um-ma-mi]*

uncooked meat. First of all, equipment for food preparation would have to be small and transportable for logistical reasons. Second, transporting meat requires a certain amount of rationing in order to limit the need for slaughter during the time of transhumance. For this reason, drying raw meat was probably of primary importance, just as even today meat is dried in many countries as a means of preservation.

The lack of knowledge about burials that is mentioned in the *Marriage of Martu* seems to be a reference to the lack of houses, because in Mesopotamia there is a long tradition of burials in the interior of houses (Novák 2000: 132–35). The Amorites' appearance, both their physiognomy and their unfamiliar clothes, also mentioned in the *Marriage of Martu*, is surely exaggerated. Nonetheless, one should bear in mind the facts that nomadic clothing had to be practical and tough and that personal hygiene could only be realized within limits. In this respect, perhaps the comparison with dogs and wolves in (g), which is suggestive of shaggy and dirty fur, can be understood. In addition, this comparison associates the Amorites with animal behavior.

An important point that the *Marriage of Martu* mentions is (the lack of) religion. The Amorites are incapable of saying prayers or knowing gods and their temples. In this context, personal names that are formed with a theophorous element are interesting. The use of a god's name in one's own name does not hint at an official cult but at personal piety. Among the 6,662 Amorite personal names listed by Gelb (1980), about 9% contain theophoric elements, and another 10% use the general term *god* without naming him or her explicitly. In the first category, about 41% contain the weather-god Haddu (241 names), 19% the grain-god Dagan (112 names), 14% the moon-god Yaraḫ (93 names), 11% the Venus goddess Aštar (67 names), 7% the sun-god Šamaš (40 names), and about 4% the goddess Išḫara (22 names). Personal names with the gods Enlil (2 names), Erra (9 names), Tišpak, Marduk, and Zababa (1 name each) are rare. These data are certainly distorted because: (1) since Gelb's analysis, the number of Amorite personal names has increased due to new discoveries; (2) the linguistic classification of a name is not always clear; (3) personal names of different chronological periods were collected and analyzed together as a single group; and (4) personal names from the Kingdom of Mari were also included, so there was no distinction from names from Babylonia. Nevertheless, it is interesting that the preferred gods were the gods who could be connected to the nomadic way of life because of their astral appearance or their function.

Personal names alone are not sufficient, however, to grasp the religious customs of the Amorites in Babylonia. Some letters from Mari grant further insight.[36] For example, tribal leaders visited the great temples to conclude treaties.[37] Smaller shrines

[X] ʾAwnāneans, who went [to the steppe] for truffles, [have brought back the following] news.

36. See Streck 2004b: 422–24.

37. For example, ARM 6 73: 10–12:

^{10} ^{I}*ás-di-ta-ki-im ù* lugal^{meš} *ša za-al-ma-qí-im*^{ki} *ù* ^{11} ^{lú}*su-ga-gu*^{meš} *ù* ^{lú}šu-gi$_4$^{meš} [*š*]*a* dumu^{meš}-*ia-mi-na* ^{12}⸢*i*⸣-*na* é ^{d}suʾen *ša ḫa-ar-ra-nim*^{ki} ^{anše}*ḫa-a-ri iq-ṭú-ú-lu-*[*n*]*im*

Asdi-takim (king of Ḫarrān) and the kings of Zalmaqum and the *sugāgū* and the oldest of the Yamīnites slaughtered donkey stallions in the temple of Sîn in Ḫarrān ("to slaughter a donkey stallion" is synonymous with "to sign a treaty").

or something similar in nomadic villages are also noted in the written documentation.[38] The performance of extispicies by Ḫanean *nabū* is also an allusion to the religious customs of the Amorites.[39] A letter mentions a *ḫumūṣum* 'memorial stone' of ʾAyyalum, which may have been a gravestone or something similar, to which four ʾUprabeans (Amorite tribe, subtribe of the Yamīnites) traveled, perhaps as part of a cult of the dead.[40] These and much other evidence reveal aspects of the Amorite religious traditions. A comparison with texts from Mari proves that the *Marriage of Martu* in no way reflects the real situation; its presentation of a lack of religiousness is an exaggeration in order to emphasize more clearly the contrast between the Amorites and Babylonians. The central idea of this literary representation is the sedentary Babylonians' perception of the strange customs of the Amorite nomads rather then the lack of religious customs.

A similar situation appears to obtain in the proverb (f), which alludes to ignorance about the cultivation of grain and therefore at general stupidity and lack of intelligence. Numerous texts from the palace archive of Mari show clearly, however, that the Amorite tribes cultivated their fields and were even asked to contribute to the harvest.[41] However, the amount of cultivation by the Amorites, who were primarily occupied with cattle-breeding, was much less than for the sedentary population of Babylonia, with its extensive field irrigation.

In conclusion, all the quoted texts present a distorted image of the Amorites through their exaggerated representations, as the texts from Mari show. These exaggerations make it possible, however, to point out differences between the sedentary

---

38. For example, ARM 14 8: 5–18:

^{5} $^{\text{lú-meš}}$*su-ga-gu ša ḫ[a-a]l-ṣí-im* ^{6}*aš-šum* dingir^{meš} *ša i-na s[a]-ga-ra-tim*^{ki} ^{7}*ù* bàd^{ki}-*ia-aḫ-du-li-im* ^{8}*ka-lu-ú i-na a-wa-[tim]* ^{9}*ki-a-am iṣ-ba-tu-ni-i[n]-n[i*$_5$*]* ^{10}*um-ma-a-mi* sís[kur$^{\text{ḪI-A}}$-*ma*] ^{11}dingir^{meš} *wa-aš-še-e[r-ma]* ^{12}*i-na* é$^{\text{ḪI-A}}$-*[š]u-[n]u* ^{13}siskur$^{\text{ḪI-[A]}}$ *[l]i-i[q]-q[ú-š]u-nu-ši-im* ^{14}*ù aš-šum be-lí la a-ša-lu* ^{15}dingir^{meš} *ú-ul ú-wa-aš-še-er* ^{16}*i-na-an-na šum-ma* dingir^{meš} ^{17}*a-na kap-ra-tim*$^{\text{ki.[ḪI]-A}}$ *ú-ta-aš-ša-ru* ^{18}*ù šum-ma la ú-ta-aš-ša-ru*

$^{5-9}$ Because of the gods who are held in Saggarātum and Dūr-Yaʾdun-Lîm, the *sugāgū* of the district addressed the following words to me: $^{10-13}$ "Release the offerings and the gods, and in their temples may they be offered as sacrifices." $^{14-15}$And because I had not asked my lord, I did not release the gods. $^{16-18}$Should now the gods be set free in the villages, or should they not be set free?

39. For example, ARM 26/1 216: 5–9:

^{5}*u*$_4$-*um a-na ṣe-er aš-ma-a[d]* ^{6}*ak-šu-du i-na ša-ni-i-im u*$_4$-*m[i-im]* ^{7} ^{lú}*na-bi-i*^{meš} *ša ḫa-na*^{meš} *ú-pa-ḫ[i-ir]* ^{8}*te-er-tam a-na ša-la-am be-lí-i[a]* ^{9}*ú-še-pí-iš*. . . .

The day after I arrived before Ašmad, I assembled the prophets of the Ḫaneans. I had extispicies done for the well-being of my lord. . . .

For the use of *nabû* = 'prophet', see Durand 1988: 377–78.

40. For example, ARM 14 86: 9–11:

^{9}. . . 4 $^{\text{lú-meš}}$*up-ra-pí-a-yu*^{ki} ^{10}*i-na ḫu-mu-ṣí-im ša* ^{I}*a-ia-lim* ^{11}*[iš]-ḫi-*{x}*-ṭú-šu-nu-ti-ma*

Four ʾUprabeans had raided them near the memorial stone of ʾAyyalum.

41. For example, ARM 3 38: 24–26:

^{24}*ù qa-tam-ma i-na e-ṣé-di-im* ^{25}*i-na a-la-ni ša* dumu^{meš} *ia-mi-na* ^{26}*ma-am-ma-an ú-ul ú-še-zi-ba-an-ni*

And likewise, nobody from the villages of the Yamīnites supported me during the harvest.

For a comprehensive account, see Anbar 1991: 170–74.

population and the nomadic Amorites. The texts do not reflect the historical situation of the Amorites who integrated quickly into the social fabric of the Babylonians, but instead refer to the nomadic Amorites both inside and outside Babylonia.

Summary

As noted at the beginning, no written documents of the Amorites exist, so one must turn to the Akkadian and Sumerian cuneiform texts to study the migration and sedentarization of the Amorites in Babylonia. Texts of completely different genres refer to the Amorites: historical sources such as royal inscriptions and year-names, literary compositions such as epics and myths, as well as administrative and economic records that were not examined in this essay due to their large number.

On the basis of the above-mentioned cuneiform sources, some general conclusions may be proposed. The term *Amorite* appears first in the middle of the third millennium B.C. in texts from Fāra and Ebla. Military campaigns into the region of the Middle Euphrates suggest contacts with the Amorite population living there during the Akkad period. However, during this period no immigration into Babylonia can be determined. During the reign of Šulgi, the number of immigrating Amorites increased enormously. Because of the increasing pressure, the king felt compelled to build a wall to bar the Amorites from entering Babylonia. Nonetheless, a mass penetration of Amorites could not be prevented. However, the literary sources do not refer to the immigration of the Amorites. These texts characterize the Amorites as mountain dwellers, which automatically excludes the area of Babylonia, due to its flat alluvial topography, and instead refers to the northern regions of Šāmīya and the Ǧebel Bišrī as well as the eastern regions of the Tigris and the Ǧebel Ḥamrīn (Streck 2000: 32; Wilcke 1969–70: 15–16). The precise migration route is unknown, but the Martu wall points to an origin of the Amonites in the north (Wilcke 1969–70: 9–12). After the fall of Ur and the breakdown of the empire into numerous local city-states, Amorite dynasties (recognizable by their names) appear in Babylonia. Their sudden appearance and the use of royal titles derived from the Sumero-Babylonian tradition demonstrate that an Amorite upper class had emerged and was already entrenched in Babylonian culture. Between the Amorite infiltration and the establishment of Amorite dynasties, we can see that a process of sedentarization must have taken place there. In addition to the name, the term martu, used to refer to Amorite persons during the Ur III period, gradually came to be used less frequently and ultimately disappeared, which is also significant evidence of their sedentarization (see Buccellati 1966: 355–62).

The mostly negative perception of the Amorites by the Babylonian population is well documented in literary and historical compositions. A comparison of these texts points to the use of stereotypical phrases to emphasize the contrasts between the nomadic Amorite population and the settled and cultivated Babylonian population. However, the cuneiform texts from Mari show that these negative representations are clichés without much basis in reality. The Amorites are described in the Babylonian sources as uncivilized and even barbaric—people who look and behave like animals.

References to their origin in the steppe plateau and their "ignorance of houses" demonstrate that these texts are describing not the already-settled Amorites but, rather, the nomadic population. Finally, I must point out that the settled Amorites did not represent themselves, nor did others describe their way of life. This "missing" reference suggests that the integrated Amorite population was considered neither strange nor uncivilized.

References

Alster, B.
1997 *Proverbs of Ancient Sumer: The World's Earliest Proverb Collections.* 2 vols. Bethesda, MD: CDL.

Anbar, M.
1991 *Les tribus amurrites de Mari.* Orbis biblicus et orientalis 108. Freiburg: Universitätsverlag / Göttingen: Vandenhoeck & Ruprecht.

Archi, A.
1985 Mardu in the Ebla Texts. *Orientalia* 54: 7–13.

Benito, C. A.
1969 *"Enki and Ninmaḫ" and "Enki and the World Order."* Ph.D. diss., University of Pennsylvania. [Sumerian and Akkadian texts with English translations and notes]

Bonechi, M.
1993 *Inomi geografici dei testi di Ebla.* Répertoire Géographique des Texts Cunéiformes 12/1. Wiesbaden: Reichert.

Buccellati, G.
1966 *The Amorites of the Ur III Period.* Naples: Istituto Orientale di Napoli.

Charpin, D., and Durand, J.-M.
1994 *Florilegium marianum II: Recueil d'études à la mémoire de Maurice Birot.* NABU, mémoires 3. Paris: SEPOA.

Cohen, S.
1973 *Enmerkar and the Lord of Aratta.* Ph.D. diss., University of Pennsylvania.

Cooper, J. S.
1983 *The Curse of Agade.* Baltimore: Johns Hopkins University Press.

Durand, J. M.
1988 *Archives Épistolaires de Mari 1/1.* Archives Royales de Mari 26/1. Paris: Éditions recherche sur les civilisations.

Edzard, D. O.
1957 *Die "Zweite Zwischenzeit" Babyloniens.* Wiesbaden: Harrassowitz.
1964 Das Reich der III. Dynastie von Ur und seine Nachfolgestaaten. Pp. 129–64 in vol. 2 of *Die Altorientalischen Reiche I. Fischer Weltgeschichte,* ed. E. Cassin et al. Frankfurt am Main: Hanseatische Druckanstalt.
1997 *Gudea and His Dynasty.* Royal Inscriptions of Mesopotamia, Early Periods 3/1. Toronto: University of Toronto Press.
2003 Enlil, Vater der Götter. Pp. 173–84 in *Semitic and Assyriological Studies Presented to Pelio Fronzaroli by Pupils and Colleagues,* ed. P. Marrassini et al. Wiesbaden: Harrassowitz.

Edzard, D. O.; Farber, G.; and Sollberger, E.
1977 *Die Orts- und Gewässernamen der präsargonischen und sargonischen Zeit.* Répertoire Géographique des Textes Cunéiformes 1. Wiesbaden: Reichert.

Falkenstein, A.
1950 Ibbīsîn-Išbiʾerra. *Zeitschrift für Assyriologie* 49: 59–79.

Frayne, D. R.

1993 *Sargonic and Gutian Periods (2334–2113 B.C.).* Royal Inscriptions of Mesopotamia: Early Periods 2. Toronto: University of Toronto Press.

1997 *Ur III Period (2212–2004 B.C.).* Royal Inscriptions of Mesopotamia, Early Periods 3/2. Toronto: University of Toronto Press.

Gelb, I. J.

1952 *Sargonic Texts from the Diyala Region.* Materials for the Assyrian Dictionary 1. Chicago: University of Chicago Press.

1968 An Old Babylonian List of Amorites. *Journal of the American Oriental Society* 88: 39–46.

1980 *Computer-Aided Analysis of Amorite.* Assyriological Studies 21. Chicago: Oriental Institute.

Gurney, O. R., and Kramer, S. N.

1976 *Sumerian Literary Texts in the Ashmolean Museum.* Oxford Editions of Cuneiform Texts 5. Oxford: Clarendon.

Jacobsen, T.

1953 The Reign of Ibbī-Suen. *Journal of Cuneiform Studies* 7: 36–47.

Klein, J.

1997 The God Martu in Sumerian Literature. Pp. 99–116 in *Sumerian Gods and Their Representations,* ed. I. L. Finkel and M. J. Geller. Cuneiform Monographs 7. Groningen: Styx.

Kramer, S. N., and Maier, J.

1988 *Myth of Enki, the Crafty God.* New York: Oxford University Press.

Legrain, L.

1922 *Historical Fragments.* Publications of the Babylonian Section 13. Philadelphia: University Museum.

Lemche, N. P.

1995 The History of Ancient Syria and Palestine: An Overview. Pp. 1195–1218 in vol. 2 of *Civilizations of the ancient Near East,* ed. J. M. Sasson. New York: Scribner.

Novák, M.

2000 Das "Haus der Totenpflege": Zur Sepulkralsymbolik des Hauses im Alten Mesopotamien. *Altorientalische Forschungen* 27: 132–54.

Römer, W. H. P.

1965 *Sumerische 'Königshymnen' der Isin-Zeit.* Documenta et monumenta Orientis antiqui 13. Leiden: Brill.

1989 Zur sumerischen Dichtung "Heirat des Gottes Mardu." *Ugarit-Forschungen* 21: 319–34.

2004 *Die Klage über die Zerstörung von Ur.* Alter Orient und Altes Testament 309. Münster: Ugarit-Verlag.

Rowton, M. B.

1973 Autonomy and Nomadism in Western Asia. *Orientalia* 42: 247–58.

1976 Dimorphic Structure and Topology. *Oriens Antiquus* 15: 17–31.

Sallaberger, W., and Westenholz, A.

1999 *Mesopotamien: Akkade-Zeit und Ur III-Zeit.* Orbis biblicus et orientalis 160/3. Annäherungen 3. Freiburg: Universitätsverlag / Göttingen: Vandenhoeck & Ruprecht.

Schwartz, G. M.

1995 Pastoral Nomadism in Ancient Western Asia. Pp. 249–58 in vol. 1 of *Civilizations of the Ancient Near East,* ed. J. M. Sasson. New York: Scribner.

Seri, A.

2005 *Local Power in Old Babylonian Mesopotamia: Studies in Egyptology and the Ancient Near East.* London: Equinox.

Sigrist, M.
1988 *Isin Year Names*. Berrien Springs, MI: Andrews University Press.
Sommerfeld, W.
2000 Narām-Sîn, die "Große Revolte" und MAR-TU[ki]. Pp. 419–36 in *Assyriologica et Semitica: Festschrift für J. Oelsner anläßlich seines 65. Geburtstages am 18. Februar 1997*, ed. J. Marzahn and H. Neumann. Alter Orient und Altes Testament 252. Münster: Ugarit-Verlag.
Streck, M. P.
2000 *Das amurritische Onomastikon der altbabylonischen Zeit, Band 1: Die Amurriter: Die onomastische Forschung. Orthographie und Phonologie. Nominalmorphologie.* Alter Orient und Altes Testament 271/1. Münster: Ugarit-Verlag.
2002 Zwischen Weide, Dorf und Stadt: Sozio-ökonomische Strukturen des amurritischen Nomadismus am Mittleren Euphrat. *Baghdader Mitteilungen* 33: 155–209.
2004a Die Amurriter der altbabylonischen Zeit im Spiegel des Onomastikons: Eine ethnolinguistische Evaluierung. Pp. 313–55 in *2000 v. Chr. Politische, wirtschaftliche und kulturelle Entwicklung im Zeichen der Jahrtausendwende.* 3. Internationales Colloquium der Deutschen Orient-Gesellschaft, 4.–7. April 2000, in Frankfurt/Main und Marburg/Lahn, ed. J.-W. Meyer and W. Sommerfeld. Saarbrücken: SDV.
2004b Die Religion der amurritischen Nomaden am mittleren Euphrat. Pp. 421–32 in *Offizielle Religion, lokale Kulte und individuelle Religiosität: Akten des religionsgeschichtlichen Symposiums "Kleinasien und angrenzende Gebiete vom Beginn des 2. bis zur Mitte des 1. Jahrtausends v. Chr." (Bonn, 20.–22. Februar 2003)*, ed. M. Hutter and S. Hutter-Braunsar. Alter Orient und Altes Testament 318. Münster: Ugarit-Verlag.
Thureau-Dangin, F.
1898 Tablettes Chaldéennes Inédites. *Revue d'assyriologie et d'archéologie orientale* 4: 69–86, 32 pl.
1903 *Recueil de Tablettes Chaldéennes.* Paris: Leroux.
Tinney, S.
1996 *The Nippur Lament: Royal Rhetoric and Divine Legitimation in the Reign of Išme-Dagan of Isin (1953–1935 B.C.).* Philadelphia: University Museum.
Whiting, R. M.
1995 Amorite Tribes and Nations of Second-Millennium Western Asia. Pp. 1231–42 in vol. 2 of *Civilizations of the Ancient Near East*, ed. J. M. Sasson. New York: Scribner.
Wilcke, C.
1969 *Das Lugalbandaepos.* Wiesbaden: Harrossowitz.
1969–70 Zur Geschichte der Amurriter in der Ur-III-Zeit. *Die Welt des Orients* 5: 1–31.
1970 Drei Phasen des Niedergangs des Reiches von Ur III. *Zeitschrift für Assyriologie* 60: 54–69.
1997 Amar-girids Revolte gegen Narān-Suʾen. *Zeitschrift für Assyriologie* 87: 11–32.

Index of Authors

Ackroyd, P. 172
Adamthwaite, M. R. 23-25, 30
Afanas'eva, V. K. 69
Akkermans, P. M. M. G. 39, 42, 54-56, 58
Albanese, C. L. 111
Allen, L. 169
Alster, B. 160, 202
Alt, S. 101
Althusser, L. 92-93
Alvarez-Mon, J. 181
Amiet, P. 101
Anbar, M. 205
Anderson, B. 91
Annus, A. 154
Archi, A. 194

Bahrani, Z. 113
Barstad, H. M. 172
Bauer, J. 101
Beaulieu, P.-A. 3-4, 12, 14, 141-143, 153, 174, 177
Bedford, P. 172, 175
Beld, S. 89, 94-95, 99, 101, 103-104
Bell, C. 92
Bellotto, N. 23, 30
Benech, C. 179
Benito, C. A. 200
Ben-Tor, A. 54, 58
Beran, T. 125
Berger, P.-R. 175, 181
Bernbeck, R. 89, 92
Beyer, D. 27, 32, 121, 128-129
Bichler, R. 171
Bietak, M. 40, 42
Bittel, K. 113, 116-117, 120, 125, 128, 131
Boardman, J. 179
Bohrer, F. N. 60
Bonacossi, M. 41
Bonatz, D. 3-4, 11, 112
Bonechi, M. 194
Börker-Klähn, J. 121
Boucharlat, R. 171, 179
Bourdieu, P. 92, 124
Bretschneider, J. 104
Briant, P. 169
Brinkman, J. A. 176
Brosius, M. 170
Brysbaert, A. 42-43
Buccellati, G. 197, 206
Bunnens, G. 23, 28
Butler, J. 92
Butler, S. A. L. 141

Cameron, G. G. 181
Cancik, H. 23
Cancik-Kirschbaum, E. 112
Cargill, J. 177
Carsten, J. 96
Cavigneaux, A. 138
Charpin, D. 143
Charvát, P. 98
Cline, E. H. 48
Cogan, M. 180
Cohen, A. 89, 95-96, 99, 101-102, 105
Cohen, S. 201
Collins, J. J. 138
Collon, D. 95
Cooper, J. S. 24, 31, 69, 93, 95, 154, 201
Cooper, L. 53-54
Cormack, M. 92

Delougaz, P. 99
Dever, W. G. 54
Di Filippo, F. 22, 28, 34
Dickson, B. 89-90
Dinçol, A. 122-123, 126
Donbaz, V. 155, 158
Drijvers, H. J. W. 152
Du Mesnil du Buisson, R. 41, 49, 51
Durand, J.-M. 22, 28, 205
Dyson, R. 179

Edzard, D. O. 194, 196, 202
Ehringhaus, H. 114, 121-122
Einwag, B. 24
Eisenstadt, S. N. 70, 83
Ellison, R. 103
Emre, K. 112

Faist, B. 22-23, 30, 32
Fales, F. M. 154
Falkenstein, A. 196-197
Farber, G. 194
Fauth, W. 125
Feldman, M. H. 3, 7, 21, 43-44, 59
Finkbeiner, U. 22, 30
Fleming, D. E. 23-25, 27, 29-31
Forest, J.-D. 101
Foster, B. R. 71
Foucault, M. 93, 102
Frame, G. 143, 146, 160, 183
Franke, S. 68, 71, 74-75
Frankfort, H. 40, 96, 98
Frayne, D. R. 143, 194, 202
Freu, J. 28
Fried, L. 175
Fuchs, A. 175, 184

Gadd, C. J. 148
Garrison, M. B. 178
Geertz, C. 97
Gelb, I. J. 67-68, 73, 76-77, 81, 100, 193-194, 204
George, A. R. 140, 143, 147-149, 151, 160, 163, 177
Gesche, P. D. 140, 142, 160
Giesen, B. 69
Gillespie, S. 96
Glassner, J.-J. 184
Goff, C. 179
Gonella, J. 133
Gonnet, H. 115, 119
Grabbe, L. L. 172
Grayson, A. K. 137-138, 180
Grelot, G. 138
Gurney, O. R. 196
Güterbock, H. G. 117, 131

Haas, V. 114-117
Hallock, R. T. 178, 181
Hansman, J. 172
Hawkins, J. D. 115, 121-123, 126, 132
Heimpel, W. 69, 96, 101, 103
Heinz, M. 3, 8, 40, 89, 130
Heltzer, M. 28, 31
Helwing, B. 95
Henkelman, W. 170, 178-179, 181
Herbordt, S. 121, 123, 126-127
Hill, H. 99
Hill, J. D. 100
Hobsbawm, E. 59
Holloway, S. W. 180
Hout, T. P. J. van den 113, 115, 119, 121, 125-127
Hugh-Jones, S. 96

Ilan, D. 54, 57
Immerwahr, S. 40, 42, 44-45, 59

Jacobsen, T. 196
Jahn, B. 5-6, 14, 16, 58
Jans, G. 104
Joyce, R. 92, 96, 101

Kempinski, A. 45, 49, 54, 57-58
Kent, R. G. 169, 181
Kent, S. 52
Kenyon, K. M. 58
Kertzer, D. 91-93
Kessler, K.-H. 177
Khayyata, W. 133
Kienast, B. 67-68, 73, 76-77, 81
Klein, J. 158, 201
Klengel, H. 28, 55-56, 128
Knapp, A. B. 59-60
Koçay, H. Z. 118
Kohlmeyer, K. 121-122, 133
Kramer, S. N. 196, 200

Kühne, C. 24, 30
Kuhrt, A. 5, 14, 151, 169, 174–177, 181

Lambert, W. G. 151, 156
Laroche, E. 120
Lee, T. G. 155–156
Leemans, W. F. 174
Legrain, L. 196
Lemche, N. P. 195
Lenfant, D. 171, 173
Levine, L. D. 179
Lévi-Strauss, C. 96
Lewis, B. 67–68
Lewis, D. M. 170
Lewy, J. 139, 163
Litke, R. L. 156–157
Livingstone, A. 150, 157
Lloyd, S. 99
Lock, G. 92
Loon, M. N. van 113, 116
Lucero, L. 93, 100–101

MacGinnis, J. 154
Machinist, P. 162
Macqueen, J. G. 116
Maehler, H. 180
Maekawa, K. 95
Maier, J. 200
Manning, S. W. 59
Maqdissi, M. al- 49–50, 57
Marchesi, G. 98
Margueron, J.-C. 22–24
Marinatos, N. 40
Marti, L. 22, 28
Martin, H. 99
Matsushima, E. 151
Matthiae, P. 49, 56
Maurer, A. 70, 82
Mayer, W. 25, 27–28
Mayer-Opificius, R. 113, 115
Mazar, A. 54, 58
Mee, C. 40
Meyer, J.-W. 100, 104
Mitchell, T. 91
Monaco, G. 40
Montag, W. 92
Moon, J. 99
Moore, W. E. 69
Moorey, P. R. S. 98
Moortgat, A. 98
Morgan, D. 111–112
Morgan, L. 40–41

Neve, P. 115–121, 125
Nichols, J. J. 53–54
Niemeier, B. 40–41, 43–50, 59
Niemeier, W.-D. 40–41, 43–50, 59
Nissen, H. 94, 97
Novák, M. 41, 50–55, 204
Nunn, A. 39, 42
Nylander, C. 179

Oates, D. 24
Oren, R. 48–49
Otten, H. 114, 116–117, 123
Otto, A. 24

Palyvou, C. 40
Pauketat, T. 92–93, 101
Pettinato, G. 78
Pfälzner, P. 41, 52–55
Pinnock, F. 95
Pollock, S. 3–4, 10–11, 90, 92–93, 96–102, 105–106
Pomponio, F. 154
Pongratz-Leisten, B. 161, 177
Postgate, J. N. 99, 154
Potts, D. 181
Pruzsinszky, R. 2, 6, 8, 21, 27

Rapoport, A. 52
Rawi, F. N. H. Al- 140, 143, 147
Reade, J. 98
Richter, T. 24, 55–56
Ricoeur, P. 92
Riegl, A. 59
Roaf, M. 179
Rollinger, R. 171, 176–177
Römer, W. H. P. 198, 202
Root, M. C. 178–179
Rosengarten, Y. 95, 101
Rouault, O. 24
Rowton, M. B. 195, 198
Rüden, C. von 42
Russell, J. M. 53

Sader, H. 39
Said, E. W. 60
Sallaberger, W. 24, 29, 31, 95, 196, 198
Salvini, M. 28, 31
Sancisi-Weerdenburg, H. 170–171, 173, 179
Scandone-Matthiae, G. 51
Schaeffer, C. F.-A. 126, 128–130
Schaudig, H.-P. 137, 139–141, 145, 148, 150, 155, 158–159, 162, 174–175, 181
Schmandt-Besserat, D. 95, 101, 105
Schmidt, E. F. 179
Schmitt, R. 169
Schwartz, G. M. 39, 42, 47, 54–56, 58, 89, 195
Scott, J. 90–93, 105
Seeher, J. 116
Selz, Gebhard 89, 93, 95–96, 100
Selz, Gudrun 95, 101, 104
Seminara, S. 22, 24, 31
Seri, A. 199
Seux, M.-J. 159
Shaw, M. C. 43
Sherratt, S. 59
Sherwin-White, S. 151, 169, 175
Sigrist, M. 197
Sjöberg, Å. 153
Skaist, A. 22, 25, 27–28, 30, 34
Smith, A. 91
Smith, S. 171, 184
Sollberger, E. 194
Sommerfeld, W. 194
Spek, R. van der 176–177, 180
Steele, C. 99
Steible, H. 69, 73
Steinkeller, P. 67, 96
Stevanovic, M. 100
Streck, M. P. 58, 138, 158, 193–199, 202, 204, 206
Stronach, D. 171–172, 179
Sürenhagen, D. 98

Tadmor, H. 162
Talon, P. 153
Taraqji, A. 39, 51, 57
Testart, A. 89, 91–92, 101–102, 105
Thureau-Dangin, F. 194
Tinney, S. 202
Tolini, G. 177
Trémouille, M.-C. 28, 31

Verbrugghe, G. P. 138, 160
Vita, J.-P. 23, 28, 30, 32
Von Voigtlander, E. N. 175

Wagner, E. 105
Walker, C. B. F. 174
Walker, W. 93, 100–101
Watanabe, K. 138
Waters, M. 181
Weber, J. A. 53–54
Weber, M. 91, 96, 101
Weidner, E. F. 180
Weissbach, F. H. 171
Werner, P. 22
Westbrook, R. 23, 27–28, 30
Westenholz, A. 196, 198
Westenholz, J. G. 21, 25, 29, 67–68, 140–141
Whiting, R. M. 58, 195
Wickersham, J. M. 138, 160
Wiesehöfer, J. 169, 173
Wiggermann, F. A. M. 156
Wilcke, C. 194–196, 201, 203, 206
Wilhelm, G. 58
Winter, I. J. 46, 53, 89, 101, 103, 112–113
Woolley, C. L. 89–90, 98–99, 103
Woolley, L. 40, 47–48, 97, 130–132
Wright, H. 101

Yamada, M. 22–24, 27–28, 30, 32–33
Yasur-Landau, A. 48
Young, T. C. 179

Zaccagnini, C. 23, 25
Žižek, S. 92

www.ingramcontent.com/pod-product-compliance
Lightning Source LLC
Chambersburg PA
CBHW081442070526
44586CB00019B/2210